CW00456863

'At last someone has undertak[en a] comprehensive history of the Eli[m in the] UK, and there is no better person [than its] official historian, Maldwyn Jone[s ...] Jones demonstrates a depth of p[ersonal ...] interacts with numerous primary sources and engages with existing historical works on Elim. He brings to life the denomination's many pioneers who sacrificially served God and proclaimed the full gospel message in word and deed. Although the book is primarily written for members of Elim churches, it also has plenty of material that will be of value to scholars of Pentecostalism. I very much look forward to reading the second of this two-volume history of Elim.'
Revd Dr Simo Frestadius, Dean of Research, Regents Theological College, West Malvern, UK

'The history of Elim has never been published before. In this book, and with detail and passion, Maldwyn Jones, Elim's official historian, tells us the story and conveys the excitement and the miracles – as well as the troubles – that attended those formative years. This is a book you will want to read.'
Professor William Kay

'Maldwyn has written the best kind of historical survey, covering the origins and early years of the Elim Pentecostal Churches. It is considered, thorough and accessible for all aspects of Elim's early years. He also manages to help us catch a glimpse of the hand of God at work in human history.'
Rev Michael Sherwood, Former Regional Leader and member of the NLT of the Elim Pentecostal Church.

And They Came to Elim

A History of the Elim Pentecostal Church
Vol 1 1915-40

Maldwyn Jones

instant
apostle

First published in Great Britain in 2021

Instant Apostle
104 The Drive
Rickmansworth
Herts
WD3 4DU

Every effort has been made to seek permission to use copyright material reproduced in this book. The publisher apologises for those cases where permission might not have been sought and, if notified, will formally seek permission at the earliest opportunity.

The views and opinions expressed in this work are those of the author and do not necessarily reflect the views and opinions of the publisher.

British Library Cataloguing-in-Publication Data

A catalogue record for this book is available from the British Library.

This book and all other Instant Apostle books are available from Instant Apostle:

Website: www.instantapostle.com

Email: info@instantapostle.com

ISBN 978-1-912726-38-7

Printed in Great Britain.

Dedications

With grateful thanks to my Lord and Saviour who, in His grace and mercy not only saved me and brought me into His Kingdom, but also brought these three special people into my life:

Eric McComb, Former Elim Irish Superintendent, whose friendship has been, and remains invaluable.

Desmond Cartwright, the first Official Elim Historian and my mentor.

Benjamin Hill, my father-in-law and one of the godliest of men.

Acknowledgements

In writing this book I have received assistance and inspiration from many people. My friend and colleague for the past fifty-six years, Gordon Neale, has constantly provoked me to write. It has taken me almost forty years to do so and I am grateful to him for his needed prods to stir me into writing. My colleagues in the Desmond Cartwright Centre, Phil and Sally Thompsett and Mike and Peggy Greenway, have been an encouragement and helped me by providing valuable personal information concerning Elim's past. Sally Gibbs, the Regents College librarian, has kindly pointed out helpful books for my research. Special thanks to David Butcher, another long-standing friend and colleague, who has supplied the photographs for the book.

Chris Cartwright, Elim's General Superintendent, has been a great encourager in my intention to write this book. I thank him most sincerely for his comprehensive and somewhat flattering preface. Also, my good friend Stuart Blount, the Director of Ministry, has given of his time in discussing Elim's history with me and shown considerable interest in this project.

Dr William Kay, one of the leading Pentecostal historians of our time, has reviewed the book and made very helpful comments. Dr Simo Frestadius has read the text and has made valuable comments, as has Mike Sherwood, one of my closest friends and best man at our wedding.

Dr John Usher's encyclopaedic knowledge of early British Pentecostal history was a great help to me. The post-graduate tutorial staff at Regent's Theological College provided me with a platform to write on Pentecostal history.

I'm grateful to the National Leadership Team of the Elim Pentecostal Church for giving me the honour of being Elim Historian in succession to my friend and mentor Desmond Cartwright and in allowing me the privilege of writing this book.

I wish to express my appreciation to Nicki Copeland and the team at Instant Apostle for their willingness to take on this project. Special thanks to Sheila Jacobs for her excellent work in the editing of this book.

Ruth, my wife of forty-eight years, has been an incredible encouragement to me, not only in the writing of this book, but also in every aspect of ministry throughout the years we have been together. I thank God for her love, patience and sacrificial support. Without her by my side, not only would I have not written this book, but many other aspects of ministry would have been curtailed.

Finally, I thank and praise my Lord and Saviour, Jesus Christ, for saving and changing me as a young man at the Elim Youth Camp in Porthpean, Cornwall, and for the support and nurture I received under the ministry and pastoral care of Pastor William Evans and the Porth Elim Church.

Contents

Preface

Pentecostals have come a long way from small beginnings in a Bible School in Topeka, Kansas, in the first days of 1901, when a handful of students were 'baptised in the Holy Spirit' and spoke in tongues. Pentecostalism has become a global movement with an estimated 500 million people drawn from every nation on earth.

The early Pentecostals were quick to recognise the importance of recording and telling their story. Driven with a mission to preach and share their new found message of the 'full' gospel and encouraged by a ready supply of testimonies of salvation, healing, experience of the baptism in the Spirit and changed lives, they began to write, to publish and to spread the news of what they believed was nothing short of a move of God for the whole world.

At first, the accounts were demonstrably pragmatic, almost totally focused on evangelistic strategy and chronicling the meetings, miracles and manifestations. Soon the early Pentecostals produced a wealth of pamphlets, magazines, tracts and promotional materials. Yet they also began to attract the attention of the world around them, quickly drawing a surprising level of press coverage and an extraordinarily rich and significant pictorial record of their growing spread and influence.

The writing of Pentecostal History is now a flourishing branch of Pentecostal Theology and Study. The sheer volume of materials that Pentecostals have generated over more than 100 years has stimulated a noticeable focus on exploring the many stories within the bigger story which has, in turn, led to a growing level of mature critical and theological analysis and reflection.

When Maldwyn Jones first told me that he had started to write a history of Elim, I was delighted. I could think of no one better to write it. I had witnessed how my own father, Desmond Cartwright, while serving as Elim's director of publications in the 1970s, had begun to research the history of the Pentecostal denomination of which he was a part, in response to enquiries that would regularly come into the office from students, journalists and scholars. Not able to find a suitable publication, he set out to put together a simple, accessible introduction. Those first forays into dusty files and conversations with veteran colleagues would lead, over many years, to an abiding passion, beyond dates and data, to explore the history of Elim and to make the story live.

I sensed that Maldwyn was also at the start of what would become an absorbing adventure, and that he and we would be the richer for it. He is uniquely qualified to tell this story at such time as this. A much loved and respected Elim minister, Maldwyn is noted for what in his native Wales is known as 'Hwyl'. The word conveys a sense of passion, energy and spirit.

Maldwyn has demonstrated that passion in decades of pastoral ministry as a caring pastor to churches large and small. He has poured it into developing others in ministry as a gifted mentor. He has carried it into the pulpit as a powerful preacher of God's Word. He has drawn from it in brilliant, impassioned speeches to Elim's Annual Conferences in the high-octane atmosphere of denominational debate.

A number of publications have sought to tell the Elim story. The early years of the growth and expansion of Elim saw an understandable focus on the defining influence and impact of the person and ministry of George Jeffreys, Elim's founder and pioneer. First published in 1928, *The Ministry of the Miraculous*, by E C W Boulton is a close-up account of George's life, including the early years of Elim, the city-wide campaigns and numerous testimonies of healings and miracles.

Aimed as a general introduction for a wider audience, Desmond Cartwright's *The Great Evangelists*, published in 1984, tells the story of Elim focusing on the remarkable ministry of George Jeffreys and his brother Stephen.

Released in the 1990s, *Pentecostal Perspectives*, edited by Keith Warrington, contains an excellent chapter from Malcolm Hathaway entitled 'The Elim Pentecostal Church: Origins, Development and Distinctives'.

More recently, William Kay's *George Jeffreys, Pentecostal Apostle and Revivalist* brilliantly brings to life George's ministry against the backdrop of changing culture and society. Lastly, the commemorative book, *Defining Moments*, was published in 2015 to coincide with Elim's Centenary.

It has long been clear, however, that there is so much more of the Elim story to be told. Building on these accounts, this study will provide us with the most comprehensive and wide-ranging account yet of the development, influence and impact of Elim.

Writing denominational history can be a notoriously challenging task. The writer may feel pressure to tone down the story, to domesticate, sanitise or airbrush the more controversial or complex aspects in order to get official approval. That's perhaps why official or definitive histories are often viewed with some suspicion.

Ironically, in the early 1980s Elim had an such an Official History prepared and ready for release. George Canty, an Elim minister known as a gifted evangelist, broadcaster and writer, had been commissioned by Elim's Executive Council to write the history of Elim. His manuscript was duly submitted, proofed and typeset for publication, but never actually printed.

Coming to the manuscript in our archives around the same time, Maldwyn and I struggled to find any record of the reason it was pulled from publication. Our best guess was that, as George Canty was known to be a straight-talking, highly individualistic and at times controversial thinker, the leaders were nervous of allowing his version of events see the light of day.

In that light, Maldwyn is released from 'official' expectations, to write with a freedom and conviction that comes from intimate knowledge and love for the Movement he is writing about. To tell the story of Elim. And it's quite a story.

Maldwyn serves as the official historian for the Elim Pentecostal Church. As such, he has been a shaping influence on developing the outstanding archive at Regents Theological College. This archival collection now houses Elim's own archive as well as a number of unique collections from British Pentecostal and Charismatic History including the world renowned Donald Gee Archive. This study draws deeply on the rich and unparalleled materials from these archive collections and brings to a wider audience aspects and shades of the story hitherto unseen.

Coming in later ministry to postgraduate study at Regent's Theological College and serving as Elim's official historian, Maldwyn has a strong conviction that understanding our history helps us to shape our destiny. Consequently, he writes this history with evident faith and purpose for the future church.

As Elim has entered its second century, we believe we are more likely to be at our best in following the call and commission of Christ in the future as we know and understand our past. The God who has poured out His Spirit upon the Church in times past, is still, as we read in Daniel 2:21, the God who 'changes times and seasons' (NIV) and calls us to a fresh season of renewed mission and ministry into every community and culture. It is my prayer that this remarkable history will contribute to that forward movement as Elim seeks to be true to its spiritual DNA as a Spirit-empowered missional movement.

Chris Cartwright, General Superintendent, Elim Pentecostal Church

Introduction

The story of the Elim Pentecostal Church in the UK is an inspirational and, at times, a miraculous one. Its beginnings, in particular, have that obvious touch of divine activity. Not only was the presence of God obviously experienced throughout the first twenty-five years of Elim's existence, but the fact that the Movement[1] survived the ravages heaped upon it by the double effect of the Second World War and a major schism that saw its founder and leader leave and start up another Christian denomination is, in itself, an astonishing witness to God's hand being clearly upon it.

To date, there has been no full historical account written concerning the Elim Pentecostal Church throughout its 105 years existence. Biographical books have been penned on the life of the Movement's founder, George Jeffreys, that give a clear account of the developing years of Elim, but little has been published on the post-war history of the Movement.[2] An early history of Elim was written and published, but covered only the years 1915-28.[3] Two later biographies on the life and ministry of George Jeffreys, by Cartwright[4] and Kay,[5] contain valuable historical information on the first twenty-five years of Elim. James Robinson, in his book *Pentecostal Origins*,[6] has devoted four chapters on George Jeffreys and the early years of Elim in Ireland that provide great historical data on the early years of the Elim Pentecostal Church. The intention in this book is to give a historical record of the Elim Pentecostal Church since its beginnings in 1915 to the year 2015 in two volumes.

In his introduction, Kay highlights the absence of Pentecostal activity in secular histories.[7] This is despite the fact that the revival campaigns of George Jeffreys received a great deal of coverage in the national press. His healing campaigns saw huge crowds and included numerous verified accounts of people being healed. The phenomenal growth of Elim during the 1920s and thirties warranted historical documentation. History must not only be documented, but observed. We ignore history at our peril. We must learn from history. Because history is an account of the past, many people are apt to consider it irrelevant.

Any written account of history inevitably bears views and opinions of the author. The challenge set before any historian is that of impartiality. 'History as a disciplined enquiry aims to sustain the widest possible definition of memory, and to make the process of recall as accurate as possible, so that a knowledge of the past is not confined to what is immediately relevant.'[8]

The Executive Council of Elim (now the National Leadership Team), commissioned George Canty[9] who was an Elim minister for more than sixty years and a past president of the Movement, to write a history of Elim which was written, but not published. Many references to Canty's manuscript and quotations from it, will be found throughout the book. However, this will not be a regurgitation of Canty's work, but will rather serve as a reference point and seek to bring to light hidden facts concerning Elim's history.

The first four chapters focus on the movements that led up to the establishing of the Pentecostal denominations in the United Kingdom. Only one of these will be the subject matter of the book, although there will be some inevitable cross-references to the others. The five movements that had a major impact on the developing Pentecostal Movement in Britain were 1) the Holiness Movements, particularly in the Wesleyan tradition, of the latter half of the nineteenth century, 2) the Keswick Conventions, 3) the Welsh Revival 1904-05, 4) the Azusa Street Revival, 5) the Sunderland Conventions.

In his excellent biography of George Jeffreys, the founder of Elim, William Kay has not gone into great detail on the 'Irish

Years' and has not provided much detail as to the names and sequence of the churches that were opened in Northern Ireland during the years 1915 to 1921, when Jeffreys moved across to England. Indeed, there is not a great deal mentioned about the Irish churches and work from that point on.[10] The author will seek to address this and remind his readers that before it became a British Movement, Elim was an Irish work with its headquarters in Belfast, from 1917 to 1923.[11]

Elim's first official historian was Desmond W Cartwright who, almost single-handedly, built up the Archives of the Elim Pentecostal Church. His contribution to British Pentecostal history is phenomenal and the Archives at the Elim International Offices in Malvern bear his name. As his successor, I acknowledge his immense work in collecting and contributing historical documentation relating to Elim that is a major foundation for this book.

The book will outline the establishment of the Elim Pentecostal Church as a major Pentecostal denomination within the United Kingdom. It will cover the remarkable campaigns of George Jeffreys held in the major halls in the country, including the majestic Royal Albert Hall and the glittering Crystal Palace. It will contain an account of the sad schism within Elim that saw the founder leave the Movement that he had commenced and start another denomination. The Second Volume will give details of Elim's struggles throughout the Second World War, hampered greatly by internal strife, as well as the Movement's survival against all odds and its steady, if unspectacular growth through the post war period and into the seventies where Elim experienced a second crisis in the form of the challenge of the House Church and Restoration movements. Details will be given of the Southport conferences that were crucial in avoiding a second major division.

There will be biographical outlines of the work and ministry of some of Elim's key leaders pointing out their contribution and impact, not only on Elim itself, but on the wider Pentecostal and charismatic scene.

The period covered in this first volume is: 1915-40. So, let the story begin.

Notes

[1] This is the generic term that will be used to describe the Elim Pentecostal Church throughout the book. This will be in place of referring to it as a denomination.

[2] Dr Simo Frestadius has included a historical account of aspects of Elim in the early eighties within his doctoral thesis. Malcolm Hathaway has included a section on the same period in his chapter 'The Elim Pentecostal Church', in *Pentecostal Perspectives* (Carlisle: Paternoster Press, 1998).

[3] Boulton, E C W, *George Jeffreys: A Ministry of the Miraculous* (London: Elim Publishing House, 1928).

[4] Cartwright, D W, *The Great Evangelists, The Remarkable lives of George and Stephen Jeffreys* (Basingstoke: Marshall Morgan and Scott, 1986).

[5] Kay, William K, *George Jeffreys: Pentecostal Apostle and Revivalist* (Cleveland, TN: CTP Press, 2017).

[6] Robinson, James, *Pentecostal Origins: Early Pentecostal Origins in the Context of the British Isles* (Milton Keynes: Paternoster, 2005).

[7] Kay, William, ibid, p1.

[8] Tosh, John, *The Pursuit of History* (Abingdon: Routledge, 2010), p2.

[9] Canty was commissioned by the Executive Council of the Elim Pentecostal Church to write a history of the Movement. The manuscript was completed in 1983 but, on the instruction of the Executive Council, it was not published.

[10] See note 6 above.

[11] Much of the information of the growth of the Elim work in Ireland after 1925 will be included in the second volume.

1
Background

There are many streams that flowed into the river of the British Pentecostal Movement in general, and the Elim Pentecostal Church, in particular. Elim was the name that was given to the denomination on its establishment in 1915. This name was given for two reasons. Firstly, it was called after the Elim mission in Lytham, Lancashire where George Jeffreys had preached on a number of occasions while he was a student at the Preston Bible School. [1]

Secondly, Elim is a biblical name taken from Exodus 15:27. This was an oasis in the desert that the Children of Israel came to on their journey from captivity in Egypt to the Promised Land of Canaan. The oasis had seventy palm trees and twelve wells. As such, it signifies a place of refreshment, a most appropriate symbol of what was to become one of the major British Pentecostal denominations.

A unique factor concerning Elim is that it is the product of pioneering evangelism and church planting by its founder George Jeffreys (1889-1962). [2] The results of his pioneering work show him to be arguably the greatest British evangelist of the last century. He occupied some of the greatest buildings in the land and conducted evangelistic crusades that established large churches throughout the country. Undoubtedly, his greatest campaign was in Birmingham in 1930 where meetings were held in the great Bingley Hall with a seating capacity of 17,000. Jeffreys filled this hall each night for a fortnight. Prior to that, services had been held at the Town Hall and the

Embassy Ice Rink in Sparkbrook, Birmingham. There were more than 10,000 converts and 1,000 baptised in water. Three large churches were established in Graham Street, Birmingham, Sparkbrook and Smethwick. Within six years, a total of eleven Elim churches had been established in Birmingham.

George Jeffreys, along with his elder brother, Stephen, was converted during the Welsh Revival under the ministry of Rev W Glasnant Jones on the 20th November 1904 in Siloh Congregational Chapel, Maesteg.[3] His pastor soon realised that there was an anointing on young George and claimed that he was 'a chosen vessel'. Boulton gives the following quotation by Glasnant Jones:

> At the open air revival services, I always found young Jeffreys at my side. I was privileged to give him his early religious tuition and a splendid scholar he was. Superior to other lads, there was a character in his face: I knew he was a 'chosen vessel.' When I left Siloh, Maesteg in 1907 young Jeffreys was in business, and had he remained in that calling, I am convinced he would have become a merchant prince.[4]

The Holiness Movements

The Holiness Movements both in Britain and America had a great influence on the developing Pentecostal Movements. It was the Wesleyan concept of a 'second blessing' that was to be most influential. The concept of 'entire sanctification' or 'perfect love' was the idea that it was possible for Christians to become so close to Christ in holiness that they would reach the place where they would be without sin. It taught an experience which totally eradicated sin from the heart.[5] The idea of perfection within the life of the believer had a profound effect upon the early Pentecostals. Charles Finney, among others, came to see it as a distinct crisis experience of sanctification, a second work of grace by which a Christian may be entirely sanctified.[6] The proliferation of the Holiness groups in America was fuelled by the 1858 revival and they strongly taught this concept of a 'second blessing'. This, in turn, matured into this being termed as the 'Baptism in the Holy Ghost'. Some historians are of the opinion that the inspiration behind the Holiness Movement was the idea of Christian perfection as embraced by John Wesley. Seeking a deeper relationship with God, like that experienced by the apostles with Jesus, Holiness Movement Christians made this idea of holiness through being sanctified by the Holy Spirit into a primary goal. This took hold in America during the first part of the nineteenth century.[7] Some Pentecostal historians believe that Pentecostalism rose out of the Holiness Movement.

More and more, the link between the 'second blessing' and a Spirit baptism became closer. A B Simpson, the son of Scottish covenanters who had moved to Canada, became a prominent figure in holiness circles at that time. At the age of twenty-one he was appointed minister of the Knox Presbyterian Church in Hamilton. It was a large church for such a young man. The church grew through his ministry and he later moved to an even bigger church in Louisville, Kentucky. He came under the influence of Major Whittle who had close connections with D L Moody. After a difficult time while leading the Broadway Tabernacle in New York, he had a breakdown, was healed, but resigned from his position and from the Presbyterian denomination. He did so on the issue of infant baptism. He started a new outreach with just a few members. In 1889, work was finished on the building that was named the Gospel Tabernacle, just one block from Times Square. He set up a Training Institute and a Missionary Home.[8]

It was clear to Simpson that healing, prophecy and tongues were an important part of God's provision to the Church at the end of the age.[9] He had an influence on Charles Parham, who was to become an important figure in the fledgling Pentecostal Movement.[10] It seemed that he believed in seeking the baptism of the Spirit which would be accompanied by the gift of tongues[11], although he did not take what was to become the classical Pentecostal view that tongues was the initial evidence of the baptism in the Holy Spirit. It was Simpson who crystalised what was to become the major focus of some Pentecostal denominations world-wide, including Elim. This was belief in the four cardinal points of the work of Christ; Saviour, Healer, Baptiser (in the Holy Spirit) and Coming King. 'It was not the uniqueness of Simpson's doctrines that marked him out, for each of his four elements was represented by a substantial spiritual movement in the late nineteenth century. Rather, it was his original combination of them ... that distinguished him.'[12]

In combining the four-fold pattern in the way that he did, Simpson elaborated on the concept that emphasised the 'full gospel' term that characteristically formulised early Pentecostal theology. It was a refinement of the five-fold theological emphasis that was adhered to by some of the early Pentecostal pioneers including Parham and Seymour. This five-fold pattern included within it the Wesleyan holiness tradition of three works of grace.[13] This is the pattern that was adopted by the Apostolic Faith Mission which traced its origin directly to the Azusa Street Revival.

> This church ... places special emphasis on the need of having three definite, separate, spiritual experiences wrought out in the heart and life: JUSTIFICATION, SANCTIFICATION, THE BAPTISM OF THE HOLY GHOST ... These doctrines concerning spiritual experience, together with the teachings on Divine Healing, the Imminent Second Coming of Jesus – premillennial ... provide the solid, scriptural foundation on which the church stands.[14]

Simpson departed from the five-fold emphasis and 'introduced a four-fold gospel of salvation, healing, sanctification and the second coming of Christ'[15] – 'emergence of this pattern is in fact, the last step in the complex process of development that culminated in Pentecostalism.'[16] The Christocentric four-fold formula presented by Simpson was adopted by many of the early Pentecostals. The only change in this formula became the substituting of 'Sanctifier' by 'Baptiser in the Holy Spirit'. This was to be popularised by Aimee Semple McPherson (1890-1944) whose claim that she had received it by divine revelation was challenged by James Bradley, who claimed that it was 'borrowed' (from Simpson).[17]

Simpson's four-fold Christocentric formula, modified by McPherson, became the doctrinal basis of the Elim Movement and Elim adopted the title 'Elim Foursquare Gospel Alliance' in 1925. Simpson, although parting company with some of the early Pentecostal pioneers in America, influenced men such as T B Barratt and A A Boddy, who were to become very influential in the development of the British Pentecostal Movement. The subject of tongues as the initial evidence of the baptism in the Holy Spirit was to become an issue in the British Pentecostal Movement. Malcolm Hathaway claims that George Jeffreys and Elim shared Simpson's view as regards initial evidence. He says that both were probably influenced in this respect by their emphasis on mission rather than charismata. This may be true, but certainly, in the early days, most Elim leaders believed that speaking in other tongues was the initial evidence of the baptism in the Holy Spirit. Indeed, in Elim's first Statement of Fundamentals published in 1922, this is clearly stated.

The Keswick Movement

The Keswick Movement was to play a seminal role in the origins of the Welsh Revival (1904-05) and the British Pentecostal Movement.[18] It was an effective counter to the rapid advance of higher criticism and theological liberalism that infected the British ecclesiastical system towards the end of the nineteenth century. The emphasis of the Keswick Conventions was the deepening of spiritual life. This was associated with the baptism in the Holy Spirit, although not with the charismata, and certainly not speaking with other tongues at the inspiration of the Holy Spirit. But the Keswick Conventions and its message, certainly prepared the way for the Pentecostal doctrine of a Spirit baptism accompanied by charismatic gifts which gave way to power for service.[19]

The major impact that Keswick was to have on the Pentecostal Movement, especially in Britain, was to view Spirit baptism, not so much in terms of holiness but as empowering for service. This was a departure from the Wesleyan holiness tradition and certainly paved the way for the Pentecostal emphasis on the baptism in the Holy Spirit. In particular, this change in emphasis was taught by Torrey, Moody's associate evangelist and successor, who wrote that 'The baptism with the Holy Spirit' was a definite experience separate from regeneration and 'always connected with testimony and service'.[20] He implied that it had nothing to do with sanctification and that the form of the power received during Spirit baptism varied according to the different gifts of the Spirit. This interpretation of the purpose of the baptism in the Holy Spirit was the groundwork that was laid for the birth of Pentecostalism, particularly in Britain.[21] Glossolalia was to be seen as the *evidence* of Pentecostalism, not its *message*. This was articulated strongly by Alexander Tee who was to become a leading evangelist within Elim in the latter half of the last century.

There were many prominent British evangelicals who spoke at the Keswick Conventions. Among them were Hanley Moule, A T Pierson, F B Meyer, G Campbell-Morgan and J H Jowett. These preachers came from various denominational backgrounds and proclaimed a message of unity among God's people. Hudson Taylor and D L Moody preached at the convention in 1892 and Andrew Murray of South Africa in 1895. The organisers proved that they saw the gospel as embracing the whole world when they invited Pandita Ramabai of India to speak in 1898.[22]

The main emphasis of the Keswick Movement was the teaching that came to be known as 'The Higher Life'. The idea was that Christians should move on from their initial conversion experience to grow and mature in the knowledge of God. This was seen as a second work of grace in the believer's life. The Keswick Movement taught, and still teaches, that Christians who receive this blessing from God can live a more sin-free life as they grow to be more like Christ. This view quickly separated Keswick from the traditional Wesleyan teaching of 'entire sanctification'. 'They managed to steer a middle road between reserved reformed views of sanctification and erroneous Wesleyan teachings.'[23]

Many early British Pentecostals attended the Keswick conventions, among them, Alexander Boddy, Smith Wigglesworth and J Nelson Parr. The Keswick Conventions had a secondary impact upon the early British Pentecostal pioneers in that it showed them the value of a national platform from which to declare their message. This was to see its fulfilment in the Sunderland Conventions that were to prove to be massively influential in the development of British Pentecostalism.

There is no doubt that the Keswick Conventions impacted not only some of the men that were to become influential in the nascent Pentecostal Movement in Britain,[24] but, in that it gave rise to the description of a second work of grace as being an endowment with power to serve and was given the designation 'baptism in the Spirit', it also proved to be one of the catalysts that caused these men to seek the experience *with* a supernatural evidence. 'Moreover, as the 19th Century drew to an end, there was a widely held desire for Christians to face the new challenges of the 20th century with fresh power bestowed by the Holy Spirit.'[25] Kay goes on to say that the phrase 'baptism in the Spirit' was used quite extensively across the theological spectrum to refer to a powerful encounter with the Holy Spirit, but beyond this, preachers did not go.[26]

Keswick certainly had an influence on the birth of the Welsh revival. Malcolmson claims that in 1905 some 300 Welsh delegates fresh from the revival held an all-night of prayer where tongues were manifest.[27] There is no substantive proof that speaking in other tongues took place during the Welsh revival. Some claim that Evan Roberts, the acknowledged leader during the revival of 1904-05, spoke in other tongues after being baptised in the Holy Spirit. According to Malcolmson, A T Pierson called the Welsh prayer meeting at the convention a 'satanic disturbance'; but that could have been with reference to the highly emotional nature of the prayer meeting.[28]

The Keswick conventions made a huge impact on Welsh evangelicals. At Keswick in 1903, two Welsh ministers recalled how thirteen Welsh people had gathered in 1896 at the convention, meeting together to pray for Wales and asking God to give to Wales a similar convention for the deepening of the spiritual life.[29] This resulted in the Welsh Keswick convention at Llandrindod Wells in 1903. Among the speakers at this convention were R B Jones and Seth Joshua who were to become influential in the Welsh Revival.

Notes

[1] Cartwright, D W, ibid, p45.

[2] Hathaway, M, *The Elim Pentecostal Church, Pentecostal Perspectives,* edited by Keith Warrington (Carlisle: Paternoster Press, 1998), p9.

[3] Hathaway, M, ibid, p2.

[4] Boulton, E C W, ibid, p1.

[5] Malcolmson, Keith, *Pentecostal Pioneers Remembered: British and Irish Pioneers Remembered* (USA: Xulon Press 2008), p73.

[6] Hathaway, M, ibid, p3.

[7] Traci Schumacher, www.newsmax.com (accessed 21st February 2020).

[8] Malcolmson, Keith, ibid, p67.

[9] Malcolmson, Keith, ibid, p 68.

[10] Robeck, Cecil M, *The Azusa Street Mission & Revival: The Birth of the Global Pentecostal Movement* (Nashville TN: Thomas Nelson Inc, 2006), p41.

[11] Malcolmson, Keith, ibid, p68.

[12] Hathaway in Warrington, p7.

[13] These works of grace are conversion, sanctification and the baptism of the Holy Spirit.

[14] Dayton, Donald, *Theological Roots of Pentecostalism* (Grand Rapids, MI: Baker Academic, 2011), p21.

[15] Anderson, Allan Heaton, *An Introduction to Pentecostalism, Second Edition* (New York: Cambridge University Press, 2014), p31.

[16] Dayton, Donald, ibid, p22.

[17] Nienkirchen, C W, *A B Simpson and the Pentecostal Movement* (Peabody: Hendrikson, 1992), p37, quoted by Hathaway, ibid, p 6.

[18] Hathaway in Warrington, ibid, p3.

[19] Hathaway in Warrington, ibid, p4.

[20] Moody's associate evangelist and successor who expressed the opinion that the baptism with the Holy Spirit was a definite experience separate from regeneration and was connected with testimony and service.

[21] Anderson, Allan, ibid, p9.

[22] Malcolmson, Keith, ibid, p72.

[23] Malcolmson, Keith, ibid, p72.

[24] A A Boddy, Smith Wigglesworth, Willie Burton, Nelson Parr and Syd Mercy all attended the Keswick Conventions.

[25] Kay, William, ibid, p23.

[26] Kay, William, ibid, p23.

[27] Malcolmson, Keith, ibid, p75.

[28] Malcolmson, Keith, ibid, p75.

[29] Penn-Lewis, Jessie, *The Awakening in Wales and Some of the Hidden Springs* (London, Marshall Brothers, 1905), p28.

2
The Welsh Revival

Wales has been referred to many times as the Land of Song and the Land of Revivals. Certainly, the Principality has had its fair measure of spiritual awakenings. There have been four major Welsh revivals since the eighteenth century of which the 1904-05 revival was the last. Although J Vyrnwy Morgan lists fourteen Welsh revivals commencing with Vicar Prichard at Llanymddyfri and district between 1620 and 1630. The other thirteen occurred during the period 1740-1905.[1] The first notable Welsh revival occurred in the middle of the eighteenth century, when 'a live coal from the altar' touched the lips of Daniel Rowlands, a clergyman of the Church of England, and inspired him with an incredible fervour in spite of great opposition. His opposers labelled him 'the cracked clergyman of Llangeitho'. But, through his preaching, all Wales became ablaze. People travelled many miles to hear him preach. There were scenes where people wept and shouted, thereby causing a stern reaction from those genteel members of the Church of England. This revival led to the establishment of the Calvinistic Methodist Church which soon became the second foremost denomination in Wales. It also gave Wales its hymnology. If Charles Wesley is the greatest English hymn writer, William Williams of Pantycelyn, certainly became the greatest Welsh hymn writer of all time. He was converted through the dynamic preaching of Daniel Rowlands.

At the beginning of the nineteenth century, another revival started. There were three main leaders to this Awakening in

Wales. John Elias with his theological sermons, Christmas Evans with his poetical sermons, and Williams of Wern with his philosophical sermons, travelled the country, proclaiming the doctrines of grace.[2] If the first revival gave Wales her hymnology, the second one gave the nation her theology. But even in this revival, there was a substantial addition made to Welsh hymnology in the person of Ann Griffiths (1776-1805) from Montgomeryshire. She was converted during this revival. Having married Thomas Griffiths, she died after childbirth in 1805 at the age of twenty-nine. Her poems were kept by her maid and later put to music. Her greatest hymn is probably the best-known Welsh hymn which is sung (in Welsh) to the tune 'Cwm Rhondda'.[3]

There was a third revival in 1859 largely through the work of David Morgan, yet another Calvinistic Methodist minister. He travelled the length and breadth of Wales preaching with great fervour and spiritual anointing. A word needs to be said here about Welsh preachers preaching with the '*hwyl*'. The closest one can get to describing it is that it was almost like an inspired chant. Christmas Evans, and later, Jubilee Young were great exponents of this type of preaching. At times, they would almost sing their sermons. The impact of this third great Welsh revival was the establishment of thousands of schools and three national colleges. According to Cynddylan Jones, this third revival gave Wales her educational system.[4] During this third revival an estimated 110,000 were added to the Welsh churches, by far and away most of them in nonconformist denominations.[5] With the exception of the first revival in the mid-eighteenth century, the revivals broke out among the nonconformist chapels of which the Calvinistic Methodist Movement was very much in the lead. This response to the moving of the Holy Spirit in revival was a repeating aspect of Welsh church life in the nineteenth century with a number of local revivals breaking out in various parts of the Principality. There were marked spiritual awakenings in Tredegar and then

Rhumney in Monmouthshire and also in Aberafan, Glamorganshire.

The first story of what became known as the Welsh Revival was told to the public in a report that appeared in the 'Western Mail' of Thursday, 10th November 1904. The reporter, writing under the pseudonym 'Awstin', told of the extraordinary meetings being held in Moriah Chapel, Llwchwr.[6] The preacher was Evan John Roberts (1878-1951), a twenty-six-year-old ministerial student. Meetings continued until 2.30 in the morning with a sermon lasting for more than two hours.[7] The length of the sermon is quite astonishing in view of the seeming lack of preaching by Roberts during the rest of the revival period.

While Evan Roberts is, undeniably, looked on as the leader during the time of the revival, there were others of whom it could be said that they were prime movers in the spiritual awakening in Wales and it could be equally said that the Revival commenced through them and not Roberts. Two men, in particular stand out: Seth Joshua (1858-1925) and R B Jones (1869-1933). Both these men were powerful players in the religious event that was to become the Welsh Revival 1904-05. The one, Seth Joshua, was influential right at the beginning of the revival, and it was during his ministry in Blaenanerch, Cardiganshire, that Evan Roberts received what he termed the 'Baptism of the Spirit'.[8] R B Jones was to become greatly used during the revival, especially in North Wales. This in itself was remarkable as there is quite a cultural difference between North and South Wales, with the Welsh language having many different words for the same thing between North and South.[9] R B Jones was born into a mining family in Dowlais, near Merthyr, South Wales.

Seth Joshua

Seth Joshua was born in Pontypool, Monmouthshire on 10th April 1858. He became a Welsh Presbyterian minister and was an influential figure in Welsh Nonconformity before, and during the Welsh Revival. Joshua spent a great deal of time in prayer and was determined to see Wales experience yet another revival. He was present at the Welsh Keswick Convention in Llandrindod in 1903 and was one of the speakers. Seth Joshua was a powerful voice in Wales. He was to be influential in the life and brief ministry of Evan Roberts. It was in a meeting conducted by Joshua in Blaenanerch in September 1904 that Roberts had an experience that was quite disturbing to some of the people there. John Thickens first noticed 'a young man sitting opposite to us in obvious distress while Mr. Joshua was speaking … a young neurotic man – that is neurotic in our opinion'.[10] Joshua had an overwhelming burden for Wales. His son, Dr Peter Joshua mentioned the time he saw his father, unbeknown to him, crying out and saying 'Give me Wales'. 'God never gave Wales to my Dad, although he gave him many souls, but one day when he was preaching when he made an appeal Evan Roberts was the only one who stood to his feet and trusted the Saviour. God never gave Wales to my Dad, but he gave Wales to Evan Roberts.'[11] The effects of Seth Joshua's praying and evangelistic preaching, it is felt by many historians, was a catalyst in the revival.

R B Jones

Another key figure in the Welsh Revival of 1904-05 was Rhys Bevan Jones, a Baptist minister who lived most of his life while in ministry in the Rhondda. It was he, at the age of thirty-five, who brought the revival to Rhosllanerchrugog, just outside Wrexham in North Wales. He was converted at the age of twelve and soon became conscious of the fact that he was being called into the ministry. He became the minister of Caersalem Baptist Chapel in Llanelli where he developed a close friendship with W S Jones of Penuel in Carmarthen. W S Jones had just returned to Wales from several years as a minister in the Welsh community in Scranton, Pennsylvania. R B became the minister at Salem Welsh Baptist Chapel in Porth, Rhondda.[12] While at Salem, he attended the convention at Llandrindod where he responded to a passionate appeal from F B Meyer to receive the Holy Spirit. Jones testified: 'A new world opened up for me. Now I saw it. I went home on Saturday and took the service as usual without telling anyone. Next Sunday I still said nothing, yet they somehow knew that they had a new man in the pulpit.'[13] Jones had a greater impact in North Wales than did Roberts, although the latter spent some two months there in 1905. Evans reckons that the main reason for this was the rapid spread of the revival independently of his (Roberts') personal appearance. R B Jones had held missions in both Rhos and Anglesey with great success. Roberts' ministry there was directed primarily to Christians.[14]

Evan Roberts

Roberts was undoubtedly the outstanding personality of the Welsh Revival. The few contemporary accounts of his childhood show Roberts to be a complex personality. His childhood friend, D R Grenfell (MP) spoke of a happy, normal lad who played rough games on the river banks at Bwlchymynydd. Another picture is of a slender young collier with piercing eyes, a lovely smile, a clean, upright look, and 'some signs of idealism and clean values'.[15]

As noted above, it was at a convention in the autumn of 1904 at Blaenanerch in Cardiganshire that Evan Roberts had an encounter with the Holy Spirit that was to change his life and, some claim, the whole of Wales. The speakers were Seth Joshua and Joseph Jenkins, minister of the Calvinistic Methodist Church in New Quay, Cardiganshire. In September 1904, Evan Roberts left his home in Llwchwr to attend a preparatory school in Castell Newydd Emlyn[16] in preparation for going to the Methodist Theological College. It was while he was at Newcastle Emlyn that he attended the convention in Blaenanerch. It was at that convention that he experienced the enormous pressure of the Holy Spirit resulting in him calling out to God, 'Bend us!'[17]

He returned to his home in Llwchwr where he was involved in conducting and speaking at a number of the chapels in the town and surrounding villages. It was in Moriah, the chapel of which he was a member, that Roberts laid down as necessary to revival blessing four key principles. These were:

1. If there is past sin or sins hitherto unconfessed, we cannot receive the Spirit. Therefore, we must search and ask the Spirit to search.

2. If there is anything doubtful in our lives, it *must* be removed – anything we were uncertain about its rightness or wrongness. That thing *must* be removed.

3. An entire giving up of ourselves to the Spirit. We *must* and *do* all he requires of us.

4. Public confession of Christ.[18]

These four cardinal points were expressed over and over in Roberts' revival meetings together with his repeated plea for the Lord to bend him, and the people gathered to hear him and witness the revival. Roberts' ministry was remarkably short-lived. By the end of the following year, the revival as such, was at an end. By this time, he was physically and mentally exhausted. He responded to an invitation from Jessie Penn-Lewis to stay at her home in Leicestershire. He stayed there until 1920 when he returned to Wales.

The 1904-05 revival has been considered by many (mostly English Evangelicals and Charismatics who have little knowledge of Welsh culture, history and ecclesiology) as the greatest of the Welsh revivals. It is the opinion of the author, who is a first-language Welsh speaker, that the last was certainly the weakest of the great Welsh revivals. In his view, the long-time effect of the 1904 revival on the Welsh chapels was that they became virtually spiritually moribund. Within forty years of the revival, Welsh nonconformity had entered a period of massive decline from which it has not recovered. It could be argued that the devastating effects of two world wars was a major contributing feature in such a decline. But it would appear that the decline in Welsh nonconformity, especially in the Welsh language chapels, has been greater than the decline in the Church of Wales and greater than Church decline in the rest of the United Kingdom.

It must be borne in mind that Welsh nonconformity was strong and largely evangelical prior to the revival of 1904-05. A large number of chapels were opened throughout Wales in the latter half of the nineteenth century (many of them had to be significantly enlarged following the 1904-05 revival). Nonconformity was, in the main, evangelical, although higher criticism and theological liberalism had affected some parts of the Church during this period. But ministers of great spirituality rose to prominence in Wales during this time. Men such as Joseph Jenkins (1859-1929), W W Lewis (1856-1938), W Nantlais Williams (1874-1959), J. Cynddylan Jones (1841-1930), and R B Jones (1869-1933) had a great impact on the spiritual health of Wales during this period. 'These men, and others like them, stood for the divine inspiration and inerrancy of the Bible and recognised its content as the divine rule for life and conduct: they made valuable contributions to Welsh Nonconformity.'[19]

It is clear that prior to the Welsh Revival evangelicalism was very much to the fore within Welsh nonconformity. Richard Owen was a Welsh Calvinistic Methodist minister mightily used of God in spiritual awakenings in North Wales towards the end of the nineteenth century. He attended the D L Moody meetings in Liverpool in February 1875 where he imbibed Moody's methodology: 'Moody taught him plainness and directness, and increased his sense of responsibility and zeal towards the unconverted.'[20] Yet, it was the pattern that was set by David Morgan, the 1859 revivalist that Richard Owen followed as being more suitable to the traditional Welsh manner of conducting divine service.[21] There was certainly revival in the

North Wales counties of Anglesey, Caernarfonshire, Merionethshire, Flintshire and Denbighshire.[22] The visits of Moody and Sankey, and Torrey Alexander to Cardiff during this period, had a galvanising effect on Welsh evangelicalism which was prevalent in the nonconformist chapels at the time. While not in rude health, evangelicalism was far from a dying cause within the Welsh chapels at the outbreak of the 1904-05 revival. One can but unfavourably compare the spiritual climate of Wales twenty years prior to the revival with the state of the Church twenty years after the Awakening.

There was considerable criticism of Evan Roberts and the Welsh Revival, not only from liberal theologians but also from fellow evangelicals. Indeed, some Welsh ministers viewed what took place in Wales during the revival as 'insanity'. In the introduction to his chapter on Evan Roberts, Morgan comments: 'Now that the excitement of the Revival is over, and the nation has regained its sanity, we are able to look more dispassionately upon the career of a man who, for a brief period, loomed largely in the imagination of the people.'[23] Like Peter Price, quoted extensively by Kay,[24] Vyrnwy Morgan was highly critical of the Welsh Revival in general, and Evan Roberts in particular. As to Evan Roberts, it can be safely said that people were moved more by the mystery of the man than by his cause.

> One of the four articles of the Revival, or confession of faith, which he has caused to be written and to be made public, was instant and absolute obedience to the promptings of the Holy Spirit. At Zion, Cwmafan, Mr. Thomas Roberts, a Wesleyan by profession of faith, an aged Christian gentleman, one of the landmarks of the valley, began to pray; but he had uttered only a few sentences when the Revivalist stopped him. The Holy Spirit prompted the one to pray, and the same Spirit prompted the other to suppress him.[25]

Most modern Pentecostal pastors would react to interruptions in their services, but one must bear in mind that this was during the time of revival when, by and large, meetings were left open for anyone to take part as the Spirit led. Also, one needs to understand that the above person was a mature Christian of considerable age. He held a high standing among the people of the locality.

Mr David Elias, a Baptist brother, offered prayers. Evan Roberts said, 'It is enough.'[26] But David Elias paid no heed to the interruption. The revivalist called for verses, and they came by the dozen; but David Elias continued to pray, his clear bell-like voice being heard above the din and clatter. Evan Roberts sat down and remained silent until Elias had finished. There was a revulsion of feeling which the revivalist did not fail to detect, and he fell in a heap on the floor of the pulpit, at the same time giving vent to the most doleful exclamations. The confusion was as indescribable as it was painful.[27]

It could be that Morgan, like Price, being a highly educated man (he was a Doctor of Divinity), was less than impressed by Roberts' seeming lack of sufficient educational and theological expertise. It is clear that Morgan, while deploring the contorted language of some revivalists on the subject of hell, had a genuine appreciation of past revivals in Wales. He was particularly impressed by the ministry of the above-mentioned Richard Owen. 'His preaching was so powerful that stalwart and hardened sinners groaned and wept. In many respects he made people think of Elijah in the Old Testament and John the Baptist in the New, heralding the coming of the Saviour into the world.'[28]

Rightful criticism can, and ought to be made of the 1904-05 revival, particularly from a Welsh point of view. As has been presented above, prior to the revival, the Welsh churches were strong and, largely, evangelical. Within a short period of time, the Welsh religious landscape had changed greatly. The major Welsh denominations (with the possible exception of the Welsh Baptists) went theologically liberal at an alarming rate. This, combined with the ravages of the world wars, the excruciating poverty in the Welsh industrial hinterland and the rise of extreme Socialism and Communism (owing to the extreme hardships experienced throughout Wales, in particular in the South Wales coalfield) had a devastating effect on evangelicalism in Wales.

There is no doubt that the revival had a very positive effect on many people during its short existence. Lives were changed, social evils declined, men stopped drinking and there was a God-consciousness evident throughout the land. But the effects were remarkably short-lived. There have been many good things that have come out of the revival, not least, a genuine hunger for God to move across our nation and the world again. But those who are embedded in the language, culture and ecclesiology of Wales are deeply saddened by the state of the churches and chapels in Wales today. Indeed, some, the author included, are of the opinion that perhaps the churches and chapels in Wales today would be in better condition had not the 1904-05 revival occurred.

On a much brighter note, the next chapters will show the positive impact that the 1904-05 Welsh Revival had on the emerging British Pentecostal Movement and, in particular, Elim. Three key leaders of the major Pentecostal Movement in the British Isles were converted as a direct result of the Welsh Revival.[29]

George Jeffreys, along with his older brother, Stephen, was converted during the Welsh revival under the ministry of Rev Glasnant Jones in Siloh Independent Chapel in Nantyffyllon, Maesteg on the 20th November 1904.[30] A fuller account of this will be recorded in Chapter 5. Sufficient to say at this point is that the Welsh Revival deeply impacted both George and Stephen, to the extent that both the Christian and the secular press referred to them as 'revivalists'. After describing George's extraordinary campaigns in Plymouth and Coulsdon in 1914, Boulton makes the following comment: 'News of the young Revivalist's successful ministry had filtered through to some brethren in Monaghan who were deeply interested in the evangelisation of Northern Ireland...'[31] It would appear that in

Boulton's thinking, there was a marked difference between evangelism and revival. In a photograph of George and Ernest Darragh, the caption reads: 'R. E. Darragh was the first member of the Evangelistic Band. He came under the influence of the Revivalist during his ever memorable visit to the Gillespie brothers.' Jeffreys is referred to as 'the Revivalist' and Darragh as 'his first Elim Evangelist'.[32] It is clear that George and Stephen Jeffreys saw themselves as 'children of the Revival' and their ministry forged in the fires of the Welsh Revival. George, in particular, was convinced that the Pentecostal Movement, of which he was to become a leading figure, was an extension and development of the revival that he himself had been converted through.

Notes

[1] Morgan, J Vyrnwy, *The Welsh Religious Revival, 1904-05: A Retrospect and a Criticism* (Chapman & Hall Ltd, 1909).

[2] J Cynddylan Jones, quoted by Penn-Lewis, Jessie, ibid, pp1,2.

[3] The name of the hymn is 'Wele'n sefyll rhwng y myrtwydd'.

[4] Jones, Cynddylan, ibid, p3.

[5] Evans, Eifion, *The Welsh Revival of 1904* (Bryntirion, Bridgend, Evangelical Press of Wales, 1993), p9.

[6] The English name for this town, situated twelve miles west of Swansea, is Loughor.

[7] Cartwright, Desmond, *Some Evangelists: The Life and Ministry of George Jeffreys and P S Brewster in the Formation of the Elim Pentecostal Church*. An unpublished manuscript, p1.

[8] Evans, Eifion, ibid, pp68-75; see also, Jones, Brynmor, *Voices from the Welsh Revival 1904-1905* (Bryntirion, Bridgend: Evangelical Press of Wales, 1995), p26, where the pastor of the church in Llwchwr writes of '30 young people being baptised in the Holy Spirit' as a result of Roberts' ministry.

[9] The author hails from North Wales and was brought up in South Wales, where his family moved to when he was aged seven. Unable to speak English until he moved to the Rhondda, he is very aware of the cultural and linguistic differences between North and South Wales.

[10] Jones, Brynmor, ibid, p 14.

[11] Jones, Brynmor, ibid, p 16.

[12] The author was, at one time, a member of Salem and grew up hearing many accounts of the ministry of R B Jones.

[13] Jones, Brynmor, ibid, p15.

[14] Evans, Eifion, ibid, p143.

[15] Jones, Brynmor, ibid, p18.

[16] Newcastle Emlyn.

[17] It was spoken in Welsh: *'Arglwydd, plyg ni.'*

[18] Evans, Eifion, ibid, p84

[19] Palmer, Chris, *The Emergence of Pentecostalism in Wales* (London: Apostolos Church History Series, Apostolos Publishing Ltd), p1.

[20] Evans, Eifion, ibid, p17.

[21] Evans, Eifion, ibid, p17.

[22] In the case of towns or places in Wales where there is a Welsh and English spelling, the author, true to his Welsh heritage, has opted for the Welsh version, as in the case of *Caernarfon* and *Llanymddyfri* (Llandovery).

[23] Morgan, Vyrnwy, ibid, p49.

[24] Kay, William, ibid, pp30,31.

[25] Morgan, Vyrnwy, ibid, p49.

[26] Morgan, Vyrnwy, ibid, p51.

[27] Morgan, Vyrnwy, ibid, pp52,53.

[28] Morgan, Vyrnwy, ibid, xvii.

[29] They were George Jeffreys (Elim), Daniel Williams (Apostolic) and Donald Gee (Assemblies of God).

[30] Another brother, William, was converted at the same time. Canty, George, ibid, p21.

[31] Boulton, E C W, ibid, p21.

[32] Boulton, E C W, ibid. Photograph between pages 28 and 29.

3
Origins of the Pentecostal Movement

A young woman by the name of Agnes Ozman became the first person recorded in the twentieth century to have spoken in other tongues as the evidence of the baptism in the Holy Spirit. It occurred at a meeting in Topeka, Kansas on 31st December 1900, under the ministry of Charles Fox Parham (1873-1929). He is seen by some as being the father of the Pentecostal Movement, although, perhaps a stronger case can be made for William Joseph Seymour. However, Parham is generally recognised as the formulator of Pentecostal doctrine and the theological founder of the Pentecostal Movement.[1]

Charles Fox Parham

Parham had set up a Bible school during October 1900 in Topeka, Kansas. Earlier that year, he had spent six weeks at the 'Holy Ghost and Us Bible School' in Shiloh, Maine, where he had been greatly influenced by Frank Sandford, an evangelist who had held a series of tent meetings in Topeka. Parham was deeply affected as a result of his visit to Shiloh and it caused him to develop his theology concerning the baptism in the Holy Spirit. 'He concluded that the baptism in the Holy Spirit was available to all who lived a holy life and sought to attain it.'[2]

In December of 1900, Parham asked his students at Bethel Bible School to search the Scriptures and see if they could discern one special sign of the baptism with the Holy Spirit.[3] It is obvious that after spending time with Sandford, he knew the answer, but he wanted his students to study the Bible and arrive at their own conclusion.[4] During Parham's absence for three days while preaching in Kansas City, his students devoted themselves to fasting, prayer and study of the Scriptures. As a result of this endeavour, they unanimously decided that speaking with other tongues constituted the one and only initial proof of the baptism in the Holy Spirit.[5]

In response to his students' revelation regarding the task that he set them, Parham called for a night-long New Year's watch service and it was during this gathering that Agnes Ozman asked Parham to lay hands on her and pray for her to receive the baptism in the Holy Spirit accompanied by the evidence of speaking with other tongues. Parham, recalling the account, said:

> I laid my hands upon her and prayed. I had scarcely repeated three dozen sentences when a glory fell upon her, a halo seemed to surround her head and face, and she began speaking the Chinese language and was unable to speak English for three days. When she tried to write in English to tell us of her experience, she wrote the Chinese, copies which we still have.[6]

Parham made the vital connection between the baptism in the Holy Spirit as a source of spiritual zeal and power, and the gift of tongues as its sign and seal.[7] In addition to this, Parham adopted the premillennialism of J N Darby and his own experience of healing.[8] After closing the mission, Parham itinerated throughout Kansas, Missouri and Texas preaching his message on the baptism in the Holy Spirit as part of what he called the 'Apostolic Faith'.[9] This was the name that was later adopted by the first American Pentecostal church in Los Angeles, and the first British Pentecostal church in Bournemouth. There is another link between Parham and William Hutchinson, the leader of the Apostolic Faith Church in Bournemouth, in that both of them were adherents of the British Israel theory. George Jeffreys was later to imbibe this doctrine, though most Pentecostals rejected it. 'The doctrines of divine healing and premillennialism became major planks of the Pentecostal platform. The scene was set for the adoption of a fourfold Pentecostal mission proclaiming salvation, healing, Spirit baptism and an imminent Parousia to usher in an earthly millennial kingdom.'[10]

In May 1905, Parham made Melrose, Kansas his new headquarters. He gathered a group of students and set up a Bible school. In July 1905, Parham and his students went to Houston, Texas where he set up another short-time Bible school where he taught on salvation, baptism in the Spirit with the 'Bible evidence' of speaking in tongues, healing and evangelism.[11]

It was to this Bible school that William Seymour came in response to an invitation from Lucy Farrow who served as a cook at the school and had been baptised in the Holy Spirit at Parham's meetings. Owing to their African–American heritage, Seymour and Farrow were aware of the limitations that their skin colour afforded them in Texas. Seymour had been excluded from seeking the baptism in the Holy Spirit at the altar of one of Parham's meetings because Parham did not allow for a racially integrated altar.[12] The 'Jim Crow' laws did not allow people of colour to mix together, and attending school together was prohibited.[13] There is a difference of opinion among Pentecostal historians as to Parham's attitude towards segregation. Some see him just as a representative of his time and social background and that there was no ingrained racism within him. They point to the fact that he was very impressed by Seymour's humility and godliness and did make provision for Seymour to take his seat in the hall outside the classroom. 'Parham would not violate the letter of the local Jim Crow laws, but he would not allow them to keep him from educating a genuine seeker, regardless of his colour.'[14]

Other historians see Parham as an inveterate racist. While he may have been a product of his culture and time, Hayford says of him, 'Without doubt Parham later became a racist, with racism so common in his time.'[15] This inbred racism is clearly seen in Parham's expressed views on 'singing in the Spirit'. While this received the almost unanimous praise of all who heard it, it was scathingly denounced in racist terms by Parham. William Manley described such singing, which he heard in the Azusa Street Revival, as the 'most remarkable incident of the sweetest singing I ever heard by about half a dozen women, all in unknown tongues, in which at intervals one voice would die away in very plaintive strains, while the others carried on the song'. This singing went by various names – 'singing in the Spirit', 'singing in tongues', the 'heavenly anthem', the 'heavenly chorus', and the 'chorus of tongues'. The faithful believed that this music was inspired completely by the Holy Spirit. Parham was having none of it. He saw nothing spiritual about it. He utterly ridiculed it and said it was nothing more than 'a modification of the Negro chanting of the Southland'.[16]

It is clear that Parham had a genuine interest in, and like of, William Seymour, but his ingrained and increasing racism became fully visible when he visited Seymour's work in Azusa Street, Los Angeles. Parham was aghast at what he saw and rebuked Seymour in very strong language. He was particularly offended at the interracial mingling of black and white people. Years later, he spoke of his disgust as 'Men and women, whites and blacks, knelt together or fell across one another; a white woman, perhaps of wealth and culture, could be seen thrown back in the arms of a big "buck n****r," and held tightly thus as she shivered and shook in freak imitation of Pentecost. Horrible, awful shame!'[17]

Parham distanced himself from Seymour and started up alternative meetings having at first tried to take over the work in Azusa Street which was resisted by Seymour and his leaders who then rejected Parham's leadership. This was a brave decision by Seymour as he viewed Parham as his spiritual leader. In fact, he had written to Parham on a number of occasions requesting him to visit Azusa Street as soon as possible to 'help set things in order'.[18] Parham started his rival Los Angeles Mission at the Women's Christian Temperance Hall, which by December 1906 claimed to have a following of 300. Hayford asserts that it was at this point that Parham lost his place of influence over the young emerging Pentecostal Movement. From this point onwards, Seymour's influence is in the ascendancy while Parham went in the opposite direction. Parham became extremely critical of the mission at this point, repeatedly complaining that 'orgies outrivalling scenes in devil or fetish worship took place in the upper room'. Over the next several years, he wrote a series of ever more scathing attacks against the mission.[19] Pentecostal historians are very much divided on their opinions of Parham. Hayford appears to be quite critical while Synan seems slightly more sympathetic. Tony Cauchi, a British Pentecostal historian, in his article on Parham appears to be the most favourable towards him. Cauchi depicts Parham as being a true prophet who was unwilling to be tied down by sectarian denominationalism. He designates him as an 'Apostle of the Spirit' who experienced two waves of revival, one in 1900-01 and the next in 1905-06 by which time he was at the height of his popularity and had between 8-10,000 followers. He puts a different slant to the rupture between Parham and Seymour: 'As Seymour's "spiritual father" in these things Parham felt responsible for what was happening and spoke out against them [the fleshly, spiritualistic controls which he felt had been allowed to develop in Azusa Street]. He held two or three services at Azusa, but was unable to convince Seymour to exercise more control.'[20]

In 1907, Parham was caught up in a homosexual scandal. He was preaching in a former Zion mission located in San Antonio when a story reported in the *San Antonio Light* made national news. Its headline read: 'Evangelist is arrested. C. F. Parham who has been prominent in Meetings Here. Taken into Custody'.

Again, there is a difference in Cauchi's reference to this compared to that of Hayford. The latter leaves less room for

Parham's innocence than does the former, although both point out that the charges were dropped. Their summation of his ministry could not be more different. Cauchi sums up Parham's ministry in glowing terminology:

> Charles Fox Parham will forever be one of the bright lights in God's hall of fame, characterised by a dogged determination and relentless pursuit of God's best and for God's glory. Despite personal sickness and physical weakness, continual persecution and unjustified accusation this servant of God was faithful to the heavenly vision and did his part in serving the purpose of God in his generation.[21]

Hayford is much less flattering in his assessment of Parham's role in the developing Pentecostal Movement:

> Parham's reaction [to the scandal] was both one of retreat and accusation. He withdrew to his one remaining stronghold, the Galena area of Kansas, establishing a base in nearby Baxter Springs. From there he bitterly denounced Seymour and other Pentecostal leaders. He became an ardent segregationist and in his later years offered praise to the Ku Klux Klan. For more than twenty years until his death in 1929, Parham was alienated from, and ignored by, the movement he helped to start.[22]

William Seymour

There has been much debate as to whether Parham or William Joseph Seymour (1870-1922) should be considered the father of the modern Pentecostal Movement. What cannot be denied, is the huge impact that this humble black pastor had on the worldwide Pentecostal Movement. He came under the influence of Parham at his Bible school in Houston in 1906. Seymour was one of the most influential African–American

Christian leaders of his time and whenever the history of modern Pentecostalism is told, his name is inevitably mentioned. Quite apart from his involvement in the development and advancement of the 'tongues-speaking' movement, his approach to Christian ministry was revolutionary on two major fronts: He advocated racial integration in worship and he also had no objections to women taking leadership roles in the church.

Seymour was born of Catholic parents on 2nd May 1870, in Centerville, Louisiana. Both his parents, Simon Simon[23] and Phillis Salaba remained slaves after Abraham Lincoln's famous Emancipation Proclamation on 22nd September 1862. Even though most black slaves were granted their liberty on 1st January 1863, Seymour's parents were not included in the emancipation for pragmatic reasons involving the impact that freed slaves from the southern Louisiana sugar plantations would have in that strategic area while the military were fighting a war. The risk being that the Union army would be immediately confronted with caring for a huge, unemployed, homeless population and it would be unable to complete its military duties. So, the status of these slaves would only be changed when the Civil War finished. However, an exemption clause was made which resulted in the immediate freedom of those slaves who would willingly join the Union army. Simon was among 15,000 African–American volunteers who made the decision to do this.[24]

Although his parents were Catholics, this would have been down to the religious persuasion of the plantation owners rather than out of their own conviction. That they came under the influence of Baptist ministers is evident from the fact that Simon Seymour was buried in the Providence Baptist Church Cemetery in November 1891. It would appear that William Seymour was raised a Baptist and had some schooling. Unlike his parents, he was able to read and write. After leaving home, Seymour lived in Indianapolis from 1894 to 1900, where he worked as a railway porter and a waiter at several hotel restaurants. It was during this time that he was converted and attended a Methodist Episcopal Church.[25] He moved to Cincinnati around 1900. It was there that he became involved with the 'Evening Light Saints', a Church of God group where he was 'sanctified'. 'Seymour struggled with a call to preach and contracted smallpox while living in Cincinnati, losing sight in one eye. Much like Parham did with his illnesses, Seymour attached spiritual significance to the sickness and felt God was judging him for not entering the ministry.'[26]

When Seymour attended Parham's Bible School in Houston (1906), he sought the baptism in the Holy Spirit with the evidence of speaking in other tongues. As a holiness preacher, he thought that he had received the baptism in the Spirit through being 'sanctified'. Parham's teaching convinced him that he had yet to receive the fullness of the Spirit. Parham took an interest in Seymour and the two of them preached to the 'coloured people'[27] of Houston.

Although strongly influenced by Parham, Seymour did not accept all of his mentor's theology. He was spiritually mature enough to make his own theological decisions. While agreeing with most of Parham's teaching, he was not convinced of Parham's claims that the language one received when he or she was baptised in the Holy Spirit was a human language intended to be used for evangelistic purposes though he was convinced that speaking in other tongues under the anointing of the Holy Spirit was the initial evidence of Spirit baptism. He also rejected Parham's notion of the annihilation of the wicked and he totally rejected Parham's Anglo-Israelite theory.[28]

Azusa Street

Revival was in the air when Seymour arrived in Los Angeles. Stories of the Welsh Revival had permeated the Christian community in the city and Joseph Smale, the Pastor of the prestigious First Baptist Church, had attended Evan Roberts' meetings in Wales and upon his return to the City of Angels,

49

Smale determined that First Baptist Church should lead the Los Angeles churches into revival, and they would do so with prayer.[29] So, the ground had been prepared for the coming of Seymour into the city with the Pentecostal message.

Seymour only stayed at the Bible school in Houston for six weeks. He had received an invitation from Julia Hutchins to lead the small Ninth and Santa Fe mission in Los Angeles. On his first Sunday there, 24th February, Seymour preached the Pentecostal message that had been taught him by Parham. He emphasised the message of being baptised in the Spirit with the accompanying evidence of speaking in other tongues and took for his text Acts 2:4.[30] The elders of the mission rejected Seymour's teachings as being counter to holiness teaching and Seymour found himself locked out of the church that he had travelled such a distance to pastor. He found temporary accommodation at the home of Mr and Mrs Edward Lee, members of the church. Although they did not accept his teaching on the baptism in the Holy Spirit, they were deeply impressed by his spirituality and humility. They gradually responded to his teaching and Seymour soon gathered a group of followers in the home of Richard Asberry, a friend of the Lees.[31] It was at this time that Frank Bartleman (1871-1936) joined the group. He was a journalist whose personal diary and regular reports in the holiness press constitute the most complete and reliable record of what actually happened in Los Angeles from 1906 to 1909.[32]

The Asberry home was situated on North Bonnie Brae Street and a number of other mainly African Americans joined the group. Frank Bartleman brought with him 'Mother' Wheaton, a nationally famous evangelist who ministered in prisons across the country.[33] Seymour had contacted two friends in Houston to join him for meetings at the Asberry home. They were Lucy Farrow and Joseph Warren. Edward Lee became the first person in the group to receive the baptism in the Holy Spirit with the accompanying evidence of glossolalia when Lucy Farrow and Seymour prayed for him. Bartleman said that the

Azusa Street revival was an example of 'the Spirit born again in a humble "stable", outside ecclesiastical establishments as usual'.[34] Bartleman points out the very humble beginnings of what was to become a worldwide revival. He expressed the opinion that this outpouring could not have occurred in an established church or even a mission. He says that all these (churches and missions) were in the hands of men; the Spirit could not work. He makes reference to the great revival in Wales where 'the great expounders of England had to come and sit at the feet of crude, hardworking miners, and see the wonderful works of God'.[35]

It was a small beginning. Bartleman found only 'about a dozen saints there, some white, some coloured'.[36] Although there was an absence of large numbers at first, there was never a lack of enthusiasm. The meetings would go on for twelve hours or more. When the Bonnie Brae location soon became far too small, Seymour and his new congregation leased a vacant building and negotiated a lease just before Good Friday, 13th April 1906. He named it the Apostolic Faith Mission – a name reflecting Parham's influence. While the revival started slowly, the *Los Angeles Daily Times* carried the headline 'Weird Babel of Tongues' and gave a very negative eyewitness account of one of the mission's first meetings. It referred to meetings being held in a tumbledown shack on Azusa Street. 'Coloured people and a sprinkling of whites compose the congregation, and nights are made hideous in the neighbourhood by the howlings of the worshippers, who spend hours swaying forth and back in a nerve-racking attitude of prayer and supplication. They claim to have the gift of tongues, and to be able to comprehend the babel.'[37] The report described Seymour as an 'old coloured Exhorter, blind in one eye'. The article ended by telling of a prophecy given at the meeting that 'prophesied awful destruction to this city unless its citizens are brought to belief in the tenets of the new faith'. The same newspaper headline of the following day reported the devastating San Francisco earthquake of 18th April. This had a galvanising effect upon the

Christians in Los Angeles and many people went to the mission as a result. They were also intrigued by the lurid descriptions given of the meetings.

According to Bartleman, Seymour would preach occasionally for an hour, though usually much shorter and the preaching was preceded by testimonies, singing, and prayer. The meetings were characterised by outbursts of jumping, jerking, dancing and singing. But sometimes, a holy hush fell on the place and there was just silence. Seymour led the meetings but did his best to make room for the Holy Spirit's leading. 'Brother Seymour generally sat behind two empty shoe boxes [crates] one on top of the other. He usually kept his head inside the top one during the meeting, in prayer. There was no pride there.'[38]

The Azusa Street revival lasted for three years with continual daily meetings occurring from 1906 to 1909. The impact it had, firstly on the United States and then worldwide, was colossal. What is clear is that there came a realignment of many denominations on Pentecostal lines. Robeck, commenting on the spread of the revival, compares it 'to a fire lit in dry tinder when nobody was looking. It exploded – billowing up and scattering its sparks in every direction'. He adds that 'some of these sparks damaged nearby holiness congregations'.[39]

The developing history of Azusa Street is beyond the scope of this book, but the importance of this incredible revival in Los Angeles was to have huge repercussions throughout the world. In the context of this book, the following chapters will reveal that just as the Welsh Revival impacted Los Angeles and the world-wide Pentecostal Movement, so did Azusa Street leap across a continent and an ocean to a north-eastern town in the United Kingdom, Sunderland, which in turn saw the rise of the three main classical Pentecostal denominations in Britain, of which Elim was the first.

Notes

[1] Synan, Vinson, *The Century of the Holy Spirit: 100 years of Pentecostal and Charismatic Renewal, 1901-2001* (Nashville, TN: Thomas Nelson Publishers, 2012), Kindle edition, Loc 851.

[2] Robeck, Cecil, ibid, p42.

[3] Synan, Vinson, ibid, Loc 872.

[4] Robeck, Cecil, ibid, p42.

[5] Synan, Vinson, ibid, Loc 872. See also, Robeck, Cecil, ibid, p43 and Hathaway/Warrington, ibid, p5.

[6] Synan, Vinson, ibid, Loc 886. See also, Synan, Vinson, *The Holiness-Pentecostal Tradition: Charismatic Movements in the Twentieth Century* (Grand Rapids, MI: Eerdmans: 1997), p101.

[7] Hathaway in Warrington, ibid, p5.

[8] Hathaway in Warrington, ibid, p5.

[9] Robeck, Cecil, ibid, p43.

[10] Hathaway, Malcolm in Warrington, ibid, p5.

[11] Robeck, Cecil, ibid, p43.

[12] Robeck, Cecil, ibid, p47.

[13] Jim Crow laws were state and local laws that enforced racial segregation in the Southern United States. All were enacted in the late nineteenth and early twentieth centuries by white Democrat-dominated state legislatures. The laws were enforced until 1965. Common Jim Crow laws included literary tests, poll taxes and the grandfather clause, which were all restrictions on voting meant to keep black men from casting a ballot. Bans on interracial marriage and separation between races in public were also common parts of Jim Crow.

[14] Robeck, Cecil, ibid, p47.

[15] Hayford, Jack and Moore, David, *The Charismatic Century: The Enduring Impact of the Azusa Street Revival* (New York: Hachette Book Group, 2006), Kindle edition, Loc 837.

[16] Robeck, Cecil, ibid, p149,150.

[17] *The Apostolic Faith,* December 1912, pp4-5, quoted by Hayford, Jack, ibid, Loc 1129.

[18] Hayford, Jack, ibid, Loc 1104.

[19] Robeck, Cecil, ibid, p169.

[20] Cauchi, Tony, *The Revival Library – Pensketches – American Pentecostal Pioneers – Charles Parham,* 2004.

[21] Cauchi, Tony, ibid.

[22] Hayford, Jack, ibid, Loc 875.

[23] William Seymour's father, Simon, was known as Simon Simon until some time between 1867 and 1870 when he changed his name to Simon Seymour. Robeck, Cecil, ibid, p16.

[24] Robeck, Cecil, ibid, p20.

[25] Hayford, Jack, ibid, Loc 988.

[26] Hayford, Jack, ibid Loc 988.

[27] Robeck, Cecil, ibid, p49.

[28] Robeck, Cecil, ibid, p50.

[29] Robeck, Cecil, ibid, p58.

[30] Hayford, Jack, ibid, Loc 952.

[31] Hayford, Jack, ibid, Loc 962.

[32] Cauchi, Tony, *The Revival Library, Pensketches – American Pentecostal Pioneers – Frank Bartleman*, 2004.

[33] Robeck, Cecil, ibid, p69.

[34] Bartleman, Frank, *Azusa Street* (South Plainfield NJ 1980, Bridge Publishing Inc), p43.

[35] Bartleman, Frank, ibid, p44.

[36] Hayford, Jack, ibid, Loc 1023.

[37] *The Los Angeles Daily Times*, 18th April 1906. Quoted by Hayford, Jack, ibid, Loc 1011.

[38] Bartleman, Frank, ibid, p93.

[39] Robeck, Cecil, ibid, p187.

4

Pentecost Comes to the UK

Just as in the United States, so it was in the United Kingdom that the first person to be recorded as being baptised in the Spirit with the accompanying evidence of speaking with other tongues was also a woman. Her name was Catherine Price and she received her Spirit baptism at her home, 14 Akerman Road, Brixton, London. Unlike many outpourings of the Spirit in Azusa Street, hers, as often befits the British culture, was received during a time of quiet worship as she began to focus her attention on Christ as the Lamb of God. When she continued in her worship of Christ, she realised that she was doing so in another language.[1] It was at this same home that Arthur Booth-Clibborn, who was to become a prominent figure in Irish Pentecostalism came into contact with Pentecostal worship.[2] The date this occurred was 7th January1907.

Thomas Ball Barratt (1862-1940)

A Cornishman by birth, he was brought up in Norway where his father obtained a position of manager at a sulphur mine. The family moved to Norway when Barratt was five years old. He was, however, educated in England. Thomas Barratt was to become one of the major figures in European Pentecostalism and had a great influence on British Pentecostals through his connection with Alexander Alfred Boddy (1854-1930) and the Sunderland Conventions. Barratt became a Methodist minister in Norway and visited America for the express purpose of raising funds to build a large mission in Oslo. Although his trip was a financial disappointment, it was to have a life-changing effect upon his ministry.[3] It was while he was staying at the New York Mission Home of the Christian and Missionary Alliance that he learned of the great Azusa Street Revival, from its newspaper, *The Apostolic Faith*, first published in September 1906. Barratt, upon making enquiries, became convinced of the truth of the baptism in the Holy Spirit with the accompanying evidence of speaking with other tongues. That he received such a baptism is confirmed by his own words:

> I was filled with light and such a power that I began to shout as loud as I could in a foreign language. I must have spoken seven or eight languages, to judge from the various sounds and forms of speech used. I stood erect at times, preaching in one foreign tongue after another, and I know from the strength of my voice that 10,000 might easily have heard all I said. The most wonderful moment was when I burst into a beautiful baritone solo, using one of most pure and beautiful languages I have ever heard. The tune and words were entirely new to me and the rhythm and cadence of the various choruses seemed to be perfect.[4]

Gee points out that Barratt was a student of the great composer Edvard Grieg and was well able to comment knowledgably on music. Barratt goes on to talk about the emotional sensations he experienced at his Spirit baptism. He mentioned the great sense of power that he experienced in prayer and felt that his whole being was at times as if it were on fire inside; then he would quieten down into sweet songs in a foreign language.

Barratt sailed from New York on 8th December 1906 and a great European Pentecostal Movement, with special emphasis on the British Isles, was about to be born. By this time, there were various pockets throughout the UK where people met for a deepening of spiritual life and the baptism in the Holy Spirit. The influence of Barratt was such that many of these people made the link between Spirit baptism and glossolalia.[5] By the end of 1906, prayer meetings were being held all over the country for yet a deeper revival than that which had so recently occurred in Wales. Prominent among these was Boddy, an Anglican vicar in Monkwearmouth, Sunderland. It soon became evident that a powerful new revival movement was about to break out. This was felt not only in Britain but with the Methodists in Norway and the Baptists in Sweden. The main emphasis on this fledgling revival movement was 'the Baptism in the Holy Spirit', which was invariably accompanied by speaking with tongues and other supernatural manifestations.[6]

Barratt was seen by some as the Pentecostal apostle to Europe. Beginning at home, a new effectiveness marked his ministry and there was undoubtedly a sense of revival wherever he ministered. Thousands responded positively to the presentation of the gospel along Pentecostal lines. 'People standing in queues to enter his services would fall under the power of God, conviction and repentance gripping them.'[7]

Alexander Alfred Boddy (1854-1930)

Boddy became the acknowledged leader on the early British Pentecostal scene. An Anglican vicar, he presided over the famous Sunderland Conventions which started in 1908. He was the third son of James Alfred Boddy, rector of St Thomas Church in the Jewish quarter of Manchester. He studied theology at University College, Durham. He was ordained by J B Lightfoot, the evangelical Bishop of Durham, in 1881 and in 1884 was appointed curate to All Saints, Sunderland. After two years, he was appointed vicar where he was to minister for the next thirty-eight years. In 1891 he married Mary Pollock, who was to prove a strong influence on him.[8]

Boddy had a colossal work to do at All Saints as the parish was quite neglected owing to the alcoholism of his predecessor. He gave himself totally to his work and, assisted by his godly wife, the church grew. Although he had given himself wholeheartedly to the work of the church, Boddy sensed that, to a certain extent, he had neglected his own spiritual care. He became a regular visitor to the Keswick Conventions and felt that at one such convention he had received the baptism in the Holy Spirit.

The parish that Alexander Boddy's father, James, ministered in was that of Red Bank in an industrial suburb of Manchester. As well as being a strong Jewish quarter in the city, the parish had a large, active Roman Catholic community. James Boddy was the vicar here from 1839 to 1871. Being brought up in such a culturally varied area where Jews, Roman Catholics, Nonconformists and Anglicans lived and worked cheek by jowl must have had a lasting effect on Alexander. The varied religious life of Red Bank obviously gave the young Boddy the ability to relate to people of many faiths 'and the social conditions he experienced also assisted his ministry later on. Evidence of this is seen in the way that he related well to people of every class during his travels and to the working-class people of his own parish of Monkwearmouth'.[9]

It would seem that Boddy had a conversion experience at the age of twenty. It is likely that this occurred while he was attending a convention at Keswick. His daughter Jane wrote: 'He had been a nominal Christian in his youth but a change came when he went to a convention at Keswick. Then he decided to prepare for ordination, but his parents could not afford to send him to Cambridge as they had done for Herbert [his brother], so my father saved up enough for him to go to Durham University and take up his L.Th.'[10] The choice of Durham might have been influenced by the fact that his father had been appointed rector of Elwick Hall, a rural parish in the County of Durham. This was after spending thirty years in the heart of industrial Manchester.

Wakefield maintains that the element of crisis was an integral part of the message of Keswick with further spiritual development expected to be seen after the point of crisis. This element of crisis was a theme which was to continue in Boddy's life.[11] His strong evangelical faith was enhanced by his visits to Keswick. The fact that he returned there after an absence of some years in 1907, just at the time that he was making steps towards the Pentecostal experience is indicative of influence that the 'deeper life' teaching of the conventions had on him.

During the course of his long ministry in Monkwearmouth, Boddy engaged on many travels and wrote books about his journeys. His writing earned him two honours: 'Fellow of the Royal Geographical Society' and membership of the 'Royal Geographical Society of Russia'. His travel journals reveal him to be an adventurous person who was prepared to take risks on his journeys. He was also a keen student of contemporary religions, in particular Islam. 'He was a man of adventurous spirit, at ease with a wide variety of people, secure in his faith, willing to learn, with integrity and humour, and taking seriously the study of ordinary life and faith.'[12]

He experienced something of a breakdown in 1901, never referring to it publicly but giving hints on the strain he felt. What became obvious in his life, apart from the deep care he had for his congregation and parishioners, was his intense desire to expand and deepen his spiritual experience. He was also an inveterate enquirer. News of the outbreak of the Welsh Revival caused him to travel to the Rhondda Valley in South Wales, where he met with Evan Roberts. Boddy saw the great move of the Holy Spirit all around him – the mysterious power gripping the sinful and causing them to call out for salvation.[13] Boddy carried with him the memories of the great Welsh Revival and that impacted his ministry at All Saints. Yet, it was clear to him that the Acts of the Apostles indicated a lost dimension. He later described the Welsh Revival as an important preparation in Sunderland, writing in an article in 1910 that 'it made hearts more hungry for the living God'.[14]

It was this constant search for a deeper experience in God that galvanised him when he read reports of the outpouring of the Spirit in Azusa Street and Thomas Barratt's account of being baptised in the Holy Spirit with the accompanying evidence of tongues. Wales had drawn him, but he felt compelled to contact Barratt and although it was winter, he travelled to Oslo where he found the Upper Room mission hall at Torvagaden 7, Oslo with some 120 people praising God and speaking with tongues. This was Boddy's introduction to the Pentecostal experience. He returned to his church in Sunderland, determined that the prayer group he led on Thursday evenings would experience the fullness of the Spirit. He was to later comment: 'I stood with Evan Roberts in Tonypandy, but have never witnessed such scenes as those in Norway.' He realised that he needed help and wrote to Barratt imploring him to visit them in Sunderland. After much pleading, Barratt agreed to come, and on Saturday, 31st August 1907, he joined the group in a Saturday night prayer meeting.[15]

Barratt stayed in Sunderland with Boddy for a period of six weeks. Among those who received their personal Pentecost at this time, and spoke with other tongues, was Boddy's wife, Mary, his daughters, Jane and Mary, and the Rev James Pollock, Boddy's brother-in-law. Pollock was, however, to later repudiate his experience, claiming that it was a demonic manifestation. Boddy himself did not receive his personal Spirit baptism until 2nd December, long after Barratt had left Sunderland.[16] 'The people were singing "O come let us adore him", and his being was moved in a way not known in any revival. Lost in wonder, he found himself prostate, lifting his voice, but not in English in a gushing fluency. When it subsided, he asked to be given the meaning and his mind went immediately to Psalm 107 and to the verse, 'O that men would praise Him for His goodness and for His wonderful works to the children of men.' He was the fiftieth (in Britain) to receive, and Pentecost means fifty.[17]

At this point, it is important that we consider the evidence of the baptism in the Holy Spirit. Most early Pentecostals accepted that glossolalia (speaking in other tongues) was the initial evidence of the baptism in the Holy Spirit. There had been times of revival and spiritual quickening when people had experienced a definite anointing that many referred to as Spirit-baptism. Although there is no reference in Elim's first written doctrinal statement as regards tongues in relation to the baptism in the Holy Spirit, the author would argue that this was a statement that was meant for a local church – there was no Movement in existence as such.[18] The Statement of Fundamentals contained in Elim's first Constitution includes tongues as the initial evidence of the baptism in the Holy Spirit. This was repeated in a statement in 1923 and 1925. It was left out of the Fundamentals in 1927 and since then has not appeared within Elim's fundamental on the Holy Spirit. The commonly accepted view within Elim for most of its existence has been that of an expected scriptural evidence of the baptism in the Spirit. Some would see that in terms of an increased power to witness and declare the gospel. Others would expect to see some manifestation of the charismata in operation.[19] Canty makes the following pertinent comment on this point:

> The Scriptural discovery in Topeka, that tongues is the invariable accompaniment to the Baptism, made the Pentecostal revival more than a subjective blessing and triggered off an intelligent acceptance of the Spirit which is the basis of the Movement. Tongues are not all there is, any more than the flag on the palace is all there is, but they indicate that the Monarch is in residence.

Cecil Polhill

Cecil Henry Polhill-Turner (1860-1938), or Cecil Polhill as he chose to be called, the Squire of Howbury Hall, was one of the famous 'Cambridge Seven'. Together with his brother, Arthur, and five others, which included C T Studd, he responded to the call to be a missionary in China in February 1885. It was Polhill's great burden to reach into Tibet. There is no doubt that he was strongly influenced by Hudson Taylor who was looked upon as God's apostle to China and was the founder of the China Inland

Mission (CIM). In 1888 he married a fellow CIM missionary Eleanor Agnes Marston. It was in the same year that he was ordained as a clergyman. They were to have two daughters and a son.

After a furlough in Britain, Polhill and his family returned to China in 1895 and settled in Szechwan. Owing to the Boxer rebellion in 1900 they were evacuated and then sent back to Britain on the grounds of Eleanor's ill-health. Once back in Britain, doctors forbade Eleanor to return to the mission field. Cecil remained in the country to lovingly look after his wife. He retained his great love for, and interest in, China and remained on the CIM board for the rest of his life.[20]

Polhill attended the Azusa Street Revival in 1908 with his good friend George Brown Studd (the younger brother of C T Studd).[21] It was here that he entered into the Pentecostal experience. Studd had by this time relocated to the United States where he helped build the Peniel Hall, a holiness mission in Los Angeles. He 'subsequently became Pentecostal and was very much involved at the Azusa Street mission before accepting the oneness-Pentecostal heterodoxy which probably explains his subsequent obscurity outside of oneness circles'.[22]

On his return from Los Angeles, Polhill met up with Alexander Boddy, and he attended the first Sunderland Convention in 1908. 'The relationship between Polhill and Boddy became central to the development of British Pentecostalism.'[23] The close relationship between Polhill and Boddy is revealed in the *Confidence* magazines that were published by Boddy from 1907 onwards. In an early edition of the magazine, reference is made to open-air meetings conducted in Bedford by Polhill. A Dutch Pastor and his wife (Pastor and Mrs Polman) were present, together with two Welsh delegates to the Sunderland Convention that had recently been held. Some thirty conversions were reported in connection with these open-air meetings.[24] In the same edition, Boddy refers to Polhill having received his 'Pentecost' in a quiet meeting in a house in

Los Angeles, 'and he believes "Pentecost" is a call to, and an inducement for, *Evangelistic Work*'.[25]

The Sunderland Conventions

The Sunderland Conventions, under the chairmanship of Alexander Boddy, were a focal point in the development of the early British Pentecostal Movement. They began in 1908 and continued until 1914. Mrs Thomas Barratt, in a report of the 1908 Conference, writes:

> Here are we then, in an Established Minister's home and church, and feel here a wonderful freedom. We came at once into an atmosphere of Christian love, and into a prayerful spirit. God has, in a wonderful way, used Brother and Sister Boddy. They believe in a whole and full salvation. They believe that speaking in Tongues is a *sign*[26] that one has received the full baptism of the Holy Ghost. It is also one of the gifts which the Spirit distributes at His will. And here they speak in Tongues and praise God.[27]

As the conventions developed, they attracted those who were to become household names in British Pentecostal history. Men such as Donald Gee, Thomas Myerscough, Smith Wigglesworth, J Nelson Parr, Arthur Booth-Clibborn, Henry Mogridge, James Tetchner, Alexander Moncur Niblock, John Leech, Mrs Eleanor Crisp, Stephen Jeffreys and George Jeffreys.

Malcolmson states that there were 500 believers present at the first Sunderland Whitsun convention, of which about 120 visitors who had travelled from all parts of the United Kingdom, and a few from Europe, were housed nearby.[28] Instruction in the exercise of the gifts of the Spirit provided needed guidance for those who were unused to such manifestations. The meetings were not particularly noisy and overexuberant, and Boddy's leadership was always calm, yet, a deep sense of God's presence ran through the conventions. Firm rules were printed and had to be accepted by those planning to attend. If people fell under the power of God they were to be left alone and not touched. If anything like display was observed, it would be corrected or even rebuked.[29]

It was at the 1913 Sunderland Convention that Stephen and George Jeffreys were invited to attend and George was asked to speak at the evangelistic services that followed on from the main convention meeting each night. He made quite an impression with the eloquence of his preaching.

Notes

[1] Gee, Donald, *The Pentecostal Movement: Enlarged Edition* (London: Elim Publishing Company, 1949), p21.

[2] Robinson, James, p49.

[3] Gee, Donald, ibid, p15.

[4] Barratt, T, quoted by Gee, Donald, ibid, p15.

[5] It would appear from Barratt's testimony that perhaps he was exercising the gift of xenolalia, which specifically designates when the language being spoken is a natural language previously unknown to the speaker.

[6] Gee, Donald, ibid, p16.

[7] Canty, George. Unpublished manuscript on *History of Elim*, p33.

[8] Robinson, James, ibid, p3.

[9] Wakefield, Gavin, *Alexander Boddy, Pentecostal Anglican Pioneer* (London: Paternoster, 2007), p13.

[10] Quoted by Wakefield, Gavin, ibid, pp20,21.

[11] Wakefield, Gavin, ibid, p23.

[12] Wakefield, Gavin, ibid, p52.

[13] Canty, George, ibid, p34.

[14] Boddy, Alexander, *Confidence, 1910*, pp192-197.

[15] Canty, George, ibid, p35.

[16] Wakefield, Gavin, ibid, p89.

[17] Canty, George, ibid, p36.

[18] Noted Pentecostal historians such as Robinson and Frestadius would disagree with me on this. Their argument is that the decision to reach Ireland with the full gospel, in Pentecostal terms, taken at Monaghan on 7th January 1915, constituted the birth of the Movement. Therefore the

doctrinal Statement published with regard to Elim Christchurch, Belfast, Elim's first church, is valid even though there was only one church in existence.

[19] The author has been an Elim minister for more than fifty years and has been an Elim member for sixty years. During that time, he has attended hundreds of meetings where people have been prayed for to receive the baptism of the Holy Spirit. In all those meetings, the gift of tongues was seen as the evidence that people had received their Spirit baptism.

[20] Malcolmson, Keith, ibid, p131.

[21] Usher, John M, *For China and Tibet, and for World-Wide Revival: Cecil Henry Polhill (1860-1938) and His Significance for Early Pentecostalism* (A thesis submitted to the University of Birmingham for the Degree of Doctor of Philosophy 2015), p164.

[22] Usher, John M, ibid, p135.

[23] Usher, John M, ibid, p174.

[24] *Confidence*, 15th August 1908, p12.

[25] Author's italics.

[26] Author's italics.

[27] *Confidence*, 15th July 1908, p4.

[28] Malcolmson, Keith, ibid, p97.

[29] Canty, George, ibid, p39.

5

George Jeffreys: The Early Years

Notwithstanding some of the negative comments made on the Welsh Revival by the author in a previous chapter, the fact is, that at the time, the 1904-05 revival had a colossal effect upon the Welsh community. The country became a seething sea of raw emotionalism as people by the thousands crammed themselves into the myriad chapels that thronged the streets of Wales, particularly the mining valleys of South Wales.

It is important for our study of Elim history that we understand something of the mindset of these proud and resilient people. Political nationalism in Wales has never had the same impact as it has in the other Celtic nations of these sceptred Isles. Welsh nationalism has existed, however, within its language and culture. Their language, more than any other factor, gave them a national cohesion; they were, and still are, a people of a language. This is loudly and musically proclaimed every time the National Anthem is sung, especially among the teeming thousands that crowd out the Principality Stadium in Cardiff, every time there is a rugby international match played there. After proclaiming the love of country and culture, the Welsh national Anthem finishes with these words: *'O bydded i'r hen iaith barhau.'*[1]

Wales was the first of the Celtic countries to be conquered and inhabited by the English. The Wales Acts 1535 and 1542, passed during the reign of Henry VIII, made Wales a part of the

Kingdom of England, 165 years before the Act of Union, 1707, that saw the Scottish Parliament and the English Parliament united to form the Parliament of Great Britain. The Act of Union, 1801, was a legislative agreement that united England (including Wales) and Scotland with Ireland under the name of the United Kingdom of Great Britain and Ireland. On 3rd May 1921 under the Government of Ireland Act, Northern Ireland was created with a devolved administration and forms part of the United Kingdom today.

Seeing then, that Wales was inhabited and governed by the English for a longer period than its Celtic cousins, one would have thought that the native language of the first kingdom thus to be assimilated, would have been the first to decline. Nothing could be further from the truth. At the turn of the last century, the Welsh language was spoken by more than 50 per cent of the Welsh population. Rapid industrialisation and the influx of families from England suppressed the language considerably and by the 1950s the Welsh language was spoken by only 15 per cent of the population. The Welsh Language Act 1933 put the Welsh language on an equal footing with the English language in Wales and according to the 2001 census 20.8 per cent of a population of almost 3 million spoke it fluently.

The Celtic languages in Scotland and Ireland are in a far more precarious position than that of their Welsh cousin. In the 2011 census of Scotland only 1.1 per cent of the population spoke Scottish Gaelic. Irish Gaelic fares better in that according to the 2016 census, 4.2 per cent of the population are fluent in the language.

The author would argue strongly that it is the Welsh language and culture that contributes to the sense of national identity in Wales as opposed to the more political factors in Scotland and Ireland. For us to understand the early history of Elim, it is important that we understand something of the background and culture of its early leaders, particularly George Jeffreys. George and his brother Stephen, indeed the whole family, were fluent Welsh speakers. The Welsh Bible was translated some thirty years before the King James Bible. The Prayer Book was also translated into Welsh. Welsh nonconformity was cradled in the Welsh language. Welsh hymns, sung in glorious four-part harmony, remain a feature of the culture to this day.

The Welsh Revival broke out in chapels where worship was conducted in the Welsh Language. Evan Roberts was a first-language Welsh speaker. The hymns in most of the revival centres were sung in Welsh. It was into this Welsh culture and language George Jeffreys was born on 28th February 1889 at 24 Metcalfe Street, Maesteg, in the Llynfi Valley, Glamorganshire. He was the fifth son of Thomas and Kezia Jeffreys. Death rates among the poor children in Wales at the beginning of the last century were 55 per cent as against less than 18 per cent among the rich.[2] By the time she died at the age of seventy-eight, Kezia Jeffreys had buried two husbands and six of her twelve children.[3] It is difficult to comprehend the curse of child mortality in Wales at that time.[4]

Cartwright describes the setting of the Llynfi valley and the enormous changes that had occurred there as a result of the industrialisation of South Wales, particularly the expansion of the coalfield.[5] Cartwright's book on the lives of the brothers George and Stephen Jeffreys was published in 1986, at the time when the Welsh coal industry was choking out its dying breath. There would have still been evidences of the coal mining activity all over South Wales at the time with rusted pit head wheels and mine carcasses still evident. The rivers would still have run black with coal dust and slurry, the coal tips would still have been evident in some parts, although, by then, they would have been reduced or partly grown over with vegetation. The valley, now, would be more akin to the scene before industrialisation raped it of its beauty.

The Jeffreys family attended the Dyffrun chapel in Maesteg. This was an Independent chapel where the local members would have had ownership of the building and would have called and appointed their minister.[6] The Dyffrun Chapel shared a minister with Siloh chapel in another part of the town and after Thomas' death, the family moved and started to attend Siloh, where George came under the influence of Rev Glasnant Jones who was the minister there from 1901 to 1907 and who was thoroughly evangelical in his presentation of the gospel.[7]

George Jeffreys was brought up in a typical coal mining family. His father, Thomas, and his brother Stephen worked in the local coal mine. 'Working underground', as the Welsh valleys inhabitants referred to coal mining, was hard and dangerous work. In winter, the miner would see daylight only for a couple of hours on a Saturday afternoon and on Sunday.[8] Life was incredibly hard for most working-class people in the early years of the twentieth century, but particularly so for the mining families. Not only were the men and boys (they left school at the age of twelve) made to work in incredibly difficult and dangerous conditions, surrounded by blackness that is difficult to describe, but they were also at the mercy of ruthless mine-owners who thought little about safe working conditions, and a great deal about the wealth that the 'black gold' would add to their already bulging bank balances. As a result of their impoverished conditions, the miners would often go on strike. They went weeks on end without work and, subsequently, without pay. Soup kitchens were a familiar feature in the South Wales mining valleys throughout the first half of the last century. Miners went on strike because of poor pay and horrendous working conditions. Sometimes, they were 'forced out' of work by the mine owners for various reasons that only benefited the owners and never the miners. The hardships encountered by the South Wales miner are well documented. The following quote gives some idea of the difficulties encountered by the Rhondda miners, but were typical of those faced by miners throughout the British coalfield:

> Right up to the 1914 war the Rhondda miners were in the van of the nationwide struggle with the coal owners, in the face of danger, hardship and dust disease. Often, there came fearful disaster. Always there was poverty in

the homes. Those who protested, any collier who stood his ground and especially the platform firebrand at mass meetings found his 'lamp stopped' and his name 'blacked' in every pit throughout the coalfield. His wife and children could only fall back on parish relief, or the galling charity of neighbours and to see whether the local grocer would give 'trust'.[9]

There is some dispute as to whether George worked underground with his brothers. Canty writes of George's employment as follows: 'George, quiet and studious grew but when the time for work came, he was too delicate for the coal face. The Caerau Cooperative Society employed him in its Nantyfyllon store, where he worked for seven years and rose to be offered its management.'[10] Cartwright quotes Glasnant Jones referring to George being 'in business'.[11] The author was of the impression that George, like his brothers, had for a time worked underground in the local colliery. Kay confirms this view by referring to the 1901 census that revealed that George Jeffreys was working underground in the coal mine as a door boy.[12] This would have been quite frightening for a boy of no more than twelve years. He would have spent eight hours a day in darkness, the penetrating gloom being only slightly lifted by the weak rays of light from his lamp. His task would have been to open and close the doors within the mine to assist ventilation and also to allow the pit ponies pulling coal carts along the rail tracks to pass. We don't know how long George worked underground, but through the aid of his mother, he was able to get an appointment working for the Caerau Cooperative Society.

Conversion

George Jeffreys was fifteen years old when he was converted in the autumn of 1904. This occurred at the height of the Welsh revival under the ministry of his pastor, Rev Glasnant Jones. He was converted at the same time as his older brother, Stephen.

Canty states that there is no record of George's conversion, but adds, 'The minister, the Rev. Glasnant Jones certainly knew that George had been converted, though no specific date is left us.'[13] Cartwright, referring to Stephen's conversion on the 20th November 1904, adds, 'Fifteen year old George made a commitment at the same time.'[14] Edsor refers to George's personal testimony of salvation, although he does not mention the date. He writes that George was gripped by Glasnant Jones' reference to Romans 10:13: 'For whosoever shall call upon the name of the Lord shall be saved.'[15]

The bond between Stephen and George was particularly close and George went to live with his brother at the time that his mother, Kezia, remarried. Both Cartwright and Canty refer to Stephen's conversion in terms of a crisis experience. Cartwright refers to Stephen's marriage to Elizabeth Ann Lewis on Boxing Day 1898. He adds that at this time, Stephen's commitment to vital Christianity could best be described as nominal.[16] It was the impact of the revival and the experience of real conversion of some of his fellow miners that caused Stephen to consider his own salvation. Canty's account is worth quoting in full:

> In the mines and everywhere, Stephen was startled by the fundamental transformation of men. They sang with hearts unburdened and he felt out of things, popular though he had been with his friends. Those who had cursed now commenced with prayer, praise and singing, and after work were not drunk but were preaching with joy on the street corners. He held out against the pressures until one week proved too much, particularly after attending a Thursday meeting. He suffered real distress until Sunday morning, November 20th, 1904, at the age of 28, he listened in the Picton Street (now High Street) chapel to Glasnant Jones on the great Welsh theme of the redeeming love of Christ. That day, opening his heart, that love took possession of him, mind and soul. His son, Edward, said, 'An indescribable

joy permeated the whole of his being.' It mastered Stephen.[17]

Over the next few months, the brothers involved themselves in the work of the chapel, although, Stephen's involvement was not quite as much as that of his younger brother owing to family commitments. However, they were both very much products of the Welsh Revival. They associated themselves with people who were anxious to keep the revival fires burning. This affected the ministry of both brothers throughout the course of their lives. They were both looked on as 'revivalists'. The revival itself was of a short duration and its effects in Wales quickly waned. But there were small groups of people within the various chapels that sought to keep the flame of the revival alive. They were often referred to as 'Children of the Revival'. George and Stephen associated with these groups. One such group met in the Duffryn Chapel in Maesteg.

Baptism in the Spirit

As has already been documented, the Pentecostal baptism in the Spirit had been experienced by a number of people in the United Kingdom through the ministry of Thomas Barratt and Alexander Boddy, among others. This 'new' revelation, accompanied by speaking in other tongues, came to the attention of Stephen and George. Pentecostalism had, by this time, broken out in various parts of the South Wales mining valleys. In a village called Waunllwyd, just outside Ebbw Vale in Monmouthshire, Rev Thomas Madoc Jeffreys (1878-1950), minister of the Tabernacle Congregational Church, came under the influence of the Pentecostal message. Having been made aware of the events in Sunderland, Jeffreys visited Boddy in 1907 and returned to Wales with 'Pentecost'.[18] Jeffreys (no relation to George and Stephen) was an avid reader of *Confidence* magazine, published by Boddy. In the first issue, Jeffreys (Thomas), states how his church had embraced the Pentecostal teaching and experience as they saw in it a return to that religious fervour and expectancy they had tasted in 1904-05. They also felt that through this new teaching, the 'lost gifts' of the Church could be regained in their search for a return to New Testament Christianity.[19] Thomas Jeffreys was to become a regular speaker and an influential presence at the Sunderland Conventions. He was certainly a prime mover of the Pentecostal message and experience in South Wales.

A Welsh Baptist minister, William George Hill, pastor of Calfaria Baptist Chapel in Cwmfelin, Maesteg, proved to be very sympathetic to Pentecostal teaching and gave considerable encouragement to some of the early Pentecostal groups in South Wales. After resigning from the denomination, he held meetings in the home of Mr and Mrs Bedford in Bridgend Road, Maesteg. They also held meetings in Oakwood School, Cwmfelin, Maesteg, which was within easy travelling distance of the home of Stephen Jeffreys. The Jeffreys brothers attended these meetings and so began their association with the burgeoning Pentecostal Movement.[20] Meanwhile, further west in Carmarthenshire, Daniel Williams was led to hold special meetings in Penygroes, where he would later establish the Apostolic Church which was to open a large number of assemblies in South Wales.[21]

As regards George Jeffreys' personal Spirit baptism, there are two conflicting accounts. What is clear is that Stephen's son Edward received a definite baptism in the Holy Spirit with the accompanying evidence of speaking in other tongues while on holiday in Crosshands, Carmarthenshire. When his parents were informed of what had taken place they were not in favour of their son's experience and neither was George, who had spoken out against the early Pentecostals.[22] However, when they saw the very positive spiritual effect that this experience had on young Edward, they began to see Pentecostal teaching in a more favourable light. In his written testimony of his Spirit baptism recorded in the *Elim Evangel*, George states that it was in the old Dyffrun Chapel that he received his baptism in the Spirit with

73

the accompanying evidence of tongues.[23] Cartwright says that George began to sing in tongues and magnify the Lord. This account is at variance with a letter written to William Oliver Hutchinson (1864-1928), who erected the first purpose-built Pentecostal church in the UK in 1908 in Bournemouth. Kay records that Cecil Polhill spoke at the dedication of the church, the Emmanuel Mission Hall, on the 5th November.

Hutchinson was to become a controversial figure in the early British Pentecostal Movement. He was a strong supporter of British Israelism. From 1910 onwards, he taught an extreme doctrine on the subject of the vocal gifts of the Spirit, especially those of interpretation of tongues and prophecy. He gave exactly the same prominence to these spoken gifts as he did to the written Word of God. 'Prophecies, in Hutchinson's opinion, should not be judged – thereby contradicting the specific New Testament injunction of 1 Cor. 14:29.'[24]

George Jeffreys visited Hutchinson in 1910 and was impressed by his experience in Bournemouth. In August 1910, George wrote to Hutchinson and his letter seems to contradict the account of his Spirit Baptism in the old Dyffrun chapel as mentioned above. Cartwright published the letter in full and it is worth recording here:

Dear Pastor Hutchinson,

I really think that God would have me bear testimony to the glorious work he has done in me. Hallelujah. Since I have been at Bournemouth 'all things are become new – old things have passed away.' Hallelujah. I have been saved, sanctified, baptised in the Holy Ghost with the Scriptural sign of tongues, Mark 16:17 and healed of sickness. This is our Lord's doing, and it is marvellous in our eyes. Glory to God: God has taken the cigarette from my lips, and put a hallelujah there instead. Hallelujah.

I have the gift of tongues and interpretation, but the latter gift must still be developed. I cannot tell you all he has done for me, as no tongue can glorify God sufficiently. I feel free and happy; so very joyful and anxious to do something. Now comes my testing. I am going home to Wales, and it is but the beginning of a mighty battle. But 'Lion of the tribe of Judah' does not tell me to fight alone but he himself will do the worse part, and victory is always his. I thank you for your prayers. GJ.[25]

A cursory reading of this letter would cause one to come to the conclusion that Jeffreys was saved, baptised in the Holy Spirit and healed while attending Hutchinson's meeting at Bournemouth. This is a complete contradiction to what he later testified of in the pages of the *Elim Evangel*. There is no doubt that George was converted during the Welsh Revival and he was active in lay ministry at that time. Probably, George received a fresh filling of the Holy Spirit in Bournemouth and was sustained in his call for ministry. Kay writes: 'The letter may simply outline to Hutchinson the spiritual credentials Jeffreys felt himself to possess in readiness for the "mighty battle" he anticipated in Wales.'[26] Hutchinson was, at the time, one of the very few recognised Pentecostal pastors with an established church and work. This letter may simply have been Jeffreys' 'letter of intent' to the fact that he felt himself called to the Pentecostal cause and ministry. His association with Hutchinson ended long before the latter developed his unorthodox doctrines.[27]

George was to confirm his decision to follow the Pentecostal line of ministry through his association with Price Davies, who was one of the young men who had been influenced by Thomas Jeffreys and who had come into the Pentecostal experience. He held meetings in Dowlais and George was baptised in water there on Sunday, 11th April 1911. This would have marked a very significant step in George's approach to Christian ministry. He was of a Congregational background and in being baptised in water by a recognised Pentecostal worker, George would have realised that the accepted norm of applying to one of the recognised denominational theological colleges with a view to enter Christian ministry was now out of the question.

Notes

[1] 'O long may the old language remain.'

[2] Cartwright, Desmond, *The Great Evangelists: The Remarkable Lives of George and Stephen Jeffreys* (Basingstoke: Marshall Pickering, 1986), p14.

[3] Cartwright, Desmond, ibid, p15.

[4] The author's grandfather (on his father's side) was Moses Jones, born in 1860. He was married in 1886 and in giving birth to their third child, his first wife died in 1891; three days later, the baby girl died. He married a second time in 1892, the same year that his first child died. Between June 1893 and November 1897, they had three daughters and a son. The two daughters died, one aged four and the other aged five. They died within nine days of each other. On 13th February 1899, my grandmother gave birth to a stillborn son. In June that same year, their nineteen-month-old son died. My father was born 23rd July 1900. My grandfather had fifteen children, of whom only six survived beyond their fifth birthday. Such was infant mortality in Wales at the beginning of the twentieth century.

[5] Cartwright, Desmond, ibid, p9.

[6] This has caused some to speculate that this chapel background played a large part in Jeffreys' split with Elim in 1939-40 on the issue of church government. However, in the twenties and early thirties, he was a very strong advocate of central church government.

[7] Kay, William, *George Jeffreys*, ibid, p10.

[8] Cartwright, Desmond, ibid, p15.

[9] Pride, Emrys, *Rhondda My Valley Brave* (Risca: The Starling Press Ltd. 1975), p65.

[10] Canty, George, ibid, p18.

[11] Cartwright, Desmond, ibid, p19.

[12] Kay, William, ibid, p19.

[13] Canty, George, ibid, p21.

[14] Cartwright, Desmond, ibid, p19.

[15] Edsor, Albert, *The Pattern 5:19*, October 1944, p5.

[16] Cartwright, Desmond, ibid, p18.

[17] Canty, George, ibid, p21.

[18] Palmer, Chris, ibid, p136.

[19] Palmer, Chris, ibid, p136.

[20] Cartwright, Desmond, ibid, p23.

[21] The Apostolic Church was to have a big influence on Welsh Pentecostal theology. Written into their fundamentals of faith is the belief that it is possible for a Christian to lose his salvation by wilful and persistent sin. They refer to it as 'falling from grace'. The majority of Pentecostal churches in South Wales leaned heavily towards Arminian theology owing to the influence of Williams and the Apostolic Church. This was the teaching that was prevalent in the home assembly of the author and he was taught this from his early days as a Christian. He repudiated this doctrine through personal study of the Bible and would describe himself now as a 'moderate Calvinist'.

[22] Cartwright, Desmond, ibid, p24.

[23] *Elim Evangel*, 25th December 1929, Vol 10, Nos 34-35, p529.

[24] Kay, William, ibid, p42.

[25] Cartwright, Desmond, ibid, p26.

[26] Kay, William, ibid, p44.

[27] Hathaway, Malcolm, in Warrington, ibid, p11.

6
Early Ministry and the Call to Ireland

By 1912, George Jeffreys was fully committed to the Pentecostal message and was determined to devote himself to ministry along these lines, but opportunities to pursue this ministry were, in those early days, hard to come by. However, George's evangelistic gifting resulted in him coming to the attention of Cecil Polhill. George was recommended to Polhill by the leader of the Pentecostal work in Swansea. As a result, he was accepted as a student at the Pentecostal Missionary Training School in Preston, under the tutelage of Thomas Myerscough. His fees were paid for by Polhill.

Ministering in Wales

Although George was only at Preston for six weeks, he met with those who were to be influential in Pentecostal circles. Among the students at Preston was W F P Burton (1886-1971) who was the founder of the Congo Evangelistic Mission (CEM). This connection was an important one, because before the foundation of the Elim Missionary Society in 1923, a number of Elim missionaries went onto the mission field under the auspices of CEM. He met with two other men who were to become leading figures in Elim: Ernest John Phillips (1893-1973) and Percy Newton Corry (1892-?). Phillips would become the long-time secretary-general of Elim, and Elim's leader in all but name, after the schism that saw George Jeffreys resign and start up a second Pentecostal denomination. Corry was an early PMU missionary to India who joined Elim and became dean of the Bible college in 1927. Robert Ernest Darragh from Bangor Co Down was another colleague that George met at Preston. The two of them were to establish a very close friendship that was to last until Darragh's death in 1959. These students were taught by Thomas Myerscough. Kay describes him as being 'known for his scrupulous attention to the details of Scripture, level-headed, trusted on all sides, thought to be originally from the Brethren'.[1] Kay sees a similarity between the sermons of George Jeffreys and those of Willie Burton where there is an obvious close attention to the biblical text and a logical approach to the meaning of the page.

Prior to his going to Preston, George had linked up with a fellowship of Pentecostal believers in Swansea and it is likely that it was this fellowship that recommended that he should be accepted as a student in Preston. There was no doubt that George carried within him a deep sense of calling to the Christian ministry. 'The conviction that God had called him to the Christian ministry had been his since childhood.'[2] Because he had embraced the Pentecostal message, however, doors which would have been open to him slammed shut. It was at this point that Cecil Polhill came forward and supplied the financial support to undergo Bible college training.

While at Preston, George's brother Stephen had commenced an evangelistic mission in Cwmtwrch, a village high in the Swansea valley. The meetings were conducted in the Welsh language. Stephen, though considerably older than George, had not had the same opportunities to preach as his younger brother, but he was a keen open-air speaker. In fact, the original invitation to Cwmtwrch had gone to George, and he, in turn, had asked Stephen to deputise for him.[3] On a previous visit to the mission at Cwmtwrch, Stephen had entered the quiet streets of the village and at 8am on a Sunday morning had, in a loud voice, called out a few verses of Scripture. It made a great impact and the congregation that day was considerably increased as a result of his bold summons to worship.[4] When the invitation came for Stephen to hold a three day evangelistic mission in Cwmtwrch, he was very conscious that this could well result in a complete change of life for him. He told his friend, Pastor W J Thomas, who at that time was also a miner: 'Well, Billy, if God blesses me this time, I shall never return to the coal-mine.'[5]

The three-day mission turned into seven glorious weeks of Pentecostal evangelism where many were saved. Stephen sent for George to help him in the mission. George at once left Preston and joined his brother in the Swansea Valley. Edward Jeffreys, in his biography of Stephen, mentions nothing of George joining his father, nor of the two of them later ministering at Pen-y-Bont, Radnorshire. Why this should be the case is a mystery as there is documented evidence of Cecil Polhill visiting the two brothers in Cwmtwrch, and of Alexander Boddy visiting them in Pen-y-Bont. Polhill mentions this in his journal in February 1913:

> Mr Jeffreys was urged to come again and take a three day mission, commencing Christmas Day. He went ... and the mission is still going on (as we go to Press). Mr George Jeffreys, brother to Stephen, and a student at the Pentecostal Training School, Preston, Lancs, was urgently called to help Stephen, and has been with him since.[6]

It was at Cwmtwrch that the healing ministries of Stephen and George were first recorded. A reporter who was present at one of the meetings described in detail the revival atmosphere that was noticeable. He comments: 'In a week or two, possibly, Stephen Jeffreys will be considered another Evan Roberts.'[7] The same report states that 'remarkable cases of healing are reported. I saw a Mrs. James today in the neighbour's cottage where she was cured. She has suffered from heart trouble for ten years. "I can tell you that I have received Divine healing," said Mrs James'. In the same article, a magistrate writes:

I was much impressed with the earnestness and sincerity of Stephen Jeffreys. He has a most winsome way, and carries his audience with him. He speaks in Welsh, but is quite fluent in English. His brother George has joined him, and he preaches in English and Welsh. They are both excellent singers, and there is a good deal of singing in the meetings. Stephen Jeffreys told me that they want this Revival to be a real one. To this end there is a good deal of Gospel preaching by George Jeffreys, who preaches the need and makes the sinner's heart bare before God. Then they are clear on the Atonement, no new theology, but the judgement to come is sounded forth with dread alarms.[8]

Following the mission at Cwmtwrch, invitations came for the brothers to hold meetings in many other places. One such invitation came from Pen-y-Bont, some five miles from Llandrindod Wells. There is some confusion as to who invited the brothers to the area. Cartwright firmly attests that it was a Quaker magistrate who invited them, but the reference in *Confidence*, February 1913, seems to indicate that the Quaker magistrate was linked with Cwmtwrch. However, the brothers responded to an invitation and made their way some fifty miles to mid-Wales. The mission in Pen-y-Bont began on Monday, 17th February 1913. The brothers must have felt similar to Philip when he stood on the road to Gaza after being greatly used of God in the Samaritan revival.[9] Added to this was the fact that this was an entirely different part of Wales to the upper Swansea Valley that they had just come from. This was a largely English-speaking area, whereas much of their mission in Cwmtwrch had been conducted in the Welsh language. 'They need not have worried, for in spite of the remoteness of the location, the crowds began to arrive from every direction.'[10] Cartwright records that there were more than fifty converts in this mission and there was also an outstanding miracle of healing.

Again, there is some discrepancy in the various historical accounts written about this healing. In the February 1913 edition of *Confidence* (thought to be written by Polhill), it is stated that 'Remarkable cases of healing are reported'. The healing of a Mrs James from a heart condition is quoted. Edward Jeffreys, who was present at both Cwmtwrch and Pen-y-Bont, states the following: 'The very first miracle of Divine healing under my father's ministry took place in this, his second campaign. Frequently he had prayed for sick people before, but he had never witnessed an instantaneous miracle of healing.'[11] He goes on to tell that his father was called upon to pray for a young girl in the area who suffered with a diseased bone in her foot. This rendered her immobile and her surgeon feared that she might require an amputation of the foot. Edward reports how his father anointed her with oil and laid his hands upon her according to the Scriptures. The young lady was healed immediately. Again, Edward makes no mention of George being there. Cartwright makes it clear that both brothers were present: 'They went to her home and she was anointed with oil in accordance to James 5:14-15.'[12]

Alexander Boddy attended the mission in Radnorshire, albeit totally unannounced. He wrote a comprehensive article concerning the mission in the March 1913 edition of *Confidence*. The brothers deferred to Boddy and insisted that he preached at each of the meetings in which he was present. Something of the immense evangelistic zeal of the brothers Jeffreys is revealed in a fireside chat that they had with Alexander Boddy in 'Llwynmelyn', the home of Owen Jenkins JP, a gentleman farmer owning 100 acres and renting another 150.

> Brother Stephen and Brother George and I had a long heart-to-heart talk. They feel that the Lord needs evangelists in Pentecostal work today. There are many teachers and would-be teachers, but few evangelists. The Lord is giving an answer through this Revival to the criticism that the Pentecostal people are not interested in

Evangelistic work, and only seek to have good times. (May the Lord shake this out of His people. Amen.)[13]

Boddy reports that the healing of Edith Carr, 'who had been lame for nine months through diseased bone in the foot', occurred three days after he had left Llandrindod. As a result of this meeting, Stephen and George were invited to speak at the Sunderland Convention that year. Following the mission at Pen-y-Bont, Stephen returned to Wales, where he was appointed pastor of a church in Island Place, Llanelli. George was invited to London and stayed there from 24th March to 16th May at 'Maranatha', the missionary rest home run by Mrs Crisp. From that base, he held services in many locations, including the Welsh Wesleyan chapel.[14]

The Sunderland Convention 1913

As mentioned in the previous paragraph, both brothers were invited to the Sunderland Convention. George was invited to preach at the evangelistic services each evening following the main convention service. There is no record in *Confidence* of Stephen attending, although there is no doubt that he was present. There is a note in *Confidence* about the Welsh contingent that were present at the convention: 'The friends were delighted with the singing of the Welsh brethren, who were with us in goodly numbers. Cwmtwrch and the Rhondda Valley and other parts of South Wales were represented, and Ivor Roberts gave a stirring testimony.'[15] It is more than likely that Stephen and George came with the representatives from Cwmtwrch. It appears that George was one of the speakers at the evening convention meeting on Monday, 12th May along with Mrs Crisp and Pastor Paul.[16] He gave a gospel address on the Tuesday evening from Isaiah 12:2-3. On Wednesday evening, May 14th he spoke from Isaiah 38:8 under the title of 'The turning back of the shadows'. His final message[17] was on the Friday where, again, it appears that he spoke at the main convention meeting along with Mrs Crisp: 'George Jeffreys gave an address on Genesis 3 and 1 Kings 19 – the call of God to the man that fell into sin and the call of God to the man that fell into discouragement.'

Three ten-shilling notes

It was at the Sunderland Convention 1913 that George made an impression on one of the Gillespie brothers (William) who were influential in the formative years of the Pentecostal Movement in Ireland. William had been converted in 1907 through the preaching of an American Pentecostal evangelist, William Anderson. Gillespie was so impressed by George Jeffreys' preaching that he spoke to his brother, George, and they invited him to Ireland to hold meetings. They enclosed three ten shilling notes for his boat fare.[18]

There appears to be a difference of opinion over times and dates between Cartwright and Canty. Canty records George Jeffreys preaching in Belfast at the Dover Street Christmas Convention. Canty's description of that meeting is worth noting.[19]

> By a remarkable providence he there met Robert Mercer, William Henderson and Robert Ernest Darragh, who spoke to him and so, for a few minutes, formed a quartet whose lives would later combine in Elim: William Henderson, the wise counsellor for early years before his untimely death robbed Elim of needed help,[20] 'Ernie' Darragh. The doyen of all song leaders, and Robert Mercer, who as a Bible teacher was a gift to the work.[21]

According to Canty, the three ten shilling notes were sent to George Jeffreys inviting him to take a holiday with the Gillespies in their home at 14 Pine Street, Belfast just after Christmas, 1914. Kay does not mention the ten shilling notes, but concurs with Cartwright that the initial invitation for George to visit

Ireland was made by the Gillespie brothers in December 1913. It had been their intention to hold an evangelistic mission in Monaghan, with George being the evangelist. Advertising literature had been prepared and the event was due to be held in the Methodist church in Monaghan. However, on discovering that the mission was to be held on Pentecostal lines, permission to use the Methodist church was denied.

George returned to Wales and took part in a ten day convention in Llanelli. There was a clear evangelistic element to the convention as George included the conversion of a noted prize-fighter who had the 'tobacco demon destroyed in him'. [22] During the first part of 1914, George held a campaign at Emmanuel Baptist Chapel in Plymouth. This was to be very significant and laid the foundation for a major crusade in the city in 1926. He returned to the same place the following year and reports of that visit were printed in *Confidence*, together with a letter of validation from the minister of the church. George's second campaign in Plymouth in 1915, seems to have set the pattern for his evangelistic strategy from the time that the Elim Movement was founded. He stayed in the city for more than six weeks. Some who were present at those meetings were later to become members of the Plymouth Elim Church which was established in 1924 following a campaign held by Stephen Jeffreys. Leon Quest, who was to become an Elim minister stated that in his opinion, Elim started not in Ireland, but in his home city of Plymouth.[23] The minister of Emanuel Baptist Church, where the campaign was held, sent a brief note that was included in the April edition of *Confidence*. The following month's edition carried a much more comprehensive report under the heading: 'A Revival at Plymouth'.

In his letter to Boddy that was published in the May edition of *Confidence*, Jeffreys points to the fact that the revival meetings had been going on for six weeks.[24] The wording in both Jeffreys' letter and that of the pastor, E M Bacon, do not just convey details of evangelistic success but contain what can only be described as revival scenes. George writes:

Sinners of the deepest dye, Magdalens, drunkards, as well as professors of religion who had no possession, have come weeping their way to Calvary, confessing their sins and making restitution of wrong things done in the past. Ungodly persons are being struck down in the meetings, while others tremble as though charged with a dynamo, caused (I believe) by conviction of sin. Members are receiving the baptism into the Holy Ghost accompanied by Bible signs in the public meetings, without any laying-on of hands. Acts 10:44 is being fulfilled, and in one meeting alone we counted over twenty who had received, and were speaking in new tongues for the first time as the Word of God went forth. Some receive the baptism on the street as they go home from the meetings, and return next day with beaming faces testifying of the blessing. Christians of all denominations join together in praising God, being knitted together in the bond of divine love, while sinners are being saved each day.[25]

In his letter, published in the same edition, Pastor Edwin Bacon states that this move of the Spirit occurred as a result of three years continuous prayer which saw him and other members of his church receiving the fullness of the Spirit the previous year. That would possibly have occurred during George Jeffreys' previous visit to the church in 1914. That this was not merely an evangelistic campaign, but one in which there was a strong Pentecostal influence, is borne out by the pastor's words towards the end of his letter. This was the second time that George Jeffreys campaigned in Plymouth. He was to conduct a third campaign in January 1926, some fifteen months after his brother Stephen campaigned and opened an Elim church in the city.

But it was in another dockyard city that George Jeffreys was to open the first Elim church; Belfast, in Northern Ireland. After campaigning in Coulsdon, Surrey, George made his way to Belfast in time for another Christmas convention. Boulton writes of the tremendous blessing that was experienced during the Coulsdon campaign. 'Souls were saved, backsliders reclaimed, and many baptised in the Holy Ghost with Bible signs.'[26]

Once again, there is a slight discrepancy in the various historical writings concerning times and places where George Jeffreys ministered. According to Boulton, Jeffreys had come to the attention of some 'brethren in Monaghan who were deeply interested in the evangelisation of Northern Ireland'. Boulton goes on to state that a revival campaign was arranged to be held in the town of Monaghan and says the Monaghan Mission yielded some excellent results. In fact, the Monaghan Mission was not held until the summer of 1915. Kay records that Jeffreys went from Coulsdon to Belfast where he preached at the Christmas convention in Dover Street.[27] It was at this meeting, according to both Cartwright and Kay, that George re-established connections with the young men that he had met up with the previous year, plus one or two others. This group of seven men invited George to a momentous meeting in Monaghan on 7th January 1915, where the Elim story truly begins.

Notes

[1] Kay, William, ibid, p51.

[2] Boulton, E C W, ibid, p12.

[3] Kay, William, ibid, p53.

[4] Cartwright, Desmond, ibid, p31.

[5] Jeffreys, Edward, *Stephen Jeffreys, The Beloved Evangelist* (London: Elim Publishing Company, 1946), pp6,7.

[6] Polhill, *Flames of Fire*, p10, p2, quoted by Kay, ibid, p53.

[7] *Confidence*, February 1913, *Wales in the Dawn of Revival*, pp27,28.

[8] There is a discrepancy between Cartwright's account of this in his book and what appears in the *Confidence* edition of March 1913. *Confidence* firmly attests this testimony as being of the mission in Cwmtwrch. Cartwright states that the person concerned was a Quaker magistrate in Radnorshire

who invited the brothers to conduct their next mission there. See
Cartwright, ibid, pp31,32.

[9] Acts 8:26-40.

[10] Cartwright, Desmond, ibid, p32.

[11] Jeffreys, Edward, ibid, p9.

[12] Cartwright, Desmond, ibid, p33.

[13] *Confidence*, March 1913, p48.

[14] Kay, William, ibid, p55.

[15] *Confidence*, June 1913, p117.

[16] *Confidence*, ibid, p114.

[17] *Confidence*, ibid, p117.

[18] Cartwright, Desmond, ibid, p39.

[19] Canty had met all four and knew three of them personally and writes
from personal knowledge of the leaders and events within Elim from 1929
onwards.

[20] He was the brother of Adelaide Henderson who became Elim's
Missionary Secretary. His spirituality was such that he was referred to as
'Henderson the Good'.

[21] Canty, George, ibid, p45.

[22] *Confidence*, May 1917, p92.

[23] Quest, Leon, personal papers in the possession of the author.

[24] The same length of time that his major campaign under the Elim banner
was held in the beginning of 1926 and of which George Jeffreys was to
write to E J Phillips, Elim's secretary-general, that he was having the time of
his life.

[25] *Confidence*, May 1915, p89.

[26] Boulton, E C W, ibid, p20.

[27] Kay, William, ibid, p64.

7

The Birth of Elim

Scarcely could any prominent work have had a less inauspicious start than did the Elim Pentecostal Church. An attempt had been made in January 1914 to hold an evangelistic campaign in Monaghan, but because of the connections of the organisers with the fledgling Pentecostal movement, the use of a building to hold the campaign was denied them. But something had touched the hearts of the group of young men that met together at the Dover Street Christmas Convention. They sensed that something spiritually significant was about to take place. There grew a certain conviction within their hearts that God was about to do a new thing in their Province.

George spent much time in the company of Ernie Darragh at 14 Pine Street, Belfast, but George also stayed in the home of the parents of Lottie Smith in County Tyrone. Lottie had received the baptism in the Holy Spirit when she lived in Philadelphia, USA. She came home to her parents' farm in Co Tyrone in 1907 with her pastor, named Anderson, whom she later married. A meeting was soon arranged in the home and present was a son named Joseph. He heard people speaking in tongues for the first time. Joseph spent a few years in the USA and then returned and joined the Elim Evangelistic Band. Joseph was to become a hugely influential leader within the Elim Movement. He had a remarkable prophetic gift. When Joseph Smith spoke, people listened.[1]

Canty is also of the opinion that the three ten shilling notes were sent to George, inviting him to come to Ireland in 1914, the same as Boulton. It could be argued that seeing as these two (Boulton and Canty) were much nearer the beginning of Elim than Cartwright, Kay or the author, their view is more than likely to be correct. However, it is clear that it was as a result of hearing George Jeffreys preach at the Sunderland Convention that William Gillespie sent the invitation for George to visit Ireland. Furthermore, they had arranged for him to campaign in the Methodist church in Monaghan, but that was cancelled by the Methodist authorities there. There is no record of George even being present at the 1914 Sunderland Convention, and he certainly did not preach there that year. It is also clear that George visited Belfast in December 1913 and went to the Dover Street Convention where he met up with Ernest Darragh.

Monaghan

George spoke at the Christmas Convention in Dover Street and met up with a group of young men who had spent a fair amount of time in prayer together. They included Robert Mercer and his brother John, as well as Ernest Darragh.[2] Again, there is a discrepancy between Canty and Cartwright. Canty states that George arrived in Belfast just after Christmas 1914. Cartwright makes it clear that George was one of the speakers at the convention.[3] In any case, George met up with this group of earnest young men and he spent quite some time praying with them. A member of the group is reported to have asked George, 'What are you going to do?' George's reply was firm: 'I am coming out for the truth of Pentecost.'[4] This was a hugely significant moment, not only for the young evangelist himself, but for the rest of that group of young men who had devoted themselves to praying for a revival, carrying with it the message of Pentecost, in Ireland. George was invited by the prayer circle to discuss evangelism in Northern Ireland; but from the minutes of the meeting that was held in Monaghan, it is clear that the group had in mind the whole of Ireland. As it turned out, owing in no small way to the partition of Ireland, almost all the campaigning in those early years was done in Northern Ireland.

It was on Thursday, 7th January 1915 that a historic gathering was held in Knox's Temperance Hotel. There were eight men present.[5] They were Albert Kerr (Co Monaghan), George Allen and Frederick Farlow (Co Fermanagh), Robert and John Mercer (Co Armagh), William Henderson (Co Monaghan), Ernest Darragh (Co Down) and George Jeffreys (South Wales). After prayer and discussion, they arrived at a momentous decision. An invitation was extended to George Jeffreys to take up permanent evangelistic work in Ireland. The minute book records that they 'came together for the purpose of discussing the best means of reaching Ireland with the full Gospel on Pentecostal lines'. The minute book then goes on to say:

> We believe it to be in the mind of God that the Evangelist George Jeffreys, of South Wales, who was present with us, be invited to take up permanent evangelistic work in Ireland, and that a centre be chosen by him for the purpose of establishing a Church out of which evangelists would be sent into the towns and villages, and that a tent be hired, for the purpose of holding a Gospel Mission during the month of July to commence the work in Ireland. We agree that God promises to supply the temporal need of every Evangelist that would be called by Him into the work, and that through prayer and faith in His promises, He would prove Himself to be to each one Jehovah Jireh.[6]

Interestingly, the meeting is titled: 'First Informal Meeting of Christian Brethren at Monaghan, Thursday, January 7th, 1915.' The minutes of that first meeting were signed by George Jeffreys, William Henderson, Frederick A Farlow, R E Darragh and A S Kerr. Strangely, neither of the Gillespie brothers were present at this meeting, although it was, they who had sent the initial invitation to George. They (the Gillespies) remained strong supporters of George Jeffreys and undoubtedly contributed financially to the work, especially in the early years. Considering that the meeting was described as being 'informal', they passed quite a formal resolution. What is very clear from this minute is that George Jeffreys was immediately recognised as their leader. He was given the right to choose a centre in Ireland for evangelising the country. They had no guaranteed income and only a small plan – namely that they would hire a tent to hold an evangelistic campaign in July.

These young men certainly had faith, but little else. They had no resources or guaranteed income. However, they recognised that in George Jeffreys, they had an evangelist of great and rare talent. They had heard Jeffreys on a number of occasions and he was obviously at ease preaching in Northern Ireland. 'He was sincere, logical, unemotional (and not English!) but also warm and determined and he could, like all Ulster's evangelical Protestants, say that he believed the Bible from cover to cover.'[7]

Although George had been given the privilege of seeking out a centre for the purpose of establishing a church from which evangelists would be sent out to reach Ireland with the gospel on Pentecostal lines, it is clear from the previous chapter that he was back on the mainland for much of the first part of 1915. Like all good leaders, he was able to delegate and William Gillespie and Robert Darragh did the investigating for premises in Belfast.

A marquee was hired and an evangelistic campaign was held in Monaghan in July 1915. A second informal meeting of Pentecostal Workers was held at the home of Jack Wilkinson of North Road Monaghan. Note the change in the title: 'Christian Brethren' had morphed into 'Pentecostal Workers'. It is worth quoting the full minutes of this second meeting.

> At a meeting of Christian workers who were interested in the Pentecostal work in Ireland, which was held at the house of Mr. Jack Wilkinson, Swann Park, North Road, Monaghan, on Sat. July 3rd 1915, we were delighted to

have with us Evangelist George Jeffreys to commence the Gospel Mission in the Tent at North Road according to previous arrangements. He informed us that God had already answered our prayers and had given a definite call to Mr. R.E. Darragh and Miss M. Straight of Bangor, Co. Down, to work in connection with the Band of Evangelists which we had claimed by faith for the Pentecostal Movement in Ireland. Mr. Darragh had kindly accepted the invitation to act as Secretary pro tem.[8]

Although George had committed himself to the work in Ireland, there is room for a certain amount of cynicism on this point because he spent as much time in England during 1915 as he did in Ireland. In fact, he conducted three campaigns in England as against only one in Ireland. He spent at least six weeks on a campaign in Plymouth in the spring and then went to London to speak at a convention. An article in the August edition of *Confidence* reported him conducting a tent mission for soldiers.

We opened our mission here to the soldiers on 27th June with Bro. George Jeffreys for the first 8 days. We had great blessings and 23 were converted that week ... Stephen Jeffreys came to conduct the meetings for a fortnight, Bro. George Jeffreys having gone to conduct tent meetings in Monaghan ... We expect George Jeffreys to return to take charge of the work later on.[9]

What is implied by that last sentence is unclear, but it would have been impossible for George Jeffreys to have been in charge of works in Ireland and England at the same time.

During the month of September, George conducted an evangelistic campaign in the city of Hereford.

May I through 'Confidence' utter a song of thanksgiving unto the Lord for His wonderful presence among us in a tent mission conducted by Mr. George Jeffreys, the Welsh revivalist, during the month of September ... On Monday October 4th, a farewell tea was held in our little church and Mr. George Jeffreys gave his farewell address to a crowded congregation.[10]

Premises had been found by Gillespie and Darragh in Belfast, which were opened in August 1915, but almost immediately George set off for a whole month campaigning in Hereford. It is the author's opinion that George Jeffreys was not, at this point in his ministry, totally committed to the work in Ireland.

The campaign in Monaghan in July 1915 went reasonably well. Kay states that this took place in the month of August.[11] But this could not be the case, as the minutes of the Second Informal Meeting of Pentecostal Workers at Monaghan on Saturday, 3rd July 1915 reveal: 'We were delighted to have with us Evangelist George Jeffreys to commence the Gospel Mission in the tent at North Road according to previous arrangement.' There was no permanent Pentecostal church established in Monaghan as a result of this campaign.[12] Jeffreys himself was quite upbeat about the campaign, as his report quoted by Canty shows:

From the first of the meetings God has been saving souls, and sinners have been trembling under the conviction of sin. One young man was stricken from his seat by the power of God, was saved and immediately delivered from sin. Next morning, he burnt a number of cigarettes, although no one had spoken to him about them. People came from great distances, and the hunger for revival is such that people come from miles around, and the cry is everywhere, 'Come over and help us.' The young men who organised this campaign are on fire for God, and have quite recently received the outpouring of the Holy Ghost, which first fell at Sunderland seven years ago. Since then, many dear saints have held on to

God for Ireland, and praise His Name, their prayers are now being answered.[13]

Canty makes the point that the choice of Monaghan was made entirely on the basis that it was in that area where the supporters lived. He goes on to express the opinion that the Irish town had never recorded to any satisfaction that the birth of Elim took place there. The first campaign inaugurated the basic problem of Elim, the care of the converts.[14] The January 1915 resolution had determined that a centre for evangelists be created. It also stated that this centre be chosen by George Jeffreys. As we have seen, George Jeffreys was back and forth to the mainland, so the work of finding a centre from which to release evangelists was left to others. The burden fell mainly on the shoulders of the secretary of the newly formed association – Robert Ernest Darragh.

Elim's very first purchase was a tent, bought for £20 from a Mr Ferguson of Bangor, to be used for evangelistic meetings. We must not underestimate the work done by the small band of young people in 1915. Meetings were conducted in small halls throughout Ulster. Joseph Smith, who died at the age of ninety, spent almost seventy years in the Elim ministry. He described the method that the evangelists would use in those early days by referencing a place in County Armagh:

> Finding a hall to rent in the Back Market, but without seating, they begged boxes from shops and planks from a wood yard to sit on. The YMCA lent 30 chairs 'which made a proud dress circle'. The weather did not co-operate, it rained. It did not, however, rain pennies from heaven despite their prayers of faith, with only fourpence in the box the first night. Somehow, bills were paid.[15]

The laundry

The search for a centre was paramount, and Darragh and William Gillespie, searched through many areas of Belfast to find a building that they could use both as a centre and a church. They decided to concentrate on the Donegal Road area of Belfast. Finally, they found a building, an old laundry in Hunter Street. Canty describes it as: 'A scarred, rough-cast and soot-covered front with five broken windows, three up and two down, facing the cobbled street and entered by battered plank doors, a one-time laundry, but now a grubby industrial abandonment.'[16] The building was secured on a three-year lease, William Gillespie and George Jeffreys being the named tenants. Two men stood as guarantors for the place and George Jeffreys was appointed Pastor.[17] A team of workers, including George Jeffreys himself, worked tirelessly to whitewash the building and make it habitable. From this point onwards in the Minute Book of the Elim Evangelistic Band, there is a change in the title given to George Jeffreys. He is no longer referred to as Mr George Jeffreys, but as Pastor Jeffreys. He was later to change the title himself by using the designation 'principal'. The reason was that Percy Parker, creator of the Christian Workers' Correspondence Course used by Elim, described himself as principal, and this suggested superiority of office. Since George was to become head of all departments, including the college, he also adopted the title. 'Somehow, it fitted and all came to call him "Principal", or "Prince" among his closer colleagues.'[18]

Kay claims that Hunter Street was the first Pentecostal church in Ireland. 'The congregation was to be called Elim Christ Church and became the first Pentecostal assembly in Ireland.'[19] However, this could not have been the case as there was already a Pentecostal fellowship in Dover Street and George Jeffreys preached there at their Christmas Convention in 1914, having also attended the previous year. Robinson refers to a group of seven or eight people who met in Cavour Street in West Belfast. In March 1911, the group moved into premises at Dover Street and called themselves 'Full Gospel Assembly'. Elders and deacons were installed and Robinson is clear that this confirmed its status as the first Pentecostal assembly in Ireland.[20]

Soon, many people gathered to Hunter Street, in spite of the cramped conditions. On Boxing Day 1915, a missionary on furlough from India, Miss Boyle, attended the evening meeting with Miss Adelaide Henderson, a Presbyterian school teacher. The only spare seats were at the front, which meant that Adelaide received the full force of the gospel message. It was so different to the services that she was used to. She was quite indignant at the very thought that she, a respectable church-attending Presbyterian needed to be 'saved'. She left the meeting before it finished. However, her brother, William, who was to become a leading figure in the young Elim Movement, stopped her and asked: 'Adsie, before you leave, have you ever been saved, do you love the Lord?' Adelaide had great respect and love for her older brother. Miss Anderson's Christmas was completely changed as she surrendered her life to Christ. She became one of Elim's first missionaries in 1920 and went to the Congo and later was to become Elim's missionary secretary, a position she held for almost fifteen years.[21] Shortly before her death, after decades of devoted Elim service, she said, 'There was extraordinary power in those early meetings. You felt it, you couldn't miss it. I've felt nothing like it since.'

George compiled a booklet containing basic doctrines that were to be proclaimed by the Church which was called *Elim Christ Church*. In this booklet was included the resolution passed at the second meeting in Monaghan 'prohibiting proselytising, deprecating any attempt to induce members of other assemblies to withdraw from their own fellowship with a view to membership in the Elim Church'.[22] In the booklet, mention is made of the baptism in the Holy Spirit with signs following. There is no reference specifically to speaking in other tongues, although this was included in Elim's first official Statement of Faith which was published in 1922.[23]

What is clear from the historical records is the extraordinary bonds that drew this small company of workers together. 'Again, and again during these early days of struggling, we find this little company meeting together to discuss their difficulties, to face their problems and form their plans, always seeking fresh guidance and grace from Him who had set them apart to this holy calling.'[24] There is no doubting that the inspiration and zeal of George Jeffreys was a huge factor in driving this small group of workers forward in their determination to reach Ireland with the Pentecostal message. At the Christmas Convention in Hunter Street, the large congregation rejoiced that under George Jeffreys' ministry many people had come to faith in Christ. At those Christmas services, it was also reported that George had held a campaign in Galway and a report was given.[25]

By the end of 1915, George Jeffreys had fully committed himself to the task of working in Ireland. It is interesting that he took on the title 'pastor' when he saw himself very much as an evangelist. Not only was he an evangelist, he was also a 'revivalist'. The references to him in the *Confidence* magazines constantly used the appellation 'Welsh Revivalist' to describe him. He was also mentioned as being one of the 'children of the Revival'. Noel Brooks, an Elim minister who stood by Jeffreys at the time of the split with Elim commented:

> One certainly cannot be long in George Jeffreys' company, whether privately or in the great public meetings which he conducts, without realising that he is indebted to the Welsh revival not merely for his conversion but also for his dominating vision and passion for revival. The scenes which his boyish eyes witnessed have ever burned within his memory as a pattern towards which he must work.[26]

Brooks' assessment of Jeffreys' great passion for revival is a true one. Also, his evangelistic drive was the major factor in the establishment of the Elim Pentecostal Church. Brooks sided with Jeffreys on the church government issue, although he had resigned from Elim in 1938 because he 'no longer accepts the Pentecostal position'. He subsequently joined the Bible Pattern Church Fellowship but was only with them for a few years.[27] Cartwright refers to a conversation that he had with Brooks over a book he had written, *Fight for the Faith and Freedom*, in which the latter stated:

> I have suffered a great deal because of that book. I very much regret that I ever wrote it. It is difficult to get things in perspective especially when one is personally involved. I no longer hold that view of church government. It may well have worked in Sweden but they had the personality of Levi Petrus.[28] It certainly did not succeed in Great Britain.[29]

Notes

[1] Canty, George, ibid, p47.

[2] Darragh was a fellow student of George Jeffreys at the PMU Bible School in Preston. It appears that he completed the two-year course, whereas Jeffreys only stayed for six weeks. There is some photographic evidence that he returned to the School for a short period sometime in 1914.

[3] See Cartwright, p43 and Canty, p47.

[4] Canty, George, ibid, p47.

[5] Cartwright and Kay state that there were seven men present. Canty and Robinson say that eight were present. The author concurs with the latter. The man whom Cartwright and Kay omit from the list is Ernest Darragh.

[6] Elim Evangelistic Band Minute Book, kept in the office of the General Superintendent of Elim, Elim International Offices, West Malvern, Worcs.

[7] Kay, William, ibid, p64.

[8] Elim Evangelistic Band Minutes of the second meeting, signed by the same five signatories.

[9] Dr and Mrs Phair, *Confidence*, August 1915, p152.

[10] Jones, Sarah, *Confidence*, October 1915, p196.

[11] Kay, William, ibid, p65.

[12] It was not until the mid-thirties (1934?) that an Elim church was founded in Monaghan, and it was not an alliance church; it remains an ECI church to this day.

[13] Canty, George, ibid, p49.

[14] Canty, George, ibid, p49.

[15] Canty, George, ibid, p52.

[16] Canty, George, ibid, p53.

[17] Cartwright, Desmond, ibid, p44.

[18] Canty, George, ibid, p54.

[19] Kay, William, ibid, p65.

[20] Robinson, James, p69.

[21] Adelaide Henderson's testimony, Elim Archives, Malvern.

[22] Boulton, E C W, ibid, p28.

[23] The author regards the 1922 Statement of Faith as Elim's first doctrinal statement. Others would disagree and point to the 1915 booklet. The author takes the view that while the 1915 booklet contained doctrinal views, it was intended for a local church and was not a Statement of Faith per se.

[24] Boulton, E C W, ibid, p29.

[25] Boulton, E C W, ibid, p30.

[26] Brooks, Noel, *Fight for the Faith and Freedom* (London: Pattern Bookroom, 1948), p22.

[27] Cartwright, Desmond, comments on *Fight for the Faith and Freedom*. Undated, written in his own hand and found in the copy of the book which he gave to the author.

[28] This was a reference to local church government, which Jeffreys came to espouse as opposed to central church government which he had set up in Elim.

[29] Cartwright, Desmond. Interview with Noel Brooks, 29th April 1970 at the Christian Bookshop, Blackpool.

8
The Irish Years: Part 1

In July 1915, a tent mission was held in Monaghan. Although there was no Elim church established in the town until the mid-thirties, the significance of the campaign held there is that it established the pattern that George Jeffreys and other members of the Elim Evangelistic Band were to use successfully in those years. George wrote a letter which was published in the August 1915 edition of *Confidence*. It is quoted here in full under the title 'Ireland: News from Bro. George Jeffreys':

> The friends of 'Confidence' will be pleased to hear of the blessed times we are having in the camp meetings which have been going on for one month. Monaghan is a place situated almost in the heart of Ireland, where John Wesley was imprisoned for preaching the same Gospel which I am now privileged to proclaim.
>
> Although many years have gone by since then, the Gospel which that saintly man of God loved, and preached with such remarkable results, is still proving itself to be just as powerful in convicting and the saving of precious souls these days in the very same town.
>
> From the first of the meetings, God has been saving souls, and sinners have been trembling under conviction of sins. One young man was stricken down from his seat under the power of God, was saved and immediately delivered from sin. Next morning, he burned a number of cigarettes, although no-one had spoken to him about them. People come from great distances, and the hunger

for revival is such that people come from miles around, and the cry is everywhere 'Come over and help us.'

The young men who organised this campaign are on fire for God, and have received, quite recently, the outpouring of the Holy Ghost, which first fell on dear old Sunderland some seven years ago. Since then, many dear saints have held on to God for Ireland, and, praise His Name, their prayers are now being answered.

God willing, early next summer, I propose going through some of the Irish districts, as I feel the need so much. For this purpose, I am purchasing the Bangor tent (at the end of their meetings). May the need of Ireland be laid upon the hearts of God's people for prayer. Thank you for remembering your Welsh brother in prayer.

George Jeffreys[1]

The nature of George Jeffreys' ministry in the year 1915 was very much itinerant. As noted above, it is not absolutely certain that he had fully committed himself to the work in Ireland at this point because he was often back and forth to the mainland. The same edition of *Confidence* carries a report of his mission to soldiers. The location is not given but it was clearly expected that he would return at a later date 'to take charge of the work'.[2]

As has been reported, the first two evangelists were Ernest Darragh and Margaret Streight. The friendship between Jeffreys and Darragh was to last a lifetime. Darragh predeceased Jeffreys by some eighteen months and Jeffreys was laid to rest in the same grave as Darragh in Streatham. Margaret Streight also maintained a very close relationship with Jeffreys. She later married Robert Mercer. They both left Elim to join Jeffreys at the time of the split with Elim.

It is interesting to note that a woman was one of the first two members appointed to Jeffreys' evangelistic team. This should not be too great a surprise owing to the Azusa Street Revival and also the early British Pentecostal meetings. Women ministered alongside men in the Azusa Street meetings, and Mrs

Eleanor Crisp was a frequent speaker at many of the early conventions in England and Ireland.[3] Mrs Crisp was a guest speaker at a number of the early Elim meetings in Belfast.

Robinson makes the following comment as regards the ministry of women in the early Pentecostal movement:

> Spirit-emphasising movements have tended in their first flush to give women a high, though rarely equal status in ministry, while it was an exceptional circumstance in mainline denominations until the latter third of the twentieth century. By 1924, of the thirty four members of the Elim Evangelistic Band, twenty two were men and twelve women a proportion matched by few other denominations at the time.[4]

Influential figures

In the early days of Elim, George Jeffreys was considerably influenced by some established figures in the early Pentecostal Movement. Two of them were Anglican clergymen, Alexander Boddy and Thomas Hackett; another, John Leech, was also a committed Anglican. Although they were very much involved in the early Pentecostal Movement, and one of them, John Leech, was to have a major influence on the theological views of George Jeffreys, all three of them died in the Anglican Communion. Another person who was to be influential in Jeffreys ministry from those early days was E C W Boulton, who was to be prominent in the development of Elim.

Thomas Hackett

Thomas Edmund Hackett (1850-1939) was the son of the Rev John W Hackett and Jane Hackett. His sister Anne was married in 1897 to Dr John Crozier who was Primate of All Ireland from 1911 until his death in 1920. Hackett was ordained to the ministry of the Church of Ireland in 1875 and served as a minister of the Church of Ireland for twenty-eight years until he retired in 1903. He identified strongly with the evangelical wing of the Church. It is thought that he was probably the first person to receive the Pentecostal experience in Ireland and he became a strong advocate of Pentecostalism.[5]

Hackett seems to have been influenced by the Keswick teaching of holiness being a crisis experience that led the believer into a deeper spiritual experience, and it would appear that he believed that one had to reach a certain level of holiness before one could be baptised in the Holy Spirit. He, along with John Leech, was one of the main speakers at the 1912 Sunderland Convention. Speaking from Acts 15:9, the theme of his message was 'heart purity'. In this sermon, he implied that achieving a certain 'purity of the heart' was necessary before a believer could receive the baptism in the Holy Spirit:

> Surely God is teaching us that once that point of heart purity is reached through simple faith in the Name of Jesus, then, and not till then, we are ready for the reception of the Holy Ghost. So, lastly, I turn once more to the 15th of Acts: 'God which knoweth the hearts, bare them witness, giving them the Holy Ghost, even as he did unto us, having first purified their hearts by faith.' God was present there, and was looking down into their hearts to see if everything was right, and He saw they accepted with open hand and open heart that great gift of full remission of sins and heart purity, and in that moment, they were ready for their Pentecost.[6]

This view of a level of personal sanctification being achieved prior to receiving the baptism in the Holy Spirit[7] with the accompanying evidence of tongues was prevalent among some of the early Pentecostals.

John Leech

John Leech (1857-1942) was an Ulsterman who became a formative and controversial figure within British Pentecostalism and was to have great influence upon George Jeffreys – in the author's opinion, one that proved to be detrimental to the Elim Movement. He followed in his father's footsteps in practising law. After a glittering undergraduate showing at Trinity College Dublin, where he won prizes in the form of First Honoursman and Plunket Gold Medallist for Oratory, he was called to the Irish Bar in 1881.[8]

Leech was a frequent visitor and speaker at the Sunderland Conventions and also appeared on many early Pentecostal platforms, including the London Whitsuntide Convention in 1915 which was organised by Cecil Polhill as a replacement to the Sunderland Convention which was suspended owing to the First World War. He was a speaker at Sunderland in 1912, 1913 and 1914. A number of his sermons were printed in *Confidence* and while he refers on more than one occasion to the law, thus revealing his profession, his sermons are easily followed and understood. Having said that, they were very much in the style of the times.

It is Leech's adherence to British Israelism that was to be highly influential upon George Jeffreys and was destined to cause great controversy within Elim. It is clear that Jeffreys was closely connected with Leech and he invited the King's Counsellor to form part of his Advisory Council for the Evangelistic Band.[9] Jeffreys' close association with Leech lasted until the latter's death in 1942 and there is no doubt that it was Leech who was the main influence on Jeffreys' British Israel views. In a letter to E J Phillips in 1934, Jeffreys refers to his views on British Israelism as being the same as they had been for fifteen years.[10]

The extent of the influence of John Leech upon the young Elim Movement is noted by the fact that both he and Hackett were appointed members of the Elim Pentecostal Alliance

Council on 6th January 1919.[11] Leech's preaching ministry was very well received throughout the early Pentecostal Movement although, in the very early years (1911-19), there appears to be little or no reference to his British Israel teaching.

George Jeffreys first met John Leech at the Sunderland Convention in 1913. This was the commencement of a long and enduring friendship and close association. In his tribute to his friend and mentor, Jeffreys refers to the early years of Elim when John Leech and his wife befriended him and were greatly involved in the work. 'When I founded the Elim Movement in the North of Ireland, both threw themselves unreservedly into the work and were not ashamed to be identified with its humble beginnings in the City of Belfast.'[12] Jeffreys goes on to express the difficulties and hardships of those early days when they had to contend with a fierce fighting opposition because of the stand they had taken for an open Bible and a Full Gospel. 'But we could always count on our beloved Mr. and Mrs. Leech for comfort, encouragement and support. They were indeed a tower of strength to us as we contended for the truths of Salvation, Healing, Baptism of the Holy Spirit, with signs following, and the Second Advent of Christ.'[13]

Leech stood firmly with Jeffreys at the time of the schism with Elim and was appointed vice-president of the Bible Pattern Church Fellowship. That Jeffreys was greatly impressed by his friend's many distinctions and achievements is seen by the inclusion within his tribute of some of them:

> He was a Master of Arts and Bachelor of Laws of Dublin University, and First Honoursman of Trinity College, Dublin; Plunket Gold Medallist for Oratory (Legal Debating), Honorary Member of the College Historical Society T.C.D., a member of the Bar of Ireland, and one of His Majesty's Counsel (K.C.), a member of the Bar of England, a Bencher of the Honourable Society of King's Inns, and a Bencher of the Inner Court of Northern Ireland. He was Senior Crown Prosecutor for County Longford. He was a leader of the Irish Bar. For over

three years he was a Judge of the Belfast Recorders Court and of the County Court of Antrim, during which period, in addition to ordinary Civil and Criminal jurisdiction, he had to adjudicate upon claims amounting to many millions of pounds sterling arising out of the disturbances in Belfast.[14]

It is interesting that within the above impressive list of distinctions, Jeffreys does not mention the role that Leech played in the British Israel Federation. He (Leech) became general commissioner of the Federation in 1926 and then its chair.

Leech was an accomplished speaker, an eminent debater and a fine preacher. Ernie Darragh, the secretary of the Evangelistic Band, reported in *Confidence* on Leech's ministry at the Ballymena Christmas Convention 1916. He writes: 'The deep, spiritual teaching which he [Leech] gave throughout the Convention has made a lasting impression, and has brought the people into a place where they have never been before.'[15] In his tribute to Leech, George Jeffreys attested not only to the oral eloquence of Leech, but also to the use of the spiritual gifts: 'Mr. Leech had given to him by the Holy Spirit the frequent manifestation of the supernatural word of knowledge, and his wealth of natural wisdom was frequently augmented by the miraculous spiritual gift of the word of wisdom.' Noel Brooks mentions a number of abiding friendships that were formed with George Jeffreys in the early days. The first one he mentions in this list is John Leech: 'Mr. J. Leech, a tower of strength and a mine of wisdom, retained until his death in 1942, his unflinching loyalty to the Revivalist whom he had sponsored.'[16] This seems to imply that Leech financed some of Jeffreys' campaigns and ministry in the early days.

The Ballymena campaign

Although the Elim Movement was founded in January 1907 and its first church, Hunter Street, Belfast, was opened in the summer of that year, the opening of an Elim Church in Ballymena seems to be the catalyst that established Elim as a Pentecostal movement. Ballymena was to become the blueprint that Jeffreys used for most of his evangelistic campaigns. Jeffreys came to Ballymena at the invitation of James and Agnes Gault. The meetings were held in the old YMCA building in Wellington Street and commenced in February 1916. Robinson reports that the Evangelistic Band returned in June of that year for more than five weeks, where the 275-seater tent was packed every evening with people coming from the town and surrounding area.[17]

George was well received and accepted in Ballymena. One reason for this could have been the great impact made on the town and locality by the 1859 revival. There were people present at the Ballymena campaign who could remember the 1859 revival and they were prepared to respond to Jeffreys who certainly campaigned along revivalist lines. He was known and acknowledged as 'The Welsh Revivalist'. This would have struck a chord with the Ballymena people.

Not only was Ballymena the first of Jeffreys' major evangelistic crusades that resulted in the establishment of a strong and viable congregation, but it also became the new centre of operations for the young movement. Boulton writes: 'Early in the ensuing year, 1916, a new centre was chosen in which to commence operations. A town situated some thirty miles to the north of Ulster's Capital, Ballymena lies in a neighbourhood which figures prominently in the religious history of Ireland.'[18] Boulton goes on to report that 120 conversions were recorded in a five-week period. He quotes words of a lady in the town, revealing what a wonderful answer to faith the coming of George Jeffreys to Ballymena was:

I do praise God for answered prayer. About seven and a half years ago I paid a visit to England and stayed at Whitley Bay. During that time, I heard of great blessing in a Vicarage at Monkwearmouth, Sunderland, and was very anxious to meet with those who were the recipients of the blessing. Praise God, the way was opened, and I found myself in the midst of the happiest band of saints that I had ever met in my life. They had received the baptism of the Holy Ghost, and were praising God. I recognised immediately that the Lord was doing a new thing in their midst, and oh, how a longing came into my heart that the blessing might reach my home in Northern Ireland. I made known my desire to the vicar and his wife, and we knelt down together and asked God to send the blessing on Ballymena. Ever since then I have kept believing that He would answer those prayers, and although it seems a long time since then, I do praise God, because I am privileged to see the answer.[19]

There was a view abroad at the time that Pentecostal people were mainly just interested in meeting together and not reaching out in evangelism. George Jeffreys' campaign in Ballymena gave the Pentecostal message an evangelistic edge. George was not just interested in Christians being baptised in the Spirit, he wanted people to come to Christ. In a letter published in the August 1916 edition of *Confidence*, George Jeffreys writes:

We have up to the present witnessed one hundred and twenty conversions, and still they come in ... this again proves that the statement some people make that Pentecostal Christians do not reach the unsaved is wrong. The desire to see souls saved is intensified in the experience of those who receive the blessing mentioned in Acts 1:8. Many have received the Baptism in the Holy Ghost in Ballymena, and they all testify of the power that they have received to witness for God.[20]

Notes

[1] *Confidence*, August 1915, p156.

[2] *Confidence*, August 1915, p152.

[3] Mrs Crisp was in charge of Maranatha, the Missionary Rest Home in London where George stayed, 26th March to 16th May 1913.

[4] Robinson, James, ibid, p132.

[5] Robinson, James, ibid, pp108-109.

[6] Hackett, Thomas, 'Heart Purity as a Necessary Preparation for Pentecost', *Confidence*, July 1912, pp156-158.

[7] The author refers to the 'baptism in the Holy Spirit'; this is the correct term. But in quoting the words of others, he has to remain true to the text, and in some cases, reference is made to the 'baptism of the Holy Spirit'.

[8] Robinson, James, ibid, p113.

[9] Jones, Maldwyn, *An Analysis of the Role of E J Phillips and an Assessment of His Leadership in the Establishment of the Elim Movement as a Coherent Christian Denomination*, MA dissertation (Malvern: Regents Theological College/Bangor University 2011), p54.

[10] Letter: Jeffreys to Phillips, 1st December 1934 (Malvern: Elim Archives).

[11] The other members were George Jeffreys, Stephen Jeffreys, William Henderson and Robert E Darragh.

[12] Jeffreys, George, 'A Prince and a Great Man in Israel Passes Over', *The Pattern*, Vol 3, No 16, Mid-August 1942, p3.

[13] Jeffreys, George, 'A Prince and a Great Man', p3.

[14] Jeffreys, George, 'A Prince and a Great Man', p4.

[15] Confidence, March-April 1915, p20.

[16] Brooks, Noel, ibid, p26.

[17] Robinson, James, ibid, p62.

[18] Boulton, E C W, ibid, p31.

[19] Boulton, E C W, ibid, p31

[20] *Confidence*, August 1916, pp130-131.

9

The Irish Years: Part 2

There is no doubt that there was a spirit of revival evidenced during the Ballymena campaign and in the weeks that followed. What is also clear from researching the history of those early days is that there was a strong sense of the Holy Spirit moving across congregations. There was a definite Pentecostal atmosphere present in meetings, with scenes reported that would not have been acceptable to Jeffreys as the work was established in England. Boulton reports one meeting when people were literally 'mown down' by the power of God:

> Among the early experiences of these times were many wonderful exhibitions of God's overmastering power. During one of the services, shortly after the Ballymena work had been commenced, whilst at prayer, the whole congregation was swept by the power of the Spirit. Fifty or sixty of the converts were literally mown down as the power of God poured itself[1] into the meeting. On this occasion, the glory of God was so great as to render further ministry in that meeting impossible.[2]

It is obvious that there was a visible manifestation of the presence and impact of the Holy Spirit in those early meetings. What is also clear, however, is the conservative evangelical presentation of doctrine. This would have been very important in Ulster where the Protestant people were well versed in Christian doctrine. Although Jeffreys and the Evangelistic Band were preaching and ministering the Pentecostal message, it was very much along 'full gospel' lines. Any deviation from biblical truth would not have been acceptable to a section of the population that was biblically literate. Boulton includes in his book a newspaper report of a convention that was held in Ballymena Town Hall a few months after the campaign and subsequent establishment of an Elim church in Ballymena. It is a lengthy report, but is worthy of inclusion in full. It shows how the town was impacted by the message that was preached in those meetings.

> The convention, under the auspices of the Elim Evangelistic Band … held in the Town Hall, continued until Sunday night, 7th inst., and was a great success. It attracted a very large and representative gathering from all denominations, and the interest which was evidenced from the beginning continued to increase until the final meetings, when the hall was not large enough to accommodate all who came, a number having to retire. The Speakers, Mr. J. Leech, K.C; M.A., and Pastor George Jeffreys clearly demonstrated by the way in which they held the attention (for periods spell-bound) of those huge assemblies for over two hours, and yet showing no symptoms of restlessness, that the power of God was with them and that a great revival spirit was abroad. Throughout the convention it was felt that the great aim and object was the exhortation of Christians to a full surrender of their entire lives to God that the Holy Spirit might lead them into all truth according to the Scriptures, and that they might be equipped by the power of the Holy Ghost to go forth as mighty witnesses for Him in this Laodicean age to stem the tide of unbelief and apostacy, experiencing and declaring the full Gospel as the apostles did … Quite a large number have professed conversion, and it is evident that those who have received the Pentecostal Baptism are fired with a zeal for the conversion of the world.[3]

Expanding in Ulster

Between 1915-1922, there were a total of twenty-nine Elim churches opened in Northern Ireland but only some were pioneered directly by George Jeffreys.[4] There is no detailed register of the churches in those early years and some of them were opened as 'works' before they became registered Elim churches. An example of this would be Bangor. The church there was officially opened in 1919, but meetings organised by members of the Elim Evangelistic Band had been established in 1917. This makes it difficult to trace the chronological opening of the Elim churches in Northern Ireland during this period.

One very important feature of the early days in Elim were the conventions. Indeed, they became a major feature of Elim church life well into the eighties. Conventions were organised by local churches and were held on an annual basis. Guest speakers would be invited and the meetings would last for three or four days around a weekend period. The larger churches would schedule their conventions around the Bank Holidays and these became a gathering point for Elim churches in a particular area. These were amalgamated into District Presbyteries in the forties.

The conventions at Hunter Street Belfast, Ballymena and Bangor became major strategic events in the young Elim Movement. These conventions drew thousands of people from all over the province. The first Easter Convention was held in Hunter Street in 1916. The building was hopelessly too small. By this time, Band members had been active in Armagh, Bangor, Ballymena and Monaghan. Three meetings were held on Easter Monday, two on the Tuesday and an evening service on the Wednesday and Thursday.[5] The conventions, particularly the summer camp in Bangor, became centres of teaching as well as evangelistic outreaches.

The conventions attracted major figures from the Pentecostal movement. Some of these had come to Jeffreys' attention through the Sunderland Conventions. There was a sprinkling of European speakers that brought a touch of mystery to the conventions, including Pastor Potma from Holland. The main speakers at the conventions were George Jeffreys, Thomas Hackett and John Leech. Stephen Jeffreys, E C W Boulton and Mrs Crisp from London, also spoke at some of the meetings. The first Hunter Street convention was held at Easter 1916. That Easter was momentous in Irish history as it was the occasion of the Easter Rising in Dublin which began on Easter Monday, 24th April 1916. The Easter Rising was an insurrection, mostly in Dublin city, that lasted from 24th April until 30th April. It was a concerted attempt to establish Irish Home Rule. An Irish Republic was proclaimed but the Rising was put down by British troops. In the week's fighting, more than 500 people were killed, half of whom were civilians. John Leech was resident in Dublin at the time, and he and his wife had travelled north to Belfast for the convention on the Good Friday, which they saw as divine providence. Their home was in Herbert Street, Dublin, which was not far from the General Post Office. This was the place where the Provisional Government of the Irish Republic was proclaimed.

George Jeffreys was the prominent figure at these conventions. His presence was charismatic and attractive. Donald Gee, a leading personality within the developing British Pentecostal Movement, says that George Jeffreys was easily the most gifted preacher that the British Pentecostal Movement has produced. He goes on to describe Jeffreys' appeal to congregations:

> He had a voice like music, with sufficient Welsh intonation to add an inimitable charm. His platform personality at times was magnetic. His face was appealing. Although lacking academic training, he possessed a natural refinement that made him acceptable in all circles. He presented his messages with a logical appeal and a note of authority that was compelling. With all that he was baptised in the Holy Spirit.[6]

Established as a denomination

In the summer of 1916, an Advisory Committee was formed consisting of Leech, Hackett and Jeffreys. This was the first step towards Elim becoming a recognised Christian denomination. It was also at this time that the four evangelists working under the leadership of George Jeffreys became known as the 'Elim Evangelistic Band'.[7] The Advisory Committee was appointed to oversee the work of the Band, but there was no doubt that George was clearly the dominant personality and he chaired the meetings. This was a clear sign of progress within the young movement, but a structure was being put in place that was to remain the norm for the next nineteen years. It was not until the establishment of the Deed Poll in 1934 that collegial leadership became a feature of Elim. Until then, George Jeffreys had the final say on all matters of government within the young denomination. It is deeply ironic that when the schism in Elim occurred in the late thirties, Jeffreys, having just two years prior signed the Deed Poll in which he was one of nine Executive Council members, albeit the chair, began agitating for the reform of the Elim Movement. Having firmly established central authority as the basis of government within the Elim Pentecostal Church, Jeffreys did a complete about turn by advocating local government for the denomination.

Towards the end of 1916, it was clear that rules and regulations would have to be put in place so that the work could progress. Leech was appointed 'president' of the Elim Evangelistic Band, but the minutes clearly reveal that an authority structure was being created. At the meeting of the Elim Evangelistic Band held in Ballymena on the 4th January 1917, the decision was taken to place collecting boxes in the homes of 'Christians interested in the work', for the purpose of 'supplying the temporal needs of the workers'.[8] According to Kay, this new basis of finance denotes a slight shift away from the faith basis on which the group first began.

The years 1917 and 1918 saw the Evangelistic Band not only making steady progress in the centres that were established, but also expanding out from those centres. By the end of 1918, churches had been opened in Belfast, Ballymena, Moneyslane, Portadown, Bangor and Lisburn. Belfast, Ballymena and Portadown especially became centres from which other churches were opened. An outreach was established in Cullybackey out of Ballymena. Trying to establish when some of the early Elim churches in Northern Ireland were opened is extremely difficult, as no documentation exists which clearly sets this out. Robinson, in his book, shows a map on which there were reportedly twenty-nine Elim churches in Northern Ireland by 1922.[9] This figure is higher than the author has been able to verify. Certainly, there was no Elim church in Monaghan until the mid-thirties, although, undoubtedly, there were small gatherings of people sympathetic to Elim that met in the area from time to time. There are no records of a church being opened in Carrickfergus during this period.

Ballymena and the area around it was certainly a place where Elim flourished. Out of the Ballymena church, assemblies were pioneered in Ahoghill, Ballymoney, Cullybackey, Eskylane, Portglenone, Randalstown, Rasharkin and Tullynahinnion. What is clear is that most of these churches were opened from Ballymena by the Elim Evangelistic Band. In time, Portadown also became a centre from which small churches were opened. Of the twenty-nine churches listed by Robinson on his map, ten of them were not in existence by 1930. It is doubtful if some were actual churches at all; mere small gatherings of people who met with a view of establishing an Elim church in the village where they lived.

Boulton reports that the first official Ordination Service was held on 17th July 1917, under the auspices of the Elim Alliance. He gives the following reason for this remarkable event which took place in a marquee that had been erected in Ormeau Park, Belfast, for the purpose of a summer mission. Boulton gives the following account:

The number of preachers joining the work was rapidly increasing, and the burden of leadership was beginning to be realised by the one who was himself directly responsible for the direction of the work. That some authoritative ordination of the leader was necessary was becoming apparent in view of the fact that he himself would soon be called upon to officiate at the ordination of those of his followers who were called into the regular ministry. Therefore, the deacons of Elim Christ Church Belfast, invited Rev. Moelfryn Morgan, an ordained minister of the Welsh Congregational Church to perform this epoch-making ceremony.[10]

Morgan was an evangelical Welsh Congregationalist minister (they were to become a rarity after 1920), who had been pastor of Sardis Welsh Congregational Chapel in Ystradgynlais, which was then in Breconshire. He then moved to Ammanford. There are no records of his connections with George, but it would appear that he had close connections with George's brother Stephen and accompanied the latter to Belfast to conduct an evangelistic mission for Elim. The most famous Welsh evangelical minister of the time was probably Rev Nantlais Williams, who was the pastor of Bethany Methodist Chapel in Ammanford from 1900 to 1910. In his report to the *Confidence* magazine (April-June Edition), Thomas Hackett speaks at some length of this great mission in Belfast although, intriguingly, he makes no mention of the Ordination Service of George Jeffreys.

Having given a synopsis of the Jeffreys brothers' introduction to Pentecost, Hackett outlines the establishment of George's ministry in Northern Ireland and the formation of the Elim Evangelistic Band. He then turns his attention to the Mission in Ormeau Park. He writes about the many who were saved and baptised in the Spirit. He also makes reference to 'many sick ones healed'. He writes: 'To be present in that tent was an inspiration; to speak in such an atmosphere was easy; bodily weakness seemed to count for nothing.'

Hackett was greatly impressed by the ministry of Morgan, and the following substantial quotation gives an insight into Welsh nonconformity at the time.

> Our brother Morgan in his own person was an illustration of this wondrous power of Pentecost. He told us he had never before addressed public meetings in English, and had come provided with a dozen or more addresses in most correct English, even to the proper accents, so that no mistake might be made in the foreign tongue! After eight minutes trial, the manuscript had to be flung to the ground, and he launched out on the power of the mighty Spirit, and found himself upborne and carried forward with astonishing ease and liberty, till it was manifest by the waning power of the Spirit and increasing difficulty of the English, it was time for his address to close. His was in truth every way a remarkable case. For twenty seven years in the ministry and not converted, yet souls were saved under his preaching, so great was the power of the Spirit and of the Word in the Welsh churches during the Revival. Brought to Christ in July 1915, he received the Baptism of the Spirit some five months later and now stands out as one the most gifted Bible teachers of our time.[11]

The intriguing fact about George's ordination in Belfast, conducted by Morgan and Stephen Jeffreys, was that this was George's *second* ordination. His first occurred in November 1912 when he was 'set apart for the regular work of the Christian ministry by the Independent Apostolic Church known as Emanuel Christ Church, in the town of Maesteg on the thirteenth day of November in the year of our Lord, nine hundred and twelve'.[12] This had been under the auspices of Hutchinson's work based in Bournemouth. By this time, Hutchinson had fallen into a measure of disrepute among British Pentecostals, so, no doubt, George took this opportunity of being ordained for a second time although, in reality, he chose not to acknowledge his first ordination.

Cartwright makes the intriguing comment that: 'Few, if any of George Jeffreys' decisive actions were carefully thought out. It would not be unfair to say that most of the decisive decisions that he made were reactions.'[13] This trait can be seen in the formation of the Elim Alliance Council. The Elim Evangelistic Band Minute Book reveals that a meeting was held at John Leech's home in Dublin on 7th July 1918, where it was decided:

> An alliance be formed for the purpose of a uniting under one name the following branches: viz: 'Elim Evangelistic Band, Elim Assemblies and Elim Missions'. The Alliance to be known as the Elim Pentecostal Alliance. That members of all churches who are born again and who stand for the full Gospel can become members of the same without leaving their own churches; the aim of the Alliance not to be that of encouraging members to leave their own denominations.

It is somewhat astonishing that for such a far-reaching decision, there were only three members present: Jeffreys, Leech and Hackett. It is also significant that the anti-proselytising clause be added to the formation of the Alliance. This, no doubt, was owing to the influence of Leech, a member of the Church of Ireland, and Hackett, an ordained minister of the Church of Ireland. The real reason for this step, according to Cartwright, was very much a pragmatic one. A Mrs Jane Rees of Glandyfi, near Aberystwyth had died on 5th November 1917 and had left a substantial proportion of her will to George Jeffreys. The will was strongly contested by members of the family until the value of the will was considerably reduced. The final settlement (of £900) was made in September 1925.[14] It was on Leech's advice that the decision was made for Jeffreys to register his group under the name the Elim Pentecostal Alliance, thus avoiding having to pay tax as he would have been obliged to do if the money had been left to him as a private individual.

A second Belfast Elim church

The Hunter Street building had become far too small and impractical for the ongoing work of the Elim Alliance. Also, the lease on the building had almost expired. Search was made throughout the city and, eventually, a disused cinema in Melbourne Street, off the bottom of the famous Shankill Road in West Belfast, was discovered. One old lady who had lived in the street for many years recounted the days when the cinema had been a church and rung out with the praises of God's people. The building seemed ideal, but the sum asked for it was way out of the ability of the young movement to pay. With a great deal of faith and very little money, the newly formed Elim Alliance paid a deposit on the building.

It was early in 1919 that the Melbourne Street building actually came into the possession of the Elim Alliance. It became more than a church; it became an important centre from which the Elim Evangelistic Band was able to outreach into the rest of Northern Ireland. It was also around this time that Elim bought a house in Belfast which was to become the administrative headquarters of the young Alliance. Number 3 University Place was to become Elim's official headquarters until 1923, when this was transferred to Clapham, London. The Melbourne Street Church was officially opened as Elim Tabernacle in July 1919 and it marked a decisive and distinctive high point in the progress of the movement.[15]

Notes

[1] The author has concerns here about this reference to the Holy Spirit. The personality of the Holy Spirit is clearly taught in Scripture. Pentecostal preachers and writers today would attest to the personality of the Holy Spirit and refer to him using personal pronouns. The Spirit is not an 'it'; the Spirit is a 'He'.

[2] Boulton, E C W, ibid, p35.

[3] Boulton, E C W, ibid, pp36,37. Report from the *Ballymena Observer*.

[4] Some of these were very small and considered to be 'works' rather than churches.

[5] Robinson, James, ibid, p167.

[6] Gee, Donald, *These Men I Knew* (Nottingham: Assemblies of God Publishing House, 1980), p49.

[7] The first two members, Robert E Darragh and Margaret Streight, were joined by William Henderson and Frederick Farlow.

[8] Elim Evangelistic Band Minute Book, GS office, Elim International Offices, Malvern.

[9] Robinson, James, ibid.

[10] Boulton, E C W, ibid, p40.

[11] *Confidence*, April-June 1918.

[12] Cartwright, Desmond, *Some Evangelists* (Being a partial fulfilment for an MA in Pentecostal and Charismatic History at Sheffield University), p10.

[13] Cartwright, Desmond, *Some Evangelists*, ibid, pp29,30.

[14] Cartwright, Desmond, *Some Evangelists*, ibid, p13.

[15] Neither the Hunter Street nor the Melbourne Street building is still standing. Hunter Street was situated in the Donegall Pass area of Belfast. The natural successor to this first Elim church would appear to be the Apsley Street Elim Church, which later became known as South Belfast Elim Church. The Melbourne Street building was sold and a building in Townsend Street was bought for the Alliance.

10
Early Prominent
Personalities

Following the meeting in Dublin, where it was agreed that the Elim work should be registered under the name 'Elim Pentecostal Alliance', a council of six came into being, which effectively provided the leadership of the movement – although there is no doubt that George Jeffreys was the 'leader of leaders'. The six were George Jeffreys, Stephen Jeffreys, John Leech, William Henderson, Robert Ernest Darragh and Thomas Hackett. The role of the Council of Six was an advisory one, with George being the one who made most of the day-to-day decisions. However, George was determined that small though Elim was, it should be wisely founded and conducted.

Stephen Jeffreys

Stephen Jeffreys (1876-1943) was the older brother of George. The two brothers were extremely close and were converted on the same day during the Welsh Revival. Stephen spent twenty-five years working underground as a collier. Physically, Stephen was very much the strongest of the two. George suffered from a facial paralysis which caused him to develop a speech impediment, but at a nine o'clock Sunday morning prayer meeting, he received a direct and instantaneous healing. In the early days, the brothers often ministered in tandem as in Cwmtwrch.

As the two of them progressed in ministry, it became apparent that George was the more fluent of the two brothers, but Stephen was the one who was most likely to preach after the fashion of the old Welsh divines, in the literary form unique to Welsh preachers and referred to as the '*hwyl*'. Someone commented: 'There is great power in George, but I feel it more intense in Stephen.'[1] Cartwright, in his book, includes the comments of a journalist who interviewed the brothers and his impression of Stephen is a very accurate summation of the man. He expressed himself as:

> favourably impressed with their natural frankness, joyousness, and eagerness to be used in the salvation of souls. Stephen Jeffreys … is a simple, humble, and yet intelligent, level-headed man of a superior South Wales miner type. He is more at home conversing in Welsh than in English, though he has a fair command of the latter language. He protested that he was not a preacher, but simply delivered what he was taught in the word of God and prompted by the Spirit to declare, together with his personal testimony the great work of grace wrought in his own soul in the Revival of 1904-05 and ever since.[2]

When he first started preaching, Stephen was much more at home in the open-air than in the pulpit. He had a deep, powerful voice that carried great distances. Stephen entered into full-time Christian ministry and became pastor of the Island Place Mission[3] in Llanelli. It was here that occurred a truly remarkable and miraculous phenomenon. Many Pentecostal writers have referred to this down through the years, but the most valid of them must be the account written by his son Edward, who was present at the service in July 1914 when a very remarkable vision appeared on the wall of the chapel during his father's sermon. This was reported in many of the newspapers during the time and was seen by too many people for it to be other than truthful.

A lady sitting next to my dear mother drew her attention to a Lamb's head which appeared on the wall at the back of my father. However, my mother failed to see the Lamb's head, but she was conscious of something very remarkable there; and presently the vision changed into the living face of Jesus Christ, represented as 'A Man of Sorrows.' During the address, which was preached in wonderful power, my father felt that there was something taking place which was having a remarkable effect on the audience. At the close of his sermon, my mother beckoned father to come down from the pulpit, and she pointed to the amazing scene on the wall.[4]

According to Edward, the vision remained on the wall for six hours. The lights were turned out, but still the vision could be seen. The news of this strange but powerful vision quickly spread through the town and hundreds of people crowded into the mission to see this incredible sight. Edward explained that his father was firmly convicted that the appearance of the face of Christ on the wall of the chapel in Llanelli was a warning concerning the Great War, which broke out in August of that same year – only one month after the vision appeared. Edward states that it made a profound impression on his father's life and ministry and greatly impacted his preaching ministry.

The closeness between George and Stephen was obvious from George's invitation to Stephen to conduct his (George's) Ordination Service in Belfast together with Rev Moelfryn Morgan. This is emphasised by George inviting his older brother to be a member of the governing council of the newly formed Elim Pentecostal Alliance. While George was ministering in Ireland, Stephen focused his attention on his homeland. In 1920 Stephen began conducting services in Dowlais, a district of Merthyr Tydfil, a large industrial conurbation, some twenty-eight miles north-west of Cardiff, known for its iron foundries and coal mines. Stephen encountered great success in the town, and eventually the Ivor Street Independent Chapel was rented and became the centre for some remarkable evangelistic and healing meetings. This was to become the first Elim church in Wales. Stephen was invited to become the pastor of the new church that was established as a result of his campaign, and it became the first Elim church outside Northern Ireland. George went to Dowlais and conducted a number of remarkable services there. For many years, the Ivor Street Chapel was festooned with crutches, spinal supports and other medical appliances that had been used by the many people who had been miraculously healed during the ministry of George and Stephen. Boulton quotes the descriptive words of one privileged participator:

> After a devastating war, and after the failure of the organised churches to meet the colossal need everywhere, there are breezes blowing from Calvary over the land of song, among the furnaces of Dowlais and in the sweet valley of Aberdare. The sick are being healed. Diamonds are being polished from the mines. The North of Ireland is being linked to South Wales.[5]

Having become an Elim minister and accepting the pastorate of the newly formed Dowlais Elim Church, Stephen was to work alongside his brother in the growing Elim Movement for the next four years. Stephen conducted a number of large and successful evangelistic campaigns, notably in Grimsby, Hull and Barking in the East End of London. Stephen left Elim in 1925 and evangelised with the Assemblies of God for many years. Stephen was not, by any means, an organiser and this caused frustrations between him and his younger brother. Donald Gee writes of him:

> Stephen Jeffreys was inimitable. That blending of humour and pathos, of unpolished eloquence with passionate evangelism was mighty in God. The repetition of many of his favourite messages never seemed to dull their intensity. He was Christ's gift of an evangelist. One of the most far-reaching effects of his

ministry was the way he seemed to trigger off so many others to follow suit, and the whole character of the British Pentecostal Movement changed.[6]

This characteristic of working as the lead, for someone else to follow is seen in his early campaigns for Elim. In Grimsby, Hull and Barking, Stephen was the prime evangelist and George followed on to finish the campaigns and establish a church. Stephen Jeffreys was a truly remarkable evangelist and a powerful preacher.

Ernest C W Boulton

Born in Hampstead, London, Ernest Charles William Boulton (1884-1959) was a prominent figure in the early British Pentecostal Movement. Philip Niblett writes of Boulton: 'He became a Christian on the 10th August 1901.'[7] According to Niblett, his early years as a Christian were influenced by E J Poole-Connor, who later established the Fellowship of Independent Evangelical Churches. He became a Salvation Army Officer and the census taken in 1911 reveals him as a married Salvation Army Officer living in Eastleigh, Hampshire. Shortly after this, he came into the Pentecostal experience and joined the Apostolic Faith Church (AFC), founded by William Hutchinson, and was appointed pastor of the branch of the work in Swansea. He clashed with Hutchinson, as he was strongly opposed to the AFC doctrine that prophecy was the infallible spoken Word of God. When the churches in Wales left their mother denomination in 1916 and formed the Apostolic Church of Wales under the leadership of Daniel Williams, Boulton sided with the Welsh churches in the division and was appointed minister of the church at Tyr-y-Dail; he was also named an assistant overseer of the new denomination.[8] The Apostolic Church emphasised the Ephesians 4:11 ministries, including that of apostle and prophet. Boulton was directed through the prophetic ministry to go to Leith, Scotland.

'However, things did not work out and he returned to Wales where he was told that he had failed to obey the Prophet.'[9] He left the Apostolic Church at this point.

Through the influence of Smith Wigglesworth, a leading figure in the young Pentecostal Movement, he was appointed pastor of a small work in Hull. He became a renowned speaker at Pentecostal conventions. He was one of the speakers at the Bradford Convention in 1918. Smith Wigglesworth writes: 'Mr Boulton from Hull, had a broken spirit. We felt God had brought him to be blessed, and thus, he was a blessing to others.'[10]

He came to the attention of George Jeffreys and was one of the speakers at the mid-summer convention held in the newly opened Elim Tabernacle in Melbourne Street, Belfast. He preached alongside George Jeffreys, John Leech and James Salter, co-founder of the Congo Evangelistic Movement. This convention was to have far-reaching consequences for Boulton. Canty writes:

> E C W Boulton by nature was cautious, not given to excited enthusiasm but prone, perhaps, by past disillusionment, to use a sharply critical judgement. It is a tribute to the tiny Elim work in 1919 that he was impressed by its leadership and solidity. He was no eager-eyed, believe-anything youth. Later, he took part prominently in Elim's fortunes, holding several of its most important offices, including that of President twice.[11]

Canty recalls that Boulton had a beautiful prophetic flow and on one occasion prophesied for forty-five minutes, overcome by the anointing of the Holy Spirit. Gee also refers to this remarkable prophetic ministry of Boulton: 'Mr Boulton himself had one of the most delightful prophetic utterance I have ever heard; it literally flowed. Charming thoughts and high devotion inspired his lips; it was religious eloquence.'[12]

Boulton joined up with Elim following Stephen and George Jeffreys' campaign in Hull. It is obvious that George held Boulton in very high esteem as just a year later, Jeffreys appointed him as one of the overseers of Elim. He was to become a prominent leader within the movement, serving as editor of the *Elim Evangel*, dean of the Bible college and field superintendent. To all the Elim family he became affectionately known as 'Pa'. His elder daughter, Ruth, became the wife of the grandson of Smith Wigglesworth, Leslie, a missionary and later the secretary of the Elim Missionary Society.

It is as a writer that Boulton is particularly noted within the Elim Movement. He contributed greatly to Elim's weekly periodical the *Elim Evangel* and wrote a number of books. He was editor of the *Evangel* for a number of years. Even for his time, his prose was somewhat dated, nevertheless it was considered greatly beneficial and spiritually uplifting to vast numbers of Elim people. His best known book is probably *The Focused Life*.[13] It is a series of devotional meditations that stem from his personal prayers. He was known throughout Elim for his devotional prayer life. His writings reflect something of his personal struggles in his early ministry and the impression one can arrive at through examining historical data concerning him is that he could, at times, be a little melancholic. Gee says: 'Ernest Boulton always gave me the impression of being a tender plant.'[14]

Boulton was a great hymn writer. Nine of his hymns were published in the original *Redemption Hymnal*. They are a mixture of devotional and inspiring Pentecostal hymns. In terms of the Pentecostal revival, his most notable hymn is 'Tarry for the Spirit', sung to the Welsh tune 'Rachie'. The words of this hymn embody the intense desire of the early Pentecostals to seek the blessing and baptism of the Holy Spirit:

Tarry for the Spirit, He shall come in showers.
Energising wholly all your ransomed powers;
Signs shall follow service in the Holy Ghost,

Then the Church of Jesus prove a mighty host

When the Spirit cometh, loosened lips shall tell
Of the wondrous blessing which upon them fell:
Life of Jesus springing, like a well within,
Hearts with loud hosannas constantly shall ring

On then Church of Jesus, claim your Pentecost:
God shall now baptise thee in the Holy Ghost.[15]

One of Boulton's greatest gifts to the Elim Pentecostal Church was his biography of George Jeffreys, *A Ministry of the Miraculous* – published in 1928. It is a remarkable, if slightly sycophantic, account of Jeffreys' ministry up to that time. Boulton was a strong and very loyal admirer of Jeffreys, even to the point that he voted against a resolution, overwhelmingly carried, that was critical of Jeffreys.[16] He remained as the pastor of the Hull Elim Church until 1928, a period of eleven years, six of those as a minister within Elim.

Joseph Smith

Joseph Smith was an Elim minister for almost seventy years, and was renowned throughout Elim for his evangelistic zeal and prophetic ministry. The writer is of the opinion that he was as close as Elim ever came to having a national prophet. He was a tall, striking-looking man with sharp features and bushy eyebrows which he was able to raise when making a pertinent point that he wanted to emphasise. I encountered him while a student at the Elim Bible College, Capel, 1967-69, when he was a guest lecturer.

The exact date of Joseph Smith's entrance into the Elim Evangelistic Band is not clear, neither is the occasion of his receiving the baptism in the Holy Spirit. According to Canty, Joseph was present at his parents' farm in 1913 when a Pastor Anderson spoke to a gathering of country folk who were sympathetic to Pentecostalism. Canty goes on to say that it was at that meeting that Joseph Smith heard speaking in tongues for the first time. He adds: 'Joseph was to live for a few years in the USA and then return and join the first Elim Evangelistic Band.'[17] Robinson, however, is of the opinion that Smith received his baptism in the Spirit in 1915, when he was in Philadelphia, and returned to Ireland where he joined the Elim Evangelistic Band in 1920.[18] Smith, in an article in the *Elim Evangel*, wrote of his family's initial connections with George Jeffreys:

> Before the foundation of the Elim work was laid in Ireland, Mr. George Jeffreys visited the home of my parents in Co. Tyrone for a time of rest and recuperation. Mr Jeffreys was then invited by my cousins, George and William Gillespie, to come and live in their home at 14 Pine Street, Belfast, which he did in company with Mr. R E Darragh.[19]

It is interesting to note that in the above quotation, Smith referred to the founder of Elim as '*Mr* George Jeffreys' (my italics) and not as 'Pastor' or 'Principal' George Jeffreys. Smith was to become a firm critic of George Jeffreys after the schism with Elim. Smith was a strong believer in central government and had no time for Jeffreys' change of heart over church government. 'Before I came to Elim I was a member of a Pentecostal church where doctrinal matters were judged by the local assembly and I know how the church was rent asunder because of that very thing ... For God's sake let us keep these things out of our local churches ... Conference is the place to settle disputes – a church is a place to worship God.'[20] Albert Edsor's retort is worth quoting fully:

> J. Smith's last two sentences, as quoted, come strangely from one who, with others from Elim Headquarters, in company with a detective, interrupted a Communion Service in a local church (Portsmouth) on a Sunday in

war time that same year (1941) and forced its minister and congregation to leave the building – which they did! – under legal threats. If, as he has written, 'a church is a place to worship God', it is surely a piece of consummate hypocrisy to cause its public celebration of Holy Communion to cease by these shocking methods. Those responsible for such actions in the Visible Church will surely be accountable to God at the last, unless they make reparation before departing from this earthly scene.[21]

Edsor was referring to one of the least savoury aspects of Elim's actions following the sad schism between Jeffreys and the Movement he had founded. This will be referred to in the second volume.

Joseph Smith was a long-standing member of the Executive Council. He was a member of the first Executive Council of Elim that was appointed following the acceptance by the Conference of the Deed Poll of 1934. He remained a member of the council until his retirement. He served as dean of the Bible college from 1946 to 1952 and was also Elim's president. His prayer life was notable as was his evangelistic zeal. He always carried some gospel tracts in his pocket which he would give away to anyone who was willing to receive them. Wynne Lewis, one of Elim's former general superintendents, referred to Smith's great faith. Smith was the dean of the Elim Bible College when Lewis was a student there in 1950-51. Smith was convinced that God had removed George Jeffreys from his position of leadership of the Elim Movement and felt that this should be articulated to the people.

Notwithstanding its sometimes bitter disagreements, Elim has always been blessed with courageous and godly leadership.

Notes

[1] Source unknown.

[2] Cartwright, Desmond, *The Great Evangelists*, ibid, p33.

[3] Jeffreys, Edward, ibid, p11.

[4] Jeffreys, Edward, ibid, p11.

[5] Boulton, E C W, ibid, pp80-81.

[6] Gee, Donald, *These Men I Knew*, p52.

[7] Niblett, Philip, *Ernest Charles William Boulton* (unpublished manuscript).

[8] Niblett, Philip, ibid.

[9] Niblett, Philip, ibid.

[10] *Confidence*, April-June 1918, p22.

[11] Canty, George, ibid, p58.

[12] Gee, Donald, *These Men I Knew*, p23.

[13] Boulton, E C W, *The Focused Life* (Clapham Park, London: Elim Publishing Company Limited, 1932).

[14] Gee, Donald, *These Men I Knew*, p23.

[15] Boulton, E C W (1884-1959), *Redemption Hymnal* (London: Elim Publishing Company, Limited, 1951), hymn number 235.

[16] Resolution passed at the 1940 Elim Conference.

[17] Canty, George, ibid, p47.

[18] Robinson, James, ibid, p183.

[19] *Elim Evangel*, 17th February 1962, p105.

[20] *Elim Evangel*, 1941, pp267-8.

[21] Edsor, Albert, *Set Your House in Order: God's Call to George Jeffreys as the Founder of the Elim Pentecostal Movement* (Chichester: New Wine Press, 1989), pp112-113.

11
1919: Double Blessing

The year 1919 was significant for Elim on two accounts. Firstly, it saw the publication of what was to be Elim's main periodical for the next sixty-five years – the *Elim Evangel*. Secondly, this year saw E J Phillips join Elim and become a member of the Elim Evangelistic Band. This appointment was to have a huge impact upon the development and history of the Elim Pentecostal Church.

The *Elim Evangel*

The first edition of the *Elim Evangel* was published in December 1919 and it was a small, twenty-page periodical with a green cover and sold at three pence (old money), the equivalent of less than one and a half new pence. This was quite expensive for that time. The average labourer's wage was £1:6d per week. The average rent at the time was one shilling and sixpence. So, the cost of the *Evangel* would have been the equivalent of about 13.6 per cent of the average weekly rent. The *Evangel* was printed by F B Phillips in Tamworth, Staffordshire.

On the front cover it had the heading '*The Elim Evangel – A Quarterly Record of Spiritual Life and Work*' inserted in a scroll-shaped block. Underneath, it had the date, volume and number of the publication, with a contents block underneath that. Also, included in that block was the design of a palm tree and well and the scripture from Exodus 15:27: 'And they came to Elim, where there were twelve wells of water, and threescore and ten palm trees' (KJV). At the bottom of the page was printed: 'Published by the Elim Pentecostal Alliance, 3 University Place, Belfast, Ireland'.

The publication of the *Evangel* was a major development within the young Elim Movement. From its humble beginnings, it grew into a major weekly Christian publication with a circulation in excess of 20,000 in the mid-1930s. The content contained not only vital information on the development of the movement, tracing its growth, but also gave direction and spiritual guidance to its readers.

The first issue gave a comprehensive list of the leadership of Elim at the time. It listed George Jeffreys as the founder and gave the names of the members of the Elim Pentecostal Alliance Council. They were: President – John Leech, MA, KC, Dublin. Secretary – William Henderson, Monaghan. Treasurer – R E Darragh, Bangor, Pastor George Jeffreys, Belfast, Pastor Stephen Jeffreys, Llanelli and Rev Thomas Hackett, MA, Bray (Advisory). The list of the current Evangelistic Band Workers was included as follows: Messrs George Jeffreys, R E Darragh, William Henderson, Frederick Farlow, R Mercer, William Campbell, Robert Tweed, Stephen Jeffreys, E W Hare, John Carter, Ernest J. Phillips, Mr and Mrs Fletcher, Mr and Mrs Enery, Miss Adams, and Miss Straight.

The first editor was E W Hare, a Cambridge university graduate. Originally from Cheltenham, Hare had been president of the Cambridge university Christian Union in his undergraduate days.[1] He was also the pastor of the Elim Church in Bangor until he left Elim towards the end of 1922. He was influenced by A E Saxby, who was a former Baptist minister who developed a prominent ministry among the early Pentecostals. He came to embrace the doctrine of 'Ultimate Reconciliation', otherwise known as Universalism. Although he did not voice his support of this doctrine until after he had left Elim, it is very likely that he espoused this doctrine all the time that he was a member of the Elim Evangelistic Band. It is interesting that in the very first edition of the *Evangel*, Hare included Bible Study Notes on 1 Corinthians 15 by Saxby. It was the first of a series that continued in the next few editions of *Evangel.*

This doctrine of Universalism was the first serious doctrinal issue to be raised within the young movement. Tweed alludes to this potentially damaging issue being raised at the Bangor Summer Camp in 1922.[2] Earlier that year, the Fundamentals had been set out in the first Elim Constitution.[3] The formations of this constitution and the subsequent ones in 1922, 1925, 1927 and 1929 were drawn up by George Jeffreys himself and were not arrived at by a consensus of the members of the Elim Evangelistic Band at the time. It is more than likely, however, that he sought the advice of Leech and possibly Hackett. In the second part of article 10 in the 1922 Fundamentals, Jeffreys had included the words: 'We believe in the eternal conscious punishment of all Christ rejectors.' Tweed observed that there was 'considerable discussion on some of the Fundamentals, some having been influenced by the teachings of A. E. Saxby on the doctrine "the ultimate reconciliation of all things".'

Saxby was highly thought of among early Pentecostals and became Donald Gee's pastor. In 1915 Saxby left the Baptist church of which he was the pastor and started a new church in Harringay, known as Derby Hall. Donald Gee and his wife became members of this independent Pentecostal assembly. It was a source of considerable anguish to Gee that Saxby became a proponent of what he and Jeffreys, representing the wider Pentecostal Movement, considered to be erroneous doctrine. The idea that everyone would be eventually saved by God was repugnant to the rank and file of Pentecostal leaders. Gee wrote an open letter that was published in the *Elim Evangel* in 1924 with the approval and support of Jeffreys.[4]

In his editorial in the first *Evangel,* he expresses the main purpose of the publications to encourage people to pray for the work in Ireland:

> We are deeply thankful to God for stirring many of His
> people to share in the burden of prayer for His work here
> in the north of Ireland, but we feel that it can only be for
> His glory that we should give regular, short reports of
> the work at the different centres. We do this with the
> definite aim of spreading the glorious fulness of His
> perfect salvation and at the same time securing the daily,
> earnest, prevailing prayers of many who are present
> more or less in the dark as to His gracious workings in
> this island.

He then goes on to provide a report of 'News from the Centres'.
These are listed as being in Belfast (two churches), Ballymena,
Moneyslane, Portadown, Bangor and Lisburn with evangelistic
outreaches in Eskylane, Cullybacky and Milford.

E J Phillips[5]

Ernest John Phillips was born in Hove, Sussex on 30th
December 1893. He was a descendant of an influential Jewish
family. He was the second son of John and Emily Phillips. He
had two brothers, Hubert C Phillips and Frederick B Phillips.[6]
All three brothers served as ministers in Elim, as did their sister
Dollie, who was for many years the pastor of the Letchworth
Elim Church. Their mother had experienced salvation at the age
of thirteen but had drifted away and married John. The eldest
son, Hubert, was converted at a children's special service
mission when he was fourteen years old. This was at an Easter
event in 1908.[7] It was about that time that their mother came
back to the Lord and their father was converted through the
ministry of the Pentecostal League, founded by Reader Harris.[8]
It is thought that E J[9] was converted in 1909 at the age of
fifteen.[10] It is significant that E J spoke more about his being
baptised in the Holy Spirit than he did about his conversion
experience. This is highly significant because in the view of most
Elim ministers who knew him, he was thought to be somewhat

aloof and unemotional. It is clear however, that E J was very much a Pentecostal in his theology and practice.

> His baptism in the Holy Spirit was in the nature of a revolution in his spiritual experience. This baptism, with the evidence of speaking in tongues, was the story of a beginning that was to affect the lives of ministers and lay brethren in many parts of the world. He says: 'It seemed to make in my life a more radical change than did conversion. It was in the nature of a revolution, everything seemed to be new.'[11]

In his tribute to E J, Greenway states that he (E J) was 'unwavering in his adherence to the truths of Pentecost. He spoke out of his own experiences'. Greenway refers to an incident that E J testified to concerning divine healing, when he was healed of a throat infection. This occurred during the time that he was seeking God's will as to whether he should join the Elim Evangelistic Band in 1919. He took his healing of a throat infection as a sign from God that he was to join the band.[12] It is evident that E J was a great believer in divine healing.

John Phillips was involved in the very early stages of the Pentecostal movement in the U.K. Rev T B Barratt, the Norwegian Methodist minister who was baptised in the Spirit while visiting New York in 1907[13] and became a very influential figure in the very early stages of British Pentecostalism,[14] visited John Phillips in Bedford and stayed in his home during a ten-day mission in July 1909.[15] Phillips was the pastor of the Costin Street Pentecostal Church in Bedford for a short period and was a beneficiary of Polhill's largesse.[16] It was in his father's home that E J received the baptism of the Holy Spirit. It is worth noting that Gee refers to E J's. seeking of the baptism of the Holy Spirit with the evidence of speaking with tongues.[17] This is interesting because of the difference between the Elim Pentecostal Church and the Assemblies of God on the matter of tongues being the initial evidence of the baptism in the Spirit. The Assemblies of God in the UK has in their Statement of

Faith stated that speaking in other tongues is the initial evidence of the baptism of the Holy Spirit. In the very first statement of Fundamental Rules published by the Elim Evangelistic Band, Statement 5 reads: 'We believe that the present latter day outpouring of the Holy Ghost which is the promise of God to all believers is accompanied by speaking in other tongues as the Spirit gives utterance.' This was changed in the 1927 Constitution where the reference to speaking in other tongues is omitted.

John Phillips died on 28th December 1931 in Letchworth. W G Hathaway, the then editor of the *Elim Evangel*, wrote a brief obituary of John under the title: 'The Passing of a Veteran in the Lord'. In the article, reference is made to 'one who was well known among those who stood for four-square Gospel truth in the early days'. The article mentions the ministry of his three sons, Hubert C, who was a missionary in Africa, E J, the secretary-general of Elim and Frederick B, the managing director of the Elim Publishing Company. Mention is also made of the daughter, Dollie Phillips, who was then in charge of the Elim church at Letchworth.[18]

There is strong speculation that E J was a conscientious objector during the First World War. His niece Mary Stormont is certainly of that opinion.[19] Michael Greenway, the son of H W who succeeded E J as secretary-general, was most definitely convinced that E J was a conscientious objector.[20] In this respect his views would have been similar to other Pentecostal pioneers, such as the Carter brothers and Donald Gee. Howard Carter was imprisoned first in Wormwood Scrubs followed by nine months in Dartmoor, one of the bleakest and grimmest prisons in England.[21]

There is some anecdotal evidence of E J's pacifist leanings in a letter sent to him by Lemuel Morris on the occasion of the latter's suspension from the Elim Movement when he affiliated with the Bible Pattern Church in 1941. He ends the letter by mentioning the fact that the Elim Tabernacle in Southampton had been destroyed by enemy action. 'From this church at

Southampton over 40 of our boys are fighting our battles on land, sea, and in the air. One is more than proud of them, more so, when one remembers the just cause for which they are fighting. We have a brother who is a "conchie" and, incidentally, his sympathy is with the Alliance.[22] Enough said – so much for the lead to our lovely boys from Elim's Headquarters.'[23] His views on war would have been quite different from the imperialistic and nationalistic views of Jeffreys and his supporters for the British Israel cause. They saw the Second World War as a defence of the British Empire.

E J had an abhorrence of war. The Christian's attitude to war was discussed at length at the 1935 Elim Conference. Pastor Moore introduced the subject and contended that a Christian should not take part in war. Mr John Leech, KC gave an address in which he supported the view that it was the duty of a Christian to fight for his country. The following proposal was put to the Conference and carried by 100 votes to two, with one abstention:

> That while this General Conference of the Elim Foursquare Gospel Alliance affirms its loyalty to His Majesty the King and to the government of our land, it believes that the Church of Jesus Christ which is called out from the world to preach the Gospel of salvation and peace to all men is based on spiritual principles which are incompatible with the Christian's participation in war. It considers, however, that this is a matter which every believer should settle for himself in the light of the Word of God.[24]

While allowing freedom of conscience, it is clear that the Conference expressed a definite anti-war tendency. There was an attempt to further debate the issue at the 1939 Conference when the matter was raised by James McWhirter,[25] who sought to reopen the discussion on the 1935 resolution concerning the Christian's participation in war. The Conference expressed its unwillingness to discuss the matter any further. A proposal by

W Kelly that it be reconsidered in view of certain points that were not adequately discussed in 1935 was also defeated.[26]

Armagh and editor of the *Elim Evangel*

E J joined the Elim Evangelistic Band in December 1919 and was appointed the pastor of the Elim Church in Armagh. Because of his connection with Armagh, the city which is the home of the Roman Catholic archbishops of Ireland, who are frequently appointed cardinals, E J was humorously referred to as the 'cardinal' by members of the Evangelistic Band. This was the appellation that Jeffreys used in his correspondence with him. Phillips, in turn, usually commenced his letters to Jeffreys with 'Dear Prince'.[27]

There is very little information on E J's ministry in Armagh. He commented positively about his time as the pastor there, although there is a comment in one of the early *Evangels* about the place being 'hard'. The work in Armagh was commenced in Milford, one of the districts. A report in the *Elim Evangel* states that: 'Mr. Ernest Phillips is the pastor of this assembly and he is deeply thankful to report continued blessing in conversions and baptisms in the Spirit.'[28] The next report refers to rising opposition with the news that the assembly will have to vacate their premises. In spite of this, however, there is great encouragement in the fact of people being converted to Christ.[29]

A room in Armagh was found to hold church meetings and then, in the autumn of that year, a disused church building in a prominent street in Armagh was rented. George Jeffreys spoke at the opening of the church and Mr Robert Smith from South Wales continued the meetings for the next fortnight. Woodroffe Hare, the pastor at Bangor and the first editor of the *Elim Evangel* continued the meetings for another week or so.[30] From the accounts printed in the early editions of the *Evangel*, it is quite clear that the work in Armagh was particularly difficult, with much opposition. It is clear that E J was sensitive to this opposition and was particularly disappointed by the comments of those who were opposed to the work, attributing natural disasters to the judgement of God.[31] The difficulties of the work in Armagh are again referred to in an *Evangel* report, when a mission conducted by R E Darragh and Miss Adams is referred to.[32] It is not certain that E J was the pastor in Armagh at this time. He was appointed joint editor of the *Evangel* alongside E W Hare in 1922 and it is thought that he spent most of his time then in Belfast.[33] From the *Evangel* reports, there is evidence to suggest that E J had a strong evangelistic spirit and was particularly anxious for people to be baptised in the Holy Spirit.

E J became sole editor of the *Evangel* in August 1922 and he set the tone for the truths that would be emphasised in the magazine: the Foursquare Gospel truths.[34] There is clear evidence from his editorials and his personal testimony that E J was a strong advocate of Pentecostal distinctives. It would appear that he looked upon tongues as being the initial evidence of the baptism in the Holy Spirit. Writing about the importance of magnifying the Lord, he lists a number of ways in which the believer can do so. 'The fourth way in which the Lord is magnified, is, we fear, an unpopular way. At Caesarea, when the Holy Ghost fell on the household of Cornelius, the inspired writer says, "they heard them speak with tongues, and magnify God."[35] And still today, Christ is magnified by speaking with other tongues'.[36] He clearly links speaking with other tongues with the baptism of the Holy Spirit. He states that the baptism in the Holy Spirit brings power with God in prevailing prayer. 'It is only those who are filled with the Holy Ghost through whom He can pray with groaning that cannot be uttered, and with words, which though unintelligible to oneself are understood by God.'[37]

There are so many references to the baptism of the Spirit, the gifts of the Holy Spirit, the need for a constant filling of the Holy Spirit that it seems as though this was not only a major plank in his theology, but that it dominated his theology. In one of his editorials he stated: 'Jesus preached the word, healed the sick, cast out demons and did many signs and wonders, not by his power as Son of God, but by the power of the Holy Ghost,'[38] Although he goes on to correctly state that Jesus' healing and miraculous ministry did not commence until He had been baptised and the Holy Spirit descended on Him,[39] the fact remains that Jesus *is* God and it is a controversial statement to make that He performed miracles not by His power as Son of God but by the power of the Spirit. Jeffreys in his teaching concerning the Holy Spirit differentiated between the Holy Spirit and the Spirit of Jesus.[40] It is possible that E J was influenced by this theory in the early years of his ministry.

The *Elim Evangel*, which became the periodical of the Elim Movement, was first published in December 1919 with E W Hare as the editor. E Woodroffe Hare joined the Elim Evangelistic Band on December 31st 1919. This was the same day as John Carter, who was later to become general secretary of the Assemblies of God. Robert Tweed also joined on the same day, together with five others. Mr Hare was the first editor of the *Elim Evangel* from December 1919.[41] It was, at first, a quarterly magazine that provided an official channel through which teaching could be given and reports of churches and campaigns circulated.[42] The *Elim Evangel* was to eventually develop a weekly circulation in excess of 20,000. When E J became joint editor with Hare in December 1921, his first action was to reduce the price of the *Evangel* by half.[43] The next significant action that Phillips undertook was to make the *Evangel* a monthly publication. He was to have a close involvement with the *Evangel* for the rest of his ministry. He was sole editor from August 1922 until February 1923 and once more became a joint editor with E C W Boulton in March of that year.

Notes

1 Robinson, James, ibid, p172.

2 Tweed, Robert, *Memoir* (Malvern: Elim Archives).

3 The writer is of the opinion that this was the first official Elim constitution, being of the opinion that the 1915 document was written not with a denomination in mind but as rules and regulations that governed the local Elim Christ Church in Hunter Street. Dr Simo Frestadius, a senior lecturer at Regents Theological College and a fellow historian, takes a different line, claiming that the 1915 document was the first Elim Constitution.

4 Massey, Richard, *Another Springtime: Donald Gee, Pentecostal Pioneer, A Biography* (Guildford: Highland Books, 1992), pp70-71.

5 This section through to the end of the chapter is taken from the author's MA dissertation.

6 Phillips, H C was born 13th February 1891 and died 12th December 1973. F B Phillips was born 23rd January 1896 and died July 2nd 1989.

7 Phillips, Hubert, *Elim Evangel*, 8th July 1961.

8 Phillips, Hubert, ibid.

9 This is the nomenclature that Phillips was known as throughout the Movement and this is how he will often be addressed throughout the rest of this book.

10 Information received from Desmond Cartwright, the official historian of Elim, in a telephone conversation on 16th March 2010.

11 Carter, J, Obituary, E. J. Phillips, The Architect of Elim, *Redemption Tidings*, 11th October 1973.

12 Greenway, H W, ibid.

13 While in New York he heard of the outpouring of the Spirit in Azusa Street, Los Angeles, which is considered as the birthplace of modern Pentecostalism.

14 He was a frequent visitor to All Saints C of E Monkwearmouth, Sunderland, speaking at two of the famous Sunderland Conventions from 1908 to 1914.

15 Usher, John M, *Prepared for Pentecost – the significance of Cecil H Polhill – 1860-1927* (MA dissertation, Regents Theological College/Bangor University, 2010), p36.

16 He received two amounts of money from Polhill, the first amounting to £88:17:8 and the second amount of £82:13:9, paid jointly to him and his co-worker James Tetchner. Usher, ibid, p35.

17 Gee, Donald, *The Pentecostal Movement*, p71.

18 *Elim Evangel*, 15th January 1932, p40.

[19] In an interview with Mary Stormont in November 2010, she referred to her uncle's strong pacifist leanings and even went so far as to suggest that he might have been imprisoned sometime between 1916 and 1917.

[20] Interview with Michael and Peggy Greeenway, in their home on 9th March 2011. Michael is Greenway's only son.

[21] Kay, William E, *Inside Story: A History of British Assemblies of God* (Mattersley: Mattersley Hall Publishing 1990), p56.

[22] This reference is to the Elim Foursquare Gospel Alliance – the official name of the Elim Pentecostal Church.

[23] Letter from Lemuel Morris to E J Phillips, 9th May 1941.

[24] Minutes of Conference, Thursday 24th October 1935, p9.

[25] McWhirter was a trusted ally of Jeffreys and left Elim to join Bible Pattern with Jeffreys.

[26] Minutes of General Conference of the Elim Foursquare Gospel Alliance 23rd November 1939.

[27] This was the manner in which they addressed each other even as late as October 1939, letter to Jeffreys from Phillips 23rd October 1939 and the reply 26th October 1939.

[28] *Elim Evangel*, March 1920, Vol 1, No 4, p23.

[29] Ibid, June 1920, Vol 1, No 3, p39.

[30] *Elim Evangel*, December 1920, Vol 2, No 1, pp4-5.

[31] Ibid. The following comment appears under Report from the Churches concerning Armagh: 'The Disappointment of Pastor Phillips and the assembly can well be imagined, and it was all the harder to hear when they had to listen to the comments of opponents to the effect that the storm was a judgment from God sent to drive them out of the village.'

[32] *Elim Evangel*, January 1922, Vol 3, No 1, p 3, 'Armagh, in which Mr. Darragh and Miss Adams have been working during the last month or so, has been proving itself once again to be a hard place.'

[33] Cartwright, Desmond, in conversation with the author 28th March 2011.

[34] These truths are centred on the Person and work of Christ: 'Jesus the Saviour, Jesus the Healer, Jesus the Baptiser in the Holy Spirit and Jesus the Coming King.'

[35] Acts 10:46, KJV.

[36] *Elim Evangel*, April 1923, Editorial.

[37] *Elim Evangel*, June 1924, Editorial.

[38] *Elim Evangel*, June 1924, Editorial.

[39] Matthew 3:16-17; Acts 10:38.

[40] Jeffreys, G, *Pentecostal Rays* (London: Elim Publishing Company, 1933). He devotes a chapter to the subject of 'The Spirit of Christ' claiming that there is a difference between the Spirit of Christ and the Holy Spirit. 'It is impossible to have an intelligent understanding of the New Testament Scriptures without recognising such a difference', p39.

[41] Cartwright, Desmond, email, 11th April 2011.

42 Boulton, E C W, ibid, p60.

43 *Elim Evangel*, December 1921, Editorial. He is introduced here as 'Secretary'. In the following edition, January 1922, he is designated joint editor with Hare.

12
Beyond Ireland

By 1920, the Elim work was firmly established in the North of Ireland. In his map of the distribution of Elim assemblies, Robinson has twenty-nine Elim assemblies in existence by 1922, as we saw earlier.[1] From historical records, it is clear that some of these assemblies were not established as churches. An examination of the database of Elim churches at the Elim International Offices in Malvern reveals that there were twenty-two recognised and established Elim churches in the North of Ireland by 1922. A number of these have since closed or replaced in nearby locations. However, Elim was clearly well established in the North of Ireland by this time and George Jeffreys was determined to expand the work in other parts of the UK.

The Welsh connection

While George had firmly established himself in Ireland, his brother Stephen had remained in his homeland and established connections with a number of independent Pentecostal fellowships in South Wales. The first edition of the *Elim Evangel* devoted four of its twenty pages to reports of revival meetings in South Wales, under the title 'Tidings from the Land of Song'.[2] The reports detail press coverage of Stephen Jeffreys' meetings in Aberaman. This was a former pit village two miles south of Aberdare.

Stephen's campaign in Aberaman was styled throughout all the reports as being a revival. This description of the meetings held here is an important factor in the ministry of both Stephen and George Jeffreys. They saw themselves as revivalists, burning coals that were ignited in the Welsh Revival 1904-05. The concept of a spiritual awakening similar to the Welsh Revival became ingrained in the ministry of the two brothers. At George Jeffreys' first campaign in Ireland (Monaghan, 1915) there were clear references to 'revival'. Jeffreys saw himself primarily as a revivalist. In his report to *Confidence*, Jeffreys refers to people having a great hunger for revival.[3] The press reports republished in the *Elim Evangel* all refer to the meetings as a 'revival'.

A new religious revival, which reproduces many of the features of Evan Roberts' revival of several years ago, has broken out at the colliery village of Aberaman, a place of some five thousand inhabitants, near Aberdare, Glamorgan. Indeed, so remarkable are the scenes of intense religious fervour, coupled with supernatural visions on the part of converts and cases of what are claimed to be divine healing of physical diseases among them, that one aged religious leader declares that he has seen three revivals but that this is the greatest of them all. For three weeks, Pastor Stephen Jeffreys, a missionary from Llanelli, has been entreating the crowds of people who have flocked nightly to the Primitive Methodist Church at Aberaman to turn from the wickedness of their ways and prepare for the Second Advent of Christ into the world, which he declares is near. His impassioned appeals have had an astonishing effect, the converts including old and young and persons professing every creed.[4]

It was through Stephen that the Elim work was established in Wales. One observer at the Aberaman meetings proclaimed: 'Another Stephen has arisen, "full of faith and of the Holy

Ghost".[5] After Aberaman, Jeffreys held campaigns in Merthyr, Cwmbach and Kenfig Hill (all in Glamorgan). The Cwmbach Baptist minister called upon the churches to back the revivalist that Wales might see a new revival with healings and baptisms in the Spirit. Dowlais became a centre of Stephen's Welsh labours, with hundreds calling upon God for salvation.[6]

There appears to be a discrepancy between Boulton and Canty in the dateline of the Dowlais church. Boulton clearly states that the Ivor Street building, where Stephen conducted his campaign in 1920, was purchased immediately after the campaign and George was invited to conduct further revival meetings in the chapel, which was subsequently bought by Elim, with Stephen being appointed as the first pastor of the Dowlais Elim Church, moving from Llanelli, where he had pastored for the previous seven years.[7] Canty, on the other hand, records the following:

> The Dowlais converts managed to work together to buy the Ivor Street Independent Chapel. In the Spring of 1922, George Jeffreys led a convention in this building and accepted the assembly into Elim, the property becoming an Alliance building. Dowlais became the first Elim in Wales and the first Elim property. On April 18th George Jeffreys performed a special task of wise practicality, ordaining church officers and forming 'an assembly on a Scriptural basis', with his brother Stephen as the pastor.[8]

This presents a historical conundrum. Canty gives specific dates, whereas Boulton does not. It is clear, however, that by 1922, Stephen was holding campaigns for Elim in Hull, Grimsby and London. He moved to England in that year. The writer therefore concludes that Dowlais was the first Elim church opened outside of Ireland and this occurred in 1920.

Through the combined ministry of Stephen and George Jeffreys, a platform for Elim was established in the Principality that was built upon by successive evangelistic campaigns. South-east Wales, in particular, was to become a stronghold for Elim, where a number of churches were established through the evangelistic ministry of Percy S Brewster. Another point to note during George Jeffreys' visit to Dowlais in 1920 was that Cyril Taylor, BA was ordained and commissioned as a missionary to the Congo mission field. In 1921, the Jerusalem Chapel, Merthyr, was acquired as an Elim church. Also, the Pentecostal church in Llanelli that had been led by Stephen Jeffreys became an Elim church around this time. Elim had three centres in South Wales before George set his sights on establishing Elim in England.

Vazon – Guernsey

There were a number of Independent Pentecostal churches that were established in the second decade of the twentieth century. One such fellowship was in Vazon, Guernsey. The Cobo Mission was a Brethren assembly that had commenced in 1905, its beginnings helped by Mr B Angel, who was later to be involved with Pentecostal evangelism. The Cobo Mission gave birth to the Vale Mission by some of its seceding members, and in 1908 the Vale Mission had a Welsh visitor, Robert Davies, who preached on the baptism in the Spirit. He was invited by the Cobo Mission the following year. He returned again in 1911, where he continued to minister strongly along Pentecostal lines. He encountered considerable opposition owing to his teaching on the Pentecostal doctrine of the baptism in the Holy Spirit, and he was unable to continue to minister there. There was, however, a small group of believers who accepted his message and a meeting was set up in the home of Mr Batiste, who was to become one of the leaders of the young fellowship. The first meeting took place on Saturday, 19th August 1911, and they met for worship the following day. Meetings were held in the packing shed of Mr Batiste's tomato exporting business. They continued to meet in the packing shed and conducted open-air meetings in the area, and so the Vazon Elim Church was conceived. The group met initially under the name of Vazon Mission.[9]

The congregation was very small with an average of just eight to ten members in attendance. The noted Welsh evangelist Seth Joshua led a seventeen-day mission in Vazon and the church took root. Things began to change when in late 1920 a Revival Mission was held in Vazon, with Stephen Jeffreys as the evangelist. Following this successful mission, a delegation from Vazon travelled to Ireland early in 1921 to examine the work of the Elim Pentecostal Alliance, which resulted in the decision by the church members to join Elim. To help establish the Elim connection in Vazon, William Henderson and his sister, Adelaide, went to Vazon for a period of ten weeks in early 1921. Joseph Smith, one of the early members of the Elim Evangelistic Band, was appointed as the first Elim pastor of the church.

In 1934, the Vazon Elim Church planted a second fellowship on the island in Delancey. This was followed by a third church, Eldad, in 1936. The three Elim churches on the island stayed open throughout the five years of Nazi occupation, when Gilbert Dunk was the pastor of the three churches. Pastor Jackson of the Delancey church was deported to a prison camp in Germany. Gilbert Dunk left Guernsey in 1952 and emigrated to New Zealand, where he established the New Zealand Elim Pentecostal Church Movement.

Leigh-on-Sea

The Pentecostal Movement in the UK was very fragmented in its early years. Apart from Sunderland and London, there seemed to be little organised efforts to bring the disparate fellowships together. Several attempts had been made to bring the scattered Pentecostal groups together, but many saw it as a matter of principle, even of theology, to retain their total independence, and even their isolation.[10] Many of the small, independent fellowships seemed to be of the opinion that somehow, smallness in size enhanced their spiritual quality. Boulton is quoted as saying: 'They were advocates of the "little flock".'[11] The presence of the crowd could not enter their Pentecostal perspective.

George Jeffreys saw in the baptism in the Holy Spirit, an empowerment to preach and spread the gospel with signs following. He had linked with the young men of Monaghan because they had accepted Christ's words: 'But you shall receive power when the Holy Spirit has come upon you; and you shall be witnesses to Me in Jerusalem, and in all Judea and Samaria, and to the end of the earth.'[12] George Jeffreys had been able to inspire a group of young people to find openings where they could preach the gospel and commence a Pentecostal witness.

This is how Elim materialised. It happened, it was not planned as such; at least, not in the early years. Canty makes the following claim: 'God made Elim. Elim did not arrive because of the sin of denominationalism, but out of the heart's love and dedication of sacrificing souls with one single aim, to save souls.'[13] While George Jeffreys was the founder of the Elim Movement, the fact is that between 1915 and 1939 approximately three-quarters of the Elim churches that were then in existence had been pioneered by people other than Jeffreys. We have already noted that Llanelli, Dowlais and Vazon Elim churches were not pioneered by George.

It was in Leigh-on-Sea in Essex that George Kingston received his Pentecostal baptism and commenced services in the locality. It became evident that a building was necessary in which to establish a permanent Pentecostal church. Thus, the very first Elim Pentecostal church in England was established through local initiative. Kingston, along with his wife, entered into the Pentecostal experience in 1911. They attended the Mitcham Lane Baptist Church, Streatham, where he became an elder. In 1918, they moved to Eastwood, Essex, and set about establishing a Pentecostal assembly. Kingston invited Jeffreys and a small party of evangelists to conduct an eight-day mission in 1921 and, having erected a building in Leigh-on-Sea, it became the first of a number of Elim churches pioneered through the Kingstons in Essex. George Kingston remained in business (he owned a chain of butchers' shops throughout Essex and the East End of London) while giving leadership and time to 'the Essex Work' as it was then known. Later, it became the Elim Pentecostal church, and these were finally added to the list of Elim Foursquare Gospel Alliance Churches.[14]

The Kingston family were well known throughout Elim. George and his wife travelled throughout the country encouraging young pastors and small churches through their caring ministry. Their son, Charles, who was converted in 1911 through his Sunday school teacher, joined the Elim Evangelistic Band in 1920 and was baptised in the Holy Spirit the following year. His contributions to Elim during its most crucial years were quite outstanding. He served as an evangelist, pastor, college lecturer and a member of its Executive Council. He served as chair of the Annual Conference on a number of occasions following the departure of George Jeffreys.

Pentecostal pragmatism

Kay, in his chapter titled 'Invading England', makes the claim that the transition from Ireland to England and Wales was carefully made.[15] The writer of this book is not convinced that this was the case. George Jeffreys was not the prime mover in the Elim churches that were opened in Wales, Guernsey, nor Leigh-on-Sea. We have seen that in the case of Wales, Llanelli and Dowlais came into Elim primarily through the efforts and ministry of Stephen Jeffreys. Vazon was already a small but established Pentecostal church that had come into existence independently of Elim. The same was true of the first Elim church in England. George Jeffreys was invited by George Kingston to hold a mission in Leigh-on-Sea, where he had already established a Pentecostal church. Although there were some twenty-two churches of various sizes in the North of Ireland, there was not much of an organised strategy and careful planning in their establishment. An absence of detailed records of opening dates makes it difficult to trace the order in which the Irish churches were opened. It would appear that only four or five churches were opened as a direct result of a revival campaign held by George Jeffreys. Most of the churches came into existence either through the efforts of the Elim Evangelistic Band or as a result of local initiative. There was no strategic plan of action, but more of a case of being led by the Spirit that resulted in a fair number of churches being opened in a relatively short period of time.

In the early years, events seemed to take place in a quite disorganised and, at times, somewhat chaotic manner. It was the arrival of E J Phillips in 1919 that resulted in some semblance of organisation. To say that George Jeffreys ministered in a pragmatic as well as a Pentecostal manner is, I believe, a fair assessment of those early days. At the 1939 Elim Conference, when Elim was in a major crisis over the subject of church government, Phillips reflected on the disorganisation that existed in the movement in the early days. In his incisive speech to the Conference, he spoke of the business and constitutional difficulties that he encountered, and referred also to the constant changes that Jeffreys had made. Phillips told the Conference that when he arrived in Belfast in 1919 there were no accounts, no list of properties and extremely deficient administration. Starting with the first constitution in 1922, there were three other constitutions published in 1925, 1927 and 1929, as we noted earlier.[16]

E J Phillips was brought on to the Elim Pentecostal Alliance Council in 1922 when he was also appointed as an overseer. The following year he was appointed to the role of secretary-general, a position that he held for thirty-four years. Phillips' great administrative, organisational and constitutional skills were a major factor in stabilising the young movement, and became crucial when Elim expanded into England. Phillips was able to analyse facts and figures in quite a remarkable way. Jeffreys wrote to him and William Henderson with two alternatives regarding purchasing property in Clapham.[17] In his reply, E J added a third alternative. In this letter he makes it clear that he had a better understanding of property and financial matters than did Jeffreys. 'I will endeavour now to go into the figures of the three schemes, rather more accurately than you did.'[18]

Notes

[1] Robinson, James, ibid, Map A.

[2] *Elim Evangel*, December 1919, Vol 1, No 1, pp16-19.

[3] *Confidence*, August 1915, p156.

[4] *Sunday Chronicle*, 16th November 1919, quoted in the *Elim Evangel*, Vol 1, No. 1, pp17-18.

[5] *Elim Evangel*, December 1919, 'Tidings From the Land of Songs', Vol 1, No 1, p16.

[6] Canty, George, ibid, p66.

[7] Boulton, E C W, ibid, p80.

[8] Canty, George, ibid, p66.

[9] Canty, George, ibid, p97.

[10] Canty, George, ibid, p60.

[11] Canty, George, ibid, p60.

[12] Acts 1:8, NKJV.

[13] Canty, George, ibid, p60.

[14] This group of churches, about a dozen in number, had their own administration and organisation while remaining in fellowship with the larger Elim denomination. It was in the late fifties that they fully amalgamated into the Elim Alliance. Although the legal name of Elim remains 'Elim Foursquare Gospel Alliance', the denomination took the name of the former Essex churches in the early seventies and became known publicly as the 'Elim Pentecostal Church'.

[15] Kay, William, ibid, p84.

[16] Phillips, E J, Speech to 1939 Elim Conference, Elim Archives, Malvern.

[17] Letter G J to E J P, 26th November 1923.

[18] Letter E J P to G J, 27th November 1923.

13

A Centre in the Capital

The year 1921 marked a significant step in the development of
Elim. This was the year that Elim invaded England. Up to now,
the movement had been confined to Ireland and South Wales.
When George Jeffreys responded to the invitation to campaign
in Leigh-on-Sea, he was determined to widen the scope of his
ministry and the Elim Movement. Boulton states that the
founder had received many urgent appeals begging him to come
over to England and commence something similar to that which
had been established in Ulster.[1] A response to such a call would
have been a great challenge. There were those who discouraged
Jeffreys from taking this huge step. The situation in England
was completely different from that in Northern Ireland and
South Wales. They insisted that the English temperament would
be far less impressionable and responsive to revival influences.

Was the civil unrest in Ireland and the partition of the
country in 1921 a factor in Jeffreys' decision to concentrate on
England? The Government of Ireland Act 1920 that saw the
island of Ireland divided into two separate legislative and
governmental parts came into being on 3rd May 1921. This act
was intended to create two self-governing territories within
Ireland, with both remaining within the United Kingdom.
However, in 1922, following the War of Independence (1919-
21) and the Anglo-Irish treaty, the southern and western part
became the Irish Free State, while Northern Ireland exercised
its option to remain in the United Kingdom.

It was necessary for Jeffreys to move cautiously. He was known in England and he returned to preach at conventions in Hull and South Wales. He relied on the funding that came mainly from the Irish congregations. The headquarters of the young movement was in 3 University Avenue, Belfast and there were two Elim churches in the city. The report on the churches in the first edition of the *Evangel* shows the progress made in the Irish churches. The opening of the Melbourne Street church in 1919 was seen as being 'the chief centre of the work'. The last sentence of the report on Belfast clearly links George Jeffreys with the city. 'Remember specially Pastor George Jeffreys and those who assist him in the city that their ministry may be increasingly fruitful.'[2] The report mentions the centres in Ballymena, Moneyslane, Portadown, Bangor and Lisburn with missions at Eskylane, Cullybacky and Milford.

There is no doubt that George wanted to expand to the mainland, but he had no organisation there. The records are somewhat unclear as to exact dates as to when the first meetings in Clapham were held. According to Kay, a disused, poorly maintained Methodist chapel in Clapham was rented for twelve months from the end of 1921. George Canty is of the opinion that the Clapham meetings started in the same year as the Grimsby campaign, which he states was held in 1922. It was inevitable that London would come into the equation and it was to become the centre of Elim's work on the mainland; indeed, throughout the United Kingdom. Stephen Jeffreys held revival meetings in Horbury Chapel, Kensington.[3] Reports in the December 1921 edition of the *Elim Evangel* state that between sixty and seventy people committed their lives to Christ in a single meeting and that many people testified to being healed. According to Kay, 'Stephen was known as a missionary of Pentecost "with signs" implying not only propagation of speaking in tongues but also public miracles of healing.'[4] Stephen was also strongly adventist and was quite colourful in his proclamation of the soon return of Christ.

While Stephen concentrated his efforts in Kensington, George focused his attention on Clapham. It is fair to say that at this stage, the idea of creating a new denomination was not the aim, though it was becoming clearer that this would be the inevitable conclusion. London presented the revivalist with an entirely different challenge. Canty makes the point that 'Revivalism was not native to the Metropolis and would have to be imported from its natural habitats of Wales and Ireland'.[5] The difficulties of pioneering in London soon became evident. Two members of the Elim Evangelistic Band, Ernie Darragh and Miss Adams, held the first meetings in Clapham and found the going very hard.

An old Methodist chapel in Clapham Crescent was discovered and recommended by a Mr and Mrs Sherlock. It was known locally as 'the haunted church'. It was in a sad state of disrepair. It represented a heart-breaking task to make anything of it, but helpers were found and set about repairing and decorating the building. A one-year rental was agreed and meetings commenced. The congregations were very small and hardly worthy of the name. Sometimes, only a handful of people gathered.

Clapham was accidentally but well chosen. It had a history of evangelical reform. The Clapham Sect or Clapham Saints were a group of Church of England social reformers based in Clapham at the end of the eighteenth century and the beginning of the nineteenth. The group consisted of men such as William Wilberforce, Thomas Buxton and Henry Thornton, who were greatly opposed to slavery. They were fired by the love of God and humanity, for the needs of their times. Other historical figures were linked with Clapham, including Samuel Pepys, Zachary Macaulay, Charles Haddon Spurgeon and Henry Cavendish.[6]

Despite this strong evangelical background, Clapham provided a huge challenge to the young Elim Movement. It must be borne in mind that there was no organisational foundation on which to establish a Pentecostal church in that area. Charles Kingston was brought in to assist Miss Adams and Darragh because the strategic importance of the new work was realised. A campaign was planned at which Stephen Jeffreys would lead, but it had to be cancelled because of Stephen's continuing success in Grimsby. George stepped in and things changed dramatically. George Jeffreys had a magnetic quality about him that attracted people to his meetings. His preaching and his excellent teaching ability directed at the spiritual level of his day, in that winter of 1922, helped to get the work on its feet.

While evangelistic missions were common enough in London then, there was a great deal of opposition to the Pentecostals in view of their emphasis on the baptism in the Holy Spirit and speaking in tongues. But those Christians who were not too prejudiced noted the new vitality and authority here. Things took form and the meetings were something new for journalists to write about, reporting 'faith cures' and happenings that were 'decidedly strange'. People with special needs were taken into a smaller hall to be prayed for. Fifty were baptised in the Holy Spirit and many healed. A woman of seventy-eight years of age claimed she had been healed of six cancers. From a very inauspicious and slow beginning, the Clapham Elim Church became established. Stephen Jeffreys campaigned there later in the year.

The chapel was rented for one year only and then had to be vacated unless it was purchased. The price for the building was £2,000. It was surely impossible to raise that kind of money – or was it? The challenge that was set this new congregation was massive. They had no reserves or large national backing of churches. A meeting was held which, in the words of a veteran member, was described as being 'critical to Elim'.[7] They prayed and believed for the impossible. Quite astonishingly, they raised the whole sum in one meeting. A wonderful foundation had been laid down. A further £1,500 was required for renovations and within one year, half of this amount had been cleared.

In seeking to understand the history of Elim, one cannot overestimate the significance of Clapham. The Clapham Elim

Church, paid for, renovated and flourishing, became Elim's citadel in the capital. George and his campaign workers lived in rooms behind the halls where the meetings were held. It was in this place that the first Elim students received a little training. From there came the backing for a major outreach to London, as support through love and prayers of the congregation made it possible. It was in Clapham that eventually the Elim Bible College would be opened and the new headquarters established.

H W Greenway, who was to become Elim's second general superintendent (then called secretary-general) and one of Elim's greatest leaders, was one of the earliest members of the Clapham Elim Church. He was a powerful preacher and writer. He was a likeable and conversational man who was known for his spirituality and his logical and scriptural defence of Pentecostalism. In his unpublished manuscript entitled *Twentieth Century Pentecostals*, he writes about his own encounter with the Pentecostal Movement. He was brought up in a Baptist church where he was converted as a young lad. There was a rather quaint old lady in the church, named Miss Woodrow, who was to play a vital role in his life and that of his friend, Herbert Court. They were both impressed and influenced by her obvious Christian joy and sweetness. Through the godly influence of this Christian lady, the two friends were introduced to the Pentecostal Movement and both became Elim ministers. Greenway's account is so vivid and gives such a clear picture of the impact that the early Pentecostal leaders had on their listeners that the account is well worth fully quoting here.

> What was the secret of this woman's influence? What was it that gave her such serenity of countenance? She spoke a lot about the Person and work of the Holy Spirit; had received the baptism in the Holy Spirit; believed in Divine Healing. She also made it clear that the Acts of the early Church should be part of the history of the twentieth century Church. But above all, she was a living embodiment of the doctrine she taught; she was the nearest personality to Jesus Christ we had met.

It became known that Miss Woodrow attended meetings near Blackfriars Bridge on Friday evenings, and it was not long before my friend and I made our way to see for ourselves what these meetings were like. A special speaker from South Wales had been announced to speak and we were anxious to hear this man who had been the centre of amazing scenes in Dowlais. It was my first introduction to the Jeffreys brothers.

The very first meeting we attended of those weekly conventions was so different from anything we had ever seen in any of our conventional churches that we were in a state of bewilderment, yet we had a desire to know more about the strange euphoria enjoyed by the people who were so devout and so fanatical. During the prayer session people around us were speaking in another language and seemed to be enjoying an ecstasy we had not seen before.

On the platform were two men who arrested our attention. Both were of medium stature, both wore dark clothes, both were striking in appearance, both took the Bible as their guide. But their styles of delivery were poles apart. We were told that Cecil Polhill came from a wealthy family and had been a member of the Cambridge Seven who suffered severely in the Boxer Rising in China. His appearance and social standing demanded some attention: but for these we would have dismissed him as not worth listening to. He had a quiet delivery and a complicated subject, speaking week by week on the Book of Revelation. We found these studies boring in the extreme.

We must not, however, allow these first impressions to obscure the valuable contribution this dedicated man of God had made in spreading the Pentecostal testimony in the London area. After receiving the baptism in the Holy Spirit in Los Angeles, he returned to work with the Rev. Alexander Boddy. He commenced meetings at nine Gloucester Place, London, and followed this effort by holding mid-day meetings for business people in

Eccleston Hall. In 1919, he started meetings in Sion College to which all who were seeking "salvation, sanctification and the baptism of the Holy Spirit and Divine Healing" were invited.

The personality who arrested our attention, however, was the one dressed in clerical garb and who came on as the final speaker. Scanning his congregation with searching eyes, Stephen Jeffreys conveyed a sense of guilt before he even spoke to us; here was a man who did not mince his words. His style we had never heard before. He was dynamic. His language was interspersed with flashes of Welsh and often rose to the familiar sing-song of the old divines.

He made no secret of his early life in the coal mines nor did he affect any claim to theological erudition. His charges to ministers who mixed worldliness with church activities and who streamlined their doctrines to prevailing modernistic teaching were delivered with scathing emphasis: the audience was carried along on a wave of tremendous enthusiasm. We felt we were listening to final truth.

At the time we little knew how far reaching would be the influence of this simple preacher in the field of evangelism. Rejecting compromise, he accepted Scriptural truth in terms of black and white. His standards were high, he swept aside all who tampered with his ideas of holiness, dubbing them wolves-in-sheep's-clothing and committing them to the limbo of the charlatan.

The preaching was not the only wonder to those of us who were in attendance for the first time: as we have already noted, we were surrounded by people who were loud in their ejaculations of praise during the time of prayer. In our church, prayer time was silent, and we associated that silence with reverence. Our first reactions to these folks, therefore, was one of incredulity. The Pentecostals of that time had no mind for the niceties of orthodoxy. They abandoned themselves to a freedom of behaviour that shocked their contemporaries to severe criticism. It is possible that we might ourselves have rejected any further invitations to return to these meetings but for the deep respect we had for little Miss Woodrow. She belonged to these people, and her life was beyond reproach. Indeed, with all the extravagance we sensed reality. There was something that attracted us and made us ask questions.

We began to look through our Bibles to see if these things were so. Were not the 120 disciples on the Day of Pentecost accused of being drunk? In the light of all that we had seen and heard we found the Bible to be a new book. It had meaning and relevance to the twentieth century. We were now able to understand passages in the Word of God hitherto avoided by our own spiritual mentors. A phase of truth had become applicable to our generation; here was the exaltation of Christ that lacked embarrassment long associated with our Christian friends.

It was not long after our introduction to the meetings at Sion College that we heard of a move to establish Pentecostal meetings in a disused Methodist Church in Park Crescent, Clapham. These meetings were to be held under the auspices of the Elim Evangelistic Band; a fellowship founded by the brother of Stephen Jeffreys in 1915.

After a short time, it was decided to hold special Bible studies at which George Jeffreys would preach. His introduction to me had an immediate effect on my life. I came under his spell, for he had a magnetic personality and a style of preaching that made the Bible come alive. His deep-set eyes seemed to penetrate and yet had a softness that carried a feeling of concern; his forehead was broad under a mop of dark curly hair. His hands were sensitive and moved in graceful gestures when he addressed his congregation. His voice was deep with a melody reminiscent of an organ that caught the timbre of the human voice. He captivated his audiences. No greater contrast could be found than in the styles of Stephen and George Jeffreys, one impetuous and forthright, the other deliberate and thoughtful.

We were thrilled when it was announced soon after the Bible studies that Stephen was coming for an evangelistic campaign, but we were disappointed, the results were minimal. It is noteworthy that efforts to reach Londoners with the Gospel did not meet with much success in the early twenties. But the meetings gradually improved and Clapham became the centre of a thriving Elim witness.[8]

It is interesting to note the final phrase of Greenway in this long narrative about the early Pentecostals and the establishment of the Elim Church in Clapham. Evangelistic campaigns and revival meetings were but the beginning. They gave an initial thrust, showing what God is like as He works in a particular way an Elim service makes possible, but there is more to be done than have these services. Pure and simple revivalism as has been described must carry with it other works of love as the gospel is declared. Canty states this concept of what we know now as discipleship very succinctly when he writes: 'Conversion means the full blossoming of personality in Christ, so that an individual's best can find satisfaction in such directions as are natural to him.'[9] Merely to sit and listen to sermons would not be a delivered life, but a constricted life. This is where the work of the pastor becomes so important. Mere professionalism can never be a true pastoral fulfilment. In the present days when this book is being written, there exists in most, if not all, Elim churches, the concept of a shared ministry. Often there are teams of ministers and church leaders who work together to guide the local fellowship.

In those early days, things were so different. There was no Bible college and little training for the work of the ministry. The pastor found himself as the one paid servant of the church, called upon to do anything. All the campaigns that have ever been held under the Elim banner would have amounted to little if the pastor appointed to follow on in the leadership of the newly opened church did not give himself completely to the task of leading his congregation; feeding them, encouraging them and exhorting them to become men and women of faith that were able to share their personal testimonies and their understanding of the Word of God with others.

Things have changed beyond recognition as far as church services are concerned, within the life and ministry of the writer. When I came into the work of pastoring a church, everything seemed to rest on my shoulders. It was nothing to preach four or five times a week to the same people. Sermons and Bible studies had to be prepared, members had to be visited and encouraged, the sick and hospitalised had to be cared for, and this burden and responsibility usually fell on the shoulders of one man.

This is the inner story of Elim, the less dramatic and less reportable side, but as essential as the historic moments described throughout this account. Without the daily pastoral toil, no evangelist could make much permanent effect; no headquarters, no paperwork, no committee, no Conference, no constitution would be of the slightest use. The pastor is the pillar, the key, the living soul of each assembly. He is not a mere cog in the machine. Elim's machine is no more than the local pastor arranges, and the Elim International Offices and Centre of Administration for the movement does not function to issue national programmes for each church to carry out as its main task. Without the local initiative of the pastors and leaders of the local Elim church, the work of the central Elim officers and national leaders would be in vain. Without the local church, pastor and congregation, there would be no call for national offices, general superintendents, regional superintendents and heads of departments.[10]

So, Elim was firmly established in the capital and in 1923, the headquarters of Elim were moved from Belfast to Clapham. The work of Norah Adams, Ernest Darragh and the Jeffreys brothers set the foundation for the opening of hundreds of

Elim churches throughout the United Kingdom, and the development of an International Missions programme that has extended throughout the world.

Notes

[1] Boulton, E C W, ibid, p83.
[2] *Elim Evangel*, Vol 1, No 1, December 1919, p2.
[3] This was a Congregational Church building which was later purchased by Elim and became Kensington Temple.
[4] Kay, William, ibid, p8.
[5] Canty, George, ibid, p71.
[6] Canty, George, ibid, p72.
[7] Canty, George, ibid, p73.
[8] Greenway, H W, *Twentieth Century Pentecostals*, Elim Archives, Malvern.
[9] Canty, George, ibid, p73.
[10] Canty, George, ibid, p81.

14

The Two Brothers and the Grimsby Campaign

The year 1922 was a significant one in the development of the Elim work. This was the year that Elim's first constitution and Fundamentals of Faith was issued. It would appear that this was put together by George Jeffreys himself. He had drawn up a statement of faith for Elim Christ Church, Belfast in 1915, entitled 'What We Believe', and made clear that the Elim Movement was taking its stand against modernism and liberalism. They regarded themselves as a spiritual movement similar in style to others that had arisen from time to time in the history of the Christian Church.[1] George Jeffreys always seemed to take a balanced approach to Pentecostal teaching. In the statement of faith drawn up for Elim Christchurch he made this 'balanced' approach obvious by including the following statement: 'We can expect the onslaught of the enemy to be furious, seeking to counterfeit and produce extravagance, which we must be careful to avoid by continuing steadfast in God's precious Word.'[2] While anxious to declare a full Pentecostal message, Jeffreys had an awareness of wild emotionalism which he was determined to avoid.

There was no mention of tongues being the initial evidence of the baptism in the Holy Spirit in the 1915 statement.[3] This is somewhat surprising, as the view taken by the vast majority of early Pentecostals was supportive of tongues being the initial evidence of Spirit baptism. Speaking in tongues was seen as the supernatural sign of the baptism in the Holy Spirit. The report of the establishment of Elim sent to *Confidence* by Thomas Hackett and which appeared in the April-June 1918 edition makes this plain:

> In 1915, Pastor George Jeffreys of South Wales, was led to open up Mission work on full Gospel lines in a small and now wholly inadequate hall, Elim Hall, Hunter Street, off Shaftesbury Square. He and his elder brother, Stephen, as many are aware were children of the Welsh Revival, and at first opposed to this Latter Rain Outpouring of the Spirit, with its supernatural Sign of speaking in Tongues. Feeling, however, their own deep need of the promised power from on high, they betook themselves to united prayer, with the earnest cry, 'Lord, baptise us with the Holy Ghost,' when, to their utter astonishment, the elder brother's little boy of nine, with a face bright as an angel's, began to speak in tongues of manifestly 'divers kinds,' and followed at great length in Welsh, with a wonderful and quite unwonted use of Scripture. A few days later, the younger brother, George, found himself one Sunday morning singing in tongues, though but a short time before he had publicly preached against it as from below.

It is clear from this account that speaking in tongues was seen as the incontrovertible sign of the baptism in the Holy Spirit. The same report features the testimony of a young Jewish lady who had come to faith in Christ and had received a remarkable healing through being prayed for by two members of the Elim mission in Belfast. The report goes on to say:

> Returning from a Pentecostal meeting one evening in deep disappointment, as she had a conviction that was to be the night of her baptism in the Holy Ghost, the same dear friend knelt down by her side, and in a few

minutes the mighty Power had descended and she was speaking in tongues.[4]

In the 1922 Fundamentals put together by George Jeffreys, speaking in other tongues is included as the initial evidence of the baptism in the Holy Spirit. This was included in the 1925 revision, but removed in 1927. This was a reflection of Jeffreys' 'middle-of-the-road' stance on the evidence of being baptised in the Holy Spirit. While being thoroughly Pentecostal in his views, George eschewed extravagance. When it came to his campaign meetings, emphasis was laid on the evangelistic message of salvation accompanied with prayer for healing.

The two brothers

In the early campaigns in England, the pattern seemed to be that Stephen Jeffreys would be the evangelist, certainly at the commencement of the campaign, and George Jeffreys would follow on and normally a church would be established. This was certainly the case with Grimsby, Hull and Barking. The difference between the two brothers was quite noticeable. Stephen was more outgoing than his younger brother. He had a very winsome personality and found it easy to make friends. In the pulpit, he was larger than life and was an inspirational preacher. He was sometimes given to flights of fancy, particularly when preaching on the second coming of Christ. He appears to have followed the futurist interpretation on the return of Christ. He was strongly adventist:

> I expect the coming of Christ very shortly. The graves will open, the bones will form together in a new spiritual body, and will ascend into the air ... Immediately among those who are left there will be fearful revolution and bloodshed, what Russia has gone through, the whole world will experience.[5]

Speculating on the identity of the coming antichrist, he dismissed both the Kaiser and Lenin and said: 'He will be of mean birth, very crafty and full of guile and will gain universal dominion over the world.'[6]

Stephen was a powerful and passionate preacher. His son Edward, speaking about the passion and energy that his father put into his preaching, wrote:

> Who could ever forget the pathos and energy which he put into every sermon he preached? I have seen his clothes so wet with perspiration that the water could be rung out. A flame was kindled in his heart at conversion which could never be extinguished. Calvary wasn't just an event in history – it was a mighty power which burned at the very centre of his being.[7]

Stephen was a fiery preacher who was most at home preaching at open-air services. On one occasion, Edward recalls his father being led of the Spirit to hold an impromptu open-air meeting one Monday in Dillwyn Street, Llanelli, at about eleven o'clock in the morning. As he preached the gospel, a housewife was busy at the washtub. As she listened to Stephen, she came under conviction of sin as he quoted the most famous verse in the Bible: 'For God so loved the world, that he gave his only begotten Son, that whosoever believeth in him should not perish, but have everlasting life.'[8] The woman went out into the street, but the preacher had gone. She was distraught. Her mother, a God-fearing old lady, went after the preacher, brought him back to the house where he led the daughter to Christ.[9]

George's preaching style was altogether different from his elder brother. Although George, like Stephen, had the God-given ability to capture a huge crowd with his preaching, he was more measured and slower in his speech than Stephen. Although there was a remarkable and deep Welsh lilt to his tone, he did not get into the '*hwyl*' as did Stephen. Stephen would, at times, get to the place in his preaching where, like the Welsh divines of old, he would almost sing some of his sentences. George was not given to 'flights of fancy' in the realms of preaching on the subject of prophecy as Stephen was. In fact, their view on eschatology was quite different. Stephen accepted what has been referred to as the Futurist interpretation of the book of Revelation after chapter 3 as being to be fulfilled in the future after the Church age. This is the view that was popularised by John Nelson Darby (1800-82). It is also referred to as the pretribulational premillennial view of Christ's return.[10]

George, on the other hand took the historicist approach to prophetic matters relating to the end times. This is also referred to as classic premillennialism. According to this viewpoint, the present Church age will continue until, as it nears the end, a time of great tribulation and suffering comes on the earth. After that time of tribulation at the end of the Church age, Christ will return to earth to establish a millennial kingdom. Those who take this viewpoint believe that the book of Revelation is an allegorical account of the entire Church age.[11] George Jeffreys was not only a historicist when it came to biblical prophecy concerning the end times, he was also a National Historicist. This refers to the British Israel view of biblical prophecy, which we will look at in a later chapter.

Although both brothers were gifted evangelists, there was a difference, not only in the style of their preaching, but also in the content. I would sum up this difference as follows: Stephen *preached* the gospel; George *taught* the gospel. Time and again, George referred to the truth and veracity of the Scriptures. His sermons went beyond preaching simple evangelistic sermons. He had a greater grasp of theological issues than did Stephen.

Physically and emotionally, they were quite different. The difference between the brothers was clearly noted by people who attended the Grimsby campaign. Stephen preached himself almost to a stand-still for twelve weeks and then George took over the services. The people wondered what the younger brother would be like. 'Those who were expecting another Pastor Stephen would be disappointed, for never were two brothers so different in features, mannerism and method.'[12] As I have said, Stephen was more outgoing and George, by nature, was rather shy. Stephen had the build of a collier stamped on him, whereas George was physically more delicate: this may well have been down to a physical affliction he experienced while young. As I mentioned earlier, he suffered with a form of facial paralysis. This affected his whole being and was an obvious serious setback to his great ambition and sense of divine calling to enter the Christian ministry. His remarkable account of healing is quoted by Edsor:

> Upon entering one of the classrooms when studying for the ministry, I found the following sentence written on the blackboard, *'He that hath an experience is not at the mercy of him that hath an argument.'* When I read these words, I could not help but say aloud, 'Yes, and especially if the experience carries with it the authority of Scripture.'
>
> I was first convinced of the Spirit's quickening power when, as a frail youth, I received the experience in my own body. My weak state began to manifest itself in facial paralysis, and I was heavily burdened, for I felt the creepiness of paralysis down one whole side. Being somewhat reticent I suffered in silence beyond measure, for I knew that unless a miracle was wrought in me, life was to be very short. When my mouth began to be affected, the one thing that distressed me greatly was the possibility of my not realising the one call and ambition of my life, the Christian ministry. From my earliest days of childhood there was the consciousness borne with me that I was called to preach the Gospel. When this affliction came, it seemed to me as if the end of all that was worth living for had come, there was no other purpose for me in life if I could not preach.
>
> We were kneeling in prayer one Sunday morning and were interceding on the subject of the services of that day. It was exactly nine o' clock when the power of God came upon me, and I received such an inflow of Divine

life that I can only liken the experience to being charged with electricity. It seemed as if my head were connected *to a most powerful electric battery*. My whole body from head to foot was quickened by the Spirit of God, and I was healed. From that day I have never had the least symptoms of that old trouble.[13]

Despite the contrasts between them, there was a strong bond between the two brothers and they worked closely together, particularly in the early years of Elim's pioneering work in England. The strategy for the early campaigns was for Stephen to go to an area first and, after some weeks, George would follow on and, more often than not, a church would be established.

The Grimsby campaign

Edward Jeffreys compares the joint ministry of his father and uncle to that of the Wesley brothers, John and Charles, in the eighteenth century. 'When they commenced their great campaigns, city after city was moved from centre to circumference.' He goes on to say: 'The largest public halls were thronged everywhere they went, because God was confirming the preaching of His Word with mighty signs and wonders.'[14]

It is this remarkable combination of 'Word and Spirit', of 'preaching and signs-following', of 'declaration and miracles' that characterised the ministry of the two brothers, particularly in the early campaigns. It was, as they saw it, a fulfilment of the Great Commission:

Go into all the world and preach the gospel to all creation. Whoever believes and is baptised will be saved … And these signs will accompany those who believe: in my name they will drive out demons; they will speak in new tongues … they will place their hands on people who are ill, and they will get well.[15]

It is not untrue to say that these brothers preached the gospel with miraculous evidence of the power of Christ, through the Holy Spirit, sent from God the Father, that had not been seen at such a level in our nation ever before.

> The preachers belonging to the various sects had preached of a Christ in history who had opened blind eyes and unstopped deaf ears in Palestine nineteen hundred years ago. But these men (the Jeffreys Brothers) went out to declare a Christ who could heal the sick today, and their preaching was a challenge to effete religion and paganism.[16]

It was on the 7th January 1922, exactly seven years after the foundation of Elim, that Stephen Jeffreys held a meeting with Mr and Mrs W Douglas at 99 Wellholme Road, Grimsby. Alec Douglas was a member of the Holiness Mission, Leicester Street, Grimsby, but it had been determined that no one who had claimed to have spoken in tongues as advocated by the fledgling Pentecostal movement would be permitted to minister to the congregation. According to Canty, he was suffering at the time from a nine-inch intestinal protrusion and was unable to stand because of the intense pain. The few believers gathered round him and Stephen laid hands upon him. He was immediately healed. Meetings had been arranged and commenced the following day. Only eleven people turned up and Stephen was greatly discouraged and declared, 'If this is it, I'm going back home.' Mr Douglas replied, 'No, you are not! God sent you and you are staying.'[17]

There is a difference between the accounts of where the first meeting in Grimsby was held. Canty states that: 'The Fringe Street auction room had been booked for special meetings and the next morning at 11 o'clock the campaign began.'[18] Edward Jeffreys, however, claims that the services were held in the Co-operative Institute, Freeman Street, Market Place, 'a large and commodious building'. He further states that there were about twenty people present.[19] Whatever, the fact is that the campaign commenced and Stephen was persuaded to stay on. It was soon rumoured throughout the area that somewhat unusual meetings were taking place at which sick people were being prayed for. We must try to understand the effect that 'healing' meetings had on the general public in the twenties and thirties. This was before the establishment of the NHS, so any kind of medical assistance had to be paid for. Also, the ailments that are considered somewhat 'normal' today, for the simple reason that there is medication available to successfully treat them, were considered to be very serious and even life-threatening in those days. So, when it was reported that meetings were taking place at which sick people were being prayed for and some were instantaneously healed, the news spread like wildfire.

Advertising posters were displayed throughout the town which made known that a 'Great Public Revival and Divine Healing Campaign' was taking place. Canty rather cynically claims that the word 'Revival' would be generally unknown to a public like Grimsby, and Divine Healing totally unheard of in all history. Someone who had been present at the meetings sent in a report to the *Elim Evangel*:

> All present at his services realise that of a truth, God is with him, and at the close of each message there is a flocking to the penitent form; among the seekers are to be seen many professing Christians and local preachers, who feel that in the past, they had nothing but an empty profession. A notable feature of the meetings has been the way God has honoured the prayer of faith for the healing of the body.[20]

There were many remarkable cases of healing at Grimsby. The following account of a press report written during the Grimsby campaign appeared in the *Elim Evangel*:

> A notable feature of the meetings has been the way in which God has honoured the prayer of faith for the healing of the body. Scores of people in Grimsby are

testifying to the marvellous way in which God has delivered them from all kinds of diseases. Last Thursday evening was devoted to healing testimonies … Four told of how they had been cured of serious ruptures: one of a tumour that had formed a huge lump under the breast which now had entirely disappeared. Many told of complete relief from heart trouble, another of restored hearing after deafness for fifteen years. A cripple who had not walked for twelve years gave his crutches to the caretaker, and a lady who had not had her feet to the ground for five years and eight months arose from her invalid chair and walked round the hall before the congregation and has walked every day since.[21]

The final weekend at the Gaiety skating rink in Grimsby saw the building packed to capacity with more than 5,000 people present. The two brothers came together for these last services. At the closing evangelistic rally on the Saturday night, the appeal was made by the wife of George Kingston. The two of them had been present during the last two weeks of the campaign. In the early years of Elim, it was not unusual for women to take leading roles in church life. By 1924, there were twelve women listed as members of the Elim Evangelistic Band. According to the *Evangel*, the response to Mrs. Kingston's evangelistic appeal was tremendous. Hundreds of people made their way to the front of the hall to give their lives to Christ.

Notes

[1] Cartwright, Desmond, *The Great Evangelists*, p44.
[2] Jeffreys, George, *What We Believe* (Malvern: Elim Archives).
[3] Although there is no mention of tongues as the initial evidence of the baptism of the Holy Spirit in the 1915 statement, it was included in the 1922 and 1925 Fundamentals but was removed in the revised constitution of 1927. The above statement is to show Jeffreys' concern at the free expression of tongues being used in his campaign meetings. Many early

leaders, E J among them, believed that speaking in other tongues under the inspiration in the Holy Spirit is the initial evidence of the baptism of the Holy Spirit.

4 *Confidence*, April-June 1918, p21.

5 *Confidence,* October-December 1921, pp53-54.

6 *Confidence*, October-December 1921, pp52,54, quoted by Kay, William, ibid, p88.

7 Jeffreys, Edward, *Stephen Jeffreys,* p4.

8 John 3:16, KJV.

9 Jeffreys, Edward, ibid, p14.

10 Grudem, Wayne, *Systematic Theology: An Introduction to Biblical Theology* (Nottingham: Inter-Varsity Press, 2003), p1100.

11 Grudem, Wayne, ibid, p1112.

12 *Elim Evangel,* May 1922, Vol 3, No 5, p74.

13 Edsor, Albert, *Set Your House in Order,* p25.

14 Jeffreys, Edward, ibid, p37.

15 Mark 16:15-18, NIV.

16 Jeffreys, Edward, ibid, p37.

17 Canty, George, ibid, p68.

18 Canty, George, ibid, p68.

19 Jeffreys, Edward, ibid, p39.

20 *Elim Evangel,* April 1922, Vol 3, No 4, p52.

21 *Elim Evangel,* April 1922, Vol 3, No 4, pp52,53.

15
Significant Beginnings

The years 1923-25 were highly significant in the foundation and development of the Elim Movement in Great Britain. It was in 1923 that the Elim headquarters were moved from Belfast to Clapham. It was in this year also that the Elim Missionary Society was birthed. Then, 1924 saw the opening of the Elim Publishing Department in Clapham. It was in 1925 that a former convent was bought in Clarence Road (later to be renamed Clarence Avenue), some ten minutes' walk from the Clapham church and preparations were made to open it as the Elim Bible College the following year. There were two other notable 'beginnings' in 1925. This was the year that Elim held the first of many celebrations in the world famous Royal Albert Hall in London. It was in this year also that Elim made a huge impact on the East End of London that resulted in the establishment of large and significant churches. But first, we must go back to the year 1922 to the city of Hull.

Expansion in Hull

Following the hugely successful campaign in Grimsby, Hull, Grimsby's rival fishing port on the opposite northern bank of the shallow Humber estuary, sent a call for help through the pastor of the Pentecostal group that met in the city that was the birthplace of the great slave trade abolitionist, William Wilberforce. The pastor, E C W Boulton, was an influential speaker at Pentecostal conventions throughout the British Isles.

He preached at a number of Elim conventions in Northern Ireland and was well thought of and respected by George Jeffreys. The Pentecostal work that he led in Hull was not large. George Canty, who came from Hull and who attended the Elim church there, describes the work at that time as 'struggling'. Boulton's request was met with an affirmative response and the Royal Institute was booked to hold campaign meetings. Apparently, the rental for such a place was very high. It was on the 28th May 1922 that a 200-strong contingent of converts from Grimsby landed from the New Holland Packet paddle steamer and marched, singing the Elim songs and choruses, the one mile to the Institute.[1]

The Hull campaign lasted a month and there were large attendances and many were healed. Hundreds responded to the gospel message. The campaign was conducted jointly by George and Stephen. Edward Jeffreys refers to the close working association that his father Stephen had with his brother George. He says that they were ideally matched for great campaigns. In his opinion, George was undoubtedly gifted as an organiser. There is no doubt that there is some truth in that, but it needs to be pointed out that E J Phillips was the one who was to become the unseen organiser and administrator of most, if not all, of George Jeffreys' great campaigns and celebrations. It was E J who booked the Royal Albert Hall and organised the great conventions that were held in them. It was he who saw to the hiring of some of the greatest and most notable halls in the land for Jeffreys to hold meetings. Edward said: 'His [George's] brother Stephen never aspired to become the leader of any organisation; he never claimed to be anything of an organiser, he knew his limitations. But as an evangelist for pioneer work he was without an equal.'[2]

While referring to the hundreds of people who responded to the gospel appeal, with as many as sixty people making their way to the front of the hall in an act of committal to Christ, Boulton's report in the July edition of the 1922 *Elim Evangel* and also in his historical work of *George Jeffreys: A Ministry of the*

Miraculous, focused attention on the incredible miracles of healing that occurred in Hull, as had been the case in Grimsby. Humberside was alert to the presence of the two evangelists, and the hall where the meetings were held was soon besieged with huge crowds waiting in anticipation. Services continued for hours as the two brothers attended to the sick, one by one, until there were too many for a single meeting. Boulton published the *Evangel* account of the Hull campaign verbatim in his biography on George Jeffreys. The *Evangel* article (written by Boulton) referred to numerous acts of healing that occurred during the revival campaign.

> Perhaps one of the cases which excited most interest was that of a young man who, in the early days of the campaign, was brought from a distance to be prayed with. His condition was pitiable in the extreme: paralysed in almost every limb, and unable to speak intelligibly; he was as helpless as a child. What a change was wrought in this young man! I remember so well the evening when, full of new life flowing through his hitherto helpless body, he swung his arms above his head, and then in the exuberance of his joy jumped again and again from his feet, demonstrating the reality of that which had been accomplished. We might continue to cite case after case of those whose lives have been changed, and whose bodies have been healed, but space forbids. The foregoing is sufficient to show the marvellous character of the work done during this month's campaign in Hull.[3]

Boulton attributes the amazing and miraculous results of the Hull campaign not to the eloquence of the preachers, nor to some strange mysterious influence which swayed the people, but clearly to the power of God. He writes of a tremendous attraction Godward which few could resist. The one word that undeniably sums up the campaigns at Grimsby and Hull, and which was to be repeated many times through the towns and cities of the United Kingdom during Jeffreys' campaigns in the 1920s and thirties was – revival.

Several hundred people were converted during the campaign, and Boulton continued to lead the church there until 1928 when he moved to Elim headquarters at Clapham. Although a very large and flourishing church was established in Hull, it was not without its struggles following the campaign, according to Canty. George Canty found Christ in Boulton's Hull assembly and added his own observed account.

> Typical of the harassments suffered by an organisation making its resources purely from its own expansion, meetings after the campaign were held in many halls, always with uncertainty as to which one. In 1926, two halls were knocked into one in Mason Street, opposite to extensive slum property of the worst kind. In 1933, the pastor (F. G. Cloke) arrived to inform the assembly that he, with George Jeffreys, had bought a large chapel some two or three miles distant in the fish dock area, and there finally, in anything but an ideal or central situation, Hull's Elim found a resting place from wanderings.[4]

This building was named 'Hull City Temple' and became one of Elim's largest churches. Mason Street was reopened as a second church in 1934.

The name of Jeffreys became widely known and George, with Ernest Darragh, who was the first evangelist to join the Elim Evangelistic Band, along with Margaret Streight, accepted invitations to Berne and Goldville, Switzerland, with offers from many towns where groups of Pentecostals wanted to see people won for Christ. A major invitation came from the USA and British plans were somewhat slowed down in the expectation that George and Stephen, along with others, would tour North America in 1923. As events turned out, this did not take place until the following year. In the meanwhile, George campaigned very successfully in Hereford without, however, forming a church there.[5] Stephen held great campaigns in South Wales (Swansea, Morriston and Ystradgynlais).

Elim's first secretary-general

It is almost impossible to overstate the importance of E J Phillips and the significance of his contribution to the development of the Elim Pentecostal Church. It was in 1919 that Ernest John Phillips left Bedford to join the Elim work in Northern Ireland. He crossed over the Irish Sea in the company of John Carter, who also linked up with Elim. John, alongside his brother, Howard, was to go on to play a very important role in the birth and leadership of the Assemblies of God in the UK. The Carter brothers came from the industrial city of Birmingham, situated in the heart of the Midlands. It was there in 1924 that the Assemblies of God was formed as the third Pentecostal Movement in Britain.

George Jeffreys soon appreciated the administrative gifts of Phillips and his penchant for fine detail. He was appointed joint editor of the *Elim Evangel* in December 1921 alongside E W Hare. A year later, Hare left Elim and Phillips was appointed the sole editor, as has been noted elsewhere in this book. This was the first of three important offices that E J occupied in his fifty-four years as an Elim minister. In 1923, he was appointed by Jeffreys to the position of secretary-general. This position, created by Jeffreys, meant that he saw E J very much as his right-hand man. This is clearly seen in the copious letters that passed between the two men. They corresponded almost on a daily basis.

It is quite evident that from the early twenties, the relationship between Jeffreys and Phillips was a close one. This is evidenced in early correspondence between them.[6] He asks Phillips' approval of his proposals to send certain ministers to Armagh and district. In the same letter, he apprises Phillips of the details of the property in Clapham.

It is interesting to note how the two signed off their letters. Jeffreys usually signed off with a remark about meetings, comments on situations, or a request for prayer. Once or twice, he used an affectionate phrase to sign off, eg 'Fondest Christian Love'[7] and 'Fondest Love'.[8] Phillips tended to use a similar phrase to sign off his letters – 'Yours in His love'. In his letters to other people, he usually signed off 'Yours truly in Christ'. What is very evident is the deep confidence, trust and genuine affection that existed between the two of them. This genuine affection the one for the other is clearly seen in the correspondence between them. In a letter of 20th January 1925, E J refers to a Miss Jones; he writes: 'You had better write her yourself, as I have already interviewed her. She has been here for some time, and both sister Hettie's and my own independent opinion of her are that she is non compos mentis!' In his reply, George Jeffreys writes: 'I see you have pronounced Miss Jones "non compos mentis". Alright old boy, I will soon settle her. There are too many like her now in the band. I will deal with this in due course.'[9] There is no doubt that there was a close affinity and total solidarity between the two men.

Phillips' knowledge of property law seems to have been great. This becomes obvious when he advises caution over the payment of a deposit for the Clapham property.[10] Also, his keen, analytical mind regarding accounts and finance is clearly seen in this same letter. He refers to the Analysis Book regarding payments from Clapham before he came into the office of secretary-general as being in 'a hopeless muddle'.

Hudson refers to the similarities between the two leaders.[11] Both were shy, determined, persistent and totally committed to the movement. E J has been described as a quiet and reserved man.[12] In almost all the photographs taken of him he appears unsmiling, stiff and aloof. Staff who worked with him, however, spoke of a kind man with a rather strange sense of humour that sometimes expressed itself in bouts of laughter at everyday mishaps such as people tripping over.[13] He was not at all a callous man, but covered up his embarrassment in this manner.

Phillips took his role of administration within the movement very seriously. His co-workers testified often of the very long hours that he put into his work. More often than not, he worked twelve-hour days in the office.[14] However, as a result of his administrative ability and clarity of mind, he was often viewed as being 'austere to the point of cold'; with some thinking that he was too fussy.[15] He was a brilliant debater at Conference as was evidenced in his debate with John Leech at the 1934 Conference over British Israelism. He took advantage of his position as secretary-general in that he usually arranged to speak last in a debate. He noted his comments on a number of cards or a small pocketbook. To these notes he would add the arguments of those who had spoken in the debate and, if he took the opposite view, would systematically demolish the arguments already put forward.[16] On one occasion, a leading minister, John Dyke, who was later to be elected to the Executive Council, reacted strongly to yet another defeat on the Conference floor at the hands of E J. It is said that he shook his fist at E J in exasperation and said, 'One of these days I'll get you yet, Mr. Phillips'.[17] 'He was deeply respected, but almost feared in Conference.'[18]

Jeffreys was equally shy. The manner in which he conducted his healing meetings and prayed for the sick sets him apart from some of his flamboyant contemporaries, such as Smith Wigglesworth. A journalist describes the scene in one of his meetings; the lengthy quotation is worth noting because it provides insight into Jeffreys' personality:

His procedure is simple. In the course of a meeting, when the congregation is 'set' and the atmosphere of faith is beginning to make itself felt, Jeffreys will ask for the sick to come forward. And while the congregation sings quietly … Jeffreys comes down from the platform and puts his hands on the heads of the sick, and murmurs a few words, 'Pray to the Lord', or 'Concentrate on Jesus Christ' or just 'Glory'. Some take it with tears, some with a smile, some go off into jerking or babbling fits, some just fall headlong and lie there. The whole thing is done without fuss or mumbo-jumbo on Jeffreys' part. He doesn't claim to heal. But the 'patients' commonly claim to have been healed.[19]

E J was able to analyse facts and figures in quite a remarkable way. George Jeffreys wrote to him and W Henderson with two alternatives regarding purchasing property in Clapham.[20] In his reply, E J added a third alternative. In this letter he makes it clear that he had a better understanding of property and financial matters than did George Jeffreys. 'I will endeavour now to go into the figures of three schemes, rather more accurately than you did.'[21] Although this comment may appear to be very much a 'put down', in the context of the letter as a whole and, indeed, of all the correspondence between them, E J clearly had the best interests of the work and George Jeffreys at heart. At the time of this correspondence, E J was in Ireland and he made a very interesting comment that showed that he felt that decisions on property and finance needed to be made deliberately and carefully: 'Really, I think it is for the best that I am not in London now, for Mr. Henderson and I can quietly talk things over and weigh everything up, which I know we could not do if we were in all the excitement that I know you are in. It is no use our rushing into this. Let us calmly consider it before we rush into anything.' This comment seems very apposite when considering the seeming financial crisis in 1937. It is quite clear that Phillips had a firm hand on financial and property matters and he was not likely to commit the movement to unsustainable debts.

E J clashed with John Leech at the 1934 Conference over the teaching of 'British Israel' interpretation of prophecy. It appears that E J was always suspicious of Leech's eschatological views. He writes: 'Remember to ask him [Mr Leech] re becoming a contributing editor [of the *Evangel*], but remember also that I am not going to commit myself as to inserting all his articles.'[22]

He was very precise in his instructions. He wrote concerning a form to be signed and also a cheque book. 'Also enclosed is cheque book; please sign this throughout on the middle of the three lines for signatures.' He continues: 'Then, I want you, please to copy out the counterfoils from your cheque book; please copy these word for word as I specially wrote them in the way I want them entered up in our account book.'[23]

E J was not afraid to bring everything to Jeffreys' notice even if it appeared to be critical of his brother Stephen. Commenting on the Forest Hill campaign, he refers to Mr Darragh and Miss Adams being very discouraged:

> They want to close down and help at Barking. They pointed out to me the way your brother is neglecting the converts there and wanted to go and help there, and then all concentrate on Forest Hill after Barking. (It is a pity, really, there is not somebody like Mr. Darragh to organise with your brother; Willie Bell, of course, cannot do much when he is glued to the piano. However, do not think I am suggesting Mr. Darragh for the job; I am not.)[24]

George Jeffreys was obviously Welsh-speaking and E J refers somewhat humorously to this fact when he writes: 'I am enclosing a letter from your brother William. There are a few Welsh names in it, therefore I require you to censor it.'[25]

It is quite obvious that E J had great freedom in taking decisions of a financial nature. In another letter,[26] he refers to the purchase of a building for the Barking church: 'I am going ahead with this. The cost, I estimate will be £1000, which will include land and building. We must have surplus cash in the Forward Movement Fund (which is very high at present) to meet the initial expenses on places like this ... Barking people are crying out for an Assembly. The meetings are now packed out. Today I have had to hire a policeman to keep the crowds away outside.'

It is clear that E J was extremely close to Jeffreys and was reluctant to sever fellowship with him. Other leading ministers within the movement at the time were less inclined to be charitable towards Jeffreys when the split occurred. H W Greenway, who succeeded E J as secretary-general, found George to be somewhat aloof and rather arrogant, preferring Stephen's company and ministry to that of his younger brother.[27]

Joseph Smith, a long-standing member of the Executive Council, as mentioned earlier, and one widely regarded throughout Elim as a 'prophet', certainly felt that E J should have been more forthright in his presentation of Elim's policy during the time of the split. Commenting on E J's report on a meeting held in Carlisle, Smith writes:

> I think this is very weak, and that more should have been made of the reason why you did not ask any questions, and the shortness of the time allowed. It should have been pointed out how deplorable it was for a man who knew what revival work was in the past, going into a town which was enjoying a real work of soul saving. He knew how essential unity is to blessing, and yet he goes there to create division, and to turn the minds of the people away from the great work they are trying to do.[28]

In the same letter, Smith argues very strongly for a more militant approach on Elim's part towards Jeffreys:

> Call a meeting of all the members of the church. Let yourself or Mr. Hathaway give an address to the people, going right through the history of the trouble, pointing out the root cause, pointing out that Mr. Jeffreys is out to smash the movement, and calling on the people to stand together in unity. Stand like soldiers in the thin red line about to receive a charge of cavalry. Let them feel that the cause of Christ is in real danger, that their church is in danger, that it is no time for internal quibbling about

minor matters – we must stand together or fall together.[29]

E J was always reluctant to personalise attacks on Jeffreys. It would appear that Smith was quite willing to counter with personal attacks. 'You would, I believe, be justified in bringing in personal things under the heading: "Why God has removed Mr. Jeffreys from the position held in this movement".'[30]

The position that Jeffreys created for Phillips was that of 'secretary-general'. This position was many years later to morph into the current name for the leader of the Elim Pentecostal Church which is 'general superintendent'. After the division that saw George Jeffreys leave Elim in 1940 and start up another denomination, E J Phillips became the de facto leader of Elim, a position he was to occupy until 1957, when he was succeeded by H W Greenway.[31]

Notes

[1] Canty, George, ibid, p82.
[2] Jeffreys, Edward, ibid, p42.
[3] Boulton, E C W, ibid, p107.
[4] Canty, George, ibid, p83.
[5] Elim's greatest post-war evangelist, P S Brewster, established an Elim Church in Hereford in 1951.
[6] Letter G J to E J P, 23rd November 1923.
[7] Letter G J to E J P, 23rd November 1923.
[8] Letter G J to E J P, 21st November 1923.
[9] Letter E J P to G J, 20th January 1925.
[10] Letter E J P to G J, 23rd November 1923.
[11] Hudson D N, *A Schism and Its Aftermath: An Historical Analysis of Denominational Discerption in the Elim Pentecostal Church, 1939-1940*, PhD dissertation (Kings College), p140.
[12] Hudson, D N, ibid, p140.
[13] Interviews with T W Walker and George Canty, November 2010.
[14] Interview with T W Walker. J C Smyth, who trained under E J at Clapham, also spoke of the very long hours that E J worked.
[15] Hudson, D N, ibid, p139.

[16] Interview with T W Walker.

[17] Information passed on to the author by J C Smyth and confirmed by T W Walker and G Canty.

[18] Interview with T W Walker.

[19] Article in *Picture Post*, 11th May 1946.

[20] Letter G J to E J P, 26th November 1923.

[21] Letter E J P to G J, 27th November 1923.

[22] Letter E J P to G J, 5th January 1925.

[23] Letter E J P to G J, 3rd January 1925.

[24] Letter E J P to G J, 23rd January 1925.

[25] Letter E J P to G J, 28th January 1925.

[26] Letter E J P to G J, 30th January 1925.

[27] Greenway, Michael, ibid.

[28] Letter J Smith to E J P, 11th August 1941.

[29] Letter J Smith to E J P, ibid.

[30] Jo Smith was revered throughout Elim as a very godly and gentle man. He was looked upon as a prophet.

[31] Jones, Maldwyn, ibid, pp17-23.

16
The Birth of Elim
International Missions

The year 1923 was a significant one in Elim's development as the first British Pentecostal Movement. As has been recorded in the previous chapter, this was the year that Ernest John Phillips[1] was appointed as Elim's first secretary-general. This position virtually made him second-in-command to George Jeffreys. When the Deed Poll of Elim was adopted in 1934 with an Executive Council appointed, two men were given ex-officio appointments. They were the founder – George Jeffreys, and the secretary-general – E J Phillips.

Elim Missionary Society

There is some debate concerning the establishment of Elim's Missionary department. In 2019, Elim Missionary department based its centenary on the visit of Dollie Phillips to India in 1919. The department settled on this event as its official centenary, though there is considerable historical difficulty in considering 1919 as the beginning of Elim's International Missions Department.

The first lies with the fact that there is no record of Dollie Phillips having been an Elim missionary. She became an Elim pastor in the 1930s where she led the Elim church in Letchworth for a number of years. Indeed, it is highly unlikely that she was even an Elim member in 1919 seeing that there were no Elim churches in England at this time. The first Elim church in England was established in Leigh-on-Sea, Essex in 1921 as a result of an invitation given to George Jeffreys by George Kingston to hold an evangelistic mission in the town. The Phillips' family home at this time was Tamworth, but the Elim church there was not founded until 1924 when a mission that had been led by Dollie's father, John Phillips, amalgamated with Elim.

In the very first *Elim Evangel*, which was printed by her brother, Hubert Phillips, in Tamworth (December 1919), extracts of a letter written by Dollie from India was published. In the letter, she refers to a protracted period of waiting on God for guidance as to the next step she should take while visiting the subcontinent. 'For a time, there was no light. Then quite suddenly the Lord showed me that I was to come here to Chandu for the present to continue the study of Marathi and enter into real mission life and work.'[2] Describing life in the villages, she mentions a little church in the compound where she was staying. A number of people attended the church from a village about twelve miles from the compound. She expresses her intention of visiting the village with the hope of sharing the gospel with its inhabitants. She ends her letter as follows: 'I should have said that I have come here for just a few months' study and practical experience before returning home, D.V. [God willing], next spring.'[3] It is quite clear from her correspondence that Dollie was exploring a possible calling to be a missionary.

The second consideration to calculate the establishment of an independent missionary policy by Elim must be the practice of seconding missionaries to other Pentecostal missionary societies. The prime example of this was the Congo Evangelistic Mission established in 1915 by Willie Burton and James Salter. Elim evangelists who expressed a call to overseas mission work were directed to such societies but financed largely by Elim churches and members. There is no archival evidence whatsoever of Dollie Phillips going out to work with such a society nor, indeed, with Elim.

Thirdly, there is clear evidence that the first recorded Elim missionaries were Cyril E Taylor and Miss Adelaide Henderson. Both joined Burton and Salter in the Congo and are listed as members of the Elim Evangelistic Band working overseas.[4] Cyril Taylor was a Cambridge graduate who offered himself for missionary service through Elim having visited the Elim churches in Ireland. He was ordained as an Elim minister at Dowlais in April 1920. 'A remarkable demonstration was held when Mr. C. E. Taylor was ordained for work in the Congo.'[5] The same edition of the *Elim Evangel* reporting the sending out of missionaries states: 'Mr. Cyril Taylor, B.A. who testifies to much blessing in the Elim work, is also going to Congo as an Elim missionary. Though he goes in an honorary capacity, he most certainly deserves the prayers of God's people.'[6] This is quite a strange statement. On the one hand, it is clear that he went out to Congo as an Elim missionary, and this was confirmed by his ordination in Dowlais; but it seems that initially, at least, he was not supported financially by Elim. It is clear, however, that from 1920 until his death while on furlough, in 1935, Cyril Taylor was an Elim missionary. It is also clear that he was the first Elim missionary as he was in the Congo some eighteen months prior to Adelaide Henderson.[7]

Cyril Taylor

Taylor's son, Sir Cyril Taylor (1935-2018) was a renowned educationalist. He was the founder and chancellor of Richmond, The American International University in London (RAIUL). 'Cyril founded the American Institute for Foreign Study (AIFS) in 1964 and he remained throughout his life committed to the benefits of international education. He was passionate about and committed to RAIUL and his support and challenging insights will be greatly missed.'[8] Taylor had a long and distinguished career in public service and was a prominent educationalist and, among other achievements, was appointed a director of Margaret Thatcher's think tank, the Centre for Policy Studies. He served on the Greater London Council from 1977 to 1986 and was elected deputy leader. He was appointed a Knight Bachelor in the 1989 Birthday Honours for services to education. In the introduction to Sir Cyril's biography, Peter Wilby makes the following enlightening comment:

> He then seemed to me possibly the most extraordinary man in British public life. He had surfed, without apparently pausing for breath, from the high tide of Thatcherism to the uplands of New Labour. Education Secretaries came and went but, for two decades, Sir Cyril was an adviser to all of them.[9]

Peter Wilby lists four qualities that were crucial to his incredible career as one of the most prominent educationalists in recent times. They were: missionary zeal, a belief in traditional values, an appetite for work and an entrepreneur's flair. Commenting on the first of these four qualities, Wilby writes:

> The first can be traced to his parents, who were evangelical missionaries, though Sir Cyril said, 'I'm not; I believe in God but I don't go to church.' Born in Yorkshire in 1935, he spent most of his infancy with his mother – his father died before Cyril's birth – in what was then the Belgian Congo. 'Kiluba was all I spoke until I returned to England when I was six.'

The story of Cyril Eustace Taylor is a remarkable one and much honour is due to Elim's (arguably) first missionary.. His son, Sir Cyril Taylor, writing about his early childhood says:

> My parents were both missionaries in Africa. That was how I came to spend my formative years in what was then the Belgian Congo, and is now the troubled nation called the Democratic Republic of the Congo.[10] But by

the time that I was born in Leeds on 14 May 1935, my father had died and it was left to my mother Marjorie, to bring up a family that now included two boys and four girls.[11]

Taylor writes a short account of his father's story and the following long quotation is worth including:

Father was a remarkable figure by all accounts. He could have settled for a comfortable life in England as a doctor. But he was within six months of finishing his medical training at Cambridge when he was gripped by the thought of serving God in the Congo. At the age of twenty-eight, he took the boat to Africa in 1920 and became a medical missionary in Ngoiamani, in Katanga. My father's inspiration was a remarkable character called James Salter, who had been born into poverty in Preston, Lancashire in 1890. Despite the difficulties of travel during the Great War, Salter managed to get himself to the Congo in 1915, driven largely by a faith in the Pentecostal cause. His followers in the Elim Pentecostal Mission claim that as a result of a constant struggle with malaria, he was raised from his deathbed six times. It was on his return to Britain to recruit more followers that my father heard this message.[12]

Adelaide Henderson

One of the missionaries that Taylor worked alongside in the Congo was Adelaide Henderson. She offered herself to Elim for missionary work in the Congo in 1920, but did not go out until 1922. She was by profession a school teacher and the sister of William Henderson, one of Elim's early and much respected leaders. She became a policewoman as part of her wartime duties, working four hours a day after school hours, using the opportunity to witness to soldiers and civilians. She was hugely influential within the Elim Missions Society. She became secretary of that organisation in 1935 and continued leading the society for about twelve years. Her testimony is recorded in *Defining Moments* and is worth recording in full here:

On a cold December afternoon, Boxing Day, 1915, we were sitting together in my home having tea with Miss Boyle, our missionary friend from India. From behind the teapot came mother's voice, 'Where would you like to go to church tonight, Miss Boyle?' 'To hear a young evangelist in a Mission Hall in the city,' came the reply. 'You will go too,' said mother, looking at me. My heart sank! Mission Hall of all places. Too hot a place for my guilty conscience. Too much of a challenge to my way of life, which was far from keeping step with my godly home.

Into the less residential part of Belfast with its cobblestone streets we went, and presently found Hunter Street and the much dreaded Mission Hall. Brilliantly lighted and packed to the door, this one-time laundry struck terror to my heart as Miss Boyle and I pushed our way to the front to get seats. Led by a fair young man with a breezy winning smile, they were raising the roof with *Rescue the perishing*. On and on they sang beating time with their hymn books, as Mr Darragh led them from the platform with his irresistible charm. How I wished myself safely back in the staid security of Old Park Presbyterian Church where I had been a worshipper with my family.

But now the dark-haired Welshman took over. It was Mr Jeffreys and how he preached! I sat shivering; conscience stricken. 'Hypocrite, hypocrite,' cried my conscience. 'Get out of this before that tornado of burning eloquence finishes you off.' I struggled toward the door with a bumping heart and stiffened as a firm hand was laid on my shoulder. I had missed my chance! 'Where are you going?' It was my brother's voice. 'I can't stand this another moment. Let me go! This place is too hot for me,' I cried.

But Willie would not let me go. Kneeling by his side and under great conviction of sin, I accepted Christ as my Saviour. Was ever a brother more pleased and was ever a sister more relieved and happy as we made our way home together. Ten days later I received the baptism of the Holy Spirit. Friends, this baptism is a sacred and blessed experience. It so revolutionised my life that after fifty years I can truly say the fires are still burning.[13]

Adelaide Henderson was not only fully engaged with the work of the Elim Missions Society, she also had a powerful prayer ministry. I met her in Eastbourne in 1969, not long after finishing Bible college. She made me kneel in front of her as she laid hands on my head and prayed fervently for me that God would use me powerfully in God's work. Shortly after that, I became an Elim minister and have remained in that capacity for more than fifty years. I have included her testimony in full, not just because of its significance within Elim missionary context, but because it also provides us with a revealing glimpse of those extraordinary early Elim meetings which were obviously so very different from the normal services provided by the established Christian denominations of the period. There was a glorious freedom and excitement in those early Elim meetings in Belfast. Not only that, but there was a clear manifestation of God's presence in those meetings that immediately affected the lives of those attendees who had not, up to then, committed their lives to Christ. It is also clear that the Pentecostal experience of the baptism in the Holy Spirit was taught and demonstrated in those early meetings.

In her tribute to Cyril Taylor, Henderson gives an account of her first meeting with him in the Congo. She had set out to work with the Congo Evangelistic Mission in 1922. Her travelling companion and fellow missionary was Miss Elsie Brooks from Tunbridge Wells. They had travelled up from Cape Town by train and river boat. It was a long and arduous journey during which both of them contracted malaria. Elsie Brooks' condition worsened considerably and she died a few miles from the settlement where the two ladies were to minister. Henderson mentions the time that she first saw Taylor in Ireland, she was clearly impressed: 'He still lives in the memory as we saw him during that first visit to Ireland, a tall, virile, manly figure. His appeal was passionate and was persuasive as he told of the hold God had got on his life … People everywhere who heard him were impressed by his earnestness, his enthusiasm was contagious.'[14]

In her tribute, Henderson recalls meeting with Taylor at the time of her fellow missionary's tragic death. She was helplessly and hopelessly crying out to God for an explanation as to why her companion had been taken from them just as they were about to commence their missionary work together. Taylor advised her to ask God to give her a message from His Word to help and comfort her in this great trial that she was going through. A short time later, the Belgian Government asked for a document regarding Miss Brooks which meant that they had to search through Elsie's trunk. They found the required document. Alongside the required document, they discovered a scroll that had a red background and in bold, white lettering, stood out the words: 'God meant it unto good.'[15] This was the word from God that they had been searching for and it gave them great comfort. This scroll was subsequently passed on to Elsie's parents, who were equally comforted.

Cyril Taylor died while on furlough from the Congo (it was the first time that they had returned since arriving there). They were ministering in Switzerland at the time of his death. In her article, Adelaide Henderson concludes with the following tribute to her colleagues and friends:

> Pastor and Mrs. Taylor's work in the Congo remains a lasting witness to their united and wholehearted effort to evangelise and Christianise the native men and women not only of their own station and its immediate vicinity but of a vast territory of hundreds of miles around. Mrs. Taylor's influence as a wife by her husband's side in

Congo has been a stimulating, noble example of what a refined, educated woman can do in helping her husband to make a home out there in the wilds of the Congo, the centre of sanctified activity and of Christian influence. She has proved herself to be a noble, true and devoted helpmate. Their united success as missionaries on their station in Ngoi-Mani will be known to the full in that day when those dark-skinned men and women, whose lives they have through grace divine been the means of redeeming, have been gathered home to God, not in scores but in hundreds. With these blood-bought trophies from the Congo these two brave warriors will stand again united in the presence of the King with exceeding joy.[16]

A remarkable sequence to Cyril Taylor's sudden death is that his wife returned to the Congo to continue her and her husband's work. In his biography, Sir Cyril Taylor writes the following:

But, remarkably, Mother was determined to continue their joint mission in the Congo. Just six months after my birth, she set sail again for Africa. She decided not to bring all six of her children with her this time. Much to their disappointment, my three elder sisters were left with their paternal grandmother in the Sussex seaside town of Worthing, the sedateness of which they saw as no match for the excitement of an African missionary village. My brother went to Fulneck Grammar School in Yorkshire where he lived with his maternal grandmother and uncle. Marjorie Taylor was then thirty-four years of age and, accompanied by my youngest sister Mary and myself, spent two months at sea travelling to the Congo via Cape Town and up Lake Tanganyika before we put in at Kabumbulu, 15 miles from the mission. Our welcome was uproarious. Crowds thronged the bank of the Congo River. Much to her embarrassment, my mother was carried aloft amid shouts of joy, songs of praise and torrents of prayer. My mother later wrote that she felt like a 'crumb seized by an army of ants'. However, the affection was genuine and made up in part for the sad loss of my father and the separation from her four older children.[17]

I have gone to considerable lengths to outline the stories of the first two Elim missionaries, Cyril Taylor and Adelaide Henderson. In the early *Evangels* where the list of evangelists were included on the second page of every edition, their names and location (Congo) appear separately from the other names. The first time this occurred was in the April 1922 edition. Also, in that same edition, the following note was included beneath their names and designation as missionaries: 'N.B. Friends desiring to support the Foreign Missionary Fund should send their gifts to Mr. W. Henderson, 3 University Avenue, Belfast.' This was the head office of Elim at the time. William Henderson (Adelaide's brother) was one of the early leaders and was a member of the Elim Pentecostal Alliance Council. In 1923, Elim's head office moved from Belfast to Clapham and it is generally accepted that this was the time that the Elim Missionary Society was officially commenced. From this period onwards, Elim sought to appoint its own missionaries who worked directly under the Elim banner. They continued to support missionaries who were seconded to other missionary organisations, such as the Congo Evangelistic Mission.

Notes

[1] He was always referred to by his initials. This was quite common in the early years of Elim and, indeed, right up until the 1970s. Older Elim ministers were seldom referred to by their first names by younger colleagues. In this book, Ernest John Phillips is referred to as E J Phillips, or simply as E J.

[2] *Elim Evangel*, Vol 1, No 1, December 1919, p9.

[3] *Elim Evangel*, ibid.

[4] *Elim Evangel*, Vol 3, No 1, January 1923.

[5] *Elim Evangel,* Vol 1, No 3, June 1920.

[6] *Elim Evangel,* Vol 1, No 3, June 1920.

[7] In the same edition of the *Elim Evangel* that reported Taylor's commission and ordination, Adelaide Henderson is mentioned as being accepted for missionary work in the Congo.

[8] www.richmond.ac.uk (accessed 25th September 2020).

[9] Wilby, Peter, introduction to Taylor, Sir Cyril, *Sir Cyril: My Life as a Social Entrepreneur* (Stroud: Amberley Publishing, 2013), Kindle edition, Loc 56.

[10] Now called Zaire.

[11] Taylor, Sir Cyril, *Sir Cyril,* ibid, Loc 208.

[12] James Salter (1890-1972) was not an Elim missionary; he was an Assemblies of God minister who was the co-founder of the Congo (now Zaire) Evangelistic mission alongside Willie Burton. He had a brief connection with the Elim Evangelistic Band in Northern Ireland. He married Alice, the daughter of Smith Wigglesworth. Although credentialled by the British Assemblies of God (he was a member of the Executive Council and chaired their conference on a number of occasions), he maintained close links with Elim and became a member of the Bradford Elim Church when he retired.

[13] Cartwright, H C and Holdaway, D (eds), *Defining Moments: 100 Years of the Elim Pentecostal Church* (Malvern: Elim Pentecostal Church Publication, 2014), p29.

[14] Henderson A, *A Tribute to Cyril Taylor, Elim Evangel,* 8th February 1935, Vol 16, No 6, p91.

[15] Genesis 50:20, KJV.

[16] Henderson A, *A Tribute to Cyril Taylor, Elim Evangel,* 8th February 1935, Vol 16, No 6, p91.

[17] Taylor, Sir Cyril, *Sir Cyril,* ibid, Loc 271.

A young George Jeffreys, circa 1917.

The first members of the Elim Evangelistic Band.

E J Phillips, Elim's first Secretary General (General Superintendent), a position he held from 1923 to 1957.

Baptismal service in the grounds of the Elim Bible College, Woodlands, Clapham.

Early Elim Leaders: Back row, Left to right, F B Phillips, R Mercer, Miss Barbour, W G Hathaway; middle row: E J Phillips, George Jeffreys, E C W Boulton; front row: P N Corry, Joseph Smith.

Signing the Deed Poll 1934: Back Row, l to r: Joseph Smith, Percy Corry, W G Hathaway, Robert Tweed. Front Row: R E Darragh, E C W Boulton, E J Phillips, George Jeffreys, James McWhirter.

Elim Ministers' Conference 1937.

Revival Party: George Jeffreys, R E Darragh, Albert Edsor and James McWhirter.

17

A Printing Press and a Tour

By 1925, Elim was firmly established in the capital and its main office had been transferred from Belfast to Clapham. Campaigns were held in Coulsdon and other areas adjacent to Clapham, but until 1925 there was nothing north of the Thames nor in the East End. This was to change dramatically in 1925. Prior to this, however, a number of significant events took place that were to have far-reaching implications in the growth and development of Elim.

Elim Publishing House

The establishment of Elim's printing press and publications centre in Clapham was a significant development in the Elim story. It is puzzling to note that Canty makes no mention of this in his detailed unpublished history of Elim. This is despite the fact that he was a prolific writer and author of a number of books. It is even more startling in the light of the fact that his account of Elim's history was due to be printed at Grenehurst Press, Cheltenham which was the final morph of the Elim Printing Press.

The intention to establish a publishing house was first noted in the January 1924 edition of the *Elim Evangel*. The following statement appeared in the 'Items of Interest' column: 'Owing to the ever increasing circulation of the Elim Evangel and the great need for literature, our readers will be interested to know that arrangements are being made to open an Elim Alliance

Publishing House in London. It will be situated in close proximity to the Elim Tabernacle (Clapham), and we hope to be able to give full particulars in our next issue.'[1] The following month's edition confirmed the plans for a publishing house attached to the Elim premises in Clapham. They were, in fact, located at the rear of the Clapham Elim Church where two houses had been purchased to accommodate the publishing house and printing works. Huge efforts were put into developing the premises ready to be opened at the Easter Convention to be held in Clapham in April 1924. The April edition of the *Evangel* had in place of the usual editorial, an article bearing the title 'Your Opportunity'. This was a direct appeal to the readers of the *Elim Evangel* to send gifts towards the cost of establishing the publishing house.[2] Boulton gives the following account of this major development:

> The Spring of 1924 brought a much-needed development in the work. The continually increasing circulation of the Elim Evangel and the growing demand for Foursquare Gospel literature had made the establishment of a publishing office almost imperative. For four years, the magazine had been printed in Tamworth by Mr. Frederic B. Phillips, but the rapid expansion of the Alliance made it necessary to remove the printing plant to London, where in the early part of the year, the foundations of the new building were laid.[3]

It was the firm intention that the publishing house would be opened during the Easter Convention to be held in Clapham. Incidentally, this convention marked the establishment of the great Easter Conventions that were to be held in London each year for the following sixty-five years. The Convention lasted for more than a week: 18th-27th April. Accommodation could be arranged by the convention secretary. The following notice was placed on the rear page of the March 1924 edition of the *Evangel* with the following offer to help with the costs of travel:

CHEAP RAILWAY TICKETS: Arrangements have been made with the Railways Companies whereby cheap tickets will be issued from all stations in England, Scotland and Wales, from the ports of Belfast, Larne, Greenmore, Dublin and Cork in Ireland, and from Jersey and Guernsey. The cost will be a single fare and a third (children half-price). Those requiring cheap tickets should write to the Convention Secretary (address below) and state the Railway Station from which they intend to travel. A voucher will then in due time be sent to them, which will enable them to purchase a return ticket at their Booking Office at a single fare and a third. With this ticket, visitors can come to London and return to their homes any days they choose from Thursday, April 17th to Monday, April 28th inclusive.

More than likely, this was an initiative by the secretary-general. It has E J's fingerprints all over it! It shows how up to date Elim were in their administration and ways and means of expanding their work – and how innovative Elim's administration was in those early days. This innovation is also seen in the relationship with the press. Whenever a major campaign was held, the press were notified and Elim benefited considerably from what was, basically, free advertising.

The publishing house was officially opened and dedicated on Easter Monday 1924 during the Easter Convention at Clapham and several of the convention speakers gave a short word. The dedication itself was led by John Leech, KC, who was the president of the Alliance Council. Leech's influence on George Jeffreys was continuing to increase at this time and was later to adversely affect Jeffreys and, in my opinion, was to have fairly disastrous consequences upon the movement.

The American tour

In 1922, George and Stephen made the first of their overseas preaching tours. The two brothers, accompanied by Ernest Darragh, were invited to speak at a Pentecostal convention in Goldiwil, a village in the lower Alps in Switzerland. They left for Switzerland on 10th August and held meetings in Berne – four meetings a day. A notice in the September edition of the *Evangel* reads: 'We hear that God is confirming His Word with signs following.'[4]

The presiding pastor of the convention, Anton Reus, wrote a full account of the meetings which appeared in the following month's edition of the *Elim Evangel*. He wrote of the immense blessing that was evident in the convention, which was expressed in a remarkable sense of joy that was demonstrably felt by the congregation. This was the first time that George and Stephen had spoken publicly through an interpreter. The comment was made: 'It was not long before they both seemed to catch on to it, and the word flowed with mighty power and conviction.'[5]

Reus, in his reporting of the convention, astutely referred to the difference in style and content between George and Stephen. This has already been referred to earlier in this book, but his comment is worth noting:

> Brother George's clear word of exposition and opening up of the Scriptures stamped him as a God-given teacher, who clearly divides the word of truth, and who with no uncertain sound promulgates the tenets of Pentecost, the faith once delivered to the saints. But he would not have been complete without his brother Stephen. Brother Stephen's word, was indeed a revival word and brought conviction home to his hearers with all the fiery passion, power and imagination of the Welsh race. But the singing was wonderful, we felt as if a bit of the Welsh revival had been brought to us in Switzerland.[6]

There are three clear observations that we can deduct from the above quotation. Firstly, George was undoubtedly the leader, even though he was much younger than Stephen. Secondly, George is viewed as a teacher and expositor, whereas Stephen is viewed as an evangelist and revivalist. Thirdly, Stephen was a more inspirational preacher than his younger brother. Greenway, Elim's second secretary-general, preferred Stephen's preaching to that of George. It is clear from the account that he gave of the first time that he heard Stephen preach, he was greatly moved by him. His son, Michael, expressed his father's preference of Stephen's preaching in a conversation with the author.[7]

The following year, the brothers responded to an invitation to preach at a convention in Stockholm, Sweden. The pastor and founder of the church, and, indeed, of the Pentecostal movement in Sweden, was Dr Lewi Pethrus. They were accompanied on this visit by James McWhirter. The convention lasted from the 5th to the 10th of September in what has been referred to as the Pentecostal Cathedral of Sweden – Filadelfia Church. It then had a membership of 2,300 and was the mother church of the Swedish Pentecostal Movement. By this time, the Pentecostal Church in Sweden was at a much more advanced stage than other European Pentecostal movements. The Filadelfia Church had its own daily newspaper that was distributed throughout Sweden. By 1922 there were more than 300 Pentecostal assemblies throughout the country. At this time, George Jeffreys was firmly committed to the concept of central government when it came to church administration. This was clearly not the case in Sweden and years later, George was to imbibe the concept of local government on the Swedish lines. While each assembly was self-governed, there was clearly a strong unity among them. 'Pentecostal work in Sweden is united throughout the whole of the country.'[8] In his report, George clearly did not want to get embroiled in the argument over church government. He did, however, briefly allude to it in his observation: 'The local assemblies alone are organised;

love is the only tie holding the many assemblies together: this, combined with strict adherence to the plain written Word of God will EVER [note the capitals] obviate the necessity for further organisation. From the commencement of the work, complete unity has prevailed.'[9]

From Stockholm, the three Elim leaders made their way to Norway where they preached at Thomas Barratt's assembly in Christiansen. This made a great impression on the brothers as it was their first meeting with Barratt, who was looked upon as the father of European Pentecostalism. Although George and Stephen had preached at the 1913 Sunderland Convention, Barratt was not present, but his influence upon those great gatherings was profound. From Christiansen, the party travelled back to Sweden where they ministered in Gothenburg and Malmo before travelling to Germany where they ministered in Berlin. The tour was completed when they visited Amsterdam and preached at a convention there.[10]

A major invitation came to the Jeffreys brothers from the USA and British plans were somewhat slowed down in expectation that 1923 would take George and Stephen across the Atlantic. When the Elim party finally responded to the invitation and went to Canada and the USA in 1924, the visit was to be a turning point in the progress of the Elim evangelistic plans. The Pentecostal expansion in the USA, according to Canty 'was remarkable, outstripping anything seen elsewhere'.[11] It is almost impossible to gauge the number of Pentecostal churches in the USA in 1924 because of the often unaligned and totally independent Pentecostal streams that existed in the country. However, I would claim that the expansion of the Pentecostal churches in Sweden at this time would bear favourable comparison with the USA. The population of the USA in 1924 was 114.1 million, whereas the population of Sweden in 1923 was just over 6 million. Sweden had more than 300 Pentecostal churches in 1923. Bearing in mind the difference in population sizes, that would have been the equivalent of somewhere in the region of 6,000 Pentecostal churches in the USA. Considering that Pentecostalism had been established for barely twenty years in the USA, I would put forward the claim that the growth of the Pentecostal work in Sweden was as great, if not greater, than that of the USA.

George and Stephen, together with E C W Boulton and two Irishmen, Ernie Darragh and James McWhirter, sailed on the *SS Empress of Scotland* on 2nd June 1924. It was to be, more or less, a voyage of discovery and establishing fresh contacts. The *Elim Evangel* carried reports of Stephen and George's preaching, especially in Canada. The first campaign was held in a large Pentecostal church in Montreal. It lasted for three weeks with healing services held in the morning and evangelistic meetings in the evenings. It seems that Stephen did most of the gospel preaching, while George concentrated on teaching and exposition of the Word of God. Once again, the difference between the brothers' preaching style was noted and commented upon: 'Pastor Stephen Jeffreys' burning ministry of the Gospel, together with Pastor George Jeffreys' clear presentation of truth is steadily making itself felt, and steadily, but surely, the tide of revival is rising.'[12] Boulton was struck by the seeming moral degeneration of Montreal:

> One is profoundly surprised at the awful wantonness and wickedness of this great Canadian City. It presents such a strange mixture of Arcadian beauty and Athenian idolatry; so completely it is given up to pleasure and profligacy of every kind that it would not be an exaggeration to describe it as a modern Sodom and Gomorrah. Every conceivable allurement and attraction is offered for the indulgence of the sinful passion of the ungodly.[13]

For what appears to be the first time, there is reference to the ministry of deliverance in an Elim publication. Boulton refers to demon possession manifested in the services at Montreal. This is the first time that I have encountered such a reference within the *Elim Evangel*, apart from references to the work of evil spirits reported from the mission fields.

> Demon possession in various virulent forms seem to be pretty prevalent out here, several desperate cases have been dealt with and in the mighty name of Jesus, the evil spirits have been expelled. In one case in particular, the evil spirits offered stubborn resistance in their endeavour to retain control of their frenzied victim. What a need of the power of the Holy Ghost when the servant of the Lord comes to grips with the powers of darkness.[14]

From Montreal, the team travelled on to Ottawa and Toronto where further campaigns were successfully held. From Toronto, they travelled west to Winnipeg, which necessitated them travelling for some forty hours on a train. After visiting Vancouver, the Elim party made their way down the west coast of the USA to the city of San Jose, where a campaign was conducted in a large tent designated 'The Canvas Cathedral'. The next place they visited was Fresno, where they ministered for a number of days.[15]

Perhaps the most important visit that George Jeffreys and his colleagues made on their North American tour, was not for the purpose of preaching, but of listening. They went to Los Angeles, which Boulton described as the 'Mecca of the Pentecostal Movement'. While there, they attended the great Angelus Temple where Aimee Semple McPherson was the founder-pastor.

> Here we found a splendid work of revival in progress. It was a most impressive sight to see that large auditorium filled with people and to witness the great number of souls seeking the Lord at the close of each service. It was the intention of the party simply to visit one of the meetings at the Angelus Temple without making our identity known, but the keen eye of Pastor W. Black quickly detected our presence, and insisted on

introducing us to Mrs. McPherson. Thus, first of all Principal George Jeffreys came into contact with this great woman evangelist.[16]

This introduction was to have a profound influence upon the Elim Movement. Aimee Semple McPherson was to visit the UK at the invitation of George Jeffreys and Elim, possibly as a result of her influence, would adopt the title 'Elim Four-Square Gospel Alliance'. More on this later.

Kay makes the observation: 'One of the unspoken purposes of the trip must have been to view the workings of Assemblies of God close-up and at first hand.'[17] By this time, there was a developing of a fellowship of independent Pentecostal churches in the British Isles. This resulted in a gathering of leaders of some seventy congregations meeting in Birmingham at the end of March 1924. An invitation had gone out from J Nelson Parr, pastor of a Pentecostal church in Manchester. The purpose of the invitation was 'to discuss the setting up of a group of churches organised on the basis that allowed local church autonomy to be retained'.[18] The proposed form of church government was in direct contrast to the one that Elim had adopted. Following on from the Birmingham Conference that saw the churches sign up to the proposals, a further meeting was arranged to be held in London in May. George Jeffreys sent a telegram to the May meeting asking why, in a discussion of unity among Pentecostal people in Britain, he had not been invited to attend. A delegation from Elim, including George Jeffreys and E J Phillips, attended the second day of the London Conference. Unsurprisingly, this caused some tension when the subject of unity between the two bodies (Elim and Assemblies of God) was considered. Surprisingly, E J was in favour of an amalgamation, with Elim becoming the evangelistic arm of a united Pentecostal movement. John Carter, a revered leader within the Assemblies of God, who was present at those inaugural meetings referred to this in his tribute to E J: 'He was a man of vision. It was he who at the meeting in London in 1924 at the formation of our Fellowship, made the startling suggestion that the two bodies become one, with Elim discontinuing their name, and Mr. Jeffreys taking the leadership of the evangelising section of Assemblies of God.'[19]

In what was to become a strange reversal of their ecclesiastical views in years to come, George Jeffreys was far less convinced of the virtue of local church government than his secretary-general. George was not impressed by what he encountered of local church government in North America. He wrote to E J from San Jose the following:

> The further I go in this Pentecostal movement, the more convinced I am that the democratic way of doing things is wrong. I am still persuaded that nothing will hinder me from going on with the Alliance as an independent work. Subject of course to the coming Band meeting. Don't have a single thing to do with them until we can meet to discuss the whole situation.[20]

It is clear that George Jeffreys was far from enamoured with the form of local church government that he had witnessed in the American Assemblies of God. Yet, he had experienced local government in Pentecostal churches while in Sweden and had not commented adversely upon it. Could the reason have been that of the strong charismatic leadership of the Swedish Pentecostal assemblies under the guidance of Lewi Pethrus?

Notes

[1] *Elim Evangel*, January 1924, Vol 5, No 1, p22.
[2] *Elim Evangel*, April 1924, Vol 5, No 4, pp73,74.
[3] Boulton, E C W, ibid, p134.
[4] *Elim Evangel*, September 1922, Vol 3, No 9, p133.
[5] *Elim Evangel*, October 1922, Vol 3, No 10, p156.
[6] ibid.

[7] Conversation between Maldwyn Jones and Michael Greenway, Elim Archives, February 2018.

[8] *Elim Evangel*, October 1923, Vol 4, No 10, p214.

[9] *Elim Evangel*, ibid.

[10] *Elim Evangel*, ibid.

[11] Canty, George, ibid, p84.

[12] Boulton, E C W, *Elim Supplement*, No 1, August 1924, p8.

[13] Boulton, E C W, ibid, p11.

[14] Boulton, E C W, ibid, p11.

[15] Boulton, E C W, *George Jeffreys*, pp153-155.

[16] Boulton, E C W, ibid, p156.

[17] Kay, William, ibid, p98.

[18] Kay, William, ibid, p96.

[19] Carter, John, *Redemption Tidings*, 11th October 1973.

[20] Telegram, Jeffreys to Phillips, 25th August 1924, Cartwright, Desmond, *The Great Evangelists*, p57.

18
Expanding and Developing in London

As we have seen in our previous chapter, the year 1924 was a significant one for Elim. The year 1925 was, insofar as expansion in the capital, even more significant. This year was to see Elim expand from their base in Clapham to the north and east parts of the capital. It was also to be the final year in which the two brothers, Stephen and George, worked together as missional evangelists. We have previously noted the difference in their characters and preaching styles. As far as campaigning was concerned, Stephen was looked upon as Elim's premier evangelist. He was the main speaker at the Grimsby and Hull campaigns and was scheduled to lead a major campaign in Clapham. When the brothers travelled overseas, it has been noted that Stephen did the gospel preaching in the campaigns, whereas George was considered to be a teacher and expositor. It is my opinion that the break between the two brothers, when it came, was necessary as far as Elim was concerned. It meant that George stepped into the evangelistic shoes of his older brother and developed his own unique style of conducting great evangelistic campaigns. But before we move on to Barking and the East End, there is another major development that occurred in 1924 that we need to highlight.

Elim Crusaders

The Elim premises in Clapham not only provided Elim's central church in the capital but, as we have seen, it housed the publishing office and printing press, and soon the Elim Bible College would be housed in Woodlands in near proximity to the Clapham church. It was from the Clapham church that Elim's first organised young people's work was birthed. It was called 'Elim Crusaders' and James McWhirter, one of the pastors at Clapham, was the founder of this work and president for many years. He, himself, was once a boy soldier. Converted under the ministry of George Jeffreys in Belfast, he became heavily involved in the leadership of the young movement and was to become a part of the 'Revival Party'.[1] Conscious of the large group of young people that were in attendance at the Clapham Church, he organised the group as 'Crusaders'. Arthur Birkenshaw, who was an early Crusader secretary at Clapham stated that the aim of the Crusaders was 'to bring others into contact with the living Christ'. Present at the first meeting of the Clapham Crusaders was the future wife of H W Greenway. Her name was Maude Frederick, and she became the first Crusader secretary in the history of Elim.[2]

Soon, many other Elim churches opened Crusader branches. The age group was very wide – between fourteen and thirty-five years of age! The Clapham Crusader branch was inaugurated in October 1924. According to a report written by Arthur Birkenshaw, it appears that the Crusaders were responsible for electing their own branch secretary, treasurer and committee members.[3]

> This band [of young people] known as the Elim Crusaders has been formed to meet the need of a definite, aggressive work for God in Clapham. The chief object of its formation is to bring others into contact with the Living Christ who has satisfied them, and who alone can meet the various needs of the human heart.

> What a testimony that Christ is the satisfier of youth is
> to be found in the fact that nearly one hundred young
> people of our Assembly can gather weekly to discuss
> how best to reach the masses that live around them.[4]

Soon, other Elim churches followed suit and started their own Crusader branches. Within the following few months, branches has been opened in Letchworth, Grimsby and Hull.[5] The Crusader movement was a remarkable phenomenon. There was nothing quite like it in the other denominations. Yes, each denomination had its respective youth organisations, but the rapidity of growth combined with strong, spiritual perspectives, set it apart. There was also great creativity within the Elim Crusader Movement that saw various 'bands' being established in various branches. Some of the larger branches had their own orchestras. There were cycling bands and walking bands. There was a social as well as spiritual aspect to the Crusader branches in the Elim churches. Within two years of the first Crusader branch being opened in Clapham, the following churches had opened Crusader branches: Barking, East Ham, Ilford, Letchworth, Grimsby, Hull, Leigh-on-Sea, Hadleigh, Winton, Parkstone, Springbourne (Bournemouth), Canning Town, Hendon and Bermondsey.[6]

The writer has very fond memories of being a member of the Porth Elim Crusaders in South Wales. I preached my first public sermon in the Crusader meeting. We were all encouraged to take part in the meetings and in that respect, the Crusaders proved to be an extremely valuable and effective training ground for young people to speak publicly. One innovation I clearly remember, was the 'matchstick testimony'. One would be asked to strike a match and while holding the lit match, give a very short testimony! It certainly encouraged us to be brief! Within four years the enrolment numbers within the Crusader movement had reached 4,000.[7]

The Barking Crusade

Two of the Clapham crusaders, Mr and Mrs Thorn, travelled regularly from the East End to Clapham. They stayed all day Sunday, bringing sandwiches for a picnic on Clapham Common, or in the winter, in the minor hall of the church. Journey by the London double-decker red bus was too far for their return after the morning meeting. If only Elim would open a church in the East End! That was their great hope. Canty points out the huge differences between life in the East End and that of the chapel culture of Wales. 'East End Cockneys, irrepressible, chirpy, earthy and irreverent, were also attractive and warm characters. But ... their built-in custom of not going to church had challenged the Church for centuries. By a kind of tribal instinct, they accepted that church was alien territory, outside their culture as a species.'[8] This was to be a great test of the evangelising strategy of Elim. Elim had been birthed in the staunchly religious province of Northern Ireland, where Protestant and Catholics alike lay great emphasis on church attendance. George and Stephen Jeffreys were children of the Welsh Revival. How would their revival-style preaching go down in the packed streets of the East End?

It was not Stephen Jeffreys' preaching that captivated the East End populace. Indeed, his preaching style would have been totally alien to anything that the East Ender would have come across. When he preached, Stephen would often drop into the Welsh language for a word or two. He would have made a strange visitor with his cheap suit and clerical collar, bearing the title 'pastor'.[9]

He appeared at the start of the campaign at Barking Baths Hall on Sunday afternoon, 18th January 1925. He was accompanied by a singer who sounded equally Welsh, William Bell. It was a cavernous hall, where about sixty people were scattered. Edward Jeffreys recalls his father's description of the scene: 'I heard father remark that the few people who were present sat like "lonely sparrows" in different parts of the hall.

But birds have a way of informing their feathered tribe when they have discovered some good food.'[10] In spite of his emotional and inspirational preaching, he appeared to make little impact upon the sceptic attitude of these East Enders. They were not impressed by the Welsh '*hwyl*' nor by the intensity of Stephen's preaching. Edward Jeffreys claims that it was the Barking campaign that laid the foundation for the great Elim churches all over London. I find myself in disagreement with this view. In my opinion, it was Clapham that was at the centre of Elim's activities, not only in London, but in the rest of the country.

That which characterised and galvanised the Barking campaign was the emphasis placed upon divine healing. There were many reports of people being miraculously and supernaturally healed at this campaign and at Leyton that was to follow where George was the evangelist. An important feature in the London campaigns was the presence of the press. They provided information about the campaigns and paid specific attention to the healings that took place. The *Barking Advertiser* gave a lengthy report of the campaign under the dramatic heading 'DIVINE HEALING AT BARKING'.

> Pastor Stephen Jeffreys, the well-known Elim Revivalist opened a remarkable revival campaign at the Baths Hall, Barking, on Sunday. Largely-attended meetings have been held nightly, and special Divine healing services took place on Tuesday, Wednesday, and Thursday afternoons. As might be expected, special interest has been taken in the Divine healing services. On Tuesday afternoon, when the first of these services was held, people arrived in bath-chairs, unable to walk: cripples came on crutches, and walking with the aid of sticks: others attended who suffered from various diseases.[11]

The first notable healing occurred on the first Sunday evening of the campaign. The afternoon service had been attended by just sixty people. There were slightly more in the evening service. One of the attendees on that memorable first night of the campaign was a crippled man by the name of Tom English, who had struggled in on crutches. An eyewitness recalls the electric moment: 'No sooner had Mr. Jeffreys laid hands on his head and uttered a single prayer, that Tom English began to shout, "I've got it, I've got it!" Mr. Jeffreys said, "Got what, man?" to which Mr. English replied "God has healed me." To the astonishment of all who were present, Tom English suddenly jumped to his feet and in pure joy ran out of the building into the street, testifying aloud what had happened to him.'[12]

> Seen by our representative, Mr. English said he had suffered from spinal paralysis, which had affected both his legs so that he could not walk. He had suffered off and on for seventeen years, but during the last two years had got much worse. Latterly, he had been under two doctors, and they had advised him to go into Bloomsbury Hospital. He went there on Friday of last week and had since been waiting for a bed. 'But I shan't want to go now,' he explained. At the close of the healings, when the missioner asked if anyone wished to give a testimony, Mr. English rose and expressed his gratitude, and then ran round the hall carrying his sticks in his hands and waving them aloft.[13]

The impact that Tom English's healing had on the campaign was phenomenal. The following night, the hall was full. Divine healing three afternoons and every night of the week attracted much press attention and a reporter wrote that though 'several failed to respond' to the healing ministry, a number 'testified that they had been healed of various complaints'.[14] The reporter for the *Barking Advertiser* made the following comment: 'Most of them afterwards declared themselves healed, but several failed to respond.'[15] This was not the comment of a cynical reporter trying to downplay the element of the supernatural so obviously present in the campaign, but a stating of the plain fact.

As powerful as the presence of the Holy Spirit was in this great campaign, the fact is, not everyone was healed. We will briefly examine the early teachings of Elim on the subjects of healing, the baptism in the Holy Spirit and the second coming of Christ at the beginning of the second volume. But, throughout the entire course of my ministry, I have always argued that it is not always the will of God for every person that is prayed for, to receive healing. When the sisters of Lazarus sent a message to Jesus, informing Him of their brother's severe illness, Jesus made the following comment: 'This illness will not end in death.'[16] The NKJV and KJV state: 'This sickness is not unto death.' The clear inference, of course, is that many sicknesses *do* lead to death. Many of the early Pentecostals taught 'Healing in the Atonement', which briefly states that believers can receive healing in exactly the same way, and on the same basis, as they can receive salvation. This caused great controversy and many problems in the early days of the Pentecostal Movement. It is a subject that even now divides many Pentecostals.

The *Barking Advertiser* carried weekly reports of the revival campaign in the borough. I quote the full report of the final week of the campaign under the title 'THE GREAT REVIVAL AT BARKING – PASTOR JEFFREYS' CLOSING MEETINGS'.

> The fourth and final week of the revival and Divine healing campaign conducted at Barking by Pastor Stephen Jeffreys will conclude on Sunday. Each week the crowds have grown in numbers and the interest in the mission has become more intense, till in the closing stages hundreds of people have, in the interests of public safety, had to be denied admission to the Baths Hall by the stewards and police.
>
> The pastor appears to have drawn the people to the meetings by some magnetic power, and, as if caught in the wave of a great religious revival, hundreds have stood in the assemblies and professed conversion. A large amount of attention has been paid to the healing part of

the mission, but in all his addresses it is the spiritual side which is specially emphasised by the missioner.

Great meetings have been held in the afternoons and evenings throughout the week, and the scenes witnessed have been absolutely without parallel in the life of the town. At each service people have sought admission long before the time of commencing. In some cases, people who have attended in the afternoon have brought their tea with them and remained till the evening meeting. Many have been quite content to stand at the back of the hall throughout the services.

A case which aroused a good deal of interest was that of Mrs Wearne, of Wilmington Gardens, Barking. Mrs Wearne, who has been suffering from rheumatoid arthritis for many years, and has been wheeled about in a chair, was taken to the mission on Monday night, and after seeing the pastor she walked round the hall and stood, without assistance, talking to her friends, telling them of the great benefit she had received.[17]

Stephen did not continue ministering in the East End, but moved to Hendon, where he had another very successful campaign. Canty makes the very interesting comment as regards to Stephen's healing ministry: 'Stephen's theology saw Divine healing as for the converted only, so he preached the need of repentance and faith in Christ. Because of the multitude, people were instructed in another room.'[18] Whether this theological view can be verified from the Scriptures is doubtful. Jesus clearly healed people before they came to a personal commitment of their lives to Himself.

Stephen Jeffreys at Hendon

George took over the campaign at Barking while Stephen moved across to West Hendon to the long-closed and neglected Alexandra Hall in Brent View Road. It did not appear to be the sort of place that was conducive to revival meetings, 'but faith suggested God could, and would work, anywhere.'[19] The Hendon campaign commenced on Sunday, 22nd February 1925. Elim Crusaders and members enthusiastically went about the work of clearing and cleaning the hall to make it presentable for the campaign. Edward Jeffreys recalls a particular sermon that his father preached at the Hendon campaign. It was based on Mathew's account of Jesus clearing the Temple in Jerusalem.[20] Edward Jeffreys points to his father's denouncement of the state of most of the churches at that time: 'With all the fiery passion of his soul, he would denounce dancing and card-playing in premises connected with the church.'[21]

> These things ought never to have been in the House of God. Do you wonder why things were at such a low ebb spiritually at Jerusalem! How could God bless such a place? Their religion had become cold and dead? The work of the church was not to produce dancers and card players, but born-again saints. Now notice what took place as the result of that clearance: and the blind and the lame came to Him in the temple, and He healed them. Glory to God – the rubbish went out through one door, and the sick and afflicted came in through another.[22]

At the same time that Stephen was campaigning in Hendon, George took over at Barking. It is interesting to compare and contrast the reporting of the two brothers in the same edition of the *Evangel*. Very little is said in the report of the context of Stephen's preaching in Hendon, while there is considerable attention given to George's preaching in Barking. Similarly, there is greater emphasis on divine healing in the report on the Hendon meetings than of those in Barking. A final observation that I would make is that two-thirds of the report of the Hendon Crusade is made up of press reports of the meetings. There are no press reports included in the Barking meetings held by George.[23]

The above observation is in stark contrast to the report given by Edward Jeffreys of his father's campaign in Hendon. Not only did he preach against the worldliness and libertine spirit which seemed to be prevailing in many of the established denominational churches but, according to his son, Stephen preached passionately on the subject of salvation from sin. Edward pointed to the fact that there is very little preaching of salvation from sin. He deplored the fact that few definite appeals were made for people to accept Christ. 'People are allowed to join the church on generation, rather than re-generation.'[24] He goes on to write about his father's preaching and practising of such a full salvation that drew such large crowds everywhere he went. He then refers to his father's great, almost child-like faith. 'He lived continually in the atmosphere of expectancy, with child-like faith in the Word of God, and his expectation was not cut off.'[25]

The *Evangel* reporter actually does not mention Stephen's name in his report, but focuses his attention on the efforts of the Crusaders and church members in cleaning the hall. He then attaches a number of press reports that focus almost entirely upon the healings that took place and almost nothing on the content of the messages preached. The report on George's meetings in Barking is much more balanced, emphasising that the gospel was preached first, followed by an appeal for salvation, and then the sick were prayed for. It is almost as if a clear distinction is being drawn between the two brothers at this point. It is to be noted that shortly after this, Stephen was to disengage from his brother and start campaigning for the Assemblies of God, where his style of ministering seemed more in line than with Elim.

Notes

[1] This was a number of men who went on campaigns with George Jeffreys. Robert Darragh was the closest companion to George Jeffreys; he was the soloist during Jeffreys' campaigns. He remained with George right up until his death in 1959. James McWhirter was the song leader and was a close friend of George and a member of the team from 1920 until his marriage in 1936. The last member of the Revival Party was Albert Edsor, who was the pianist at Jeffreys' campaigns from 1928 to 1962 and was the last surviving member of the Revival Party.

[2] Canty, George, ibid, p87.

[3] *Elim Evangel*, December 1924, Vol 5, No 11.

[4] *Elim Evangel*, ibid.

[5] Reports of these new branches appeared in *Elim Evangel*, 15th January 1926, Vol 6, No 2, p17.

[6] Elim Crusader Movement, *Elim Evangel*, 6th December 1926, Vol 7, Nos 23,24, p283.

[7] Canty, George, ibid, p87.

[8] Canty, George, ibid, p88.

[9] Canty, George, ibid, p 88

[10] Jeffreys, Edward, *Stephen Jeffreys*, p50.

[11] *Barking Advertiser*, 24th January 1925.

[12] Canty, George, ibid, p89.

[13] *Barking Advertiser*, ibid. Quoted by Edward Jeffreys, *Stephen Jeffreys*, p53.

[14] Canty, George, ibid, p89.

[15] *Barking Advertiser*, ibid.

[16] John 11:4, NIV.

[17] *Barking Advertiser*, 14th February 1925, quoted by Jeffreys, Edward, ibid, p56.

[18] Canty, George, ibid, p90.

[19] Canty, George, ibid, p91.

[20] Matthew 21:12-13.

[21] Jeffreys, Edward, *Stephen Jeffreys*, p57.

[22] Jeffreys, Edward, ibid, p57.

[23] *Elim Evangel*, 16th March 1925, Vol 6, No 6, pp67-68.

[24] Jeffreys, Edward, ibid, p58.

[25] Jeffreys, Edward, ibid, p58.

19
Revival in the East End

The Barking campaign was the spark that set the East End of London ablaze with revival fire. It is interesting to note the description given in the *Evangel* of the impact that Elim was having on the capital. Under the title 'Revival Fires in London', the report was written in a very dramatic style, using the picture of a huge gun blasting for the truths of Pentecost over the city. 'London! yes the full Gospel guns are firing and this mighty metropolis is being attacked from every side. Shell after shell is bursting right in the midst of the enemy camp, and great is the spoil for the Kingdom of God.'[1] Elim certainly saw itself as being engaged in a mighty battle against evil forces.

The report contains a foreshadowing of what was to become a creedal foundation within the Elim Pentecostal church – the Foursquare Gospel. Elim's leaders had visited Los Angeles and made contact with Aimee Semple McPherson, the founder of the Foursquare Church, based in the USA. This denomination was founded in 1927 with its headquarters in Los Angeles. Angelus Temple, the mother church of the denomination, was opened in 1923, through the ministry of Aimee. Foursquare refers to the four-fold ministry of Jesus.[2] The *Elim Evangel* first carried the Foursquare motto in its January 1925 edition. This also marked the occasion of the *Evangel* going to a fortnightly publication as opposed to monthly.

The report described four great canon-fire shots aimed at the great metropolis. The first shell was that of repentance: 'The old fashioned Gospel of repentance toward God and faith toward our Lord Jesus Christ is effecting the same results in this great city as it did when sounded out in Jerusalem some two thousand years ago.' This emphasises the role of Christ as Saviour. The second shell was said to be that of healing: 'The smoke is scarcely cleared before another, more startling, is released and HEALING of the body falls like a thunderbolt into the centre of counterfeit healing.' The reporter had in mind, particularly, the teachings of Mary Baker Eddy, the founder of the Christian Science movement.

The third shell is that of the baptism in the Holy Ghost.[3] 'Pentecostal showers are falling, and the same signs are given because the same loving Christ is still upon the throne.' It is interesting to note that this appears to be the first time within the *Elim Evangel* where reference is made to the baptism of the Holy Spirit without speaking in other tongues as being the initial evidence. The fourth shell is the proclamation of the coming of the Lord: 'Its searching message, supported by unmistakable signs in these last days declares to one and all that His coming is at hand.'[4]

Parting of the way between George and Stephen

While Stephen campaigned in Hendon, George continued at Barking. As has already been noted, Hendon was one of the last campaigns Stephen undertook for Elim. From 1926 onwards, he ministered almost exclusively within the ranks of the Assemblies of God. It would appear that Stephen was not altogether suited to work within the structures of what was increasingly becoming a centrally governed movement. He was altogether different from his younger brother. George was meticulous and precise in his administration. Together with E J Phillips, he developed a sound administration. Stephen chafed at such organised administration. There was also a difficulty regarding the provision of a house for Stephen and his family in

London. Cartwright reports that during the time that the Elim delegation was in Canada and the USA, it was agreed that Stephen should be more fully linked with Elim. He had been listed as a member of the Elim Pentecostal Alliance Council in the first edition of the *Elim Evangel*, but there is no record of him ever being ordained as a member of the Elim Evangelistic Band.[5] The confusion over dates of ordination and such matters, was typical of Stephen's casual approach. He was not an organised person.

There was voluminous correspondence between George Jeffreys and E J right until the time that George left Elim. The two corresponded with each other on a regular basis, sometimes corresponding daily for a protracted period of time. The huge amount of correspondence between them[6] revealed the frank, but close, manner of their relationship. 'Although Jeffreys was the leader, and E J carried out his policies, they would disagree on many topics and sometimes E J would persuade Jeffreys of a particular course of action, and, at other times, it was the other ways round.'[7] It is important to understand the nature of the relationship between Jeffreys and E J. The latter was certainly not a blinkered civil servant. He was a brilliant administrator who carried out Jeffreys' instructions to the letter. In his communications with E J over his brother Stephen, George lets E J know what he really thinks, 'being fully confident that E J will behave honourably and in the best interests of the Movement.'[8]

George agreed that Elim should take responsibility for Stephen's ministry. A group named 'The Full Gospel Forward Movement' was formed. This group consisted of E C W Boulton, E J Phillips and Ludwig Naumann. The latter was a businessman who worked for the Baltic Exchange. Signed on the 18th June 1925, the Agreement read as follows:

> Pastor Stephen Jeffreys agrees to devote his full time to conducting the missions or other appointments arranged for him by the said Council, to preach the Full Gospel.

For this, he shall receive a salary of Five Pounds (£5) per week, in addition to being allowed all necessary travelling expenses and the occupation of the house free from rent, rates, or taxes.[9]

In consideration of the above, all collections and offerings at all missions, together with all private gifts whatsoever to pastor Stephen Jeffreys or his wife are to be put to the funds of the Full Gospel Forward Movement Council. All correspondence addressed to Pastor Jeffreys to be opened by the said Council.

This agreement may be terminated by three calendar months' notice being given on any date by either party thereto.[10]

This agreement makes very interesting reading. It shows that there was some concern over Stephen's willingness (and his wife's) to keep any personal gifts to himself. The ink had hardly dried on the paper when Stephen wrote to Phillips informing him that he was unable to take on another large mission during the hot months. He conducted meetings at Surrey Tabernacle, a large, former Baptist church in South London. He then held a campaign in Pontypridd during his holidays in September, following which he held meetings in Notting Hill Gate to fulfil a promise he made to his friend Ben Griffiths of Peniel Chapel, which was not an Elim church. Stephen then went to Margate in November to conduct a campaign that was not associated with Elim. By this time, it was quite clear that the brothers were operating on different lines. Cartwright makes the observation that Stephen was being manipulated by those outside Elim, causing friction between himself and his younger brother.[11]

Inevitably, there came a parting of the ways between the two brothers that resulted in Stephen ceasing his campaigns for Elim and linking up with the newly formed Assemblies of God. Edward Jeffreys makes the following comment in his biography of Stephen: 'When my father left the Elim Movement it was for them a great loss, and many of God's dear saints were deeply grieved. They wept at his departure. But he had no alternative under the circumstances which existed at this time.'[12] However, the letters between George and E J reveal a different view to this. Stephen had clearly breached the agreement that had been signed by him under which he agreed to campaign for Elim. Edward Jeffreys is correct, however, in his statement that the departure of his father from Elim was a 'great loss' to them (Elim).

Stephen's departure as Elim's prime evangelist saw George taking over the evangelistic campaigns and becoming Elim's most active pioneer. But of Stephen, Canty writes movingly; writing in the 1980s, he comments:

> Stephen is remembered and loved until now for his compassion, wit and eloquence. His faith is still a standard to emulate. He is often in the mind's eye of hundreds, singing the old hymns, maybe bouncing on one foot, wiping his forehead which glistened with perspiration, then using his handkerchief above his head to the rhythm. His friend and pianist, Llewelyn Bell, would help him take off his shirt, which clung to him saturated with sweat, and use a towel upon him in the vestry.
>
> Twice daily, several days a week, perhaps every day, for weeks or months, sick people waited in endless lines to call upon his help, taking enormous toil of his concentration of mind and physical energy, either at home or abroad. His bodily resources were too small for his big heart and finally were exhausted, with a crippling form of arthritis being the price paid for his relief to thousands of such sufferers. He would rise to minister after having to rest in bed all day, ill.
>
> In 1934, the man whose face was often like that of his namesake's, Stephen the martyr, that of an angel, died aged 67.[13]

It is quite puzzling to the human mind that both George and Stephen, two of the greatest healing evangelists in British

Pentecostal history, suffered extreme physical illnesses. George developed diabetes. Yet, despite their own physical conditions, they were instrumental in the healing of many who suffered similar and sometimes, more extreme illnesses. One is reminded of the words of St Paul, when afflicted by a thorn in the flesh:

> Therefore, in order to keep me from becoming conceited, I was given a thorn in my flesh, a messenger of Satan, to torment me. Three times I pleaded with the Lord to take it away from me. But he said to me, 'My grace is sufficient for you, for my power is made perfect in weakness.' Therefore I will boast all the more gladly about my weaknesses, so that Christ's power may rest on me.[14]

East Ham

When Stephen went to conduct the campaign at Hendon, George continued at Barking for a final week. This was to be a major development within the advancement of Elim. As has been noted above, the two brothers were to end their working together in ministry and this meant that George took the role of leading evangelist and campaigner within Elim. For the rest of 1925, George concentrated on the East End.

At the end of April, George held a campaign in East Ham Town Hall. The *Evangel* carried the title: 'Revival Scenes at East Ham – George Jeffreys at the Town Hall'.[15] The report was written by E W Hare, the first editor of the *Elim Evangel* who left Elim in 1922 having been persuaded to believe in the doctrine of Ultimate Reconciliation (Universalism). He later repented of this aberration, and was received joyfully back into the Elim family. He did not, however, take up a position with Elim, but in 1926, went to Japan as an independent missionary.

The East Ham meetings continued for at least two months and a church was finally established there. A report appeared in the *Evangel*,[16] written by a local resident. In it, reference is made to a number of conversions and comments made on the joyful nature of the meetings. A somewhat cryptic comment is made concerning the effect of the meetings on those who were already Christians: 'We realise the difficulty at first of some of our Christian citizens in grasping the truths from the Word as preached by Pastor George Jeffreys, but the "Truth" is making them free. They have found that to be four-square on the Word of God, their blessings are multiplied to the full proof assurance of God's abiding presence and His cleansing, keeping and healing power.'

Ilford, Forest Hill and Canning Town

The new Elim Hall in Ripple Road, Barking, was opened on 17th May at which both George and Stephen ministered. The services were then led by Ernest Darragh and Miss Adams, both being members of the Elim Evangelistic Band. The following report appeared in the *Evangel*:

> We rejoice to report an ever-increasing spirit of revival at Barking where evangelists R.E. Darragh and Miss Adams have been labouring for a few months. The new Elim Hall is packed at every meeting, and often, large numbers are turned away unable to gain admittance. Since the campaigns in the opening months of the year, about four hundred have been baptised in the Holy Ghost, speaking in other tongues. Souls are being saved and bodies being constantly healed.[17]

An Elim Crusader branch was formed on the 24th August with 171 members joining that day. Within a few weeks, it had grown to more than 200.

Stephen Jeffreys held his last campaign for Elim in Forest Hill in August 1925. Henry Proctor, an elder of the Clapham church and a frequent writer in the *Evangel*, challenged a local newspaper concerning healing. A reporter expressed much cynicism concerning healing. He wrote a letter to the editor of the *Referee*, a local newspaper, as follows:

> In further reply to your challenge to Pastor Stephen Jeffreys in your issue of 2nd August, in which you promise that 'Should he make one single cure, we undertake to offer him our most sincere apologies, and to announce his success to all the world.' I have to inform you that on Sunday, 23rd August, Mrs Lilian Knowles, of 33 Kangley Bridge Road, Sydenham, demonstrated to a crowded audience such a case as you 'demand'. She testified that her daughter Queenie, now ten years of age, had been deaf and dumb from birth, and at about two years of age had been declared by Dr W J O'Brien of Sydenham, to be a permanently 'deaf mute'.
>
> The child, not only repeated from the platform at Trinity Church, Forest Hill, words she had been taught by her mother, but counted up to ten, as fingers were held up to her own initiative.
>
> We ask then, that you make this case known to all your readers, for the sake of thousands of sufferers who may also likely be healed through your kindly doing so.[18]

Stephen commenced the campaign, before George took over. This was to be the last official campaign that Stephen undertook for Elim. We must, before writing Stephen out of Elim history, mention his campaign at the Surrey Chapel, situated behind Walworth Road. The building seated in excess of 2,000 but was almost derelict. George Jeffreys wrote the report of his brother's campaign at the Surrey Tabernacle which commenced on 29th March. The report contains a great deal of military imagery. The opening sentence spoke of 'the pastor [Stephen Jeffreys] turning the Full Gospel gun among a most enthusiastic congregation something like eight hundred in number'.[19] Although in the report George mentions the great deal of work and planning that the overseers had put into renting the Surrey Chapel, most of the work was carried out in meticulous fashion by E J Phillips. George carries on with his military terminology:

> The whole land was surveyed, strategic points given much attention to, and ways and means of keeping the gunners well supplied carefully considered, while scouts and outposts were not forgotten. The launching of such a daring attack upon a stronghold of such magnitude called for great foresight by the Overseers including the busy Editor of the *Evangel*,[20] who had taken on the Herculean task, which could only be tackled in an atmosphere of prayer and faith.[21]

William Kay refers to the contrasting accounts of the reports of the Surrey Tabernacle meetings in Edward Jeffreys' book about his father and those of the same meetings in the *Elim Evangel*. In the first, there is no reference to George. 'This is Stephen's ministry and glory.'[22] Edward writes: 'The campaign went on each day for some months, and the Surrey Tabernacle became a spiritual rendezvous.'[23] In the *Evangel* report, George is given equal billing with his brother, even though, according to Kay, he preached less frequently.

The *Evangel* carried reports of campaigns held in Ilford and Canning Town in the same edition.[24] Both campaigns were conducted during the month of October. The Ilford campaign was conducted after the Canning Town campaign and George Jeffreys took over the Town Hall, which was filled to capacity. The doors were closed with hundreds of people unable to get in. An impromptu open-air meeting was held at which six people accepted Christ as Saviour. So great were the crowds that 'a large number of policemen were present to keep order'.[25]

The *Evangel* report includes local press reports of the campaign. They contain a description of the crowds who patiently lined up outside the Town Hall, waiting for the meeting to commence. With divine healing being advertised in the many posters and pamphlets displayed and distributed by the enthusiastic Elim Crusaders from Barking, and joined by students from the Elim Bible College, the report gives a description of the abject physical condition of many in the crowd:

> Pastor George Jeffreys, the Elim revivalist, held healing meetings at the Town Hall on Thursday. At half-past four in the afternoon, a dozen or so had lined up, and by six o'clock, the crowd was being controlled by half-a-dozen policemen, it extending halfway down Oakfield Road. Men arrived with children held lovingly in their arms, with bandages on their heads and legs. There also were cripples and others who obviously were suffering acutely from maladies of divers forms. A few minutes past six the crowd immediately outside the hall in the High Road, began humming a revivalist hymn, and before long there was a chorus of voices singing, 'All my sins are blotted out'.[26]

An Elim church was soon established in Ilford which has continued to grow for almost a century, and is today one of the largest Pentecostal churches in London.

It would appear that the Ilford and Canning Town campaigns were held almost in conjunction with one another. Canty states that the campaign in Canning Town commenced with an afternoon meeting in the Central Hall on the afternoon of 4th October 1925 and in the Town Hall at night. Canty comments: 'Sixty people came forward for salvation and [there was] no greater test of George Jeffreys' attempts to plant Welsh revival in spiritually arid country than that.'[27] Two local Methodist ministers were very supportive of the campaign and allowed their church buildings to be used for meetings when the Town Hall became unavailable owing to a trade union dispute.

By the end of 1925 there were seven Elim churches reported in London. There were large congregations at Clapham, Barking, East Ham and Ilford, and slightly smaller ones at Hendon, Canning Town and Forest Hill. Elim was certainly expanding.

Notes

[1] *Elim Evangel*, 16th March 1925, Vol 6, No 6, p67.

[2] Jesus Christ: The Saviour, the Healer, the Baptiser in the Holy Spirit and the Coming King.

[3] In this book, I use the terminology that is included in the original material from which quotations are taken. It was common parlance within the early Pentecostal Movement to use the designation 'Holy Ghost' where we would now use the term 'Holy Spirit'.

[4] *Elim Evangel*, 16th March 1925, Vol 6, No 6, p67.

[5] Cartwright, Desmond, *The Great Evangelists*, ibid, p62.

[6] This correspondence was collected by Desmond Cartwright and placed in chronological order and placed in the archives at Malvern.

[7] Kay, William, ibid, p104.

[8] Kay, William, ibid, p105.

[9] This was quite a substantial weekly payment in those days. E J himself took only £1:10 shillings (£1.50) at that time.

[10] Cartwright, Desmond, ibid, p62.

[11] Cartwright, Desmond, ibid, p63.

[12] Jeffreys, Edward, ibid, p69.

[13] Canty, George, ibid, p92.

[14] 2 Corinthians 12:7-9, NIV.

[15] *Elim Evangel*, 1st May 1925, Vol 6, No 9, pp106, 107.

[16] *Elim Evangel*, 1st September 1925, Vol 6, No 17, pp203, 204.

[17] *Elim Evangel*, 15th September 1925, Vol 6, No 18, p215.

[18] *Elim Evangel*, 15th September 1925, Vol 6, No 19, p214.

[19] *Elim Evangel*, 1st May 1925, Vol 6, No 9, pp104-105.

[20] This was a great understatement. 'Busy' hardly began to explain the immense amount of work that was being done in the background by E J. It must also be borne in mind that, at this time, he fulfilled three major roles within the growing denomination: secretary-general, editor of the *Elim Evangel* and principal of the Elim Bible College.

[21] *Elim Evangel*, 1st May 1925, ibid.

[22] Kay, William, ibid, p115.

[23] Jeffreys, Edward, ibid, p63. This creates the impression that Stephen, almost single-handedly, conducted the meetings. This is far from the case. Stephen campaigned in Pontypridd, Notting Hill Gate and Margate during this time.

[24] *Elim Evangel*, 16th November 1925, Vol 6, No 22, p256.

[25] *Elim Evangel*, 16th November 1925, ibid.

[26] *Ilford Recorder*, 6th November 1925.

[27] Canty, George, ibid, p94.

20
'Having the Time of My Life'

These are the words that George Jeffreys used to describe the sheer exhilaration that he experienced during the Plymouth campaign held in January 1926. The following note appeared in the second edition of the *Evangel* in the year 1926 and it included details of meetings held by Stephen Jeffreys in Greengate and George in Plymouth: 'Signs and wonders are being wrought in the name of the Lord by Pastor Stephen Jeffreys at Greengate Congregational Church and by Pastor George Jeffreys at Stonehouse Town Hall, Plymouth.'[1] These seemingly inconsequential references to the ministry of the two brothers reveal the chasm that was growing between their respective ministries.

Having been a former pastor of the Plymouth Elim Church (1981-86) I had wrongly believed that the Plymouth Elim Church was established as a result of George's phenomenal campaign in the city in January 1926. In researching for this book, I came across the fact that Elim had actually commenced in Plymouth in the autumn of 1924, when Stephen conducted a most successful campaign in Stonehouse, Plymouth. An Elim church was commenced in Stonehouse with Joseph Smith as its first minister. Some papers written by Leon Quest[2] came into my possession and they reveal a certain antagonism towards George Jeffreys. The information in the papers is difficult, at times, to comprehend owing to the somewhat rambling style of the writer. What is evident, and substantiated by reports in the *Evangel*, is that Stephen left a solid work in Plymouth which was greatly enhanced by the ministry of one of Elim's early leaders, Pastor Joseph Smith.

Stephen Jeffreys campaigned in Plymouth in the late autumn of 1924 and held his meetings in Stonehouse Town Hall, a suburb in the west of the city and near the large naval dockyard of Devonport. The *Evangel* reported on this campaign under the title 'Revival at Plymouth', with the subheading: 'Pastor Stephen Jeffreys in the Stonehouse Town Hall'.

> Most encouraging reports of the Plymouth Revival Campaign are to hand. At the time of writing it has only been in progress for one week, and it has been attended with remarkable conversions and healings. We are glad to say that up to the present, those deciding for Christ number four hundred, and this is being added to daily. The Town Hall is crowded out with people, who, as of old, are attracted to the services by the miracles wrought in the name of the Lord. In some services, the means of bringing them to the services are remarkable. One example, a lad of about sixteen years of age came last night (he could not find anyone to bring him to the afternoon healing service) seeking healing. He asked me to get the missioner to pray with him: soon after, he was walking without crutches. He had not been on his feet since he was an infant.
>
> Another lady, whose paralysed legs had to be supported with irons was prayed for. She was instantaneously delivered and was able to carry the irons home. A man who was bent was able to straighten himself after prayer and anointing. Another, from Devonport, came to one meeting doubled with arthritis and was healed after being ministered to. He walked round the hall, a free man, as the people clapped their hands at the demonstration of Divine power.[3]

The following month's *Elim Evangel* carried a well-written and full report by Mrs Howard Evans. The report referred to the very large number of responses to the gospel appeal and further substantiated the healings reported above. In addition, she wrote: 'Cancers and tumours were entirely removed, sight was restored and stammering tongues unloosed.'[4]

The author had for a long time believed that the Plymouth Elim Church was founded by George Jeffreys in 1926. After researching for this book, it is evident that the Plymouth Elim Church was established through the campaign held by Stephen Jeffreys which commenced on 8th November 1924 in the Stonehouse Town Hall. The campaign by George Jeffreys in 1926 (which commenced in the same hall) was a great expansion of the work commenced by his brother Stephen, some fifteen months previously. Leon Quest was at pains to point this out in his papers.[5] It is historically important to bear this in mind when considering George's campaign in Plymouth, which marked the commencement of his major campaigns outside London and brought him huge national press coverage. But before we embark on the Plymouth campaign, there is a further vitally important development that occurred around this time that we need to report.

The Elim Bible College

In his comprehensive work on the life of George Jeffreys, William Kay suggests that the commencement of the Assemblies of God in 1924 and the desire of the Carter brothers (Howard and John) to form a Bible college to train Pentecostal ministers was the spur that persuaded George Jeffreys and E J Phillips that Elim must do likewise.[6] I believe it was already in the hearts of Jeffreys and Phillips to start a Bible College. The following comment appeared in the November 1924 edition of the *Elim Evangel*:

> During the last eighteen months, the question of a Bible Training School for Elim has been before our minds, and at last, we have decided to venture in this, as we have

in other things, in the name of our Lord. We ask our readers to pray for three things: (1) That suitable premises be acquired for this purpose; (2) that funds for this most needful work be forthcoming; and (3) that wisdom be given to those responsible for the choice of the staff.[7]

In an article in the same edition, George Jeffreys states clearly the need for a Bible college for Elim, under the title: 'Send forth Labourers'. In this article, he sets out the need for trained workers to fulfil leadership roles in the new churches being planted and also to have trained ministers at hand so that the Elim work could be progressed throughout the nation. 'To expedite this work, we need a Training School, a place where the study of the Word of God can be combined with the practical side of evangelism.' He further states in this article that Elim's progress has been greatly hindered by the lack of such training facilities. The fact that this had been in the minds of Elim's leaders for a period of eighteen months shows that they did not proceed to such a decision by the determination of the Carter brothers to provide a similar training school for the newly formed Assemblies of God. Jeffreys concludes his article by imploring the readers of the *Evangel* to support Elim in this vital development:

The need is great and we must forge ahead. Suitable premises must be secured for the purpose of making it possible to speed up and take advantage of the soon-passing privileges. The call for training comes from those in all spheres of life. It demands our attention, and we supply the answer in the most practical form by procuring a Training School that stands foursquare on the Word of God. As I look back over the past, I cannot but feel grateful to God and our Elim friends for their faithfulness in prayer and practice. I have been more than encouraged by the measure of their support that has been given when I have deemed it necessary to appeal for a forward movement.[8]

A note was included in the following month's *Evangel* to keep the project of the Bible college very much in the minds of the readers.[9] The first *Elim Evangel* of 1925 reported a gift of £14:9:6d from the Letchworth Elim Church which was given towards the establishment of the Bible college project. It was a thanksgiving offering on the occasion of being able to open a building extension without having to incur debt. This shows that the Bible college project had struck a chord with the Elim family.

The Elim Bible College commenced in April 1925 and met in the minor hall of the Clapham Elim Church. The principal was E J Phillips. A notification appeared in the 1st May edition of the *Elim Evangel* with the news that the college had started. 'Like many other Elim undertakings, the school has begun in an unostentatious manner with five students.'[10] The report went on to express the following intention regarding the college: 'The Overseers of the Alliance are looking to the Lord to supply the need of a suitable home in London where the students can live and study under the same roof.' The first students were charged twenty shillings (£1) for board and lodgings with free tuition provided. While no guarantee was given that students would receive appointments with Elim after training, with each case being decided on its merits, the report made it clear that preference would be given to those who graduated from the school. The only reference to anything that could be remotely identified with a curriculum was the following: 'Studies in all things essential to the four square ministry of the Word will be given, as well as practical training in the ever increasing centres in London and elsewhere.'[11]

Later that year, the *Evangel* reported that a former convent had been purchased in Clapham; it was to become the home of the Elim Bible College for the next forty years. It was in Clarence Road that the Roman Catholic convent of the

Redemptorist Order was situated. Renamed 'Woodlands', it was said to be haunted and, according to Canty, 'some odd experiences did occur'. A magnificent gift of £1,200 came in with a perpetual mortgage from a private mortgagee. The cost of the convent was £6,350. The following typical Canty comment is worth including in full:

> Two men were sent to live there and work on cleaning and painting. One was a young Clapham Crusader, Herbert Court, and the other a former alcoholic now delivered and saved. They saw the nuns leave with a backward glance at the gloomy residence which would soon be filled with most un-nun-like student noise. The first batch were anything but sanctimonious, one of them walking on his hands on the parapet of the roof three floors above destruction.
>
> The college became a general centre for visitors from around the world. To make it pay, residents were accepted as well as students, often retired missionaries, mostly ladies, but also some young single working men. The students were not always happy to serve them, especially if they had been in charge of a church for a couple of years. 'Are you one of the washers-up?' asked such a boarder of one student. 'No, Madam, I am the Head Student!' he retorted indignantly. Another, bidden by the cook to clean her greasy pans, blandly asked if she had made the rock cakes for tea? He commented, 'My dear, look after yourself, you are far too delicate for such heavy work.' Perhaps such reactions can be forgiven in such very young men.[12]

The Plymouth campaign

George Jeffreys went to Plymouth in January 1926 to consolidate the work that had been commenced by his brother Stephen. It was not the original intention to commence a major campaign in the city. The meetings were held in the Stonehouse

Town Hall, a suburb of Plymouth, and were originally intended to last just a few days. What transpired in Plymouth was to set the pattern for Jeffreys' subsequent campaigns in major British cities from 1926 through to 1934. The *Evangel* report stated: 'The primary object of the special effort now on foot was to consolidate the assembly by a series of Bible Studies, and this has been established more quickly than anticipated by the extraordinary blessing of the Lord. The meetings are now in the full swing of a Foursquare Gospel revival.'[13]

Accompanying this report, and subsequent ones, in the *Evangel*, were a series of press reports, both local and national. Elim had learned very early on the importance of harnessing the press to its advantage. Leon Quest, however, was not greatly enamoured by the reported miracles in Stonehouse under George's ministry. He comments:

> I have the 1926 Elim Evangels of G. Jeffreys and the Plymouth campaign. What upset me is that most of the miracles that happened under S. Jeffreys were put into print (photo's) [sic], as if they had happened under G. Jeffreys. George Jeffreys was a man of print and publicity; Stephen never bothered, but I knew and saw the people healed and kneeled at their side as they breathed in the breath of Divine healing.[14]

Quest was an Elim minister for almost sixty years and was highly respected in Elim. Having experienced at close hand the difficulties that Elim went through in the late thirties and forties owing to the resignation of George Jeffreys and its impact on the Elim Movement, it is necessary to bear in mind his personal bias. Also, he had joined the Elim church in Plymouth shortly after it had been established through the campaign held by Stephen in 1924. However, personal bias can be a two-way issue. Boulton, in referring to the great Plymouth campaign, refers to the work 'already in existence'. However, this remark is slightly disingenuous as he prefaced his account of the campaign as follows: 'Eleven years had now elapsed since

Pastor George Jeffreys conducted his last special services in Plymouth.' He then refers to the 'remarkable happenings which took place at that time'. The inference is that George Jeffreys' campaign in 1926 was connected with his last visit to Plymouth. 'The presence of many of those who had been so richly blessed and healed in the 1915 meetings bore eloquent witness to the enduring character of the work then wrought.'[15] There is no reference in Boulton's book to the campaign held in 1924 by Stephen Jeffreys, nor to the assembly that had been established with Joseph Smith being the first pastor.

Notwithstanding Quest's cynicism on the one hand, nor of Boulton's unrestrained adulation on the other, it is undeniable that the Plymouth campaign conducted by George Jeffreys in January and February 1926 was quite sensational. The campaign, having commenced in the Stonehouse Town Hall, moved to the prestigious Plymouth Guildhall. This was filled to capacity. Apparently, the first week of the campaign was somewhat difficult: 'The first week of the campaign was what one might term "uphill work", although many precious souls were saved, bodies healed and several brothers and sisters received the baptism of the Holy Ghost in accordance to Acts 2:4.'[16] There was a notable change in the second week of the campaign. Ernest Gorringe, the writer of the *Evangel* report, refers to the second week as 'being the commencement of the revival we had all been praying for'. His report suggests that the meetings were quite different from the usual church services of the day. He notes that a woman who had been prayed for lay prostrate on the platform for about an hour. The following night, she testified of being healed from breast cancer.[17]

What was to be the final night of the campaign was held in the Plymouth Guildhall. A remarkable feature of Jeffreys' campaigns in the twenties and early thirties was the very favourable press attention he received. Gorringe includes in his report to the *Evangel* a cutting from a Sunday newspaper; Boulton includes the same report in his book, but makes no mention of its original source. I include the press report in full, as it gives us a valuable insight into how Jeffreys' campaigns galvanised towns and cities and had such a big impact upon the community within those places:

Not since Charles II, summoned his afflicted subjects to the old Church of St Andrew's to be cured of the 'King's Evil' by the touch of his royal hands, has Plymouth witnessed such scenes as have occurred at the faith-healing mission conducted by Pastor Jeffreys, a young Welsh revivalist. The culminating point was reached at a meeting held in Plymouth's historic Guild-hall,[18] situated but a few yards from where Charles officiated as a faith-healer many centuries ago. The sick, halt, blind and lame flocked from over a wide area, charabancs even being run from Cornwall, to participate in the streams of healing power which are declared to flow from the pastor's hands.[19]

Such wonderful things have been claimed that many ministers were included in the vast congregation, and medical men were also numbered among those who had been attracted there by curiosity.

The healing was not performed until the end of the service, which was characterised by great earnestness occasionally rising to the heights of typical Welsh revivalism. Pastor George Jeffreys is 'powerful in prayer', as he would be described in his native Wales, and his Gospel addresses are charged very fully with that cascade-like eloquence and picturesque idiom which marked Evan Roberts and all his successors in religious revivalism.

A woman, bed-ridden for thirty-eight years with an internal complaint which necessitated the wearing of instruments, presented herself on his platform to thank him publicly for what he had been able to do. 'I am cured', she said to him, 'but what am I to do about the instruments?' The revivalist replied, 'The faith which cured your disease can also remove the instruments,' and the woman went home fully believing. That night she slept as she had never slept before for thirty-eight years, and in the morning, so it is declared, she found the instruments on her bed when she awoke.

Even sceptical policemen, whose duty it is to regulate the throng, have been swept off their feet by what they have seen and heard. One night two girls, one blind and the other dumb, inquired their way to the service, of the officer nearby. An hour or so later he was amazed when the couple returned to him, literally dancing for joy, the dumb girl speaking and the blind girl seeing. A young woman tells how a serious affection of the eyes was banished by the Divine power wielded by the Pastor, and dozens of others relate stories of how he cured them by like means of weak lungs, gastric troubles, bronchitis, catarrh and neuritis, as well as many other complaints.

Faith and prayer are the two great ingredients of the missioner's prescription. Those who have visited his extraordinary services say that they are pervaded by an atmosphere that is too elusive to be pictured in words.[20]

What was intended to be the last night of the campaign became the stepping stone for a huge advancement in that the massive Drill Hall was booked for two weeks and was filled to capacity each night. While writing to E J from Plymouth, Jeffreys reported:

I am having the time of my life. Souls are continually flocking to Christ, most startling and marvellous healings, whilst yesterday hundreds were turned away from the town hall an hour before starting time. An average of about forty souls a day are being saved. Those who were cripples walked in the service last night. The ambulance brought one and arrangements had been made for it to come for her. However, she walked home. This is the greatest healing service yet.[21]

The Plymouth campaign was foundational in that it set a pattern for further major campaigns throughout the country that climaxed in the great Birmingham campaign of 1930. The beginnings were difficult and somewhat small, but following miraculous healings, the numbers grew so dramatically that larger and larger halls in the same city were hired and filled to capacity.

Notes

[1] *Elim Evangel*, 15th January 1926, Vol 7, No 2, p23.
[2] Leon Quest was a much-respected minister within Elim and served on a number of Conference committees. He, and his brother-in-law, Fred Cloke, were members and trustees of Plympton Free Methodist Church. Cloke, was to serve for a short time on the Executive Council of Elim. Douglas served for almost sixty years as an Elim pastor.
[3] *Elim Evangel*, December 1924, Vol 5, No 12, p282.
[4] *Elim Evangel*, 1st January 1925, Vol 6, No 1, pp4,5.
[5] Quest, Leon, *The Early History of the Elim Pentecostal Church as I knew it* (22nd May 1982) and *Precious Memories of Elim* (November 1980). Papers held by the author which will be transferred to the Elim Archives, Malvern, on completion of book.
[6] Kay, William, ibid, pp119,120.
[7] *Elim Evangel*, December 1924, Vol 5, No 12, p256.
[8] Jeffreys, George, 'Send Forth Labourers', *Elim Evangel*, November 1924, Vol 5, No 11, pp258,259.
[9] *Elim Evangel*, December 1924, Vol 5, No 12, p281.
[10] *Elim Evangel*, 1st May 1925, Vol 6, No 9, p102.
[11] *Elim Evangel*, 1st May 1925, ibid.
[12] Canty, George, ibid, p86.
[13] *Elim Evangel*, 1st February 1926, Vol 7, No 23, pp26,27.
[14] Quest, Leon, ibid.
[15] Boulton, E C W, ibid, p186.
[16] Gorringe, Ernest, *Elim Evangel*, 15th February 1926, Vol 7, No 4, pp39,40.
[17] Gorringe, Ernest, ibid.
[18] Point of interest: the author, while being the pastor of the Plymouth Church (1981-86) conducted carol services and a number of Sunday evening celebration and evangelistic services in the same Guildhall, which was filled on each occasion.

[19] Unlike the response to Charles, Plymouth remained loyal to Elim and a very strong and large congregation remains in the city to this day. Plymouth was not a royalist city and fought for Cromwell in the civil war.

[20] *Birmingham Sunday Mercury*, 31st January 1926, quoted in the *Elim Evangel*, 15th February 1926, Vol 7, No 4, p40.

[21] Letter from G J to E J P in January 1926.

21
Aimee Semple McPherson and the Royal Albert Hall

Following on from Jeffreys' very successful campaign in Plymouth, the revivalist went to Vazon in Guernsey for a few days. Although he conducted a short campaign there, it was a much lower-key affair and it gave him opportunity to have a much-needed rest. This was a turning point in George's approach to campaigning in the major cities of the country. Kay makes the pertinent comment: 'This campaign, now that George was out of the shadow of Stephen, was the first that seems to have brought about the realisation that whole cities could be stirred by the spiritual excitement of these huge meetings.'[1]

Canty also refers to the Plymouth campaign as being 'Elim's full arrival'.[2] A brief crusade was held in St George's Hall, St Peter Port, Guernsey's capital. More than 100 people received Christ and as many as 900 of the island's small population attended the meetings. George was to return to the island in 1934 and 1936. Vazon, the first church, was followed in 1934 by Delancey, which began as a Sunday school in the Wesleyan Church which had just been bought by Elim. Then the Eldad Congregational Church, Union Street, St Peter Port was established as an Elim church. In 1950, St Helier, Jersey came into the Elim list. Canty comments: 'These bare bones of facts and dates have to be clothed with the fullness of the work of the Holy Spirit over the years through loyal prayer, work, preaching, pastoral care, many a campaign, with many a pastor and dedicated members.'[3] My next volume will contain a chapter on the remarkable story of the preservation of the Elim churches in Guernsey from 1940 to 1945 when the Channel Islands became the only part of the British Isles that suffered from Nazi occupation.

The period between 1926 and 1930 was undoubtedly George Jeffreys' 'golden era'. Great annual conventions were held at the Royal Albert Hall, sometimes three times in one year. He travelled the length and breadth of the United Kingdom, going 'from the south coast of England up to Scotland and from Yorkshire to Ireland'.[4] He attracted huge crowds, and some of the most prestigious halls in the country were hired and filled. Halls such as the Cory Hall, Cardiff, Brangwyn Hall, Swansea, the Drill Hall, Bournemouth, the Guild Hall, Southampton, Portsmouth City Hall, the Usher Hall, Edinburgh, the Queen's Hall and Drill Hall, Carlisle, St Andrews Hall, Glasgow and Birmingham Town Hall, followed by the Odeon Ice Skating Rink, Sparkbrook, culminating in a two weeks campaign in the huge Bingley Hall, Birmingham.

The social conditions in the country at this time were very challenging indeed. 'The war had bled Britain almost white in money and man-power. Hollow-cheeked unemployment haunted the streets. The coal strike and General Strike in this year of 1926 saw mobs smashing up vehicles, police charging them with batons, and the economy sinking.'[5] Kay provides us with a comprehensive account of the historical and social conditions that were prevalent in Britain at the time. Referring to the General Strike of 1926, he writes:

> A bitter and mounting dispute between mineworkers and owners came to a head. It had simmered in the background during the first part of the 1920's but negotiations eventually foundered. 'It would be possible to say without exaggeration that the miners' leaders were the stupidest men in England', said Lord Birkenhead, 'if

we had not frequent occasion to meet the owners.' Both sides were intransigent, the miners toughened by their hard labour and the owners for greed by high profit. The Government attempted to head off the action until, with Churchill as Chancellor of the Exchequer and after a debate in the House of Commons, it came to a point of decision: no fresh money to buy time for additional negotiation. The strike was called for 3 May 1926 and, although it centred on the mineworkers, spread out to other unions and so became general.[6]

Although the General Strike lasted for only two weeks, after which the TUC called the strike off, it had a profound effect upon the morale of the working class throughout the country. Class distinctions seem to have become more entrenched and the teachings of Marx and Engels seemed to resonate within sections of the working class, particularly the miners of South Wales. 'It left a legacy of bitterness in the coalfields, and both the Jeffreys brothers must have been acutely aware of feelings within the mining community even if they themselves, at this stage in their lives were largely detached from it.'[7]

Liverpool

It had been intended that later in the month of January 1926, Jeffreys would have campaigned in Liverpool. Such was the blessing and success in Plymouth, however, that E J advised the postponement of the Liverpool campaign. The campaign eventually commenced on Sunday, 14th March, at a disused chapel in Windsor Street, formerly used by the Holiness Movement. The initial report in the *Evangel* is quite short, but accompanied by a number of press reports. *The Yorkshire Observer*, 26th March 1926 under the title 'Remarkable scenes at Disused Chapel', gives a description of what must have been extremely strange goings on in a Christian service in those days:

> Extraordinary scenes are reported at a disused Liverpool chapel, formerly belonging to the Holiness Movement, where services are being conducted by a young pastor named George Jeffreys. Members of the congregation claim that, by anointing worshippers with olive oil and praying over them after the laying-on of hands, the pastor has effected miraculous cures of various ailments. One man and several women, after the anointing, are said to have fallen on the floor of the church and, at the end of a period of apparent unconsciousness, declared that they had benefited.[8]

Another press report in the same edition of the *Evangel* heads up a paragraph with the dramatic and startling title: 'Patients Swoon at Pastor's Touch'. The press reports all spoke of the huge crowds of people that attended the services and described the unabated joy and enthusiasm of those in attendance. After a short while, the Windsor Street chapel became far too small to accommodate the huge crowds that were attending the services, but unable to get in. Eventually, the services were moved to a boxing stadium in the city and George preached from the ring. The local newspapers, and some national ones, posted photographs of the scene with headings such as 'Jeffreys in the Ring Again'.

Aimee

Jeffreys, along with his brother Stephen and Boulton, McWhirter and Darragh, had visited the USA and Canada in 1924, where they not only campaigned, but also acquainted themselves with the various American Pentecostal movements. They visited Los Angeles and attended services held at the newly built Angelus Temple in Echo Park. Jeffreys did not preach at the Temple, but he was introduced to the young evangelist that had brought this huge church complex into existence – Aimee Semple McPherson. To say that she was a phenomenon in the Christian Church in the US is a vast understatement. She created a mixture of wild adulation to outright cynicism and opposition. She not only thrilled the crowds, but also managed to create a scandal that shadowed her ministry from that point onwards.

It is claimed that she changed the traditional Church scene in America to a huge extent. Matthew Avery Sutton, in his book, gives evidence to this claim in the very title: 'Aimee Semple McPherson and the Resurrection of Christian America'.[9] Aimee Elizabeth Kennedy was born to James and Mildred Kennedy near Ingersoll, Ontario, Canada on 9th October 1890. Her father was a farmer, and her mother worked for the Salvation Army. She was raised in the Canadian countryside and this background helped her to forge a resolute, determined and tough personality that was often underrated because of her very feminine appearance and outlook. In 1908 she married Robert Semple, a fiery young preacher and Irish immigrant. 'A local newspaper described the 'very popular' bride as a gold medallist in elocution', who 'has always been a cheerful contributor at local entertainments.'[10]

Semple responded to God's call to mission work in China and Aimee, conscious of God's own call upon her life for ministry, accompanied her husband when he left Chicago for China in 1910. Within a few months of arriving in China, however, Robert contracted malaria and died. A short time after her husband's death, Aimee gave birth to a daughter, whom she named Roberta. Her situation was grim, to say the least. She eventually managed to return to California and continued to New York where she met up with her mother and the Salvation Army. Her tragic circumstances caused her to doubt her calling and question her Pentecostal experience. 'Lonely and desperate, she met Harold McPherson, a middle-class business man who provided the security she wanted. They were soon married. She gave birth to a second child, Rolf, yet she remained unhappy.'[11]

According to her own personal testimony, Aimee became increasingly aware of God's call to leave her comfortable situation to preach the Word. According to Sutton, 'the hound of Heaven kept after her'.[12] She took her children and left McPherson to return to her parents' home in Canada. She never returned to her husband, but it is unclear whether they became divorced. Aimee set out to evangelise America and crisscrossed the nation in her 'Gospel Car'. After travelling along the eastern seaboard and the southern states, she headed west and arrived in Los Angeles in December 1918 and felt the Lord calling her explicitly to remain and minister in the 'City of Angels'. There she evangelised with astonishing results and developed a healing ministry. She soon gathered a large following and determined to build a large wooden tabernacle for worship. The plans changed as she felt that the structure needed to be more permanent and elaborate. She appealed for finance and gained the support of wealthy benefactors. She travelled a great deal and held revival meetings where she was able to raise funds for the building of Angelus Temple. The elaborate and huge building, seating more than 5,000, was dedicated and opened in 1923.

Jeffreys obviously made an impression on Aimee and he was influenced by her four-fold presentation of Christ as Saviour, Healer, Baptiser in the Holy Spirit and Coming King. It appears that Aimee Semple McPherson was the first person to use the term 'foursquare' in her title. Jeffreys had also begun to emphasise the foursquare aspect to his preaching. This was in contrast to the five-fold gospel[13] that was prevalent in the earliest Pentecostal churches that had the name 'Apostolic Faith' connected with them. These churches included within their Fundamentals a definite experience of sanctification.

Jeffreys introduced the 'foursquare' concept into his teaching and his campaigns and in 1926 he set up the Foursquare Gospel Churches. This was with the purpose of attracting independent Pentecostal churches into Elim. This was to be the forerunner of Elim Church Incorporated, which has a number of independent churches that are linked to Elim but retain the trusteeship of their own buildings and are not part of the Elim Full Gospel Association. Tom Walker, a past general superintendent of Elim, described it as being 'a part of the wheel, but not in the hub'.[14]

George was aware of his detractors and wrote to Phillips from Plymouth with the complaint: 'We hear down here that I have made a new sect, of which I am the pope and my aim is to smash the Assemblies of God.'[15] There was a desire to incorporate into Elim those churches that had not been founded by Jeffreys nor the Evangelistic Band. The setting up of the Foursquare Gospel Churches of the British Isles was intended to solve that problem but was later to contribute to the dispute that caused huge governmental problems for Elim. It created two sections within the one movement 1) Those churches under direct Elim government, and 2) Self-governing churches. The reporting of this organisation in the 1st July 1926 edition of the *Evangel* shows both the strength and weakness of the organisation:

> The Church of the Foursquare Gospel with its comprehensive evangel of Saviour, Healer, Baptiser and Coming King, is now fairly launched. The word 'Foursquare' is catching like wildfire, as the happy acknowledgement of a faith in the full Gospel of our Lord Jesus Christ. Those churches and ministers who have already perused the constitution, will have been impressed by the gracious reconciliation of the *real spirit of liberty* and *constitutional government*. As has already been pointed out, every encouragement is given to ministers to spread the glorious message along the lines of their personal vision. The only bonds in this new union of churches and ministers are the bonds of Christian love and fellowship…There is now an open door for a *common platform for all* who preach the full Gospel. No church or assembly would be debarred from entering, providing of course its teaching and practice is in accordance with the Constitution of the Foursquare Gospel Churches. [original italics]

A definite link was established between George Jeffreys and Aimee Semple McPherson around the term 'foursquare'. The year 1926 was already turning out to be an astonishing one of growth and advancement for Elim when, quite unexpectedly, Aimee phoned the Elim offices and offered to preach for the movement. This offer was immediately accepted and Elim's planned convention was radically changed. The planned Easter Convention was to be at the Surrey Tabernacle that seated 2,000. Kay states simply that the housing of the convention was changed from the Surrey Tabernacle to the Royal Albert Hall. Canty, in his unique style, presents a far more appealing element to the decision to hold the Easter Convention in the Royal Albert Hall.

But first, we must chronologically present the events. Aimee Semple McPherson had been given a holiday to tour the Holy Land by her church. She phoned the Elim offices in London, offering to hold evangelistic services in the capital. Charles Kingston gave a full, if somewhat mystical, report of the background to Mrs McPherson's short campaign in London. He gave full details of the circumstances that led to the services at the Surrey Chapel in early March. Aimee had crossed the Atlantic and visited Paris. She was inundated by requests for meetings, including one from Elim. All were turned down. Kingston records that she had left Paris on a transcontinental express train when, in the middle of the night, she became conscious of the fact that God had work for her to do in London. She returned to Paris and made her phone call to the Elim offices. Elim (or should I say, E J!) had just five days to put on the campaign. An enormous amount of work was completed in a remarkably short period of time, and Kingston added the following brief newspaper report:

> A whirlwind revival struck Walworth yesterday afternoon, when Mrs Aimee Semple McPherson mounted the pulpit of the Surrey Tabernacle and delivered a 15,000 word sermon under the hour – a

veritable Niagara of eloquence during which she never once hesitated for a word. She spoke of her great ambition – to proclaim the name of Jesus to every creature in the world.[16]

Kingston goes on to give a brief description of each of the four evening campaign services. In the first service she told her life story. Kay comments: 'She was a thoroughly Pentecostal evangelist who prayed for the sick and spoke in tongues, and she brought with her the uncompromising vehemence of the cultural wars she felt herself to be fighting for America's soul.' This echoes Sutton's premise that Aimee Semple McPherson was a major player in what he termed 'the resurrection of Christian America'. Kay adds the following comment: 'Evolution and all its implications were, to her mind, alien to the central founding narrative of the Pilgrim Fathers and godly America, and it is likely that her anti-modernistic attitudes rubbed off on Jeffreys and early Elim.'[17] Jeffreys and 'early Elim' were thoroughly fundamental in their beliefs, so I do not think that Aimee's anti-modernistic attitudes rubbed off on them but, rather, confirmed their already established theological positions.

Aimee's preaching was both simple and profound. She avoided theological clichés and got straight to the heart of her subject. On the third night of the campaign, she focused on prayer, a subject that is not usually one that would be the major topic in an evangelistic sermon. She presented the subject in a novel way. Kingston gave the following summation of her sermon:

> The next day, the crowds gathered again. At the afternoon service, the subject 'Prayer' spoke to all hearts. 'It was,' said the evangelist, 'like pulling the bell rope, and way up in heaven, the bell began to ring. Ding-dong, ding-dong, and God said "Hush you cherubim, keep quiet you seraphim, lay down your harps, you angels. There is a soul pulling on the bell rope of prayer." The rope,' continued the speaker, 'hangs just over your head.

Lift up your hand, brother, sister, and somewhere up in heaven the bell will ring ding-dong! ding-dong!' Many at the end of this service came to the altar and reached up their hand to pull the bell-rope of prayer for salvation.[18]

At the end of the campaign, Aimee agreed to return to London following her vacation in the Holy Land. The problem facing Elim was where to find a hall large enough to house the anticipated thousands who would want to attend.

The Royal Albert Hall

We return to Canty's explanation and description of how it came about that Jeffreys came to agree to booking the Royal Albert Hall for the annual Easter Convention. According to Canty, the key player in this decision was Herbert Court, a young Elim probationary minister who, while wielding a paintbrush in his hand at Elim Woodlands, the home of the Elim Bible College, entered into conversation with George Jeffreys. Court had his mind on conventions. He had attended the Aimee Semple McPherson campaign at the Surrey Tabernacle where 2,000 seats were filled and hundreds of people came to faith in Christ. 'Conventions had been, and still were, the main Pentecostal occasions by which the Movement not only progressed but virtually existed. Churches were few, and those hungering and thirsting after righteousness, especially leaders of small groups, longed for help, instruction, teaching and fellowship.'[19] Conventions seemed to provide the answer to these needs.

Canty claimed that Jeffreys saw further than this. Conventions were more to him than a good time being had by all. 'He had swung the Surrey Tabernacle event in a new direction – a demonstration of Pentecostal things for the benefit of the world in general.'[20] It would appear that from this point onwards, Jeffreys treated conventions and campaigns alike. Whether it was called a convention or campaign, Jeffreys was determined to declare and demonstrate Pentecostal truths embodied within the Foursquare Gospel. Canty states that Court had a mind which approached things from unexpected angles, and already had thoughts about conventions past and conventions present, when George Jeffreys walked in on him to see how work was progressing on the college. Their chat led to the Surrey Tabernacle convention and George voiced his problem of finding a venue large enough for the next London attraction and public enough to make it a true demonstration. Court, who knew London very well, said: 'You won't find many places bigger than what you have used already, except, of course, Kensington, the Royal Albert Hall.' Apparently, Jeffreys did not snatch at the proposal for it would have been a very bold preacher who would commit himself to London's largest concert hall.[21]

The Royal Albert Hall consumed George's thinking and excitement grew within him as he pondered further on the prospect of holding a great convention in the nation's premier concert hall. The availability and willingness of Aimee Semple McPherson no doubt allayed his concerns about filling the great hall.

> Prayer was added to thought. Faith was added to prayer. On Sunday night, Easter 1926, for the first time 'the tongues people' presented themselves before London's limelight. Thousands streamed in, filling boxes, galleries, stalls and arena, while Elim music flowed from the famous organ under the fingers of Ron Cooper. One thing everybody felt – the Elim family had come home. It had begun in a far-off Welsh village, and now had burst on the fashionable scene of west London.[22]

The Royal Albert Hall was booked for Easter Sunday evening and all day Monday. The theme of the convention was, naturally enough, the Four-Square Gospel. Aimee McPherson spoke on the subject of 'Jesus the Saviour' on the Sunday evening. John Leech spoke on 'Jesus the Baptiser' on Easter Monday morning, followed by George Jeffreys in the afternoon speaking on 'Jesus the Healer'. Aimee spoke again at the final service, on the subject of 'Jesus the Coming King'.

> She dealt with this entrancing subject in a masterly manner, first sweeping away 'the refuge of lies' ... by proving from the Scripture that it was neither at Pentecost, nor at the fall of Jerusalem, nor is it at conversion, nor at the death of the believer, nor by the world-wide preaching of the Gospel, that the Coming is fulfilled, but that there will be a literal coming of 'this same Jesus in like manner as He went up into heaven'.[23]

From that moment, the Royal Albert Hall became a prime feature in Elim's history. George Jeffreys preached there nearly fifty times until 1939. War and internal strife halted the demonstrations, but in 1945 Elim begun its festivals again. Elim continued to use this great hall for its Easter Monday celebrations right up until the end of the century. It was a place of pilgrimage to many of us who made the annual visit to London from all parts of the United Kingdom. The memories of those great annual celebrations in Britain's premier concert hall remain indelibly in the minds of those of us who had the privilege of attending them.

Notes

[1] Kay, William, ibid, p136.
[2] Canty, George, ibid, p98.
[3] Canty, George, ibid, p98.
[4] Kay, William, ibid, p126.
[5] Canty, George, ibid, p98.
[6] Kay, William, ibid, pp140,141.
[7] Kay, William, ibid.
[8] *Elim Evangel*, 1st April 1926, Vol 7, No 7, p77.

[9] Sutton, Matthew Avery, *Aimee Semple McPherson and the Resurrection of Christian America* (London/Cambridge, MA: Harvard University Press, 2007), Kindle edition.

[10] Sutton, Matthew Avery, ibid, Loc 94.

[11] Sutton, Matthew Avery, ibid, Loc 118.

[12] Sutton, Matthew Avery, ibid, Loc 126

[13] The five-fold gospel was the addition to the four-fold (Saviour, Healer, Baptiser and Coming King) of Jesus the Sanctifier.

[14] The author heard Mr Walker say this on many occasions, especially in his lectures to his students at the Elim Bible College. I was a student at the college, then at Capel, 1967-69.

[15] Letter G J to E J, 20th January 1926.

[16] Kingston, Charles, *Elim Evangel*, 15th March 1926, Vol 7, No 6, pp61,64.

[17] Kay, William, ibid, p123.

[18] Kingston, Charles, *Elim Evangel*, ibid.

[19] Canty, George, ibid, p102.

[20] Canty, George, ibid, p102.

[21] Canty, George, ibid, p103.

[22] Canty, George, ibid.

[23] Proctor, Henry, *Elim Evangel*, 1st May 1926, Vol 7, No 9, p101.

22
Expansion in the Provinces

In recording the many achievements of Jeffreys in his revival campaigns throughout the country, Kay refers to the immense efforts and support of those who worked behind the scenes. He shares a great admiration with the author of the highly gifted secretary-general – E J Phillips. He was the organising genius behind the campaigns and arranged matters from the hiring of the great halls, especially the Royal Albert Hall, to the striking floral arrangements at the Royal Albert Hall meetings. Kay refers to the large volume of correspondence that passed between Jeffreys and Phillips, mostly to do with money and finding the right pastors to be appointed in the new churches that were opened as a result of Jeffreys' campaigns. The letters between them show how financially tenuous things were at this time.[1] The correspondence between the two leaders was voluminous and shows the depth of the relationship between them, as we have already seen above.[2]

George Canty wrote of E J:

> He was logical and methodical despite being pre-
> occupied with details. He wore butterfly collar fashion
> of a slightly earlier day. His rather small eyes in his lean
> countenance (always with a high colour), gimleted you
> through his steel rimmed glasses and, as one man said,
> as if the butterfly collar was about to fly at you. I would
> judge it a false impression as I found him very nice to
> work with.[3]

Bournemouth

As already noted, 1926 proved to be a truly momentous year in Elim's history. Apart from the campaigns themselves, churches were established and buildings erected or bought. In the final *Evangel* of the year, a member of the Elim Evangelistic Band (most likely, E J Phillips) reported on ten buildings that had been dedicated to the Elim work during the year. They included purpose-built halls at Barking, East Ham, Rayleigh (Essex), and Bangor. Another Elim Tabernacle was opened in Belfast. It was to become known as the Ulster Temple. This magnificent building is situated on the Ravenhill Road, opposite the Ormeau Park. For many years, this was the largest Elim building in Northern Ireland and was used for the great Christmas conventions. It was to become, for many years, Elim's largest church in the Province of Ulster.

Joseph Smith wrote a report of the opening of the Ulster Temple. 'Pastor George Jeffreys in Ulster where he first hoisted the Elim Flag' was the title of his report. E J added an editorial comment: 'Pastor George Jeffreys, Founder and Leader of "Elim" in the British Isles, conducted last month, the opening campaign of the new Belfast Tabernacle. He was assisted by evangelists R.E. Darragh, James McWhirter and Mr. Carey Davies, accompanist of the Party. The first meeting was on Sunday, June 13th.' In his report, Smith explained that the purpose in erecting such a large building was to hold major campaigns and also to accommodate the ever increasing crowds that gathered for the Belfast conventions. The campaign lasted for eighteen days and the new building was filled to capacity each night. In his report, Smith includes the words of a chorus that was very popular and sung each night of the campaign. It was written by Mr Norman Black (1903-93) a Crusader and organist of the Elim Tabernacle, Belfast. (I understand by this that he was a member of the first Elim tabernacle in Melbourne Street.)[4] The words of the song are as follows:

The Foursquare Gospel is true, yes, I believe it, don't you?
That Jesus saves me from all sin, gives His Holy Spirit to dwell within.
He heals my body from all pain, and soon He's coming back again,
Hallelujah! Hallelujah! I believe the Foursquare Gospel.[5]

In addition to these newly built churches, five other buildings were either bought or leased and housed large congregations. These were at Bournemouth, Plymouth, Bermondsey, Liverpool and Hull. Large congregations were established in these churches following campaigns led by George Jeffreys. The *Evangel* reported that there was a weekly congregation of 1,000 following the great Plymouth campaign. The pastor that was eventually appointed there following the 1926 campaign was Percy LeTissier, a Guernsey man who became well known throughout Elim.[6]

After the Royal Albert Hall, Jeffreys turned his gaze southwards, once more. This time it was to the beautiful seaside town of Bournemouth. 'He encouraged Elim people to combine attendance at his Bournemouth campaign with their summer holidays.'[7] This was done through a prominent advertisement placed in the 15th May edition of the *Evangel*. It read as follows: 'During the months of July and August, A GREAT REVIVAL AND HEALING CAMPAIGN will be conducted by Pastor George Jeffreys in a large tent IN BOURNEMOUTH. *Arrange to spend your summer holidays at Bournemouth*.' The tent was situated at the tram terminus in the seaside town.

The challenges that faced Elim in establishing viable churches with healthy congregations following Jeffreys' great campaigns were enormous. 'The real story of Elim is its struggles after campaigns to keep together immature converts who had no previous Christian loyalties. Buildings became a critical, if sometimes uninteresting chapter.'[8] Although, as we have seen, a few new buildings were erected, in the main, Elim could only take over discarded chapels. Canty's comment is wry and telling: 'It was like dressing in cast-off clothing.'[9] These buildings had to be paid for, and this burden was laid largely on the converts and new members themselves. There were some gifts and legacies given and these were greatly appreciated and ploughed directly into Elim's property portfolio. It must be also borne in mind that the Irish churches numbered around twenty-four by this time, and a number of these were large and established congregations. They contributed in no small part to the finances required for Elim's building programme.

The tent, pitched at Moordown, at first seemed a somewhat unsuitable location. Canty, in his own inimitable style, describes the seating arrangements in the tent: 'The seating, consisting of seven-foot planks with three-inch back rests supported on iron bar frames, was known to leave weals on the human anatomy. The same seats were sometimes installed in Elim halls, proving the sterling Christian saintliness of the users!'[10] George Jeffreys had commenced his Elim campaigns using a tent in Monaghan which they later purchased and used on many occasions in his Ulster campaigns. But this was respectable, middle-class Bournemouth!

Elim's offer to respectable Bournemouth residents of a long ride in a chattering tram to a flapping tent and seats as bad as a hair shirt, no great organ, no surpliced choir and no beauty, only to hear sermons, lacked something of the science of show business. However, as a tent, it was done as well as tents could be done. Not as one has seen some Gospel efforts, with seats of every type spread around – camp stools, armchairs, kitchen bentwood; spindle, deck and upholstered chairs – like a furniture auction sale room perched the best way possible on the bumps and waves of brick sites and with a D.C. generator throbbing incessantly for the preacher to do battle with, plus crackling PA equipment. George

> Jeffreys hated the primitive loud speaker systems of
> those days. But you didn't get rained on in his tents![11]

Canty was himself a noted evangelist within Elim and conducted many campaigns, a number of them in a ubiquitous tent. He had a unique style in which he used his many talents in the proclamation and demonstration of the gospel message.

After the usual slow start, the campaign soon began to make its mark on Bournemouth and the tent was ultimately packed to its 1,200 capacity. George Jeffreys held an evangelistic service each evening as well as afternoon healing meetings. George not only preached the gospel, but also gave lengthy Bible teaching. It was not long before upwards of 600 people had responded to the gospel invitation and the campaign continued to make a huge impression on this sedate seaside town. After seven weeks in Moordown, the tent was moved to Boscombe, even though by then it was September and by the ninth week, 1,500 people had turned to Christ. As a result of the many healings and miracles that took place, the tent became far too small. The following report appeared in the Bournemouth *Guardian*, 31st July 1926:

> The vicinity of the Moordown tram terminus has assumed an aspect of considerable activity during the last week, and scenes of religious enthusiasm has been witnessed, conducted by Pastor George Jeffreys, of the Elim Alliance of Preachers, in a large tent which has been erected there. He is a Welsh revivalist who believes in Divine healing. Large congregations have assembled and large numbers of people suffering from all kinds of bodily afflictions have been making their way to the tent with the aid of walking sticks, whilst others have been pushed in bath chairs. Pastor Jeffreys is the Founder of the Alliance and the Elim Bible College, London, where ministers are being trained to send all over the country with their message of Divine healing.

Many miraculous healings have been achieved, and 70 conversions have taken place. At a well-attended meeting on Thursday afternoon, a 'Guardian' representative heard many testimonials given by a number of Winton and Moordown residents. One lady remarked that she had not been able to walk for five years, and as a result of her faith and attendance at the services she had been restored. Another, a girl of tender years, intimated that she had suffered from a curvature of the spine since she was three years of age. She was attended by doctors in the hospitals for seven years, but to of no avail, but on Sunday last, attended the mission and secured her 'deliverance'. Other instances of cures from deafness, rheumatism and neuritis were given, and many others signified that they had benefitted from the services.

Pastor Jeffreys addressed the meeting and said the reason why he believed in Divine healing was because God had declared Himself to be a healer. Another reason for his belief was that it was in a commission given to everyone in the Bible. 'I believe myself that the Church should have the power to heal today as it had in the days of old,' he observed. 'I believe that the miraculous should accompany the preaching of the Gospel as it did in the early days. Take the miraculous away from Christianity, and you have no Christianity left.'[12]

This report was written on the first week of what turned out to be a nine-week campaign which concluded in the largest possible venue, the Drill Hall with thousands present during these last meetings. Not one, but several churches were opened in the Bournemouth area as a result. 'Quietly, because of the possible multitude who might overwhelm the accommodation, on October 3rd a chapel was opened by the Principal at Springbourne. Soon, Parkstone, West Howe and Verwood were also settled in and three new Crusader branches created from the many young people won to Christ in the campaign.'[13]

Aimee reported 'drowned'

The 1st June edition of the *Evangel* carried the distressing news of the death by drowning of Aimee Semple McPherson who, just a couple of months previously, had preached for Elim at the Surrey Tabernacle, the Royal Albert Hall, Hull and Belfast. She was a controversial figure in evangelical circles on both sides of the Atlantic. George Canty was an obvious admirer of Aimee and was appalled at the venom that was unloosed against this lady; this caused him to reveal certain facts in the section of his manuscript that dealt with the Royal Albert Hall meetings:

> Aimee handled every situation with charm and composure, and thanked the smoking, hats-on journalists and photographers for their 'truly British attitude', an ambiguity of which they could make what they wished, but she showed no resentment and attempted no self-defence. Students arriving to 'tear her limb from limb', she disarmed so effectively they were rendered speechless ... the spite of the Press became revealed the next day in a headline which shook one's faith in the veracity of the Press evermore: 'Hot Gospeller fails to strike fire.'

Aimee Semple McPherson clearly captured and captivated the hearts of Elim people, and she was to return in 1928 for a week-long campaign at the RAH. Canty was clearly of the impression that Elim leaders were hesitant in their attitudes towards her. Boulton, a long-time member of the Executive Council and one of Jeffreys' inner circle, never even mentioned Aimee's appearance at the Royal Albert Hall in his biography of Jeffreys.

On 20th May, George Jeffreys received a cablegram from Aimee's mother, informing him of Aimee's drowning. In it,

Mother Kennedy implored Jeffreys to go over to Los Angeles immediately to take over Aimee's role as the pastor of Angelus Temple. The cablegram read as follows:

JEFFREYS ELIM CLAPHAM LONDON: SISTER MCPHERSON DROWNED WHILST SWIMMING TUESDAY. SOUL GLORIFIED SISTER HAD ANNOUNCED YOUR CAMPAIGN. WHOLE WORLD LOOKING TO ANGELUS TEMPLE. FOURSQUARE EVANGELIST IMPERATIVE NEED YOU HERE IMMEDIATELY THIS CRISIS HOUR. EARLIEST POSSIBLE DATE YOU CAN LEAVE. MOTHER KENNEDY.[14]

This request caused huge consternation within the Elim leadership. In correspondence between Jeffreys and Phillips, the latter advised caution. This was a critical period in the development of Elim. A wrong step at this point would have greatly hampered the work of the young movement. As it turned out, the cautionary approach was completely justified as six weeks later Aimee reappeared with harrowing tales of her kidnap. What is obvious is the fact that George Jeffreys' standing in Pentecostal circles was such that only he was deemed worthy to fill the McPherson pulpit. Notwithstanding the dilemma caused by the invitation, almost a command, to go across to Los Angeles and fill McPherson's pulpit, her reported death was a great shock and caused Jeffreys personal grief. This is clear in his tribute to her in the *Evangel*:

Words are inadequate to express the deep regret experienced by myself and all the Elim workers. We felt that one of ourselves had been called home. She loved Elim and Elim loved her. Like all the triumphant pioneers that had gone before, she was loved by countless multitudes everywhere, and was also the target for the poisonous arrows of envy and jealousy. Today, she is beyond the aim of those who hurled them, and who, if they are determined to continue in this sordid business, will have to find another to take her place.

The hundreds of thousands led to the Saviour through her loving ministry will look forward with joy to the bright and happy reunion with her in the presence of the Lord.

As one who was privileged to gain her confidence whilst working with her in the British Isles, I can truly say that Aimee Semple McPherson was not only a princess among preachers but also one who behind the scenes of public life was a really humble soul and a true saint of Jesus Christ. Our heartfelt sympathy goes out to 'Mother Kennedy' and the darling children, whom we prayerfully commend to the God of all consolation and hope.[15]

At the end of the tribute, the following note is added: *('Pastor George Jeffreys has cabled intimating the impossibility of his going to the Angelus Temple at present – Ed')*. The editor of the *Evangel* was E J Phillips and it is the author's personal supposition that he included this note to ensure that Jeffreys did not leave for the Angelus Temple at this crucial time in Elim's history.[16]

Opinions among Elim historians of the effect of Aimee's ministry for Elim are varied. As has already been noted, Canty was a great admirer of her ministry and was very positive about her ministry for Elim in 1926 and 1928. He wrote elaborately about the Royal Albert Hall meetings, describing the excitement and the wonder of a single, small, young denomination having the effrontery to book the Royal Albert Hall and fill it to overflowing. He points out that Elim hired the great hall on many occasions other than at Easter. He adds: 'But of all the exciting events the outstanding one would certainly be that which drew national attention, the visit of "Sister Aimee".'[17] Canty mentions the unbridled venom that was unloosed against her (as already noted) and he obviously felt that this was very unfair. Cartwright, on the other hand, was much less positive towards McPherson's ministry and effect on Elim. Referring to the note in the 15th June issue of the *Elim Evangel* and the request that Elim people pray much about the invitation extended to George Jeffreys to take over the Angelus Temple, he writes:

> The cause of all this activity was the disappearance of Aimee. The possibility of going to Los Angeles and of taking over the Temple would occupy the mind of George Jeffreys more than once during the next few years. Involvement with Aimee was to have repercussions that were not always beneficial. Some of his closest associates, especially William Henderson, urged caution. For a new religious movement, almost any publicity had a value, but some of the more flamboyant activities of Aimee did not help George Jeffreys.[18]

Six weeks after her reported drowning, Aimee was found near to the Mexican border with the USA, claiming to have been kidnapped. This was ridiculed by the press, who claimed that she had been conducting an illicit sexual affair. Scandal surrounded her, but Jeffreys accepted her account and the 15th September issue of the *Evangel* contained in detail, in Aimee's own words, her harrowing experience. While swimming in the ocean, her secretary had gone into the nearby town for some shopping, Aimee heard her name called and she was confronted by a man and a woman who told her that their daughter was very seriously ill nearby and would she come and pray for her? It was a ruse and she was drugged and kidnapped. She was taken into Mexico and moved from one lodging place to another. She was being held for a ransom of half a million dollars. The account she gave in the *Evangel* was an extremely detailed one. Eventually she was able to escape and made her way to a town right on the Mexican-Arizona border. Telephone calls were made to Los Angeles and, finally, she was able to speak with her mother.

This account was met with a great deal of cynicism from much of the press on both sides of the Atlantic. She continued to contribute articles for the *Evangel* and made one further visit to the UK in 1928 where she again preached in the Royal Albert Hall. Cartwright quotes Donald Gee, who expressed the opinion that her visit in 1928 'more than the first two appearances [1926] revealed that she could never have the same magnetic appeal to the more conservative British temperament'.[19]

Whatever conclusion the historians may come to as regards Aimee Semple McPherson, surrounded as she was with Hollywood glamour and the whiff of scandal, there can be no denying the fact that she made quite an impression on Elim and her appearance at the first of Elim's Royal Albert Hall conventions gave George Jeffreys the confidence to hire this great hall on numerous occasions.

Notes

[1] Kay, William, ibid, pp144,150.

[2] The author has had access to the letters between Jeffreys and Phillips and has seen the correspondence that Kay refers to. Unfortunately, access to the Elim archives has been hampered owing to the COVID-19 pandemic. I am therefore reliant on Kay's meticulous research of the correspondence which is placed in chronological files put together by Desmond Cartwright.

[3] Canty, George, unpublished paper written on the request of Gordon Hills, former field superintendent of Elim.

[4] Norman Black and his wife became members of the new tabernacle, later to be known as the Ulster Temple. He became an elder and secretary of the church, as did his son Cecil, who occupied those two roles when I was the pastor there in the mid-1980s. His other son, David, was the Sunday school superintendent.

[5] *Elim Evangel*, 15th July 1926, Vol 7, No 14, p161.

[6] *Elim Evangel*, 6th December 1926, Vol 7, Nos 23, 24, p280.

[7] Kay, William, ibid, p137.

[8] Canty, George, ibid, p99.

[9] Canty, George, ibid.

[10] Canty, George, ibid, p99.

[11] Canty, George, ibid, pp 99,100.

[12] *Elim Evangel*, 16th August 1926, Vol 7, No 16, p188.

[13] Canty, George, ibid, p100.

[14] *Elim Evangel*, 1st June 1926, Vol 7, No 11, p122.

[15] *Elim Evangel*, 1st June 1926, Vol 7, No 11, p122.

[16] The author wrote his dissertation for his MA on the work and leadership of E J Phillips and has read all the correspondence between Jeffreys and Phillips over this period. Phillips most certainly advised great caution on a positive act by Jeffreys to the request to go immediately to the Angelus Temple.

[17] Canty, George, ibid, p105.

[18] Cartwright, Desmond, *The Great Evangelists*, p82.

[19] Cartwright, Desmond, ibid, p82.

23
Going North

The first major Elim campaigns in England were held, as we have seen, in Grimsby and Hull, two cities in the north-east. Following those first campaigns, George, together with Stephen, concentrated on London. After the break with Stephen, George campaigned in Plymouth, Guernsey and Liverpool before returning south once more and campaigning in Bournemouth. Between the campaigns in Liverpool and Bournemouth, George held a brief campaign in Belfast at the opening of the city's second 'tabernacle', soon to be known as the Ulster Temple.

This year (1926) proved to be a major one in the establishment and growth of Elim. The Bournemouth campaign was George's longest, lasting for a total period of nine weeks. This campaign saw the establishment of four new Elim churches in the Bournemouth area. George Jeffreys kept up a hectic schedule throughout that incredible year. He also convened the five-day campaign at the Surrey Tabernacle at which Aimee Semple McPherson spoke. In addition to this, the first of Elim's many Easter conventions was held at the Royal Albert Hall where Aimee Semple McPherson was the main speaker, with George and John Leech being the others.

Carlisle

After summer in a huge tent in Bournemouth, capped with thousands packed into the Drill Hall, came autumn in 'an ill-lighted basement with a congregation less than a score'[1] in England's closest city to Scotland – Carlisle. As usual, Jeffreys commenced his campaign in this northern outpost in a quiet manner. He went to Carlisle as a result of an invitation from a small group of Pentecostals who gathered there. The article carrying the first report[2] of the campaign in Carlisle shows a group of enthusiastic students outside the Bible college in Clapham, waving their arms in expressing God's blessings on the Revival Party as they leave in a very large car for the north. J Welsh reported on the first week of the Carlisle campaign, stating: 'Over fifty precious souls have accepted salvation through faith in the Saviour.'

Although the meetings started with a score of people, they soon grew at a fantastic rate. To understand this phenomenal growth of attendances at Jeffreys' campaigns, we must bear in mind that by now, he was something of a national figure. National newspapers as well as scores of local press publications had reported on his campaigns. They majored on the healing reports at the various revival meetings. In this respect, Jeffreys hardly had to do much by the way of advertising. Having said that, a large number of leaflets giving details of the campaign were distributed throughout Carlisle.

It was not long before the 'score' became hundreds, then thousands. Someone claimed that 'the whole district is charged with the spirit of revival'. This required a succession of ever-larger buildings to house the congregations – a Methodist chapel, the Queen's Hall, the Drill Hall, the latter having never before been used for such a purpose, and still people pleading for admission could not be allowed in because literally every space was filled by people standing. Welsh includes a most interesting note at the end of his report: 'All denominations are participating in the meetings, and are on the tip-toe of expectation of a mighty outpouring of the Spirit of God. Hallelujah! Pray!! Pray!! Pray!!'[3] This was most uncommon in Jeffreys' campaigns as many clergymen of all denominations, together with their churches, usually either ignored the campaigns or vociferously spoke against them and discouraged their people from attending. Quite often, this had the opposite effect upon many people, as they became intrigued to find out what Jeffreys was doing that was so wrong!

According to evangelist J Welsh, who provided the reports of the Carlisle campaign in three successive editions of the *Elim Evangel*, the whole area around the city of Carlisle was greatly affected by the campaign. People were travelling from more than thirty miles from the city to attend. 'The Lord is blessing Pastor George Jeffreys and we are in the midst of the greatest move of the Spirit Carlisle has known for over 30 years.'[4] By the end of the second week, more than 500 people had turned to Christ for salvation. Underneath a photograph taken of the meeting in the Drill Hall and included in the same edition of the *Evangel*, the following editorial comment is attached:

> The older inhabitants say that they never remember such a visitation from God. The whole district has been stirred, hundreds have been converted and marvellous cases of healing witnessed. People have been delivered from all kinds of diseases. The largest halls in the town have been crowded to the doors. Here is the view of the front section and platform of the big military drill hall at one of the revival services. As we go to press, the great Military Riding School is contemplated for the final rally.[5]

The Military Riding School could accommodate 3,000 people, but it had no seats. Some chairs were hired, but it was announced that those who wished to be sure of a seat should bring their own. They did, which was a 'never to be forgotten sight', as James T Bradley put it.[6] He was new to the Pentecostal revival, but would later become secretary-general of Elim.[7]

By November, a delighted Jeffreys reported: 'The whole town[8] is a stir. I can see that Carlisle will probably eclipse Bournemouth. There are hundreds of young people captivated, the like of which I have never seen before.'[9] Chris Cartwright includes an addition (presumably from the same letter) to the above comment:

> The salvation of souls is marvellous in every meeting, I cannot keep count ... the cream of the city is now clamouring to get in ... The healings are more and more and greater than anywhere. Today, the place was stirred by a young lad whose arm was in splints and broken. After he was prayed for, his mother took off the splints and the arm was perfect. I cannot possibly tell you how we have gripped the city.[10]

The 1st January 1927 edition of the *Evangel* carries another report of the Carlisle campaign. Evangelist J Welsh informs us that the last five nights of the campaign were conducted in the Military Riding School on the outskirts of Carlisle. The weather was typical November weather for Carlisle. There was no heating in the vast hall and many people had to bring their own chairs with them. Welsh informs us that more than 1,200 people gave their lives to Christ during this campaign. His short report of the afternoon healing service on the final day is worth including here:

> The last healing service on the Sunday afternoon would have melted the heart of a Stoic. Rows upon rows of kneeling figures, suffering from various complaints, and waiting for a healing touch from the Great Physician. Dozens had taken tea with them and remained in the building ready for the evening service. It was estimated that well over 3,000 listened to the dear Pastor's last message. Eternity alone will reveal all the results of this time of God's special visitations.[11]

As well as J Welsh, three others wrote reports on their observations of the great Carlisle campaign. One of them, Rev J D Hurst, was a Church of England clergyman. His observations are written in full as they reveal to us the orthodoxy of Jeffreys' preaching. His reference to the way and manner in which the campaign was conducted would have come as a surprise to many non-Pentecostal church folk who would have, no doubt, heard of the strange and most unconventional 'goings on' in some Pentecostal meetings. His report is included in full:

Speaking from the point of view of one who knew something of the revival meetings recently conducted in the City of Carlisle, yet as one not directly connected with it, will you please allow me to place down a few impressions I received during my four days attendance at the meetings. As to the meetings themselves, there was nothing sensational whatever. Pastor Jeffreys and his splendid band of evangelists impressed me very much and their method of conducting the crowded congregations was marvellous. The enthusiastic singing was another feature; it was good to be there, no critical or sceptical spirit could possibly live in that heavenly atmosphere for one moment!

The pastor's addresses were listened to with deep earnestness, he did not preach the opinions of men, or even his own, but loyally held fast to the Word of the Lord. Had Mr Jeffreys been an Anglican, we should have labelled him a first rate Gospel preacher, definitely evangelical, doctrinally sound and holding fast to the thirty-nine articles of our Church's belief.

His Gospel for sinners and saints alike was as clear as crystal. His heart was all fire for God. His desire was not to be known by men in the popular sense, but that men may know Jesus as their Saviour, Lord and King. He had the joy of seeing hundreds respond to his appeal for full salvation in Christ Jesus. The sick were healed, others broken in body and mind were delivered. Carlisle will remember the Foursquare Gospel campaign for years to come, and praise the name of the Lord. Hallelujah![12]

Not everyone was as positive in their comments about the Carlisle campaign. Desmond Cartwright mentions that there was 'some opposition especially from the Railway Mission, whose pastor was a Keswick stalwart. He condemned them publicly'.[13] There may have been some anger and sorrow behind his words, as apparently a large number of the young people who attended the Railway Mission transferred their allegiances to Elim. Among them was the said James T Bradley.

Cartwright refers to James Walsh. This would appear to be a mistake in the surname, as in the three reports of the campaign in successive editions of the *Evangel*, he is referred to as J Welsh. It would be too much of a coincidence for there to have been a J Welsh and a James Walsh closely connected with the campaign. Taking it that the two names refer to the same man, Cartwright informs us that it was he (James Welsh) who had given the original invitation to George Jeffreys to conduct the campaign. He died in Carlisle on 19th February 1927. 'Two months later the converts moved into their own building on the West Wall, where they were to remain for the next fifty years.'[14]

In the year 1926, George Jeffreys had held seven major campaigns, four of them being pioneer campaigns that resulted in the establishment of new Elim churches. The seven campaigns were held in Plymouth, Vazon, Liverpool, Belfast, Bournemouth, Carlisle and Ilford. New Elim churches were established in Liverpool, Belfast, Bournemouth and Carlisle.

There appears to have been a flexible approach for the holding of campaigns. Plans were sometimes changed at the last minute as in the case of Liverpool. Plymouth was not intended to be a major campaign by George Jeffreys. His original intention had been to go down there for a few days to hold Bible studies and encourage the young assembly there that had been established as a result of Stephen's campaign in the city in the autumn of 1924. It had been George's clear intention that Liverpool would be his first major campaign of 1926, but such was the response of the people of Plymouth to George's ministry, accompanied by hundreds of clearly testified healings, that E J advised him to postpone the Liverpool campaign and continue in Plymouth. So, George had a 'busman's holiday' in Vazon, Guernsey following his time at Plymouth. Although he drew large congregations to his short campaign in Vazon, he was able to recuperate and re-energise after his hectic schedule in Plymouth.

The Liverpool campaign was postponed yet again, when the opportunity arose for Aimee Semple McPherson to evangelise for Elim in the spring of 1926. Similarly, the Ilford campaign was postponed as a result of George Jeffreys' extended campaign in Carlisle. The following note appeared in the *Evangel*: 'Pastor George Jeffreys' Ilford campaign was postponed owing to the Carlisle revival. It is to be held from the 8th to the 19th of December.'[15] It was while George was campaigning in Carlisle that the decision was made to hold a major campaign in Glasgow. It would appear that this was not in his original schedule, but as Carlisle is so close to the Scottish border, he may well have been persuaded to turn his attention to Scotland and to establish Elim churches there. Plans were often changed at the last minute. Sometimes it was the invitation of a friend or acquaintance that took him from one place to another. This was the case in Carlisle when it is evident that he responded to the invitation of James Welsh.

The rapid development of the work caused him to marvel at what God had done in, and through, Elim in such a short time. Writing his New Year message for 1927, George expressed his bewilderment at the pace of development within the young movement since its unsteady and unspectacular birth in 1915. He writes:

Little did we dream of an Elim Movement of present-day dimensions, with preachers scattered all over the British Isles and witnessing in foreign lands. Within the limited scope of our vision, we did not see the radiant beams of a Foursquare Gospel message falling upon countless multitudes throughout the length and breadth of the land, penetrating the regions beyond. The work as we know it today is not the result of any carefully laid plan, neither has it materialised as a result of us copying any other work. By God's grace we have been carrying on from one step to another, quite unconscious of the divine programme. While God was pleased to do the planning, we were privileged to do the praying.[16]

Another momentous year in the history of Elim was 1927. George's increased activity during this year led to the holding of nine pioneer campaigns.[17] The first of these was held in Rochester, Kent in January 1927. Jeffreys had, as was usual for him, chaired the Christmas Convention at Belfast. This was a standing arrangement and it enabled him to 'refresh the Irish roots of his ministry'.[18] Kay highlights the importance of the Irish section of the work by his following comment: 'We learn [that] the Belfast believers were willing to loan substantial sums of money to support Elim's full Gospel evangelism.'[19] The establishment of the Elim churches in Ireland provided a stable foundation for the development of the burgeoning Elim work on the mainland.

In an attempt to integrate the Elim churches in London and to create a bond of fellowship among them, a weekly convention rally was organised. Services were held in the Memorial Hall, Farringdon Street every Friday night. These services commenced on 14th January 1927 and were conducted by George Jeffreys. 'Elim saints in London are praising God for a weekly convention.'[20]

The Glasgow and Paisley Campaigns

Following the short but successful campaigns in Bermondsey and Rochester, where Elim churches were established, George turned towards the north once more. But this time, it was to a different country – Scotland. Here he would be presented with altogether different challenges than those he faced 450 miles away in southern and south-western England. The time had come to cross the Scottish border, the land of Presbyterian and Calvinistic strictness. 'Here the national disposition was not marked by exuberance nor was it likely to respond to lighter Gospel choruses.'[21] In this, Canty was proven to be 'out of kilter', as it were. The Glaswegians took to the Elim choruses with great joy. This was in no small part owing to the influence of Seth Sykes and his wife, Bessie, who were well-known evangelists in the Glasgow area.

Seth Sykes (1892-1950) was an evangelist from Springburn, Glasgow. He worked for Glasgow Corporation Tramways. He was secretary of the Tramway Christian Association. In 1929, Sykes left his job to become a full-time evangelist. Sykes fully endorsed the Jeffreys' campaign in Glasgow, which had started off quite slowly. The *Evangel* report states that the first week was uphill work and wonders whether this was down to the nature of the 'canny Scotch'.[22] However, attendances soon increased and the St Mungo Grand Hall was filled to capacity from the second week of the campaign onwards. The following report by Seth Sykes (1892-1950) was published in the *Evangel*:

> I can praise God for the visit of George Jeffreys and helpers to Glasgow. After one week's plodding, God blessed the faithful ministry of the Foursquare Gospel, and hundreds have been saved and healed of such ailments as asthma, rupture, varicose veins, blindness, deafness, paralysis and heart trouble. At one evening service, 56 people testified to healing.[23]

Sykes wrote a number of choruses that became extremely popular within Elim and appear in the Elim Chorus Book.[24] Perhaps his most popular chorus is: 'Thank You Lord for Saving My Soul'.[25] Other choruses that he wrote that were very popular among Elim congregations were: 'God Has Blotted Them Out';[26] 'I Took a Plunge in the Crimson Flood'[27] and 'Running Over'.[28] He also wrote the hymn 'Love, Wonderful Love', which is number 514 in the *Redemption Hymnal*.[29]

The campaign then moved to Paisley and St Andrew's Hall, seating 5,000 people. Still, seating was so limited 600 men occupied the platform, some clinging to the very edge. Some 1,500 decisions for Christ were registered. When the time came for the party to leave Glasgow, police help was called for as 5,000 Scots surged around their car. Elim revival meetings continued in the Corporation Hall, with 800 people in regular attendance. A fine and large former church building was purchased and renamed 'Glasgow City Temple'. So began Elim's permanent work in Scotland, the first minister being G T Fletcher. He had been appointed the pastor of the new Carlisle church just a few months previously, but it was felt that he was more needed in Glasgow. Canty includes in his manuscript a most interesting account that will resonate with Pentecostals:

> The power of God did not depart with the George Jeffreys team. In the subsequent services, for instance, a girl baptised in the Spirit gave a clear utterance in tongues, and a man stood to ask who she was. On being told she was a poor girl who had scarcely been outside of Glasgow, he was staggered. He had been living in Italy, but in perfect Italian she had, he said, revealed all God's dealings with him throughout his life.[30]

Notes

[1] Canty, George, ibid, p109.
[2] Welsh, J, *Elim Evangel*, 15th November 1926, Vol 7, No 21, p263.
[3] Welsh, J, ibid.
[4] Welsh, J, *Elim Evangel*, 6th December 1926, Vol 7, Nos 23,24, p301.
[5] *Elim Evangel*, 6th December 1926.
[6] Canty, George, ibid, p109.
[7] James Bradley and his brother Robert played a large role in Elim. Robert was for many years a lecturer at the Elim Bible College and was a well-

known convention speaker throughout the movement. His older brother James served for more than thirty-five years on the Executive Council and ended his ministry as Elim's secretary-general. The Bradley family hailed from Carlisle.

[8] Carlisle, at the time, was a town, the County town of Cumbria. It was granted city status in 1974.

[9] G J to E P J, 11th November 1926. Quoted by Kay, ibid, p140.

[10] Cartwright, H C and Holdaway, D (eds), *Defining Moments*, p42.

[11] Welsh, J, *Elim Evangel*, 1st January 1927, Vol 8, No 1, p9.

[12] *Elim Evangel*, 1st January 1927, ibid.

[13] Cartwright, Desmond, ibid, p85.

[14] Cartwright, Desmond, ibid.

[15] *Elim Evangel*, 6th December 1926, Vol 6, Nos 23,24, p304.

[16] *Elim Evangel*, 25th December 1926, Vol 9, Nos 51,52, p801.

[17] 1927 was a special year for supporters of Cardiff City, of which the author is one. They won the FA cup for the first and only time in their history when they beat Arsenal 1-0 at Wembley stadium. It is the only time the FA cup has resided outside England for a twelve-month period.

[18] Kay, William, ibid, p155.

[19] Kay, William, ibid, p155.

[20] *Elim Evangel*, 1st February 1927, Vol 8, No 3, p47.

[21] Canty, George, ibid, p109.

[22] It should have read 'Canny Scots'. My many Scottish friends and colleagues would quickly point out that Scotch is an alcoholic beverage; Scots are Scottish people.

[23] *Elim Evangel*, 15th March 1927, Vol 8, No 6, p84.

[24] *Elim Chorus Book* (Eastbourne: Victory Press Evangelical Publishers Ltd, 1966).

[25] Ibid, No 519.

[26] Ibid, No 6.

[27] Ibid, No 337.

[28] Ibid, No 8.

[29] *Redemption Hymnal.*

[30] Canty, George, ibid, p110.

24

The Most Productive Years

The five years from 1926 through to the end of 1930 inclusive, are generally accepted as being the most productive years for George Jeffreys' ministry, culminating in what was undoubtedly his greatest campaign, in the UK's second city, Birmingham, in 1930. The reports of these huge revival crusades make truly staggering reading for those of us who have grown up in days when the Church has been in perpetual decline since the end of the Second World War. The press reports themselves are mind-blowing. There was a degree of cynicism expressed by some reporters, but generally they gave fair presentations of the campaigns, concentrating on the sensationalism in the form of the thousands of reported healings, emphasising repeatedly, however, the words 'it is claimed'. There is no doubt that the many hundreds of press reports were extremely influential in attracting the huge crowds that attended Jeffreys' campaign meetings.

An exception to the above was the scurrilous report published in *John Bull*, a popular jingoistic periodical that was popularised under the editorship of Horatio Bottomley (1860-1933) who became a Liberal MP. Kay gives a comprehensive account of this vicious attack on Elim, and George Jeffreys in particular, in his book.[1] The nub of the article's attack on Elim was that 'the movement was set up to rob the gullible of their savings'.[2] This attack on the integrity of Elim and its leaders, especially George Jeffreys, must have shaken the movement to its core. The attack was utterly false and could have caused irreparable damage to Elim and the wider British Pentecostal denominations. The article condemning Elim appeared in the 18th January 1930 edition of the magazine. At this time, George was in Glasgow, preaching at the City Temple. George dealt with an interruption in a service in which he was speaking. 'A member of the congregation caused a disturbance and demanded that Jeffreys provide a public answer to the printed criticisms.'[3] George's response was to remind people that they could press charges with the public prosecutor against Elim – nobody did.

The attack caused great consternation among Elim's leaders. They were strongly of the opinion that they needed to rebut these scurrilous accusations but were not in full agreement as how to set about doing so. Consideration was given to addressing them through the legal system, but that would have involved them in a continuing legal battle with an organisation that was well practised in such confrontations. Eventually, it was decided that George should write a disclaimer which was published in the *Elim Evangel* on 21st February 1930. E J made a revision to the disclaimer after he had consulted with Elim's solicitors.[4] Kay states that the denial of wrongdoing was absolute.[5] Canty, however, comments: 'Elim's timid reply consisted of one short, mild piece in the "*Elim Evangel*".'[6]

The author is of the opinion that Canty was harsh in his assessment of Elim's reply to the article. Elim's leaders had to traverse the extremely torturous pathway of maintaining the integrity of the movement without getting embroiled in an ongoing debate. Jeffreys' denial of the charges was firm and to the point:

> Principal George Jeffreys and the Elim Foursquare Gospel Alliance absolutely deny each and every one of the charges made against them in the *John Bull* article. Such methods and practices have never been known in the organisation, and would not be tolerated in any one of its churches or missions. We make no apology for the

Scriptural supernatural manifestations in our services; such have characterised revivals of religion down through the ages. The multitudes of changed lives and the testimonies of those in all parts of the British Isles who have been healed of physical ailments is the best answer to all who object to this aspect of our ministry.[7]

The language of the *John Bull* article was, for those days, highly provocative and designed to ridicule and belittle the ministry of the Jeffreys brothers and to cause distrust among would-be attenders of the campaigns. However, typical of this kind of scurrilous journalism, they could not even get their basic facts right. They said that 'their leaders are three brothers, George, Stephen and William Jeffreys'.[8] William was never involved in the leadership of Elim and, by this time, Stephen had left Elim and joined the Assemblies of God. The article ends with cutting sarcasm: 'They forsook the perils of the pit for the profits of the pulpit.'

The fact that Elim came through this bitter attack was owing in no small measure to the meticulous work of Elim's secretary-general, E J Phillips. In his assessment of the relationship between Jeffreys and Phillips, Kay suggests that there was friction between them that had arisen over the need for exactness and meticulous financial accounting. 'Phillips not only counted for every penny but also made sure every law was kept.'[9] Having written my Masters dissertation on E J, and focused on his leadership of Elim in the post-Jeffreys era, I do not concur with Kay's observation of there being friction between the two men during the twenties. Their relationship with each other, at that time, was extremely close and warm. Any disagreement between them would have been that which is common among friends. Kay is obviously an admirer of Phillips, and in that respect shares the opinion of the author of Elim's unsung hero.

From Glasgow to Leeds

The impact that Elim had on Glasgow and other cities and towns in Scotland was quite remarkable. The church that was formed in Glasgow as a result of Jeffreys' incredible campaign there, numbered in excess of 800 people. In the 1930s, Elim had a number of churches with Sunday congregations hovering around the 1,000 mark. Included in these were three churches in Scotland: Glasgow, Greenock and Dundee. There were three Elim churches in Birmingham that also came into that category: Graham Street (now Birmingham City Church), Sparkbrook and Smethwick. Clapham, Kensington Temple and Barking had huge congregations, certainly in excess of 600. The famous Cardiff City Temple (Cardiff City Church) was another church with a congregation in excess of 1,000 every Sunday.

A very large church was established in Carlisle following the campaign there. This was clearly evidenced by the huge numbers of people that left Carlisle in a hired train to attend the Glasgow campaign on the first Saturday. The train had allocated nine of its eleven carriages to the members of the newly formed Elim church in Carlisle, 650 of them!

> Anyone walking down the platform as the train stood in the station, would have seen over a hundred labels bearing the words 'Reserved for Elim', pasted on the windows, so we are correct in saying that this was an *Elim train*. Think of it – a train load of saved and happy people, mostly converts of the recent great revival services conducted by Pastor George Jeffreys in Carlisle.
>
> On arrival at the Glasgow (Central) station we noted the great crowds of people hurrying to the trains, trams and buses for the purpose of attending one of the great football matches for which Glasgow is so keen, but our train-load was hastening to St Mungo's Hall, to see our beloved pastor and co-workers and to spend 'a day with God.'

What a sight! Pastor's car, skilfully piloted by our dear brother Fred Bell, moved slowly at the head of the procession, and with songs of Zion, the saints of God moved on through the busy Glasgow streets. The police were kind, helpful and so clever at handling the traffic and clearing the way for Elim. Eyes turned to see this great sight; crowds formed up to watch the procession; great interest was aroused as the march progressed.[10]

One of the great problems that was caused by the establishment of these huge congregations was finding pastors to lead them. The Elim Bible College was barely two years old! Maintaining the fervour and interest of such huge gatherings of people, mostly new converts but many of mature Christian experience, was more of a challenge than the initial breakthrough. The number of capable and experienced men for 800-strong churches was virtually nil.[11] This was clearly revealed in the fact that the newly appointed pastor of the Carlisle church was whisked north to take over the Glasgow church. He left a church of 600-700 hundred to take charge of a church with 800-1,000 members! The logistics of founding such large churches from scratch are truly mind-boggling! Elim was a very young movement, just twelve years old at the time of the Glasgow campaign. It had very little by way of departments, activities and provisions. Those that it had were a miraculous provision – two head offices (Clapham and Belfast), a printing press and a Bible college.

There can be no doubt that the genius of E J was a major factor in the establishment of these huge congregations and the forming of them into large churches. The correspondence between him and George Jeffreys clearly reveal his involvement in the purchasing and leasing of buildings. That was one of the first problems that faced a pastor appointed to one of these mega-churches. But, somehow, the buildings were either bought or leased and pastors appointed to them, some of whom were very young and hopelessly inexperienced, but with the fire of God burning within them and a clear sense of calling. I recall speaking on one occasion to Samuel Gorman, who had faced such a challenge. Gorman was a member of Elim's Executive Council for many years. He was a godly and humble man who was gifted with a remarkable ability of teaching the Scriptures. He was a faithful pastor and a great preacher. After very limited Bible college training, he was appointed an Elim pastor. When I was a very young probationary minister, just a couple of months fresh from Bible college, I visited him at his home in Eastbourne on a number of occasions. On one such visit he told me how, at the age of twenty-four, he married his dear wife, Marjorie. On return from their honeymoon, they were instructed to make their way to the town of Greenock, situated at the mouth of the River Clyde, some twenty-five miles west of Glasgow. They were met at Glasgow by two leading members of the new Greenock church and taken to Greenock straight to the Saturday evening service at which more than 800 people were present. What a terrifying prospect for a young minister not long fresh from Bible college!

When George Jeffreys moved on to Leeds, direct from Glasgow, he found that the situation in this northern city was somewhat different. On this occasion, a gifted leader happened to be ready-made on the spot, as it were. In Leeds, there was a businessman named Jewitt, a gifted preacher, who already had an assembly some sixty or seventy strong. Canty claims that the two weeks that Jeffreys spent in Leeds exceeded everything up to that time, with 2,300 being brought to Christ and some of the most spectacular healings wrought. Under the title: 'Over 2,000 Converted *in* Two Weeks', Pastor T H Jewitt wrote a report for the *Evangel*:

> The greatest feat of modern evangelism was the overwhelming success of a fourteen days' mission conducted by Pastor George Jeffreys and party when two thousand, two hundred and ninety professed conversion and hundreds were healed of all kinds of diseases. Why such a glorious triumph of the Gospel over sin and sickness in a few days? Not because it was

an easy field of labour ... The why and wherefore of this remarkable victory is that God answered prayer. The prayers of local saints that had been expressed in groans and tears for many a year, and the prayers of thousands of God's people throughout the land. Pastor George Jeffreys preached the Word of God with great power, every address had a message for saint and sinner. Thousands praise God for his able and faithful ministry of the Foursquare Gospel.[12]

Accompanying the report of the Leeds campaign in the *Evangel*, were a number of reported healings printed by the *Leeds Mercury*. Canty states that one of the most spectacular healings was that of Jim Gregson, a shattered cripple. 'Instantly, as if by a hundred hands on his body, Jim was made whole.'[13] A *Leeds Mercury* investigation later found that all claims of healing were substantiated and still standing, while congregations of 1,000-1,500 for years afterwards testified to the work of God.

The most astonishing healing during the Leeds campaign was reported in a much later edition of the *Elim Evangel*. This particular healing revealed that Elim members did not merely rely on the prayers of the revivalist, but availed themselves of the teaching of the apostle James as taught them by Elim pastors:

> Is anyone among you sick? Let him call for the elders of the church, and let them pray over him, anointing him with oil in the name of the Lord. And the prayer of faith will save the one who is sick, and the Lord will raise him up. And if he has committed sins, he will be forgiven.[14]

Harry Toft was a famous Welsh rugby union player who played for the famous Swansea All-Whites before the First World War. Known as the 'human corkscrew', he played at inside centre or fly-half.[15] He played alongside Dicky Owen, the Swansea and Wales scrum-half who went on to captain his country. Owen won five triple crowns and captained his country on three occasions. But he is most remembered as a member of the historic Welsh team that beat the first All-Blacks touring team who were previously unbeaten in their tour of Britain in 1905.

Toft was paid the then huge sum of £170 to turn professional and he signed on for the Hunslet Rugby League club, just outside Leeds. Pastor T A Carver gives an account of his conducting services not far from Leeds, meeting with Harry Toft while he was in the area. Reading the article, it would appear that the chronology set the testimony that Harry Toft gave of his healing to have occurred shortly after George Jeffreys' campaign in Leeds. He told Carver that after retiring from rugby he developed cancer of the tongue, which spread to his mouth and throat. This terrible disease caused him months of fearful agony. It was at this time that George Jeffreys held his great campaign in Leeds, and Harry Toft returned to the gospel that he had forsaken. I now take up Carver's own account of his conversation with Toft which was replicated in the *Herald of Wales* newspaper:

His physical condition grew worse, and ultimately the doctor pronounced that he had only a few weeks at the most to live. 'But – Man's extremity is God's opportunity!' At the revival meetings, the old three-quarter had been told that Christ still heals today as of old. His words to me were these:

When the doctor told me there was no hope, I just cried to God, 'Lord, if you will give me another chance, I will live an out-and-out life for Thee.' Then immediately I felt an urge in my soul. I asked my family to send someone to the Foursquare Church and fetch the elders so that they might anoint me and pray according to the Scriptures. 'I was sure God would heal me,' continued Toft. 'In due time, the elders came and prayed over me in the name of the Lord. I shall never forget it. Immediately, I felt divine power enter my body. The pain ceased, and I, a dying man, was instantaneously healed, when I had passed beyond all human aid. And since that day I have never had any trouble and today, over fifty years old, I feel fitter than in the St Helen's days.'[16]

Between campaigns, Jeffreys conducted the second great Easter Convention at the Royal Albert Hall. This time, there was no Aimee present to guarantee a full house; George was on his own! The hard-bitten Fleet Street reporters announced that '10,000 people were mesmerised by his preaching'.[17] Boulton, in the colourful and somewhat poetic style of writing which was the typical fare of religious magazines of the day, writes: 'No pen could picture the events of the wonderful, epoch making day. It baffles description! It is beyond portrayal! A veritable pageant of Pentecostal power!'[18]

Kay quotes extensively from Rom Landau's book, *God is my Adventure*.[19] He devotes a chapter (twenty pages in length) to the Annual Elim Demonstration at the Royal Albert Hall. He entitled the chapter 'Miracle at the Royal Albert Hall: *Principal George Jeffreys*'. It is not at all certain that the 'Demonstration' referred to in this chapter is that of the 1927 Easter Convention. Indeed, there are a few indications that this is a compilation of a number of such conventions that Landau attended. The baptismal service that he refers to in his chapter on Jeffreys did not take place at the Royal Albert Hall, but at the Crystal Palace, and it was there that he was granted an interview with the revivalist.

Landau writes that he arrived at the Albert Hall soon after ten 'on a brilliant Easter Monday morning, to find a jumble of taxis, bath-chairs and even ambulances in the street outside'.[20] The building was already half-full when the great organ began to play and five thousand voices responded to the lilting tune:

There never was a sweeter melody,
It's a melody of love.
In my heart there rings a melody,
There rings a melody.[21]

By 10.30, there was not a seat left. There were crowds of young people in the stalls and rows around the platform. The boys were in dark suits and the girls in white dresses, and they had sashes of silk with the words 'Elim Crusader' emblazoned on them. Landau makes the following comment concerning the class of people present:

> The audience consisted mainly of working-class people. Many of them had come from Wales, from Yorkshire, from the Midlands, and much less Cockney was heard than is usual on popular occasions at the Albert Hall. Food and bottles containing tea or coffee, were stowed under the seats.[22]

Some of the Elim leaders were particularly sensitive to the claim that Elim was predominantly a working-class movement. As one who has taken considerable pride in being numbered among such wonderful people, I have no problem with such a designation, and neither did Canty. But this seemed to have irked Boulton somewhat, as he wrote in his report:

> Some of its enemies have hurled at this Movement the cutting criticism that its appeal is confined to the ignorant and the illiterate,[23] that amongst its adherents the emotional element predominates. We are convinced that the most censorious critic would acknowledge that the character and composition of this mighty meeting constituted a complete refutation of such a false valuation of the work. Undoubtedly, there was emotion and enthusiasm, but it was of the intelligent type, emanating from those in whose lives God had wrought wonders of blessing and healing.[24]

Boulton comes across in these words as a bit of an intellectual snob! It is interesting that Canty (who came from Boulton's assembly in Hull), while lecturing students at the Elim Bible College on the subject of 'Church History', was adamant that

Elim was the only Christian denomination to have had its roots planted firmly in the down-to-earth, genuine working classes of our country.

Notes

1 Kay, William, ibid, pp204,206.

2 Kay, William, ibid.

3 Kay, William, ibid, p205.

4 Cartwright, Desmond, ibid, p101.

5 Kay, William, ibid, p205.

6 Canty, George, ibid, p118.

7 *Elim Evangel*, 21st February 1930, Vol 11, No 8, p121.

8 Cartwright, Desmond, ibid, p101.

9 Kay, William, ibid, p206.

10 *Elim Evangel*, 1st March 1927, Vol 8, No 5, p77.

11 Canty, ibid, p110.

12 Jewitt, T H, *Elim Evangel*, 2nd May 1927, Vol 8, No 7, p107.

13 Canty, George, ibid, p110.

14 James 5:14-15, ESV.

15 Most commonly referred to as outside-half. Fly-half is the name that most Welsh rugby aficionados give to this, the most revered rugby position in Welsh rugby folklore.

16 St Helen's here is not a reference to the famous Lancashire Rugby League team, but to the ground where Swansea RFC still play their home games.

17 Canty, George, ibid, p111.

18 Boulton, E C W, *Elim Evangel*, 16th May 1927, Vol 8, No 10, pp145-148.

19 Landau, Rom, *God is My Adventure: a Book on Modern Mystics, Asters and Teachers* (London: Faber And Faber, Ninth Impression), p121.

20 Landau, Rom, ibid, p120.

21 This song was a popular hymn written by Elton Roth (1891-1951) and it appears with permission in the *Redemption Hymnal* (597).

22 Landau, Rom, ibid, p121.

23 The fact is that at this time, a considerable number of working people had left school almost unable to read or write. This was not down to ignorance, however, but to the fact that many had to leave school at the age of twelve or thirteen to work so that they could earn money for their impoverished families.

24 Boulton, E C W, *Elim Evangel*, 16th May 1927, ibid.

25
Sweeping the South

As I have pointed out, a huge problem that Elim faced in the opening of new, some of them very large, churches, was the shortage of experienced and qualified pastors to take charge of the congregations. Elim's ecclesiastical structure was still evolving in the late 1920s and early thirties. While there had been changes to the Constitution in 1919, 1921, 1925 and 1929, all these had been formulated by George Jeffreys himself. It was not until 1934 and the formulation of the Deed Poll that Elim's governing structure became formalised, and remains today the basis of the governmental structure of the Alliance.

The role of women

One of the ways in which Elim addressed the shortage of ministers in the late twenties was to allow women to be involved in leading churches, sometimes as assistants to male pastors, but there were some notable occasions when women led churches, a few of them being large churches, on their own. Elim's stance on women in ministry has, throughout its 106-year history, been pragmatic. In the early years, Elim had only one pastor, George Jeffreys. The others were considered 'evangelists', and together they formed the Elim Evangelistic Band. As late as 1927, many who led churches were referred to as 'Evangelist'. Those men who had been with George since the early years were referred to as 'Mr'. These were the ones that were usually appointed to the larger churches.

The earliest expression of governance within the Elim Pentecostal Church was the formation of the Elim Evangelistic Band in January 1915. The first members of the Band were George Jeffreys, Ernest Darragh and Margaret Streight.[1] Other women were added to the Band – Miss Adams and Miss Adelaide Henderson. When the *Elim Evangel* was first published in December 1919, the names of female members of the Band were included in the list of evangelists but after those of the male members. This seemed to indicate that while there was a degree of male ascendancy, women had the same status as their male counterparts when it came to ministry. This situation continued through to 1923, when according to Carter, there was a significant change:

> With various changes in categories and presentation in subsequent editions, the next major significant change with the presentation of names at the beginning of the Evangel occurred in the February 1923 edition. The categories were re-worked, for the sake of this paper the major change was within the largest and most graphically central category of 'Members of The Elim Evangelistic Band in The Regular Work of The Ministry'. This was the first time that there was an explicit demarcation of the men from the women; after the listing of men, a sub-category was introduced of 'Sisters'. No similar gendered term (eg, Brothers) was used for the men.[2]

The first Ordination Service took place during the London Easter Conventions in 1928 when eighteen men were ordained. There had been some discussion as to whether 'sisters' should be ordained, but a decision on this was deferred, and a committee consisting of six men and three women was appointed to consider the subject. Carter points out that at this time there were two bodies of government within Elim, the Executive Presbytery and the General Presbytery. The latter comprised of all ministers, and included women who were able to take part in debate, but not allowed to vote.[3] The three women on the committee were Mrs Charles Kingston, Miss Adelaide Henderson and Miss N Kennedy. Carter sums up Miss Kennedy's arguments, and they were drawn from Church history, Scripture and current practice.

> Miss Kennedy, at one instance, argues from early Church history, saying 'I understand from a record by an early historian that women were ordained by the laying on of hands until the Church council of Laodicea forbade it in 360AD.' She does take a more primitivist approach to the discussion, looking for examples in Scripture and early Church practice. She also includes an explanation of the term 'ordination' as one who is elected or appointed. She then focuses on Phoebe as a deacon whom, she argues, must have been elected/appointed (hence ordained), and was viewed by Greeks, Romans and Barbarians 'as a succourer, LEADER' (emphasis in original).
>
> Biblical and early Church practice are important parts of this short correspondence; however, the main focus is upon a person's gift. Miss Kennedy refers to 1 Corinthians 12:11 as an inclusive verse with regards to gifts and ministry, arguing that God gives gifts to whomever according to His will. She ties this in with the current situation within Elim, arguing that women are being elected and appointed to the 'oversight of churches', and even if they do not publicly receive the 'laying on of hands' their 'gift and ministry' is recognized by the appointment.[4]

Miss Kennedy's argument was a very valid one. A Miss Buchanan was in charge of the new Carlisle church for a short while after Pastor Fletcher had been moved to Glasgow.[5] Miss M B Ewes is reported to have been in charge of the Forest Hill Elim Church[6] and Miss Kennedy herself was appointed to have 'oversight' of the Portsmouth church, with Miss Thompson as her assistant.[7]

The proposal to ordain women was soundly defeated. One member of the committee who was strongly opposed to the ordination of women was P N Corry, who was the dean (principal) of the Elim Bible College. In 1936, the college suspended the admission of female students. Corry seems to have appeared somewhat suddenly on the Elim scene. There is little information concerning him prior to the announcement in the *Evangel* appointing him as dean of the Elim Bible College. The title 'principal' was dropped in relation to the college and transferred to George Jeffreys.

> To one and all, the announcement that Percy N. Corry is the new Dean will be received with great joy and satisfaction. He is undoubtedly one of the most able Bible students and teachers of our land. He is of the same school as W.P.F Burton, and James Salter, Founders and Pioneers of the Congo Inland Mission, E J Phillips, our efficient Secretary-General; R E. Darragh, the first Evangelist to join our Pastor's Evangelistic Band, in Ireland; and our own beloved leader himself. Corry's splendid talents, his manliness, combined with his influence, especially with young men, will be conducive to the strengthening of character such as is needed for our ministry today.[8]

He was elected onto the first Executive Council in 1934, and served both as dean of the Bible College until 1942, when he was forced to leave his positions and Elim under controversial circumstances.

Women continued to be involved in leading churches, although this decreased greatly towards the end of the 1930s. Incongruously, however, they were allowed to vote in the famous debate on British Israelism in 1934. The minutes reveal that seven women voted in this debate; five were against the identity and two abstained. The voting results were separated into various categories including 'Sisters in the ministry'. 'It is likely that these seven "Sisters in the ministry" had been Elim workers for more than six years.'[9]

Five south coast campaigns

In 1928 and 1929, George held campaigns in five cities and towns along the south coast. The first of these was in Southampton, the great seaport city. It was also the place where Isaac Watts (1674-1748), the great English hymn writer, was born. The nine bells in the Civic Centre Clock sound Watts' probably best known hymn: 'O God, Our Help in Ages Past', every four hours until 10pm.

Canty says that 600 Bournemouth converts and supporters set forth to open the campaign in Southampton.[10] He adds a typical Canty comment: 'The support was needed, for only four people responded to the Gospel in the first meeting. But after the first sufferer was healed, walking and kneeling after two years of trouble; that was enough, in those days, to begin the rousing of this great port.'

The Southampton campaign was a great success and a strong church was established in this major seaport. There were many outstanding healings that took place in this campaign. Among them was Mrs Cox of Romsey, partially paralysed, who went home without her wheelchair, and other Romsey residents saw and believed.[11] A number of churches were opened in the vicinity of Southampton as a result of this campaign. They included Romsey, Eastleigh, Salisbury, Verwood, Canada (in the New Forest), Andover and Grinstead. This was a common feature in many of Jeffreys' campaigns. Canty comments:

> So the fire spread from larger Elim centres, though sometimes only kept alight by the sheer determination and character of typical Elim members in war days, and

in those times of difficulty which inevitably pass over all institutions and human beings.[12]

There were a number of remarkable testimonies recorded in the *Evangel* that took place in Southampton. One of them has intrigued me greatly:[13] 'One young man who said he came from Eastleigh, told the Pastor he was taken to the mission on the Tuesday evening, stone deaf, but after prayer and being anointed by Mr. Jeffreys, received his hearing.' Eastleigh is a railway town about eight miles from Southampton and I had the privilege of being the pastor of the Elim church there in my early years of ministry. I was greatly helped and encouraged by the members of that small church. We must always be aware that the church is not a building, but people. The work of a pastor is not primarily to lead, but to serve. In that small but wonderful Hampshire church, I found it was often the other way round. People there helped and served me. By their kindness and encouragement, I took my early, faltering steps in the ministry.

The most startling reported healing that took place in the Southampton campaign was that of Miss Florence Munday: her personal testimony is well worth recording in its entirety. In a letter to George, she wrote these words:

> How overjoyed I am that you came with your little band to Southampton. Glory be to God! My cup is full and running over, for just one week ago I was an invalid having been wheeled about in a bath chair between fourteen and fifteen years suffering from a tubular knee. I was lying ill in London when your campaign started, and the doctors there gave me to understand the knee was absolutely destroyed and that I should never walk again.
>
> My mother brought me home as soon as I was able to travel, to talk it over with my doctor in Southampton, to have my leg amputated. But praise be to God, I never saw my doctor, but came in my bath chair to the Central

Hall for the Divine healing service, and on that Thursday afternoon when you laid your hands upon me, I was healed. The power of God came upon me, and as I lay there in my chair, my knee lifted three times in the splints, and afterwards, I was able to step out of my chair without aid and I was able to walk across the hall – I was healed. That night, I slept without my splints for the first time in fourteen years. The knee which seemed to be destroyed and would never bend again is bending beautifully, and the leg which was so wasted is gaining and already, there is a big improvement.[14]

In early June, 1927, the next major centre along the south coast that Jeffreys campaigned in was Brighton and Hove. Again, only a handful greeted the Revival Party in the Hove Town Hall, though a now familiar pattern showed itself. Ever-increasing attendances resulted in the meetings being transferred to the larger and famous Dome in Brighton. People queued at the three entrances for hours; one woman apparently did so for seven hours. Twelve hundred people confessed Christ as Saviour and 300 testified to healing. A Baptist minister wrote his impressions of the revival meetings in the *Evangel*.[15] He was deeply impressed by the singing, joy and enthusiasm that was evident in the great gatherings. There was an obvious spirit of praise in the great congregations in Brighton. In one of the meetings a pianist was needed, and a request made from the platform brought forward a young musician, Albert Edsor. According to Canty, he soon joined the Revival Party and throughout the rest of George Jeffreys' life remained his admirer and inseparable friend, rarely absent from his side.

Edsor was not only Jeffreys' pianist, but also his chauffeur. His loyalty to Jeffreys was total and he, with the three other members of the Revival Party, left Elim along with their leader in 1940. Edsor was fierce in his defence of Jeffreys and took great exception to some of the writings of Desmond Cartwright in his book *The Great Evangelists*. Having succeeded Cartwright as Elim's official historian, I am of the opinion that many of

Edsor's objections were highly prejudiced. Cartwright's book was the first historical publication on Elim's history since Boulton's which only went up to 1928, and the movement is deeply indebted to the incredible research into Elim's history that he made, together with the preservation and collection of archival material without which it would have been impossible to write this book. The basis of Edsor's grievance was Cartwright's comment: 'We pass over the remaining years of George Jeffreys' life in a few words. After he left Elim he spent time in the wilderness.'[16] In comparison with the twenty-five years that he led Elim, Cartwright's summation of Jeffreys' last twenty-two years of ministry is correct.

Edsor was embittered in his attitude towards Elim in general and towards the leaders of the movement at the time of the division. The Elim Executive Council were sarcastically referred to as 'The Elim Governors'. His attack upon the writings, and by implication, the integrity of a man lauded and acknowledged as one of the foremost British Pentecostal historians and a mentor to the author of this book is, in my opinion, to say the least, scurrilous.

Canty was obviously favourably impressed by Edsor. I speculate at this point as to the reasons why the Executive Council of the day who had commissioned Canty to write the official history of Elim decided at the last minute not to publish it. Could it be that one of the reasons might have been his commendation of Edsor? Canty wrote:

> As George Jeffreys' pianist and private secretary and resident with him he had a unique opportunity to know the revivalist, the real man. It would be impossible to find higher testimony to George than that, after knowing him to the day of his death. Albert Edsor remains to the hour that these words are being written, as warm in affection for George Jeffreys and as alert in his defence and honour as any man ever could be. Time has not diminished, as intimacy did not tarnish, the lustre of

George Jeffreys in the eyes of the man who knew him the best.[17]

As to the last point in Canty's above statement, surely the man who knew him best was the man who knew him the longest and who was also resident with Jeffreys but for a much longer period of time than Edsor. I refer to Ernest Darragh, who was the first member of the Elim Evangelistic Band, along with Margaret Streight. Jeffreys is buried in the same grave as Darragh, as noted before in this book.

Elim were able to purchase the Glynn Vivian Hall in the Lanes, Brighton, an old nonconformist building. This was able to accommodate up to 1,000 people. 'So the Elim voice was heard where also had been heard the men of the calibre of John Newton, Wade Robinson and evangelist Henry Varley. Soon 2000 witnessed 300 baptisms, of all classes.'[18] Canty is here referring to the fact that Jeffreys' appeal was not just to the working class, but that people of all backgrounds were attracted and influenced by Jeffreys' ministry.

From Brighton, George Jeffreys went fourteen miles west along the coast to Worthing. 'This was a sedate town and a place to which Jeffreys would return two years later.'[19] Jeffreys set up his evangelistic marquee in the Ore Valley Farm. The tent was soon too small and the campaign moved to the Elite Picture Theatre which, although accommodating three times more, was soon also too small.

This was in spite of financial pressures that the principal mentioned in his end of year message in the *Elim Evangel*.

> We have passed through the troublesome waters of financial difficulty, we have our testing times, we are called upon sometimes to stand with our backs against the wall – but we stand together. In answer to the prayers of God's people, deliverance comes.[20]

The final south coast campaign of the year was held in Portsmouth, hailed at the time as 'the greatest naval port in the world'. Jeffreys and his Revival Party were overwhelmed by the reception they received first in the great tent on Southsea Common and finally in the 2,000-seater Guildhall. Canty comments: 'Having converted men, Elim now converted a cinema to godly purposes.'[21] The first pastor was a woman, Miss N Kennedy, the sister of a former president and Executive Council member, James Craig Kennedy. The building held some 400 seats which were fully occupied until the events of 1939-45 nearly terminated activities In four weeks, there were 900 conversions.[22]

Following the Portsmouth campaign, Jeffreys returned to London, where he launched evangelistic attack after attack at Wimbledon, Hammersmith, Shepherd's Bush, Kings Cross, Islington, Finsbury Park and Croydon. Part of his Hammersmith campaign was held in the old 'Alley Palley' (Alexandra Palace). This part of London had seen nothing like it. Conquering the East End was one thing, but capturing the sophisticated West End of London was something else. Twice, 4,000 people made the lofty reaches of Alexandra Palace echo with praise to God as 1,200 were seen accepting Christ and others being miraculously healed. From these various efforts, churches were opened in Somers Town, Hornsey, Holloway, Tottenham, Muswell Hill, Islington and Wood Green.

Notes

[1] Elim Evangelistic Band Minute Book, 3rd July 1915.

[2] Carter, Jamys, 'An Historical Overview of women in ministry within the Elim Pentecostal Church in the first half of the twentieth century' (*Journal of the European Pentecostal Theological Association*), August 2018, p3.

[3] Carter, Jamys, ibid, p4.

[4] Carter, James, ibid, pp7,8.

[5] *Elim Evangel*, 2nd July 1928, Vol 9, No 13, p208.

[6] *Elim Evangel*, 1st January 1929, Vol 10, No 1, p16.

[7] *Elim Evangel*, 1st March 1929, Vol 10, No 3, p47.

[8] *Elim Evangel*, 16th May 1927, p141.

[9] Carter, Jamys, ibid, p10.

[10] Canty, George, ibid, p111.

[11] Canty, George, ibid, p111.

[12] Canty, George, ibid, p111.

[13] *Elim Evangel*, 1st June 1927, Vol 7, No 14, p163.

[14] *Elim Evangel*, ibid.

[15] His name was Algernon Coffin. There was a minister in Elim with that same surname. On one occasion he appeared on the same convention platform as another Elim pastor with the surname 'Way'. One can imagine the amusement of hearing Pastor Coffin and Pastor Way being announced as the speakers. Pastor Jack Way remarked: 'Call me Rev Way rather than Pastor Way. I am revving up, not passing away!'

[16] Cartwright, Desmond, ibid, p158.

[17] Canty, George, ibid, p112.

[18] Canty, George, ibid, p112.

[19] Kay, William, ibid, p171.

[20] *Elim Evangel*, 10th December 1927, Vol 8, No 23,24, p354.

[21] Canty, George, ibid, p112.

[22] *Elim Evangel*, 15th October 1927, Vol 8, No 20, p305.

26
Further UK Campaigns

The years 1928 and 1929 were phenomenal ones in the history of Elim. George Jeffreys was at the height of his revival ministry. In 1927, he had held campaigns in Glasgow, Paisley, Leeds, Southampton, Worthing, Portsmouth, Wimbledon, Hammersmith, Shepherd's Bush, King's Cross, Islington, Finsbury Park and Croydon. In addition to these, he conducted and preached at the great Easter Convention at the Royal Albert Hall. This, in itself, was a great step of faith. In the previous year, Aimee Semple McPherson preached at London's and the nation's premier concert hall. This time, George was on his own. Would he fill this huge hall with a seating capacity of 10,000? He most certainly did. The response of the press was a clear indication that Elim's founder had stunned the capital with his profound, yet straightforward gospel preaching. They were fascinated by the huge numbers of people that came out for healing and reported many of the healings that took place. Apart from the attack upon Jeffreys and Elim in the *John Bull* magazine, the press were, at best, positive in their reporting of Jeffreys' campaigns and rallies, and at worse, they were neutral. It is clear that Principal George Jeffreys had touched the heart of the nation.

Time and space prevents me from examining Jeffreys' scriptural emphases. His teaching on the Foursquare Gospel will be dealt with in the first few chapters of the second volume on Elim's story. It should be noted, however, that some of his theological views were not orthodox either from the conservative evangelical viewpoint, nor indeed from the Pentecostal norm. His view on British Israelism was certainly not standard Pentecostal fare. This will be examined later in this volume.

Jeffreys' views on the baptism in the Holy Spirit could be said to have become less obviously Pentecostal than at the beginning of his ministry. It is my personal view that this was to have a long-lasting effect on Elim in future years. There is no doubt that in the early years of Elim's history (certainly into the early thirties) the established position on the baptism in the Holy Spirit was that speaking in other tongues was the initial evidence of such a baptism. This was clearly stated in the movement's earliest Fundamentals until 1927, when Jeffreys changed the fundamental on the baptism in the Holy Spirit by substituting the phrase, '... accompanied by speaking in other tongues ...' with '... with signs following'. Subsequent changes to the statement of fundamental beliefs have maintained this view.

It would seem that, with the exception of his views on healing and miracles, Jeffreys became less Pentecostal as the years went on. It is certain that his views on the initial evidence of the baptism in the Holy Spirit and his eschatological views separated him from many established Pentecostals of his generation. E J Phillips was one who majored on his experience of the baptism in the Holy Spirit. He spoke more about this than he did of his conversion. 'This is highly significant because in the view of most Elim ministers who knew him, he was somewhat aloof and unemotional. It is clear, however, that E J was very much a Pentecostal in his theology and practice.'[1]

In the very first article on the baptism of the Holy Spirit,[2] Thomas Hackett, a Church of Ireland clergyman, and a member of the first Elim governing council, clearly associated the baptism in the Holy Spirit with the identifying evidence of speaking in other tongues.[3] 'This mighty Baptism was originally by the speaking in other tongues as the Spirit gave utterance ...

we believe the speaking with other tongues to be the Bible evidence of the baptism in the Holy Ghost.'[4]

Following the resignation of W Hare, the first editor of the *Evangel*, E J Phillips was appointed as his successor. In May 1924, Boulton wrote the editorial for that month and it was taken up with the baptism in the Holy Spirit. The following month, E J wrote the editorial on the same subject. In his editorial, Boulton made no reference to 'tongues' being the initial evidence of the baptism of the Holy Spirit. Phillips, however, wrote the following:

> You will find when the Holy Ghost comes in and takes possession that you will be filled with the glory of God, and the Holy Ghost will manifest His presence by speaking through you in other tongues the wonderful works of God. Your very spirit, soul and body will be permeated with His presence.[5]

It should be noted that Boulton was less critical in his views of Jeffreys than was Phillips. There is no record of Boulton speaking against the principal at the time of the division within Elim. On the subject of the baptism in the Holy Spirit, Boulton's views appear to be similar to those of Jeffreys'. Jeffreys did not believe that speaking in other tongues was the initial evidence of the baptism in the Holy Spirit. Boulton became the editor of the *Evangel* and dean of Elim Bible College. Both these offices would have given him the opportunity to influence many post-war Elim ministers. It is the author's opinion that Phillips was far more orthodox in the Pentecostal sense than was Jeffreys. In his book *Pentecostal Rays*, Jeffreys names three schools of thought on the effect of the Spirit on the mortal body. The first is that those who receive the gift of the Holy Spirit will have the sign of speaking in tongues. The second view is that everyone who receives should have some definite supernatural manifestation of the Spirit in the mortal body, not necessarily the sign of speaking in tongues. The third view stands for the reception of the Spirit by faith without any outward sign.[6] He is clearly referring here to the baptism in the Holy Spirit. He states categorically: 'The second view is the scriptural one.' In reading his views on the evidence of the baptism in the Spirit, it is quite clear that Jeffreys went a considerable distance from the accepted norm within Pentecostal circles. He seems to differentiate speaking in tongues as an evidence of the baptism with the gift of tongues mentioned in 1 Corinthians 12. It has long been my view that there is no scriptural difference between the two. Once a person has spoken in tongues, he or she has the ability to give a spoken message in tongues during public worship, which will then be interpreted. There is no difference between tongues as an *evidence* of the baptism of the Spirit and the *gift* of tongues when exercised in public worship as a message from God to be interpreted.

> Insistence upon this particular sign [tongues] for every seeker, in face of these positive and negative affirmations of Scripture on the subject, means the violation of the reasonable and logical law that should govern the right dividing of the Word of truth. The claim based upon precept and example is that tongues is the initial sign of the Baptism is not valid, because it is not stated to be the example in Acts 4, nor in Acts 8.[7]

He goes on to argue, however, that in the case of the Samaritan revival, there was clearly some kind of an evidential sign of the receiving the baptism in the Holy Spirit, for Simon saw the effect of the laying on of the apostles' hands.[8] Unlike his view on Church government, Jeffreys' view on the evidence of the baptism in the Holy Spirit is one that has prevailed and become the accepted norm in Elim to this day. It is the author's opinion that this has had a detrimental effect on Pentecostal distinctives within Elim. In my early days in Elim, believers were taught to seek the baptism in the Holy Spirit as a distinct, personal experience. They were taught to seek an initial evidence. The evidence that was invariably looked for was that of speaking in other tongues by the inspiration of the Holy Spirit. It would appear that clear teaching on the baptism in the Spirit is seldom given in Elim churches at present, and fewer opportunities are given to those seeking Spirit baptism.

Jeffreys taught a distinction between the Spirit of Christ and the Holy Spirit. The two proof texts that he uses are Romans 8:9 and Acts 19:2. He argues that the Spirit of Christ enters the believer at the point of conversion and that the Holy Spirit can only be received by those already regenerated.[9] 'Jeffreys continues to hold his position about the distinction between the Spirit of Christ and the Holy Spirit, the former being responsible for regeneration and the latter for empowerment.'[10] Kay deals comprehensively with Jeffreys' doctrine on healing, the Holy Spirit and the second coming of Christ. He includes Jeffreys' views on three baptisms.[11]

1928

The first revival campaign of 1928 was held at the Caledonian Road Baths, King's Cross, in January. The *Evangel* reported that up to the time of going to press, some 400 decisions for Christ had been recorded.[12] The *Evangel* report contained a press cutting from Islington Press, 14th January 1928 that included a number of testimonies of divine healing. The following edition of the *Evangel* carried a report by Miss Hamilton Hunter who stated that more than 1,200 people had surrendered their lives to Christ and the meetings had transferred to the Alexandra Palace. Some four pages in the *Evangel* are devoted to this great campaign.[13] Included in this was a very positive report by Rev W H Stuart-Fox, vicar of St Saviour's, Crouch Hill, titled: 'A-Never-to-be-forgotten-climax to a Wonderful Campaign.'

> How many are saying today, 'Thank God for this campaign!' I do for one, I am quite sure that our churches, many of them, are going to be rocked by the waves of blessing, set rolling by the manifestation of the

presence of the Risen Christ, rocked until the sleepers awake. Too many of our churches have run into a form, and have put up denominational fences which even the Holy Ghost can't get through, and the liberty of the Spirit unknown and His power unrealised.

Then on Sundays, that great home of the 'Pictures' – the rink Finsbury Park – was witness to moving pictures of a new and much more startling character than had ever been seen there before. Here was fact, not fiction. Here was life, not mechanism. Here were miracles, not produced through the art of photography, but by the vital force of the living Saviour.[14]

From King's Cross, Jeffreys moved south of the Thames to Croydon. As a result of this great campaign, Elim churches were established, not only in Croydon itself, but also Thornton Heath, South Croydon, Wallington and Woodside.[15] The 15th March edition of the *Elim Evangel* carried the following title on its opening page: 'Croydon *in the* throes of *a* Revival: Principal George Jeffreys' Campaign Extended' – it lasted for a period of six weeks.

The greatest revival we have witnessed in the London district is now in progress in Croydon. Owing to large crowds being turned away from the meetings, the members of our churches in London were requested not to attend the services. And yet, the spacious North End Hall was packed and the doors locked long before the time for the meetings to commence. The campaign was announced for three weeks, but so great was the blessing that Principal George Jeffreys consented to forego a short rest in order to continue the meetings for another week. At the end of this week, he was persuaded to allow other evangelists to commence his next campaign while he continued another fortnight in a still larger building. In these meetings, there is a constant stream of salvation and healing. At the time of going to press, over 1,100 have professed conversion. Croydonians of every denomination say that they have never seen such a movement of the Spirit of God.[16]

Following on from the Croydon campaign, the great Easter demonstration was held in the Royal Albert Hall. The great hall was booked for two days – Good Friday and Easter Monday. The press were staggered at the great baptismal service that George Jeffreys conducted on the Good Friday. More than 1,000 believers were baptised. It must have been a huge logistical challenge. The tank that was brought in was of considerable size. In the photograph published in the *Evangel*, two sisters are about to be baptised; also in the tank is George Jeffreys and four assistants to help him with the baptisms. One of them is a very youthful Harry Greenway, later to become secretary-general in succession to the formidable E J. Questions were raised about the hygiene risks of so many people being baptised. But a very well designed drainage system was in place so that water constantly ran in and out of the tank. The press were beside themselves in reporting the incredible scene. All the major national newspapers covered this remarkable event.[17]

There were three services on Easter Monday, the first being a communion service. Again, the logistics of serving communion to 10,000 people must have been immensely challenging. Behind these great celebrations we detect the careful planning and organisational skills of the redoubtable secretary-general. He arranged matters to the finest detail. Nothing escaped his scrutiny. Jeffreys was the great evangelist who led the campaigns, but without E J working so hard behind the scenes, his campaigns would not have been anywhere as successful as they were.

Whitsuntide saw Elim holding another convention at the Royal Albert Hall. They were to hire this great hall on two further occasions in 1928. This was a phenomenal achievement. No other Christian denomination has managed what this young Pentecostal movement did in this respect. We must remember that Elim was only thirteen years old in 1928. From a disused laundry in a Belfast backstreet to four occasions in one year at the nation's premier concert hall seating 10,000 people is a truly staggering achievement. John Leech once again spoke at the communion service in the Royal Albert Hall on Whit Monday. This clearly shows his ever-increasing influence on George Jeffreys. The convention continued for a further three nights in the Queen's Hall, London.

The lovely south coastal town of Eastbourne was the next centre of Jeffreys' campaigns. It was a community noted for its businessmen's long-settled attitudes and respectability. It was a place that was hardly conducive for a Jeffreys' revival campaign, and at first, things were very quiet. But the Pier Pavilion and then the Winter Garden soon became too small. Converts were eventually numbered in four figures.

When regular Elim services were held following the campaign, only the Town Hall could cope. The pastor appointed to follow up the crusade had an enormous task before him. Pastor LeTissier, originally from the Channel Islands, was sent from Plymouth to lead the new Elim congregation in Eastbourne. He was assisted by the boy preacher Frank Allen.

If Eastbourne responded extremely well to George Jeffreys and Elim, the story of the Bath campaign is quite different. About eighteen people had left one of the churches in Bath on account of the 'worldliness' and Bible criticism. When George arrived in September 1928, these were the first people to attend his campaign. Two weeks of meetings proved hard-going and only about a 100 responded to Christ. 'He shook off the dust of his feet then, so to speak, though he had had higher success than he supposed.'[18] Canty attributes the establishment and survival of the Elim work in Bath to the efforts of the very young and later, highly successful, pastor W G Channon, who went on to become pastor of Spurgeon's Metropolitan Chapel. The new Elim congregation had to carry their sole Elim accessories in a tin trunk from hall to hall. For a time, they had the lease of the

Assembly Rooms, but it was decided to restore the rooms to the style of the mid-eighteenth century. Eventually, the historic Percy Chapel was bought. Canty highlights some of the enormous difficulties facing new Elim congregations. The task of forming a group (some of them many hundreds strong) was a herculean challenge. That many young and inexperienced Elim pastors rose to the occasion and established strong Pentecostal churches is down to the work of the Holy Spirit.

Despite difficult days in Bath, George struck more deeply into the West Country, to the Devon county capital of Exeter. Although the Exeter campaign was a great success, it is clear that there was strong opposition to this Elim campaign from more than one section of the Christian Church in the city. James McWhirter, a member of the Revival Party, made this clear in his report in the *Elim Evangel*:

> Here, Principal George Jeffreys' Revival and Healing campaign has been fighting its way to success. Yes, *fighting* – as pioneers of truth have always had to fight … It has been a fight too! Through a hide-bound ecclesiasticism and priest-craft of which our Divine Lord was the greatest foe. Through the ignorance and prejudice and the heartless lukewarmness of Laodicean Churchianity. Through the jealousy and popery of small sects. But all this makes the victory more gratifying and glorious. A gentleman in the Civic Hall – who is not a professed Christian – said to me in a confidential and sympathetic manner: 'The people who were in this hall before you (a Christian Convention) have been giving it to you.' At this, I smiled, and replied: 'They were only advertising us.'

It was during the Exeter campaign that Albert Edsor was asked by George Jeffreys to join the Revival Party as pianist and chauffeur. He wrote to his mother: 'I am playing here for the campaign and last night we had a marvellous time … close on 2000 in the all for the service … after the service I had a talk with the Pastor (George Jeffreys) and I am going with him as his pianist.'[19] This was the commencement of a lifetime's service for Edsor. He became Jeffreys' staunchest ally and Elim's sternest critic. He was inspired to write a book[20], largely as a result of the book *The Great Evangelists* written by Desmond Cartwright, and also, the book *Restoring the Kingdom* by Dr Andrew Walker.[21]

Edsor took great offence at Andrew Walker's comment about Jeffreys that hinted at a consideration of the evangelist's sexuality. What would have further annoyed Edsor is that throughout his section on Elim and Assemblies of God, Walker mis-spelled Jeffreys and rendered it as *Jeffries* (author's italics). He writes: 'George Jeffries was a shy man ... he never married. Despite his rather effeminate looks in his early days (at least against his miner brother), and despite the occasional whiffs of scandal surrounding his sexuality, there is not the slightest historical evidence that Jeffries was homosexual.'[22] Such a statement would immediately cause some to consider as to whether there was some truth to Walker's suggestion.

Following the Exeter campaign, Elim did the unthinkable by hiring the Royal Albert Hall for a seven-night campaign with Aimee Semple McPherson and George Jeffreys. This was truly a monumental step of faith. The *Elim Evangel* carried a report of the remarkable Royal Albert Hall campaign with the following title: 'SISTER MCPHERSON IN LONDON – Remarkable Campaign at the Royal Albert Hall'.

> Another Foursquare Gospel campaign has passed into the history of a Movement which, although barely twenty years old, yet can already lay claim to many a magnificent evangelical exploit ... Seven days in a building of such capacity as the Royal Albert Hall, with all the expense involved, without anything in the nature of an actual guarantee, seemed to have been a risk that might have shaken the confidence of the most intrepid Christian workers.[23]

Following this great campaign, George and Aimee went on a whistle-stop tour of the provinces holding revival meetings at Glasgow, Carlisle, Leeds, Hull, Sunderland, Brighton and Bristol. Two further campaign meetings were held in the Royal Albert Hall on 14th and 15th November, with an afternoon and evening service on both days. It is difficult for us to comprehend the immensity of this evangelistic endeavour.

The last campaign of 1928 saw Jeffreys in Bradford during the month of December, when 1,400 people accepted Christ as their Saviour and another great assembly blessed another great city.[24]

1929

In January 1929, George Jeffreys laid the foundation stone of the Elim Church in Eastbourne. On the campaign front, things were a little quiet in the first four months of 1929. Elim held its fourth consecutive Easter convention at the Royal Albert Hall. The *Daily Chronicle* reported that some people waited from 7am until the doors were opened. 'There were scenes of religious fervour.' The *Daily Telegraph* reported: '10,000 attended the Foursquare Demonstration at the Royal Albert Hall yesterday … sixty-six testified that they had been healed of cancer and other crippling diseases.'[25] The same edition of the *Evangel* carried the interesting news that Elim had opened a bookshop in Paternoster Road, London.

The first major campaign of 1929 took place in Greenock, Scotland. Although there was a write-up of the campaign in the 1st June edition of the *Evangel*, with a glowing report from the former provost of Greenock, Canty refers to it as being 'of the power of a limited effort'.[26] He does add that the campaign was such that 'the first pastor, Samuel Gorman, expressed the view that it could have been the mightiest of all campaigns'. Thomas Baxter, JP, Hon Sub-Sheriff of Renfrewshire and Bute, Provost of Greenock (1921-24), in his report to the *Evangel* wrote that he had witnessed all the major evangelistic crusades in

Greenock during the previous fifty years, including the Moody and Sankey and Torrey-Alexander campaigns 'but we have not witnessed anything like the present … A special feature of the meetings was the large number of young men and women who attended. More and more they were in evidence as the work progressed'. Some of these young men were to become Elim ministers and influential lay members of the Elim Conference for many years. Among these young people were Tommy Stevenson and John MacInnes, both of whom were to become presidents of Elim. Also, Willie Hilliard, a pastor of the church at the time, served as president of Elim. The Greenock church produced not only fine pastors, but influential lay members of Conference. These included Robert Campbell (who was an Elim pastor for a period of time and the father of David and Ian, two current Elim pastors).[27] Nine hundred people were converted in quick time and a congregation founded, having five hundred in the morning and 1,400 at night. In private conversations with Samuel Gorman, the author can testify to the fact that he (Gorman) was astounded at the work of God going on before and around him.

Notes

[1] Jones, Maldwyn, ibid, p 9

[2] *Elim Evangel*, December 1920.

[3] Hackett, T E, 'The Baptism of the Holy Ghost and Gifts of the Spirit – Why Now?', *Elim Evangel*, December 1920, Vol 2, No 1, p10.

[4] *Elim Evangel*, 'The Baptism in the Holy Ghost', June 1920, Vol 2, No 3, p50.

[5] *Elim Evangel*, Editorial by E J P, June 1924, Vol 5, No 6, p118.

[6] George Jeffreys, *Pentecostal Rays* (London: Elim Publishing Company Ltd, 1933), p36.

[7] George Jeffreys, ibid, p37.

[8] George Jeffreys, ibid, p38.

[9] George Jeffreys, ibid, pp39,40.

[10] William Kay, *George Jeffreys*, p234.

[11] William Kay, *George Jeffreys*, chapter 11

[12] *Elim Evangel*, 1st February 1928, Vol 9, No 3, p44.

[13] Elim Evangel: 15th February 1928, Vol 9, No 4, pp56,60.

[14] *Elim Evangel*, ibid, p57.

[15] Canty, George, ibid, p113.

[16] *Elim Evangel*, 1st March 1928, Vol 9, No 6, p81.

[17] *Elim Evangel*, 1st May 1928, Vol 9, No 9, pp134,135.

[18] Canty, George, ibid, p114.

[19] Edsor, Albert, *Set Your House in Order*, p20.

[20] *Set Your House in Order*.

[21] Walker, Andrew, *Restoring the Kingdom* (London: Hodder & Stoughton, 1985).

[22] Walker, Andrew, ibid, p249.

[23] *Elim Evangel*, 1st February 1928, Vol 9, No 8, pp246,247.

[24] Canty, George, ibid, p115.

[25] Both newspapers were dated 2nd April 1929, reported in *Elim Evangel*, 1st May 1929, Vol 10, No 5, p65.

[26] Canty, George, ibid, p115.

[27] David is (at the time of writing) the Regional Leader for London and the South East; Ian is the Pastor of the City Church Greenock (an Elim Church) and a member of the influential Audit Committee.

27

George Jeffreys' Greatest Campaigns

By the late twenties, Elim was growing at quite a rate. Jeffreys' campaigns were attracting small, indigenous efforts at church planting. For instance, the following report appeared in the *Elim Evangel*: 'Verwood: a very gracious work for God is being sustained in the very heart of Dorsetshire. A small, but nevertheless enthusiastic and consecrated company of God's children are standing staunchly for the Foursquare Gospel, and God is honouring their witness.'[1] The March edition of the same year carries a report of the Worcester church that had been opened independently of George Jeffreys.[2] The April edition of the *Evangel* reported the news of the establishment of an Elim church in Hornsey as well as in Bridgewater.[3] The May edition carried news of a further four churches that had been commenced by local initiative – Rayleigh, Wood Green, Rathfriland and Devonport.[4] At the time of the severe internal dissention that led to the division within the movement, W G Hathaway, the field superintendent, referring to the number of churches that had been established in Elim as a result of George Jeffreys' campaigns, noted that the total number was forty-seven. At this time, there were approximately 215 Elim churches so, according to Hathaway, 168 Elim churches had not been founded by the principal.[5]

The above is by no means an attempt to minimise Jeffreys' great campaigns, but simply to point out the fact that it would have been impossible for all, or even the majority of Elim churches between 1915 and 1939, to have been established as a direct result of George Jeffreys' revival campaigns. The effect of those campaigns, however, was not just to establish strong and large Elim churches in the major conurbations of the land, but also to encourage the opening of smaller churches as a result of local initiative. This was particularly the case among the Essex churches.[6]

The *Elim Evangel* had gone from a fortnightly to a monthly publication in August 1928 when the *Foursquare Revivalist*, a weekly newspaper publication, was launched. This was not a great success and commencing in June 1929, it was incorporated into the *Elim Evangel* which then became a weekly publication. The *Evangel* was not above making political observations and E J (the editor), being himself of Jewish descent, was pro-Zionist in his views of the Jewish people returning to Palestine (as it was, Israel as it now is). In the February 1929 edition, an intriguing article appeared concerning Mussolini. Reference was made to a huge statue that was built in his honour. A direct quote was taken from the *Christian Herald* and printed as part of the article. When Hitler became chancellor of Germany, Phillips made his opinions known as to the plight of Jewish people in Nazi-controlled Germany and Italy.

In an editorial comment, Phillips writes under the subheading, 'The sigh of the Jew'. In this article, he refers to the fact that the kingdom of God has been taken away from the Jewish people. He looks forward to the day 'when Jewish hearts will welcome the Christ of God'. But, almost as a foreshadowing of the dreadful Jewish pogrom that was to come to fulfilment under Hitler, E J refers to the present appalling situation in Poland with regards to suicide among Jews:

> We are told that another epidemic of suicides among the Jews in Poland during 1927. During the first half of that year there were 140 such suicides in the City of Warsaw alone, and among them were two Rabbis. There has

never been another instance in Jewish history in which Rabbis of thirty years of official service have killed themselves, and the Jews all over the world, especially in Poland, were greatly shocked.[7]

In June 1929, the Labour Party, under the leadership of Ramsay MacDonald, became the Government. This was the second time that MacDonald became Prime Minister, having led a minority Labour Government for nine months in 1924. He headed a national Government from 1931 to 1935, dominated by the Conservative Party and supported by only a few Labour members. MacDonald was expelled from the Labour Party as a result. E J's editorial comment makes interesting reading.[8] He implies that the reason that the Government was changed that year was due, in no small way, to the controversial defeat in the House of the proposed revision of the Prayer Book that had been advocated by the Bishops of the Church of England with the support of the Conservative Party. He goes on to say:

As a movement, we have no conscious political opinion, being occupied more especially with spiritual issues: notwithstanding, we are loyalists who pray for and are submissive to His Majesty's Government in so far as its rule is not at variance with the Word of God. The Government has our sincerest wishes for success in dealing with the pressing problems with which it is pledged to grapple.

The years 1929 and 1930 were to witness probably the three greatest Elim campaigns, certainly in the opinion of the author. The Birmingham campaign of 1930, discussed previously and in the following chapter, is recognised by Elim historians and researchers as Jeffreys' finest and greatest campaign.[9]

Following the campaign at Greenock, George turned his attention back to the south coast, where he conducted a short campaign in Hove. After crossing the Irish Sea for a convention in Bangor, he returned to the Royal Dome in Brighton (5th-7th

August).[10] He set up his Campaign Tent in Worthing from the end of July through the month of August. This was another successful campaign on the south coast, with the newspapers reporting a large number of conversions and many people testifying to being healed. The next place on Jeffreys' campaign map was the town of Ipswich (2nd-15th September). There were 250 converts registered during the Ipswich campaign.[11]

Cardiff

As wonderful as the campaigns in Hove, Worthing and Ipswich had been, nothing could have prepared George for the great campaigns at Cardiff and Swansea. Of the two, Cardiff, as befitting the city that was to become the capital of Wales in 1955, having had city status conferred upon it in 1905, was the premier of the two South Wales campaigns, with the Swansea campaign evolving from Cardiff. The torrent of revival seemed to be sweeping back to the place where it began, in Wales, at the turn of the century.

The attendances at Jeffreys' meetings in Cardiff were huge, surpassed only by the vast crowds that would attend the great Birmingham campaign the following year. The accessibility of Cardiff to the famous South Wales mining valleys of Rhondda, Dare, Cynon, Merthyr and Rhymney meant that thousands of people streamed from those places to Cardiff to hear George preach and pray for people to be healed.

The *Daily Express* carried a bill-board notice with the following words: 'HEALING CAMPAIGN IN CARDIFF: TENSE SCENES'.[12] The *Evangel* carried the newspaper report with this startling and emotion-filled first paragraph: 'A wave of emotion ebbed and flowed through the Cory Hall here this afternoon and finally filled the building. Men sobbed out prayers, women fell on their knees, and rose again to lift eager hands.'[13]

The Cardiff campaign opened on the 22nd September in Cardiff's premier Conference Hall. The Cory Hall was next door to the YMCA in Station Terrace, opposite the entrance to Queen Street Station. According to Kay, Jeffreys had responded to an anonymous postcard that had reached Clapham with the words: 'Cardiff needs Foursquare Gospel'. George, being a first-language Welsh-speaker from South Wales, responded to the suggestion. Kay makes a mistake in his assumption that the Cory Hall housed the YMCA and the Wood Street Congregational Church. While the YMCA was situated right next door to the Cory Hall, they were, nevertheless, separate buildings. As for Wood Street Congregational Church, that was situated opposite Cardiff General Station (now called Cardiff Central Station) some mile and a half away from Queen Street Station.[14] The Cory Memorial Temperance Hall was built at a cost of £5,000 and presented to the temperance societies of Cardiff by John Cory (1828-1910) as a memorial to his late father, Richard. It was in this great hall that the Miners' Conference was held on 21st July 1915, when terms for settling the South Wales coal strike were accepted after negotiations with Lloyd George. It was later to become a concert hall featuring brass band competitions.

Jeffreys was booked for three weeks but stayed for seven. He spoke every night as well as twice on Wednesdays, Thursdays and Sundays.[15] As was quite a familiar occurrence, only a few people were present in the first meetings and George wrote to E J: 'It will take time.'[16] After campaigning for three weeks, the *Evangel* reported: 'The Revival in Cardiff is proceeding with ever-increasing blessing. Over five hundred souls have been saved, and over forty have testified to the experience of Divine healing.'[17] As usual, there appears to have been considerable opposition to Jeffreys' campaign in Cardiff, as there had been in Exeter. The reasons would have been similar in both cities: opposition from ecclesiastical circles. But whereas the opposition in Exeter would have been largely from the established Church, in Cardiff it would have most likely come from the nonconformist chapels. Although Wales was famous for the great 1904-05 revival, there had been a strong reaction to the emotionalism of those days. The Welsh theological colleges were, by and large, modernistic and liberal, and this was transferred to the congregations. The *Evangel* comment was: 'Opposition is gradually breaking down before the message of the Foursquare Gospel, which is being attested by signs and wonders.'[18]

By the fifth week of the campaign, 1,600 decisions for Christ had been registered and countless people healed. The Cory Hall, although it seated 1,200, became too small to contain the vast crowds eager to gain admittance. The officers of Wood Street Congregational Church offered their building to Jeffreys. This was the largest nonconformist chapel building in the whole of Wales. Splott Road Baptist Church, which was almost as large as the Wood Street building, was also used for the revival meetings.[19] The effect on Cardiff was enormous. Sympathetic press coverage ensured that the campaign meetings continued to overflow each evening. The pressure on George Jeffreys must have been immense. He preached a total of sixty-three times in seven weeks. There was no let-up. There was no time for a break even when the Cardiff campaign finished, because he immediately commenced the Swansea campaign.

Compared to Evan Roberts, George was less emotional and certainly preached a great deal more. Although he was Welsh-speaking and his accent while speaking and preaching in English carried a very discernible Welsh lilt, his style was not typical of that associated with Welsh revivalists at the turn of the nineteenth century. 'We can say that the preaching of the Gospel was not harsh and condemnatory but, on the contrary, warm, clear, and bringing the promise of new spiritual life and health.'[20] George's preaching was very biblical and expositional. He emphasised, time and again, the full and supreme authority of the Scriptures. Noel Brooks wrote of Jeffreys: 'He continually exalted Holy Scripture as the sole and absolute authority in the church. He constantly warned his followers not to place the gifts of the Holy Spirit either above Holy Scripture or on a level with it. Only the Bible is authoritative'.[21] Brooks added: 'The conviction that Scripture is supreme – controlled George Jeffreys' powerful ministry throughout his career.'[22]

Although by nature shy, as noted before, George Jeffreys filled the platform from which he preached. He was no showman, and sometimes came quietly on to the platform with anyone hardly noticing him. But when he preached, it was quite obvious that God was in the house. His preaching was direct and clear. I have spoken to many people, mostly Elim pastors, who heard him preach. While some thought that his brother Stephen's inspirational preaching was more to their liking, George's preaching and teaching caught people's attention. There was a clarity to his voice that was profound. He had a rich baritone voice and when he uttered brief sentences of introduction, the presence of the Holy Spirit was evident. One of his favourite phrases was 'The Master is here' – and He certainly was! As a first-language Welsh-speaker, when preaching in English, he pronounced every syllable. There was no slurring over words. The Welsh language is a phonetic one and there are no silent letters in it. The tendency is that those of us Welsh people who learned English as a second language make sure that we clearly enunciate every letter, vowel and syllable that needs to be pronounced. An added factor to this, and quite noticeable in George's preaching, is that a first-language Welsh speaker tends to speak English a little slower than the average native speaker.

Rom Landau was deeply impressed by the timbre of Jeffreys' voice: 'The voice of Jeffreys was strong, it was a baritone, and full of the melody which we are accustomed to find in a Welsh voice.'[23] Landau refers to the unobtrusive way that George appeared on the Royal Albert Hall platform: 'Though my eyes had rarely left the platform, I did not see the entry of George Jeffreys … and I only discovered later that he had been sitting for some time among his friends in the front row.' But it was the tone of Jeffreys' voice that captured Landau's attention: 'I did not doubt that the strong and sincere tone of Jeffreys was responsible for much of the veneration in which his followers held him. There was in it the reassuring note of fatherly advice ... A George Jeffreys with a high-pitched tenor might never have become known.' Landau was struck not only by the quality and timbre of Jeffreys' voice, but also by his biblical preaching:

> The contents of his message were not new. At times their crude fundamentalism was irritating. So was the somewhat childish emphasis on the necessity of real baptism instead of 'the pagan Catholic sprinkling of children', as Jeffreys called it. But I was struck by the way in which he spoke. There was a quality in his delivery which I can only describe as biblical. The Bible was obviously the source from which he had derived his knowledge and his powers as a speaker. But the main feature of his style was not merely the right adaptation of biblical knowledge: there was in his words a natural persuasiveness which can be derived only from full identification with the Bible.

Landau, while being something of a mystic, was not a Christian by declaration. He was a secular writer and reporter. But he grasps something of the essence of the biblical Christian evangelist when he cuts to the heart of Jeffreys preaching. Would that it were said of gospel preachers everywhere today what he said of Jeffreys:

> The whole philosophy of Jeffreys was neither emotional nor intellectual – it was just biblical. The man has identified himself with the spirit of the Gospels speaks as though from another level. His reasoning does not come from his intellect but from a 'higher order of reality', and thus he becomes in a way above argument. It seemed that the Scriptures had become the very life-blood of George Jeffreys.[24]

There were many and incredible healings that took place during the Cardiff campaign as they had in other campaigns. A reporter for the *Evening World* writes of the healing of Mrs Elizabeth Wood, School Street, Abertridwr, whom he had known for some years. She had been a cripple and had moved about on crutches with the utmost difficulty. 'After being anointed and prayed for, she arose and placed her crutches on one side. I could hardly credit it when she walked to the front of the hall without assistance.'[25] The result of the Cardiff campaign led to the formation of a 1,000-member church and a building was erected in Cowbridge Road East and was known as the 'City Temple'. It was the only Elim church that maintained its congregation at pre-1939 levels and remains the largest Pentecostal church in Wales. Much of this is down to the work of its long-time pastor, Percy S Brewster. His story will be told in the second volume of Elim's history.

Swansea

The Swansea campaign commenced on 11th November 1929. The weather that day was not conducive for people to be out of doors, yet the Central Hall was full to capacity. The report in *Defining Moments* is slightly incorrect in that it said of George Jeffreys that he 'was largely unknown' in the district. The Welsh newspapers, particularly the *Western Mail*, were full of reports of the Cardiff campaign. Swansea was a town[26] very close to Llwchwr (Loughor), the birthplace of the Welsh Revival (1904-05). As such, it would have been aware of news of revival accounts in other parts of Wales.

The first reports of the Swansea campaign appeared in the *Elim Evangel* dated 29th November 1929:

> The Foursquare Revival in Wales has spread to Swansea in the west, for Principal George Jeffreys and the party are continuing the revival campaign. Expectation is running high that Swansea will have a great spiritual awakening that will equal Cardiff, if not eclipse it. From the first service the atmosphere was pervaded with the

spirit of revival. Many wonderful healings have taken place. Among the most remarkable was that of a young man with a deformed back, whose hump has completely disappeared. One woman was healed of an obnoxious growth of twenty years standing, and another of a poisoned stomach. Daily, men, women and children are touching Christ by faith, and are being made perfectly whole. Nearly one hundred have already been converted. One great feature of the opening week of services is the large number of young men who attend. In this it resembles the Cardiff campaign.[27]

It was in Swansea that the same reporter from the *Daily Express* who had recounted Evan Roberts' meetings in the Welsh Revival described the Elim meetings and interviewed George. Glyn Thomas was the young man referred to in the above *Evangel* report. He was well-known in Swansea as a newspaper vendor whose hunchback deformity was obvious to all. Thomas had attended the campaign each night and on Thursday, 14th November, he went out for prayer. 'After prayer, the jacket he was wearing hung limply on his back and the huge hump completely disappeared. He was also healed of severe epilepsy.'[28] Glyn Thomas went on to study for the ministry, pastoring a number of churches in the UK, and also travelled abroad, preaching the gospel.

Present at the Swansea campaign was Rev Glasnant Jones, under whose ministry George and Stephen Jeffreys had both been converted in Siloh Chapel, Nantyffyllon, Maesteg. A report under the heading: 'HIS CONVERTS BECAME REVIVALISTS' appeared in the *News Chronicle* (Welsh Edition) on 20th October 1947 where the 'veteran of Dunvant' spoke movingly of the two brothers: 'And here I am. Like Goldsmith's old soldier who shouldered his crutches to show how fields were won. Without a doubt Stephen and George Jeffreys were the means of converting a great multitude of unbelievers, and perhaps I may have a mark or two to my credit in the "grand inquest" for bringing the two brothers into the fold.'[29]

The Swansea campaign continued into the month of December and George questioned whether he should withdraw from the Annual Christmas Convention in Belfast, but after consultation with E J Phillips, decided to fulfil his arranged schedule. It was only occasionally that George visited Wales after this, on private visits to family, preaching in places such as Cwmtwrch in the Swansea valley. The end result of the Swansea campaign was yet another large church established in Dyfatty Street, near the railway station. It also bore the name 'City Temple' for many years and remains a thriving Elim church to the present day.

Notes

[1] *Elim Evangel*, 1st February 1929, Vol 10, No 2, p31.

[2] *Elim Evangel*, 1st March 1929, Vol 10, No 3, p43.

[3] *Elim Evangel*, 1st April 1929, Vol 10, No 64.

[4] *Elim Evangel*, 1st May 1929, Vol 10, No 5, p80.

[5] This was communicated in a letter sent from Hathaway to Phillips sometime in 1939 which is in the Elim Archives in Malvern. The author has seen this letter but, owing to the COVID-19 restrictions, is unable to include its exact date.

[6] These were the churches that had been pioneered largely through George Kingston and were a body of churches that were a part of Elim but were not Alliance churches. They developed separately under the title 'Elim Pentecostal Church'. They joined the Alliance in the mid 1950s, and Elim adopted their name a as their official name. The legal name still remains: 'Elim Foursquare Gospel Alliance'.

[7] *Elim Evangel*, 1st February 1928, Vol 9, No 11, p164.

[8] *Elim Evangel*, 14th June 1929, Vol 10, No 7, p104.

[9] Cardiff and Swansea were the other two of his greatest campaigns.

[10] Kay, William, ibid p189.

[11] *Elim Evangel*, 4th Oct 1929, Vol 10, No 23, p359.

[12] *Daily Express*, 3rd October 1939.

[13] *Elim Evangel*, 18th October 1929, Vol 10, No 25, p387.

[14] The author went past the Wood Street Congregational Church every day on his way to his first job after leaving school, in Westgate Street after alighting from the General Station. The Wood Street Congregational Church building was demolished in the early 1970s.

[15] Kay, William, ibid, p193.

[16] Cartwright, H C and Holdaway, D (eds),, *Defining Moments*, ibid, p46.

[17] *Elim Evangel*, 25th October 1929, Vol 10, No 26, p404.

[18] *Elim Evangel*, ibid.

[19] *Elim Evangel*, 8th November 1929, Vol 10, No 28, p434.

[20] Kay, William, bid, p195.

[21] Edsor, Albert, *Set Your House in Order*, pp10,11.

[22] Noel Brooks wrote a book on George Jeffreys, *Fight for the Faith and Freedom* (London: The Pattern Bookroom, 1948).

[23] Landau, Rom, *God is my Adventure*, p122.

[24] Landau, Rom, ibid.

[25] *Elim Evangel*, 8th November 1929, Vol 10, No 28, p434.

[26] Swansea achieved city status in 1969.

[27] *Elim Evangel*, 29th November 1929, Vol 10, No 31, p487.

[28] Cartwright, H C and Holdaway, D (eds), *Defining Moments*, p46.

[29] Edsor, Albert, *Set Your House in Order*, p29.

28

The Birmingham Campaign

The exhilarating, but ultimately hugely challenging decade of the thirties, began with Fascism, Nazism, world economic difficulties and swift religious decline, and for Elim, its own tragic upheaval lying ahead.[1] However, the wave of revival had not spent itself. The Elim churches, many of which had begun as a result of George Jeffreys' campaigns, were flourishing. It had been three years since the beginning of the Glasgow church, and on the first day of 1930, Hogmanay was celebrated by George Jeffreys opening the City Temple. 'A building admired by Ruskin, the St. John's and Renfield Street Church had been acquired for the Movement.'[2] The 'tragic upheaval' referred to above, together with the onset of the Second World War, resulted in the demise of the huge congregation that gathered weekly in this fine building. The building was eventually lost to Elim, and just a small congregation continued steadfastly over many years in the West of Glasgow. But that small congregation not only survived but grew until presently, there is a large and thriving Elim church in a large, modern building in this great Scottish city.

An invitation came to George Jeffreys to hold a campaign in Birmingham. There was certainly an interest among Elim leaders for a church to be established in the second city. At the end of 1929, a large church building had become available in Broad Street, but Elim were unsuccessful in purchasing it. They then turned their attention to nearby Smethwick where another building had come up for sale, and E J Phillips went to see it.

Cartwright reports that the city was very crowded and E J was unable to find a hotel, so he spent the night on a seat at the station![3] The building was purchased for the bargain price of £1,225. It was anticipated that Phil Hulbert should hold meetings there at first. Phillips was concerned about these plans and wrote to Jeffreys: 'It seems to me that all campaigns are practically a failure on new ground, unless they are conducted by you.'[4] In the meanwhile, the idea of holding a campaign in the heart of the city took hold.

This was a city that had a population of more than a million. It also had a strong Christian tradition and was known for its support of radical nonconformity. Birmingham had been represented by two great Congregational preachers and theologians: Dr R W Dale and Dr J H Jowett. Dale had a great influence on the city and was well-known for his many books, the chief one being his epic *The Atonement*,[5] which holds a cherished place in the author's book shelves. It was in Birmingham that the British Assemblies of God came into being in 1924. It was the birthplace of John and Howard Carter, two highly influential leaders of the Assemblies of God. 'The assemblies were not well established there however and they remained small, lacking any real leadership after the Carter brothers moved away.'[6] The campaign conducted by George Jeffreys in 1930 would have a dramatic effect not only on Elim, but on the future of the Pentecostal churches in the city.

The campaign commenced in Ebenezer Chapel, Steelhouse Lane. It was in the very same place that Charles Finney (1792-1875) had held protracted meetings in 1850.[7] The venue was booked from 26th March to 13th April. Apparently, there was some heated discussion between the deacons, some of whom were unsure as to whether George Jeffreys should be allowed to hold his meetings in their church. The decision to allow him to hold his campaign there was allowed by a casting vote.[8] Cartwright gives a different perspective on this. He states that the Elim leaders learned that the church was to close, and it became available for meetings while its future was being decided.[9]

It was felt by many Elim historians, including Canty and Cartwright, that the Birmingham campaign, though Jeffreys' greatest triumph, marked the beginning of the end of his great revival and church-planting ministry. Yes, there were notable campaigns in places such as Dundee, Nottingham, York and Huddersfield that were still to come, but from 1935 onwards, as we shall see, Jeffreys diverted his attention away from church pioneering and concentrated instead on what he saw as church reformation.

The principal had campaigned in Birmingham, at Duddleston, for John Carter in 1919. Now, on 26th March, he faced a small company of people scattered across the pews of this large church building. Letters to E J Phillips revealed how discouraged he was at the end of that first night. He wrote the following to Phillips:

> My meetings opened yesterday with a real backwash in Dudley (where Eddie Jeffreys opened meetings on March 16th – such crowds attended his meetings that many were left standing outside). All the people that could not get, or had already received the tickets they had used for healing in Eddie's meeting came to me. It was a real uproar when I invited people out for healing. Although the ground floor of the Church only was full yet they rushed out like wild Indians. Ho, my what a place. In Eddie's meetings he prays with a certain number *one* by one on a *chair*. When they found I invited them all out, it came as a surprise. One man said at the end, 'This man is a better preacher but the other performs more than he does.'[10]

The front page of the *Evangel* of 28th March 1930 hardly bore any resemblance to the small gathering at Steelhouse Lane on the first night of the Birmingham campaign. The whole page was taken up with notices for the coming Easter celebrations in

London, Belfast, Glasgow and Cardiff – the Foursquare Gospel conventions for the four countries of the United Kingdom. The list of speakers at the London convention makes interesting reading. All of them were close friends of Jeffreys and with one exception, they were all lost to Elim in 1940 when George made his final breach with the movement that he had founded.[11] George Canty takes up the story:

> Within five days, the Steelhouse Lane walls echoed less emptily for 'Brummies' were trekking to a venue they would never have dreamed of finding a week before and 600 had already said 'Yes' to the Gospel offer. The meetings should have ended on 13th April, but the chapel was almost constantly surrounded by a sea of humanity. Converts were being numbered now into the thousands. The historic Town Hall, with 2000 seats, became ridiculously inadequate.[12]

The first hint of what was happening in Birmingham, appeared in the 11th April edition of the *Elim Evangel* under the title: 'Principal George Jeffreys at Birmingham' and a subtitle: 'Over 600 converts and many healings'. The report was written in capitals, as follows:

> Foursquare Gospel revival fire has broken out in the City of Birmingham where Principal George Jeffreys and his revival party are holding forth. The campaign started as usual with a comparatively small congregation but the power of God was present. Day by day the Principal has been laying a solid and sure foundation whilst the congregation has been steadily growing until today, the fifth day, the place is packed to capacity. The Ebenezer Congregational Church in Steelhouse Lane has become a live centre of Foursquare revival activity. Over six hundred have been saved and many testify to miraculous healings. One gentleman who attended the Welsh revival meetings said Why, this is like Cardiff over again.

> Another who had been present at the Principal's
> campaign at Leeds declares it is another Leeds revival.
> Great conviction rests on the people and the deep
> spiritual atmosphere is sensed by the best of Christians.
> The Word of God is being sounded out with grand
> results.[13]

The following week's edition of the *Evangel* reported that more
than 2,000 converts had been registered in the Birmingham
campaign. The meetings at that time were still being held in
Steelhouse Road. Something had to change. That change came
when on 24th April the meetings were transferred to the Town
Hall for four nights. The Birmingham Town Hall was famous
for its concerts and political meetings. It was in this hall that
David Lloyd George had spoken against the Boer War. Lloyd
George was then a thirty-eight-year-old radical MP, and he took
his opposition to the Boer War right to the lair of the colonial
secretary and one of the architects of Britain's colonial policy –
Joseph Chamberlain. The crowd outside the Town Hall rioted.
Every window in the building was broken and Lloyd George
was forced to flee, dressed as a policeman, before he gave his
address. The riot resulted in the death of one man, and forty
people received hospital treatment.

There were far more people present at the Town Hall on the
occasion of George Jeffreys' campaign there in April 1930, but
the only protests came not from the crowd, but from many
pulpits in the city and, according to Canty, a religious counter-
attraction was put up by a leading nonconformist to occupy
Christian interest.[14] It was totally ineffective. Hundreds were
receiving their salvation and hundreds were receiving healing.
Ministers were confronted by their own members reporting
how they found Christ and were delivered from their sicknesses.

Soon, even the Town Hall became too small. The Sunday
services in May were transferred to the Embassy skating rink in
Sparkbrook. This was then the largest skating rink in Europe
and could accommodate 8,000 people, and 5,000 flooded into

this cavernous hall for the first meeting there on 4th May. At the Royal Albert Hall Easter Demonstration, Jeffreys announced that conversions in Birmingham totalled 4,000, with 2,000 turned away from the last Town Hall service.

The Bishop of Birmingham, E W Barnes, was a modernist theologian who caused quite a stir among the city's evangelicals by denying the virgin birth and the physical resurrection of Christ in his book, *Should Such a Faith Offend?*[15] He organised a response from other churches in the city who united in a 'Back to Church' campaign. He organised a march through the city led by the Salvation Army band. Cartwright comments dryly: 'The effort was not a success.'[16]

Despite opposition from so many ecclesiastical quarters in the city, the campaign continued, with thousands being converted and many hundreds testifying to being healed. Among them was the family of Eldin Corsie, a later principal of Elim Bible College and general superintendent of Elim.

The final two weeks of the campaign were held in the Bingley Hall, a low roofed-in exhibition hall occupying an entire block, dingy and draughty with a kind of gallery around the space, which was broken by roof supports. They talked of room for 18,000. Canty adds the following wry comment: 'The architectural atmosphere did not suggest the feel of the Divine quite so much as Westminster Abbey ... but something else was found there, the real, not the simulated presence of God. The Bingley Hall became hallowed.'[17] Soon, more than 6,000 decisions had been counted and there were hundreds of healings. Others shared the ministry, such as Frankie Allen, the boy preacher.

The 6th June edition of the *Evangel* displayed a cleverly worded announcement of the Birmingham campaign being transferred to the Bingley Hall. It had the following dramatic title: '19th Centenary of Pentecost'. 'For the Nineteen Hundredth Anniversary of the Outpouring of the Holy Ghost, the great Bingley Hall, Birmingham has been taken for two weeks (28 May to June 9).' Special trains were organised so that

Elim people from various parts of the country could attend. Canty suggested that James McWhirter, George Jeffreys' song leader and a member of the Revival Party, was the organising genius behind the hiring of the Bingley Hall. There is no doubt, however, that the negotiations with the railway companies were made by E J. It was his extraordinary administrative gifts that were the unseen hand behind the platform created for the Revival Party. There was a further report of the Birmingham campaign, again in capital letters to denote the thrill and excitement of what was going on in the second city: 'Birmingham Revival Sweeps On'.

> Crowds queued up early for the last days revival meetings in the large skating rink in Birmingham today. The monster congregations were swayed by the power of God. Principal George Jeffreys, choosing a message on the great miracle of the near future, penetrated all hearts and, one hundred and forty-eight souls were added to the many thousands coming together day after day for weeks strikes people as the greatest of all. Everyone now talks about the Bingley Hall and the proposed meetings for the last two weeks. Critics say the Bingley Hall cannot possibly be filled as in days of Moody and Torrey. Prayer warriors are convinced it will, and that the power of God will sweep through the building in greater measure than ever before. One thing is certain: God will honour His word with signs following.[18]

The reference to Moody and Torrey is to denote the only times that the Bingley Hall was used and filled for religious services, when D L Moody and Ira D Sankey were there during Moody's second visit to Britain in 1875 – Dr R A Torrey and Charles Alexander had used the building again in 1904. The great difference between those campaigns and Elim's campaign in 1930 was that the two previous occasions had the wide support of a great number of churches. Jeffreys had no such support.[19]

The Bingley Hall filled up twenty-six times (an aggregate of 250,000) and the final service began half an hour before time, since the place could not possibly hold another individual. George Jeffreys reached out to the Midlands in a way that none other ever did. During that incredible campaign, more than 10,000 conversions and many hundreds of healings took place. Eleven hundred people were baptised in water, and three large churches were opened in Birmingham as a result.[20] Each of these three churches had weekly congregations in excess of 800. Robert Tweed was appointed the pastor of the new Sparkbrook church and he baptised 450 people in one service, held at Hall Green swimming baths. By 1936, there were eleven churches in Birmingham.[21]

After a short break in Switzerland, George returned to London, where twenty-five churches were now active. He held campaigns in Wandsworth, Kingston and Ealing, where new Elim churches were established. An important step followed in Kensington. In 1921, Stephen Jeffreys had campaigned in the Horbury Chapel, with Donald Gee as his pianist. The minister of the chapel, F W Pitt, was opposed to the Pentecostal Movement and would not allow the chapel to be used for Pentecostal gatherings after this occasion. On 30th October 1930, Jeffreys bought the building for Elim from the Congregational Union and held a campaign there. Named Kensington Temple, it had to be enlarged, with meetings suspended until it reopened the following year.[22]

In September 1930, George Jeffreys made the very bold decision of hiring the Crystal Palace – possibly the largest hall in Britain. Elim would hire the place and fill a whole day with attractions and great services.[23] With an Elim brass band playing and Crusader banner flying, George led his legions into the Crystal Palace. 'Colossal congregations and monster crowds' are referred to in the *Evangel* report.[24] The 30th October 1930 edition of the *Evangel* is given over in its entirety to reports and impressions of the celebrations at the Crystal Palace. A hundred more converts were added to the kingdom that day, and some 500 sought healing.[25]

On 29th October 1930, the Nottingham campaign commenced in the massive Halifax Place Chapel, a former Methodist building. It was purchased by Elim. The campaign continued for several weeks and drew large crowds. The *Evangel* reports played heavily on the Methodist connection: 'Halifax Place, the grand old sanctuary of Nottingham Methodism is the scene of an old-time revival'.[26] Some 1,200 converts were recorded during the campaign and W G Channon was appointed as the first pastor. He, like Gorman, was a young pastor appointed to lead a huge congregation, but he filled the enormous chapel week by week, with more attending than had been converted in the campaign. Apparently, if he had less than 400 at the weekly prayer meeting, he would be worried![27] The Nottingham church was to be very seriously affected by the problems within Elim at the end of the decade and the congregation splintered. The vast building became an albatross around Elim's neck and incurred substantial losses to the movement after the war.

The year 1931 saw George campaign once again in Ulster. There can be no denying the fact that the work in Ireland had been neglected, and the churches there felt a sense of grievance at the fact that Jeffreys had concentrated almost entirely on the mainland and had not given more of his time to them. Phillips commented on this in his letter to Jeffreys on 17th October 1933: 'The people think they're neglected while we are pushing ahead in all other parts of the British Isles. Of course this is true – there has been practically no advance in Ireland for ten years or more.'[28]

The campaign in Belfast lasted three weeks. Elim had started in Northern Ireland, and Jeffreys' campaigns there in the early days of Elim had established a number of the churches. Although he was the founder of Elim, and after moving to London in 1922 he was very much the 'face' of Elim to the outside world, being the figurehead, such was not the case in the early days in Ireland. In those early days, there were other evangelists who worked alongside George and conducted campaigns and opened churches. There had been no campaigning on the scale of Plymouth, Barking, Leeds, Glasgow, Bournemouth, Cardiff and Birmingham within Ulster, although Belfast was a large city. The meetings in Belfast in 1931 were certainly greater than Jeffreys had held while campaigning there in the early days. 'Extraordinary scenes have been witnessed in the Ulster Hall, Belfast, during the past ten days, while Principal George Jeffreys conducted his revival and Divine healing campaign.'[29] Unusually, E J Phillips accompanied the Revival Party to Ulster, where he spoke at the Christmas Convention in the Ulster Temple. He remained in Belfast for the first few meetings of the campaign and made the following observations: 'Two unusual features of this campaign are the very large proportion of born-again people attending the meetings, and the large proportion of men.'[30]

It was around this time that George started revisiting churches that he had pioneered where he preached at conventions or special weekends.[31] Although he was to hold successful campaigns in Dundee, Sheffield and York in between the years 1931 and 1934, his revival campaigning slowed considerably.

Notes

[1] Canty, George, ibid, p117.

[2] Canty, George, ibid.

[3] Cartwright, Desmond, *The Great Evangelists*, p103.

[4] Cartwright, Desmond, ibid, p103.

[5] Dale, R W, *The Atonement, The Congregational Union Lecture for 1875* (London: Congregational Union for England and Wales, Sixteenth Edition, 1895).

[6] Cartwright, Desmond, *Some Evangelists*, p25.

[7] Cartwright, Desmond, *Some Evangelists*, pp25.

[8] Fawcett, R, *The Elim Movement in Birmingham* (Grad Cert Ed, May 1976), p3.

[9] Cartwright, Desmond, *The Great Evangelists*, p103

[10] Letter from Jeffreys to Phillips, quoted by Cartwright, ibid, p104.

[11] The exception was Percy LeTissier, who, being close to Jeffreys, left Elim with him and became pastor of Kensington Temple as a Bible Pattern minister. He returned to the Elim fold a few years later.

[12] Canty, George, ibid, p118.

[13] *Elim Evangel*, 11th April 1930, Vol 11, No 15, p227. In the *Evangel*, this quote appears in block text.

[14] Canty, George, ibid, p118.

[15] Barnes, Ernest William, *Should Such a Faith Offend?* (London; Hodder & Stoughton, 1928).

[16] Desmond Cartwright, *The Great Evangelists*, p103.

[17] Canty, George, ibid, p109.

[18] *Elim Evangel*, 6th June 1930, Vol 11, No 23, p361.

[19] Cartwright, Desmond, *The Great Evangelists*, p105.

[20] Graham Street (now Birmingham City Church), Sparkbrook and Smethwick.

[21] Cartwright, Desmond, *The Great Evangelists*, p106.

[22] Canty, George, ibid, p121.

[23] Canty, George, ibid.

[24] *Elim Evangel*, 26th September 1930, Vol 11, No 39, p609.

[25] Canty, George, ibid, p121.

[26] *Elim Evangel*, 14th November 1930, Vol 11, No 46, p729.

[27] Canty, George, ibid, p121.

[28] Kay, William, ibid, p245.

[29] *Elim Evangel*, 23rd January 1931, Vol 12, No 4, p49.

[30] *Elim Evangel*, 23rd January 1931, Vol 12, No 4, p52.

[31] Kay, William, ibid, p246.

29
Rows and Revivals

This chapter will briefly cover the years 1931-34, years when the shadow of division began to descend upon the Elim Movement.

Jeffreys had conducted a three-week campaign in Belfast in the month of January 1931. George had spent very little time in Ireland and, as mentioned in the previous chapter, the Irish churches felt neglected. William Henderson, one of the overseers appointed by Jeffreys, had been appointed Irish superintendent in 1929, but he was also in charge of the Southern district in England from June 1929 to April 1930.[1] The sudden death of Henderson resulted in Joseph Smith being appointed Irish superintendent, but he was based in London. The death of Henderson was a serious loss to Elim. His was a steadying hand on Elim, and he worked closely with Phillips. He was close to Jeffreys, but was not afraid to speak his mind. He was a humble, godly man and was referred to as 'Henderson the good'. What an accolade! Jeffreys consulted both Henderson and Phillips on all major decisions. 'It is probable that many of the decisions that were made after his death would have been different if he had lived.'[2]

In February 1931, George wrote to Elim headquarters to report that there were 'rows and revivals everywhere'.[3] The changes brought in by the new rules in 1929, at the time of the revision of the Elim Constitution, caused particular unrest in the Irish churches. These churches had been in existence much longer than the churches on the mainland. The church officers were, as a rule, more biblically knowledgable than those on the mainland, and had a wider experience of local church matters. Issues that were of concern to the Irish churches were lay representation, ownership of property and local control, as distinct from central control from Clapham. These matters contained the seeds that would, in just a few years' time, cause a crisis in the movement.[4]

While in Ireland, Jeffreys conducted a short campaign in Armagh, the ecclesiastical capital of Ireland, with two cathedrals. Coming back across to England, he conducted a pioneer crusade in Southport. Some 600 people responded to the gospel appeal, and a church was established. Blackpool was to have been next, but Edward Jeffreys stepped in with a rival tent causing the following comment in the local newspaper: 'The piquant spectacle of uncle and nephew conducting rival revivalist campaigns is to be a feature of the season in Blackpool.'[5] George had actually changed his plans when he discovered that Edward was going to be in Blackpool, even though he had been the first to arrange his meetings there. He withdrew and Phil Hulbert went instead. It had been planned that the Blackpool campaign would run from 4th July through to September.[6]

A convention was held in the Birmingham Town Hall on Whit Monday and the *Evangel* carried on its cover the following newspaper report. The heading was: 'Nine Hour Queue for Religious Rally in Spacious Town Hall'. The report ran as follows:

> Remarkable scenes were witnessed in and around Birmingham Town Hall on Whit Monday. While the majority of the people was on holiday, followers of Principal George Jeffreys, of the Elim Foursquare Gospel Mission, rallied in great numbers to hear the founder of the most emotional revival movement in modern times, and give expression to their religious fervour. There were afternoon and evening rallies, and the Town Hall which seats over 2,000 persons, was too small to accommodate the crowds seeking admission.

A small group of people arrived at six a.m., and by ten o'clock there was a lengthy queue. Before midday, the building was surrounded, and until three o'clock, when the first rally commenced, the waiting crowd indulged in hymn singing. In both audiences, there were many people in wheel chairs and their sustained enthusiasm was a tribute both to the personal magnetism of Principal Jeffreys and the appeal of his virile Gospel.

Last year, it will be remembered, principal Jeffreys conveyed a great convention in the Bingley Hall, which he filled to overflowing. The present position in Birmingham is that four permanent centres of the mission have been established, and more than 10,000 converts have been registered. Over 1,100 candidates have been baptised by immersion in water, and in over 1,000 cases, it is claimed, miraculous healings have taken place.[7]

In July 1931, George conducted a short mission on the Isle of Wight, and an Elim church was established in Ryde. He also presided at the opening of the Elim church in Portsmouth, and opened the Elim church in Worthing in August. Jeffreys was finally able to hold a campaign in Blackpool in August and this was followed by one in Sheffield. The *Sheffield Independent* newspaper reported: 'Conversions in a fairground', 'Crowds flock to hear Principal – strength restored to cripples'.[8] The campaign was held in a tent that was pitched on Smithfield Fairground, near to Victoria Station. Phil Hulbert continued the campaign in Sheffield while George held meetings in Glossop. Richard Howton had founded a church there in 1888 and had actually inscribed the word 'Foursquare' inside the building long before it was adopted for the Alliance. This pastor anticipated Pentecostal faith, had healed the sick, had exercised various gifts of the Spirit and founded a healing home. Elim now accepted this work, and George held a campaign in the town's largest cinema.[9] It was in Glossop that the first conference of ministers took place under the direction of Robert Tweed, who was the northern superintendent. It was confined to those in the northern region. Among some of the discussions that were held was whether or not Elim churches should hold harvest festivals. The majority of the ministers felt that such services should not be encouraged. During the early part of the Second World War, some of the departments of Elim headquarters were transferred to Glossop for a short time.[10]

Between campaigns, another day was spent at the Crystal Palace, with 150 believers being baptised by full immersion on the confession of their faith. This was in addition to the Easter and Whit Monday gatherings at the Albert Hall. The press reported the presence of Sir P Holland-Pryor and Lady Holman, daughter of General H C Holman and Lady Holman, the general's wife having been miraculously healed in Eastbourne. They also noted twenty-eight one-time cripples doing a demonstration act.[11] The *Elim Evangel* of 9th October was given over entirely to the reports of the Crystal Palace meetings when there were three meetings held that day. The speakers were Percy Corry in the morning and James McWhirter at the evening service. The afternoon service was devoted to the baptisms which had been originally arranged to be held outside, but because of the inclement weather had to be brought inside. George conducted the appeal and altar call at all three meetings. The reports were long and rich in biblical language and allegories. The editorial dwelt on the aspect of 'witness' and is worth including in full:

> The greatest privilege in the Christian Church in this present world is to witness to the power of her risen Lord. This year's demonstration in the Crystal Palace was certainly a gathering of individual witnesses into a corporate witness for Christ. Thousands were there to witness to his saving and keeping power, hundreds openly testified to deliverance from disease and infirmity by the hand of the Great Physician, while hundreds glorified Him as the One who had baptised them in the Holy Spirit with signs following. Over the whole

gathering too, there was a keen note of expectation; it was heard in the prayers, in the praises, in the addresses – the expectation of the soon coming of the Bridegroom for His own. The Principal is never happier than when leading others in their witness and that day will live in the memory of those who were present, as a day of witness for the Master.[12]

Another Elim church building was opened in London. This time, in Bermondsey, where a former Methodist building was leased. The secretary-general, E J Phillips, presided at the opening of this church on 14th October 1931.[13] This was quite a departure from regular church openings, as these were almost always conducted by George Jeffreys. It clearly shows that E J was looked upon as the second-in-command in Elim.

Meanwhile, George was concentrating on Yorkshire, where a number of short campaigns were held, with other ministers coming in to continue the work and allow the principal to move to another place. The longest he stayed in this series of campaigns was in Huddersfield, where a thriving church was established in October 1931. 'I have spoken to many Christians who have followed Christ for years, and their testimonies have all been the same, "We can see a glorious Foursquare Gospel Centre in Huddersfield in answer to the prayers of years." We have never seen anything like it!'[14] Knottingley was a town where George commenced the campaign for another of his evangelists to continue. Halifax came next, where the Halifax Free Church council president agreed for his Stannary Congregational Church, seating 2,000, to be used. Services were also held in the spacious Trinity Hall Baptist Church.[15]

Yorkshire was indeed fertile ground for George Jeffreys and Elim. His second major campaign in England had been in the city of Hull. He was to return there in 1933 for a five-week campaign where there were 1,500 conversions and a large church opened in Hessle Road, near the fish docks; it was named Hull City Temple. The front page of the 4th December

Evangel carried the following report under the title 'Revival Fires in Yorkshire':

> The Foursquare Revival that broke out in Yorkshire some three months ago, when Principal George Jeffreys and Revival Party came to Sheffield, is spreading like a prairie fire. The Principal has carried the torch from town to town, and at each place there is a burning bush that is not being consumed. Sheffield, Glossop,[16] Huddersfield, Halifax, Barnsley – everywhere there are crowded gatherings. Hundreds of converts are turning to Christ in one day. Miracles of healing are given in answer to prayer, and miraculous signs are confirming the Foursquare Gospel message. Unbounded enthusiasm prevails all around; people drawn from all stations of life are entering wholeheartedly into the revival. The services are held in churches, theatres and public halls, and Foursquare Gospel hymns and choruses are sung by full-throated congregations in the vice-like grip of the glorious revival. Conviction of the old fashioned type is resting on the district, and there is great rejoicing on the part of saints who have prayed, as they see the object of their prayers enter the Kingdom. Readers, pray on that the Principal shall be led of God, and for the ministers in charge of the revival centres.[17]

Visits to Lurgan, where a short campaign was held, and Belfast for the Annual Christmas Convention, took place in December 1931. Then it was off to Scotland for the New Year Convention at the City Temple, Glasgow, and back to London, where Jeffreys held the Crusader rally at the Kensington Temple on 8th January 1932, followed by a campaign in King's Cross. This was held in the Spa Fields Church (a Countess of Huntingdon's Church)[18] in Wharton Street.[19] The three 'c's' were present at this campaign as in all the others – 'converts, cures, crowds'.[20]

The editorial in the 14th February edition of the *Evangel* had a section in it that was almost prophetic. Under the heading

'Preach Peace', it informed *Evangel* readers of the dangers of a new bomb where it would be possible for twenty-five aeroplanes to start 4,000 fires in a great city. Various means of starting fires including fire-tipped arrows, explosive bullets and flame-throwers 'have been known in warfare from earliest times but surely, incendiary bombs on such a colossal scale have not been known before'. The article went on to almost paint a prophetic picture of what would happen in London during the Blitz that was to take place in the Second World War, in just over seven years' time. 'One fleet of such machines above London could bring death and destruction by fire to such an extent that the Great Fire of 1666 would seem a small thing.' The writer then spoke of the need for humankind to turn to encouraging peace, rather than war. 'Let us the more speak peace by Jesus Christ, and look to the coming of Him who is the Prince of peace.'[21] This editorial was probably written by E J, who had very strong pacifist opinions. The same edition of the *Evangel* advertised the London Easter Convention which would be a week-long affair. Two of the advertised speakers were young Elim pastors who were to become prominent in the leadership of the movement after the war. They were James T Bradley, who was to become Elim's third secretary-general, and J J Morgan, then the very young pastor of the new and large Elim congregation in Brighton, who would become a member of the Executive Council and field superintendent.[22]

George Jeffreys next turned his attention northwards to Scotland. On this occasion he concentrated on the eastern part of the country with a campaign in Perth, commencing on 6th March in the City Hall.[23] It would seem that this pioneering effort was not as successful as Jeffreys' campaigns in Glasgow and Greenock. 'The brief visit of the Principal to Perth was blessed of God in the salvation of souls and healing of bodies. Although the congregations were unusually small, being chiefly Christian, the people revelled in the ministry of the Word.'[24] It seems likely that owing to the small crowds in Perth, George turned his attention back to the west coast, and a campaign was held in the town of Ayr. The report of this appeared underneath the Perth report and it has an altogether different tenor to it: 'Glorious scenes of revival [are] being witnessed in the campaign at Ayr. At service after service souls are saved and remarkable healings are being witnessed.'[25] Jeffreys then turned north-east once again, this time to Dundee, the city of jute, jam and journalism. According to Kay, the June meetings were held in the Caird Hall, *Edinburgh* (author's italics). He refers to the front page of the *Evangel* of 10th June, but that is clearly with reference to Dundee, not Edinburgh. The Caird Hall was in Dundee, and not Edinburgh as mentioned by Kay.[26] Apparently, only eleven people turned up at the first meeting in Dundee, but the crowds soon gathered and a number of halls were hired in the city, moving eventually to the largest building in Dundee – the Caird Hall, where attendances swelled to 3,000.[27] A large church was established in this city and a prominent politician became a member. He was Edwin Scrymgeour (1866-1947) who was the city's Member of Parliament from 1922, when he ousted Winston Churchill, until 1931. He is the only person ever elected to the House of Commons on a prohibitionist ticket, as the candidate for the Scottish Prohibition Party. He established a close relationship with George Jeffreys and when the latter left Elim, Scrymgeour left also and became a leading member of the Dundee Bible Pattern Church.

It was in the month of October 1932 that George held his campaign in Edinburgh where 400 converts from Dundee visited the meetings and he had to move his meetings to the 2,200-seater Usher Hall for the last six days of his campaign.[28] After ministering as usual at the Christmas Convention in Belfast, George returned to Scotland and campaigned in Aberdeen on 4th January 1933 in the city's Music Hall. The revival meetings continued until the beginning of March. Albert Edsor, a member of the Revival Party, comments: 'The Revival and healing campaign held in Aberdeen by Principal George Jeffreys has been an untold blessing to the city.' He reported that there were in excess of 250 conversions with fifty-five being baptised in water.[29] Canty reports that a church was founded in the city and 'under Sam Penney, the first young pastor, Aberdeen's Elim had three hundred in attendance'.[30]

It was around this time that Jeffreys' attention began to focus on the issue of local church government. Having been in Belfast at the beginning of 1933, George was greatly concerned about the state of the churches there. Hudson states that many of the people who had joined Elim churches earlier now seemed to have left and there were complaints about headquarters.[31] George began agitating for a structured leadership for the Irish churches and, after the establishment of the Annual Conferences, advanced the case for lay representatives to be appointed in the Irish churches. From this time onwards, it would appear that Jeffreys was as taken up with the idea of reforming the churches as much as he was engaged in evangelism. York was the scene of his last major church pioneering campaigns, where 1,500 responded to the gospel invitation.

The first Elim Conference was held in London in 1933. According to Canty, the vexed issue of lay representation was brought up. Also, in this Conference, discussion on the interpretation of biblical prophecy took place. This theme was to recur in successive Conferences and according to E J Phillips, Jeffreys attachment to the National Historicist interpretation of prophecy was a major reason for the split that was to take place in the Elim Movement at the end of the decade. It is this and the subject of church government that will be largely the content of the concluding chapters of this book.

Notes

[1] Cartwright, Desmond, *The Great Evangelists*, p109.
[2] Cartwright, Desmond, ibid.
[3] Cartwright, Desmond, ibid.

[4] Cartwright, Desmond, ibid, p110.

[5] Cartwright, Desmond, ibid, p122.

[6] *Elim Evangel*, 22nd May 1931, Vol 12, No 21, cover ii.

[7] *Birmingham Gazette*, 26th May 1931. Printed on the cover of the *Elim Evangel*, 5th June 1931.

[8] *Elim Evangel*, 11th September 1931, Vol 11, No 37, p577.

[9] Canty, George, ibid, p122.

[10] Cartwright, Desmond, *The Great Evangelists*, p111.

[11] Canty, George, ibid, p122.

[12] *Elim Evangel*, 9th October 1931, Vol 12, No 41, p646.

[13] *Elim Evangel*, 23rd October 1931, Vol 12, No 43, p674.

[14] George Edwards, *Elim Evangel*, 20th November 1931, Vol 12, No 47, p742.

[15] *Elim Evangel*, 27th November 1931, Vol 12, No 48, p761.

[16] Glossop is in Derbyshire, not Yorkshire.

[17] *Elim Evangel*, 4th December 1931, Vol 12, No 49, front page.

[18] The Countess of Huntingdon was a prominent evangelical who was deeply influenced by the Methodist Revival of the eighteenth century. She established what became known as the Connexion, a group of twenty-two churches in England. It seceded from the Church of England and founded its own training establishment – Trevecca College.

[19] *Elim Evangel*, 29th January 1932, Vol 13, No 5, cover ii.

[20] Canty, George, ibid, p123.

[21] *Elim Evangel*, 14th February 1932, Vol 13, No 8, p120.

[22] *Elim Evangel*, ibid, cover ii.

[23] *Elim Evangel*, 4th March 1932, Vol 13, No 10, cover ii.

[24] *Elim Evangel*, 22nd April 1932, Vol 13, No 17, front page.

[25] *Elim Evangel*, ibid, front page.

[26] Kay, William, *George Jeffreys*, pp251,252

[27] Canty, George, ibid, p123.

[28] Kay, William, ibid, p252.

[29] *Elim Evangel*, 7th April 1932, Vol 14, No 16, p243.

[30] Canty, George, ibid, p123.

[31] Hudson, D N, ibid, p169.

30[1]
The Constitution

E J Phillips held three leading positions within the Elim Movement – secretary-general, dean of the Bible College and editor of the *Evangel*. But it is in his role as Elim's first secretary-general (general superintendent) that he made a lasting impression on the history of Elim. He was an administrative genius and, in conjunction with George Jeffreys, wrote the 1934 Deed Poll.[2]

The Constitution

E J was a great constitutionalist. He was greatly involved in the Deed Poll of 1934 which became the basis and foundation of the Elim Constitution. The earliest Elim Constitution was written in 1922 with revisions made in 1925, 1927 and again in 1929.[3] There is little documented evidence of E J's involvement in these documents and it is highly unlikely that he contributed much to the 1922 Constitution. He stated that, on average, there had been a major revision to the Constitution every three years.[4] According to E J, Jeffreys was agitating for a new Deed Poll in 1938, which was just four years after the original one.[5] E J made the claim that the 1922 Constitution was drawn up entirely by George Jeffreys without any reference to the overseers.[6] It would appear that E J was referring to the Elim Alliance Council, because overseers were not appointed until 1923, with himself being one.[7]

Deed Poll 1934

E J was the architect of the 1934 Deed Poll which, to this day, is the basis of the Elim Constitution. There was a Deed of Variation passed in 1942, which was largely drawn up by E J and the Executive Council of the day in the aftermath of the split with George Jeffreys.[8] Although E J was the architect, it is clear that throughout the consultation with solicitors regarding the 1934 Deed Poll, he was in close touch with Jeffreys and consulted with him throughout the whole procedure.[9] He made it clear in his correspondence with the solicitors that he conferred with Principal Jeffreys on constitutional matters.[10] The importance of consultation with Jeffreys over the Deed Poll is again stressed in later correspondence.[11]

It is obvious from the notes of E J's speech to the 1939 Conference that by the time of the drawing up of the Deed Poll, there were some serious concerns over Jeffreys' introduction of new policies and changes almost at random. Reference is made to the changes in the constitution. In the drawing up of the Deed Poll, it would appear that E J was determined to bring in a sense of permanency to the Constitution. He wanted to make it difficult to vary the Constitution at the founder's whim. For this reason the Constitution was sectioned into three parts: the Deed Poll, General Rules and Working Arrangements. The first section would be more difficult to amend than the other two sections. Changes to the Deed Poll require a 75 per cent majority of Conference in two successive years.[12] This was established in the 1934 Deed Poll, but as the Executive Council was then the governing body of the movement, the schedule is different because it applied first of all to the Executive Council, but the principle is clearly established there and transferred to the Conference with the Deed of Variation of 1942.[13] Changes to the General Rules require a two-thirds majority of Conference and have to be by means of a Special Resolution. The third section – Working Arrangements – requires just a simple majority for any changes to be made.

The Third Schedule within the Deed Poll sets out amendments to the Deed. Before any amendments could occur to the Deed Poll, it had to be approved by a Special Resolution of the Council and a Special Resolution of the Ministerial Conference.[14] Following this, there had to be a further Special Resolution passed not less than three months or more than fifteen months after the passing of the aforesaid Special Resolution of the Ministerial Conference.[15] A major provision within the Deed Poll was the protection of the Fundamentals of the Alliance. The Fundamental Truths was one of six provisions which 'cannot be added to or revoked or otherwise amended but they shall for ever be as they are now hereinbefore expressed'.[16] It is highly likely that E J was influenced to place this provision within the Deed Poll because of the British Israel teaching which the founder was advocating. In so doing, he was seeking to protect the doctrinal integrity of the movement and also to ensure, as far as possible, constitutional and governmental stability.

E J interpreted the many demands for governmental change as a means on Jeffreys' part of bringing British Israelism (BI) into Elim. In his handwritten notes written on the Sunday before the start of the 1939 Conference, E J writes: 'Candidly [I] do not believe that G.J. [is] concerned as to form of government provided it brings liberty for B.I. to be preached in the churches.' The way that the Deed Poll was set out shows that E J was determined to make the constitution of the Alliance, so far as the major elements were concerned, as inflexible as possible. There was a greater degree of flexibility within the General Rules and even more within the Working Arrangements, but the Deed Poll itself had to be strong and not easily changed.

The main reason for the Deed Poll was the necessity of Incorporation owing to the growth of the work. This was accepted in a meeting held at Elim Woodlands[17] at which G Jeffreys, E J Phillips, E C W Boulton, P N Corry and W G Hathaway were present. Other reasons for Incorporation were the present personal financial responsibility of the overseers, and the need of making adequate arrangements for the carrying on of the work after the days of the founder.[18] This statement is quite ironic in view of the schism that was to come that saw the founder leave the movement that he had started.

There were difficulties within the movement owing to the types of churches involved in the Elim Church Incorporated. The majority of the churches were centrally governed, but there were some local government churches as well as others, such as the Essex Elim churches, that had their own trust and were outside the governance of the Alliance but were in fellowship with Elim. One of Elim's former general superintendents, commenting on the confusion within the government of the movement in the mid to late thirties, stated that there were too many categories of churches.[19] There were churches under direct government, churches that had greater local freedom to determine their local policies and some churches that were under the jurisdiction of the minister.[20] The Deed Poll of 1934 was a genuine attempt to regularise the government within the movement, but its main weakness was that it could only apply to directly governed churches.

Commenting on the passing of the Deed Poll, George Jeffreys wrote as follows: 'It is obvious that the rapid growth of a work such as Elim necessitates changes in government. Expansion is impossible without wise adjustment and revision of existing arrangements.'[21] He went on to inform the *Evangel* readers that the overseers of the Alliance had been carefully considering certain changes in the administration of the movement – changes which he felt would make even more rapid progress possible.[22] In the same article, Jeffreys informed the movement that the Constitution of the Elim Foursquare Gospel Alliance had been set out in the form of a Deed Poll. In his words, the main reason for such a Deed Poll was to provide a satisfactory system of government for the continuance of the work following the death of the present leaders. Jeffreys informed his readers that the whole movement would now be governed by an Executive Council which would be appointed by the Ministerial Conference. This was not altogether accurate, as only four of the nine members of the first Executive Council were appointed by the ministers. The president and secretary-general were ex-officio members of the council. The founder was given the power to appoint three members[23] so that left four Executive Council members to be appointed by the Conference.

The Deed Poll is dated 10th April 1934. In his *Evangel* article, Jeffreys lists the eight men who will serve alongside him in the first Executive Council.[24] The Ministerial and General Conference of the Alliance was held from 17th to 21st September 1934 and there is no record of an election of Executive Council members at that Conference.[25] It is obvious, therefore, that the original Executive Council were all chosen by Jeffreys. The first election took place at the 1935 Ministerial Conference when Boulton (sixty-eight votes), Hathaway (sixty-three), Corry (forty-eight) and Smith (forty-one) were elected.[26]

The Deed Poll clearly sets forth the position of George Jeffreys as the founder and leader of the Elim Foursquare Gospel Alliance.[27] The preamble was drawn up by E J and passed on to Bulcraig & Davis.[28] In this letter E J informed the solicitors of the fact that the recent Conference had unanimously approved 'our suggestions for the future government of the work'. It is obvious that E J did a thorough search of the Deed Poll and Constitution of other Christian organisations and consulted with a number of professional bodies before finalising the Deed Poll. He refers to difficulties that arose in the Salvation Army when they formed a company called 'The Salvation Army Trustee Company' for holding their property in Trust. He says that he examined their file at Somerset House, and also that of 'Friends Trust Ltd', a somewhat similar holding company for the Society of Friends.[29] This shows the meticulous detail and research that he went into in drawing up the Deed Poll.

The first statement in the Trust Deed is the name of the religious denomination concerned. The name so described in the Deed Poll is the 'Elim Foursquare Gospel Alliance'.

The objects of the Alliance were set forth as follows: 'To spread and propagate the full Gospel of our Lord Jesus Christ and the Fundamental Truths hereinafter fourthly set forth.'[30] By the term 'full Gospel' it is generally meant the gospel from a Pentecostal perspective. Many Pentecostal churches were designated 'full gospel' churches because they not only preached an evangelical message, but preached the truth of the baptism of the Holy Spirit with signs following.[31]

The main aspect of the Deed Poll was the granting of authority to the Executive Council to carry out the objects of the Alliance through the training and sending out of ministers and evangelists, the establishment of churches, the formation of Sunday schools and the issue of religious publications throughout Great Britain and elsewhere.[32] This particular clause seems inhibitive as far as its geography is concerned, because it omits to specify Ireland, where the work started.

The 1934 Deed Poll clearly established the primacy of the Executive Council. The powers of the Executive Council were set out in the fifth declaration:

> The Alliance shall be always hereafter under the direction and control of the Executive Council hereinafter mentioned whose duty it shall be to uphold and enforce the discipline and superintend the operation and working of the Alliance and to conserve the same to and for the objects and purposes hereinbefore set forth.[33]

The powers and responsibilities of the council were elaborated in the Second Schedule, 'Constitution, Powers, Duties and Discretions of the Executive Council'.[34] The duties and responsibilities of the Executive Council were set forth in the eight declarations, which gave them power to make and publish General Rules for the governance of the Alliance, these rules to be binding on all ministers and churches of the Alliance.[35] This clause also set out the means by which General Rules might be established, revoked or amended.

An important aspect of the work of the Executive Council as defined by the Deed Poll was to be the formation of a Ministerial Conference.[36] This was to have far-reaching consequences for the movement because, as will be seen, it was the Ministerial Conference that ultimately rejected Jeffreys' attempts to reform the government of the Alliance and which eventually led to a split within the movement. The first Ministerial Conference was held in Clapham from 18th to 22nd September 1933. There was a forerunner held in Glossop from Monday, 24th October to Wednesday, 26th October 1932 but this was only for the Northern Division of ministers. The government of the movement was discussed at length at this Conference. The minutes record that it was felt that there should be a General Presbytery consisting of all ministers and a Ministerial Presbytery consisting of all who had been in the work for six years, with an Executive Presbytery being elected from the latter body.[37]

One of the duties of the Executive Council under the Deed Poll was to appoint one of its members to be secretary-general. The wording is significant: 'He shall have such authorities and shall perform such duties as may from time to time be delegated to him by the Council and shall hold that office at the will of the Council.'[38] There is clear evidence here that the position of secretary-general was a case of 'first among equals' although, as far as the original Executive Council was concerned, it would have been 'second among equals', with George Jeffreys being the first and primary office holder. What is clear is that the position of the secretary-general was given clear prominence over the other Executive Council places. It must be further noted that until 1940, the position of secretary-general was held at the will of the founder.

Clause 23 in the Second Schedule outlines the power of the Executive Council. Such powers were extremely wide. Many of the powers were passed on to the Ministerial Conference in the Deed of Variation of 1942. These included the appointment, suspension and dismissal of ministers and also the authorisation for the ordination of ministers. Other powers, such as the appointment of headquarters officers and making and amending General Rules were passed on to the Representative Conference, which was comprised of ministers and lay representatives from each local church.

The result of the 1934 Deed Poll was that the Executive Council became the governing body of the movement. This changed in 1940 when the Representative Session of the Conference became the governing body. However, the Executive Council[39] was the de-facto leadership of the movement in-between Conferences. 'The National Leadership Team (formerly Executive Council) is accountable to the Conference and is subject to any direction as may be proscribed by the Conference, but no such direction shall invalidate any prior act of the NLT which would have been valid if that direction had not been given.'[40] The basic meaning of this clause in the Constitution is to establish the primacy of the NLT. They have the power to decide on policy on behalf of the Conference, but the Conference has the right to rescind such policy but it would not make the original decision of the NLT illegitimate.

In notes on the Deed Poll, E J clearly states that the Executive Presbytery is the governing body except as provided in this Deed Poll and General Rules.[41] In the same document he outlines the powers of the Ministerial Presbytery. It would appear that they were limited to three main functions: 1) To annually elect a president, 2) Annually elect members to the Executive Presbytery, 3) To confirm the acceptance of ministers by the Executive Presbytery and to authorise their ordination and to recognise any ordination by an ordained minister at request of a properly constituted church or governing body.[42] From these notes written by E J, it is clear that the Ministerial Conference would have no power to purchase property; this was all to be done by the Executive Council.

Jeffreys was to claim that he was unaware of the extent of the powers given to the Executive Council under the Deed Poll, but as has been noted, E J kept the founder informed right throughout the negotiations. In any case, E J was acting on behalf of the leadership appointed by Jeffreys. In a reply to a pamphlet issued by the Executive Council in January 1941, Jeffreys stated that he had, for some years, been deeply convinced that it was wrong for a mere handful of men to have such control as he, and a few others, had over the ministers, the people, the property and the finance of the whole movement.[43]

At the same time that the Deed Poll was drawn up, E J was involved in the drawing up of a Model Trust Deed whereby local churches could be involved in the financial arrangements for their buildings. The Model Trust Deed was a method of holding property by local trustees on behalf of the Alliance.[44] It is arguable that it granted a greater degree of local autonomy.

E J outlined the new system under which church buildings could be purchased or erected by Local Trustees.[45] Up until that time, the financial responsibility for every new church building purchased or erected had been under the responsibility of individual trustees at Elim headquarters. E J claimed that there were two advantages in setting up a Model Trust Deed. They were: 1) Less responsibility on headquarters trustees, and 2) More local effort to clear the cost resulting from local instead of headquarters responsibility.[46]

Notes

[1] The final chapters of this book contain mainly the transcript of part of the Author's Masters dissertation previously referred to. The dissertation was written from a definite pro-Phillips perspective. It is the author's opinion that the success and continuation of Elim as a major Pentecostal Movement was owing in no small part to Phillips' outstanding skills and dedication to Elim.

[2] Hudson, D N, ibid, 138.

[3] Notes of E J P's speech to Conference on 21st November 1939 (Malvern: Elim Archives).

[4] E J P, ibid. This was actually an incorrect statement because the first constitution in 1922 was merely a 'book of rules' for ministers and churches. The 1925 and 1929 editions were merely that: revisions of the 1922 rules.

[5] E J P, ibid.

[6] E J P, ibid.

[7] *Elim Evangel*, April 1923, List of Overseers.

[8] There was a Deed of Variation in 1942 and a further Deed of Variance signed on 12th September 2007.

[9] The solicitors that were used for constitutional purposes were Bulcraig & Davis of the Strand, London. They were used from 1929 onwards.

[10] Letter from E J to Bulcraig & Davis, 25th November 1933.

[11] Ibid, 28th February 1934.

[12] Elim Pentecostal Church *The Constitution* – Schedule Amendments to the Deed Poll 1, 2010 Edition, p10.

[13] This is a reference to the provisions within the Deed Poll. There are three of them: The Governance of the Alliance, Exclusion re Ireland (the Irish Constitution) and Amendments to the Deed Poll.

[14] At this time there was only a ministerial Conference; the Representative Conference which consisted of ministers and lay representatives was not established until 1940.

[15] Elim Foursquare Gospel Alliance: Deed Poll by George Jeffreys, 10th April 1934 (The Third Schedule: Amendments to this Deed 1), p14.

[16] Deed Poll 1934 (Amendments 4), p15.

[17] Elim Woodlands was the home of the Elim Bible College.

[18] Notes, *Incorporation etc* by E J Phillips, Elim Archives.

[19] Lewis, I W, unpublished account of Elim History (Malvern: Elim Archives), p15.

[20] Lewis, I W, ibid, p15.

[21] Jeffreys, George, 'Our-ever-enlarging Elim', *Elim Evangel*, 15th June 1934.

[22] *Elim Evangel*, ibid.

[23] Cartwright maintains that Jeffreys wanted the right to appoint four members but eventually settled on three.

[24] R E Darragh, Robert Tweed, Ernest J Phillips, James McWhirter, Joseph Smith, Ernest C W Boulton, Percy N Corry, W G Hathaway. This is the order in which the names appear on the Deed Poll, with the name George Jeffreys at the head of the list.

[25] Conference Minutes, 1934.

[26] Conference Minutes, 1935.

[27] Elim Foursquare Gospel Alliance, *Deed Poll by George Jeffreys*, 10th April 1934.

[28] Letter and Enclosures, 7th November 1933.

[29] Letter E J P to Bulcraig & Davis, 25th July 1933.

[30] In a Deed of Variation in 2007, the Objects of the Alliance were added to in a significant way. In the first instance, spreading and propagating of the full gospel of Christ was to be primarily, *but not exclusively* the Fundamental truths. Added to this was a declaration of some of the means in which the gospel could be demonstrated through social action, community action, the provision of recreation facilities, advice and support services, as well as by the advancement of education. Elim Foursquare Gospel Alliance, Deed Poll by George Jeffreys, 2.

[31] The Constitution of the Elim Pentecostal Church, Secondly: 1, 2, 3 p1.

[32] Deed Poll 1934, p3.

[33] Deed Poll 1934, p4.

[34] Deed Poll 1934, pp6-15.

[35] Deed Poll 1934, p4.

[36] Deed Poll 1934, p5.

[37] Ministerial Conference Minutes 1933: Tuesday Morning, *Government of Denomination.*

[38] Deed Poll 1934, Second Schedule 5, p6.

[39] The Executive Council was renamed the National Leadership Team in 2007 in a Deed of Variance.

[40] The Constitution of the Elim Pentecostal Church, General Rules Part 1, Section 3, sub-section 15, Clause (c), p17.

[41] Notes on Deed Poll sent to Solicitors, November 1933 (Elim Archives).

[42] Notes on Deed Poll, ibid.

[43] Jeffreys, G, *Why I Am Outside Elim* (London: Bible Pattern Church Pamphlet, March 1941).

[44] Hunter, B, Administrator Elim Pentecostal Church International Office. Telephone conversation 4th May 2011.

[45] Phillips, *General Notes re. Model Trust Deed* (Malvern: Elim Archives, 1934).

[46] Phillips, *General Notes.*

31
Division

There is a suggestion among some Pentecostal historians that E J usurped Jeffreys' leadership within Elim. As Liardon says in his book, *God's Generals: The Healing Evangelists*:

> While Phillips was a dedicated worker in building up the kingdom of God, sacrificing years of his life to the Elim movement, his skills in the areas of administration and helps were service gifts as found in Ephesians 4:11. I believe that this is where the Elim collision took place. Administrators thrive on order and precision; apostolic leaders must step out in faith and will occasionally make mistakes. In some ways, it is inevitable that these two temperaments would have found it hard to co-exist.[1]

Liardon, however, completely misses the point in that he fails to appreciate that these two did not only coexist for twenty years, but were, for most of that time, in constant daily communication with each other and were very close friends.

The division in the movement is seen by some as the result of a power struggle between E J and Jeffreys. 'As Jeffreys gained notoriety and attracted the spotlight of success, their close friendship dissolved into a power struggle over the organisation they led.'[2] The implication here is that E J was somehow jealous of the success and ministry of Jeffreys: that is not the case. E J was not a platform man. He was not a great preacher and seldom preached at national events or conventions. E J was a man who seemed at ease with his own personality and ministry.

He was content to leave the platform to others with differing talents from his own. 'But of his organisational genius men will talk for years to come.'[3] In his tribute, Greenway adds: 'And despite his different role in the work of God, many will be found in glory as a result of his labours.' There is no doubt that E J was a man who was completely comfortable in his role and was content in carrying out the work for which he was best suited.

Hudson refers to the striking similarities in the personalities of E J and Jeffreys. 'Both were shy, determined, devoted to the Movement and its development and both suffered periods of severe illness.'[4] They were both wholly dedicated to the movement, persistent and single-minded, unwilling to allow illness to render them marginalised from the activities of the movement. He comments that Phillips, in his total commitment to the movement, protected the churches from the perceived dangers of Jeffreys with fanatical zeal.[5] Such a statement could create the impression that Phillips was slightly 'unhinged' and saw dangers lurking where perhaps, the situation was not as dire as he anticipated. It is quite clear that from 1936 onwards, the dangers were not merely perceived, they were very real. Some have suggested that Phillips was a manoeuvrer who was determined to fulfil his self-appointed role as protector of the movement. While the author clearly sets out to positively examine E J's role in the preservation of the movement, there is little evidence to suggest that his position was a self-appointed one.

To suggest that E J manoeuvred situations in his struggle with Jeffreys is harsh and suggests that he was a manipulator. The tributes paid to him and the opinions of those who knew him on a personal level do not suggest that he was in any way manipulative. He is described as being courteous, well-mannered and dignified. He was strong-willed but not stubborn. Where principle was involved, he was adamant.[6] A strong-willed and adamant approach to principle, however, is not a platform to suggest that the person concerned would manoeuvre to get his own way. In fact, the very descriptions themselves would seem to militate against such action. Carter, in his obituary, adds: 'In character he was high principled. E.J. was a righteous man; one could never think of him being other than what he professed to be.'[7] While it could be argued that men like Greenway, Bradley, Walker and Smith, who at one time or another worked very closely with E J, were somewhat biased in their assessment of his character and work, the same could not be said of Carter, who was one of the main leaders in a movement that was locally governed – the very form of church government that Jeffreys advocated from 1935 onwards.

The differences between Phillips and Jeffreys

As has already been noted, Hudson refers to the many similarities between E J and Jeffreys. Both men were considered to be 'shy, determined, devoted to the Movement' and both 'suffered periods of severe illness'.[8] The fact that both men were determined is clearly shown in their actions. Molly Phillips, when interviewed by Hudson, refers to the time that her husband first proposed to her and, after seeking God's guidance, she declined the proposal. E J accepted this from her, though disagreed with her that it was God's will. Ten years later, he approached her again, and this time she accepted his proposal and they married that year.[9] Jeffreys' determination is clearly seen in his efforts to bring about reform to the government of the movement.

An important factor that must be considered in the personalities of the two men is their national and cultural make-up. E J was a phlegmatic Englishman; Jeffreys was an emotional Welshman. It is quite evident from an examination of their respective lives that E J was steadier and more consistent in his approach to matters, whereas Jeffreys tended to be far more likely to be governed by his emotions and circumstances. E J referred to this aspect of Jeffreys' personality in his speech to the 1939 Conference. He talked about Jeffreys often changing mind and plans.

The other great difference between E J and Jeffreys is that the latter allowed himself to be cocooned by the Revival Party to such an extent that he was cut off from some of the realities of the time. So, when he did confront problematic situations, Jeffreys was inclined to see the worst in them because he had been protected from any form of criticism or debate by members of the Revival Party. Among these people, in particular, Jeffreys commanded immense devotion;[10] he was seldom seen on a personal level without members of the Revival Party being at hand. Phillips, on the other hand, worked long hours on his own. He spent a great many hours at his office desk, and the light in the secretary-general's office could often be seen burning after midnight: his devotion was complete.[11] Smith speaks similarly of the long hours spent in the office. 'He never shirked any duty no matter how he felt. I think that he worked too hard. When coming home at night from taking meetings in distant parts of London I could see the light still burning in his office. He never seemed to spare himself.'[12]

E J was quite a private man, unlike Jeffreys; he did not surround himself with a small and close company of friends who would protect him from criticism and opinions that did not fit in with his philosophy of ministry. The Revival Party was a group of workers who became Jeffreys' close friends, and who organised his evangelistic meetings, led the singing at those meetings and arranged for adequate follow-up arrangements for his converts.[13] Jeffreys was assured of the tremendous loyalty of this small group of men all his life. Robert E Darragh was the first worker who joined Jeffreys in 1915. He became a very close friend and lived with him for forty-four years until his death at the age of seventy-two in 1959. Darragh was the song leader at Jeffreys' meetings. James McWhirter joined the Evangelistic Band in 1919 and became the campaign organiser and the one who dealt with newspaper reporters.[14] McWhirter was a member of the Revival Party until his marriage in 1936. He also, along with Albert Edsor, lived with Jeffreys. McWhirter sided with Jeffreys and left Elim in 1940 and became a minister with the Bible Pattern Fellowship.[15] Edsor joined the Revival Party in 1928 as the pianist. He lived with Jeffreys until the latter's death in 1962. This very close-knit company surrounded Jeffreys and poured adulation upon him.

It is evident that E J did not see himself as a figurehead, but as a leader among others. Some students of Elim's history are of the opinion that the schism was assisted to some extent by a dispute between the two leading figures – Jeffreys and Phillips. Hudson views the situation as a power struggle between the two. Referring to the physical illnesses that the two men suffered in 1938,[16] Hudson comments: 'They were both weakened men, each struggling to retain power from the other, each believing that they had a divine mandate to lead the Movement, despite being debilitated by their illnesses.'[17] There is nothing to suggest that E J saw himself as the leader of Elim. That he was the de-facto leader after Jeffreys left was the result of his extraordinary gifting as an administrator and constitutional expert. He made it clear that at a time when the office of president was one that was unlimited in length, he emphatically ruled himself out of consideration. Later, when the presidency of the Movement became an annually elected position, he did not allow himself to be elected until he had retired as secretary-general.[18] Phillips' dignified persona has often been interpreted as being aloof and cold. In the opinion of those who knew him well and worked alongside him, he was neither.

Phillips' view of the reasons for the split

From 1936 onwards, Jeffreys began to agitate for changes in the government of the movement. This was completely at odds with the Deed Poll of 1934, which he had instituted with the help and direction of E J. The issue as far as Jeffreys and his close supporters were concerned, was the right of the local church to own its own property and be largely in charge of its own affairs. One of Jeffreys' eight points was the right of the local church to take its own decision with regard to supplementary doctrine. E J was adamant that this was the main reason for Jeffreys wanting to change the governmental structure of the movement. In his opinion, this was Jeffreys' way of introducing British Israelism into Elim.

The books written by supporters of Jeffreys downplay the role of British Israelism. in the split. Edsor has a small section in his book entitled 'False Presentation of B.I. Controversy'.[19] He accuses Elim of clouding the far more important issue of what George Jeffreys was striving for in his reform governmental policy for the Elim Movement, by emphasising the British Israelism controversy.

The financial crisis

The financial state of the movement was a main reason for the differences between E J and Jeffreys that was to have a considerable effect upon the future of Elim. The movement's policy of paying salaried ministers out of central funds was contributing to its deficit. According to Hathaway, in 1936, ministerial payments exceeded ministerial receipts by £1,345. In the eight months up to 30th June 1937, a deficit of £1,417 was being carried.[20] It was evident that Jeffreys' view of the financial situation was a great deal more pessimistic than that of E J. He refers on more than one occasion to the time that he became aware of the fragile state of the movement's finances during the time that E J was away from the office for a prolonged period of time in 1938 owing to ill health. E J was far more sanguine in his approach to the movement's debt than was Jeffreys. This may be owing to the differences in their backgrounds. E J came from a moneyed family; they were used to handling finance and would have been comfortable with having a debt on their property as long as the capital value exceeded the amount of the mortgage. Jeffreys came from a working-class Welsh family, where debt was considered a curse and every effort would have been made not to go into debt.

E J was incapacitated owing to illness from September 1937 and was hospitalised for a long period. W G Hathaway was appointed to provide cover for E J. Hathaway wrote to E J when he was in hospital in Ventnor on the Isle of Wight, informing him of the proposed Special Resolutions that were to be placed before the Executive Council at their quarterly meeting to be held on 19th November 1937.[21] Enclosed with the letter was the wording of five Special Resolutions that would have had the effect of drastically curtailing the payments of salaries made to ministers.

E J wrote a lengthy reply to the letter and proposals, in which he clearly stated his view that there was an overreaction to the financial difficulties that the movement was currently faced with.[22] He felt that the proposals were too drastic and would come as a great shock to the ministers. He suggested that the best approach would be to write frankly to every minister and probationer, pointing out the seriousness of the financial situation and stating that unless there was a considerable increase in the offerings in the churches, it would be necessary to make an all-round reduction in salaries.[23] E J clearly saw the proposals as having the effect of seriously reducing the number of direct government churches and creating a new section that would be outside direct government control.[24] He addressed the issue on the third page of his letter by suggesting that if such drastic action was required, it should be done by transferring the eighty or so men to the unsalaried Section of Direct Government instead of making a new section for them. 'Instead of the double blow of ministers being unsalaried and removed from the Ministerial Conference, they would then be saved the latter.'[25]

The main thrust of E J's opposition to the proposals is the fact that they raised once more the question of doctrine to be taught in the churches. He referred to the decision of the 1935 Conference, which was reaffirmed at the Conference that had recently been held, which was to protect the work as a whole. Once the relationship between himself and Jeffreys had deteriorated, E J perhaps saw Jeffreys' plan to bring British Israelism into the movement in almost every situation. He argued that the Special Resolutions would limit the application of that resolution[26] to about forty churches, whereas the Ministerial Conference intended that it should apply to the majority of the churches. He further argued that the Executive Council would therefore be betraying the Conference unless it would allow the next Ministerial Conference to decide whether that resolution should apply to the new section as well as to Direct Government Churches. He concludes this section of the letter by re-emphasising the point that if it were necessary to take the drastic action proposed by these Special Resolutions it would be better for them to be taken by transferring men to the unsalaried section, altering, if necessary, some of those rules.[27] It would seem that E J was a little suspicious about the framing of these resolutions. In his letter of 12th November, Hathaway suggests that he, along with Jeffreys and Boulton, would be prepared to visit him at Ventnor. In his reply, E J suggests that if he (Hathaway) felt it necessary to come to discuss the matter with him before the meeting of the council, it would be perfectly agreeable to him, but adds: 'I should imagine it would be sufficient if you came alone.'[28] Perhaps he was more confident of influencing Hathaway if he were on his own.

There was no visit made to E J and the Executive Council meeting was put back to the following week. Apparently, E J's advice prevailed. Hathaway wrote to him informing him of the decision of the Executive Council not to pass the Special Resolutions that had been previously sent to him.[29] The letter contained details of a 'much more moderate scheme'. The most important decision, in the writer's opinion, made by the Executive Council was the second one in the letter; namely: 'That we accept the principle of self-supporting churches and thus eliminate subsidies.' This was the beginning of the end of paying ministers' salaries from central funds. Subsidies would still be given to very small churches to allow a minimum salary of £3 per week to married ministers and half of that to single ministers; such subsidy to end when the church offerings rose above the minimum. In his reply, E J expressed complete satisfaction with the proposed changes.[30]

Jeffreys produced an article for the *Evangel* on the financial position in Elim.[31] In this article he attributed his physical breakdown to the threatened financial upheaval within Elim. This financial upheaval had been miraculously averted and Elim would be able to face the future with absolute confidence. Reference is made to the newly elected Executive Council. In the article, he quotes the opening sentences of the comments he made at the first meeting of the newly elected Executive Council in November 1938:

> The personnel of the present Executive is God's answer to prevailing prayer, for on it depends the shaping of Elim's future policy. Personally, I feel the right men are in the right place, and I believe that each one of you will wholeheartedly engage to make the necessary reforms in the work that will remove once and for all the positive hindrances to the progress of the Foursquare Gospel message in this and other lands.[32]

One of the first actions of the newly elected Executive was to pass a number of Special Resolutions that showed how determined they were to deal effectively with the existing obstacles to progress. A resolute effort was made, according to Jeffreys, to place all churches in Elim on a purely self-supporting basis, thus eliminating the paralysing system of deficits which had been obtained for so long.[33] Jeffreys claimed that the total debt within Elim amounted to £44,000 at the end of the financial year which terminated in October 1937, which had been reduced to £37,500 by the end of March 1938.

E J took strong exception to the article, as his handwritten notes attached to a copy of the article reveal.[34] On the phrase 'Threatened financial crisis with its inevitable upheaval', he writes: '[there] never was one.' He adds that there probably would have been one if the doctrinal issue had been fuelled. Here again it is obvious that the main reason for the difficulties, as far as E J was concerned, was the British Israelism controversy. In his opinion, the phraseology used in the article would be likely to make the readers judge the Executive of financial incompetence. He comments on the figures mentioned, and with reference to the sum of £44,000, states that the article does not say that this was a debt on buildings. As regards the allowances made to the Revival Party, he comments that there was no mention of other sources of income. E J was aware of Jeffreys' financial position because he filled in his income tax forms. Jeffreys had two personal bank accounts and on 7th June 1935, he had £2,033:10:2d in the one account and £1,238:10:3d in the other.[35]

E J interpreted the article as an attack upon his financial and administrative competency. He claimed that the article presented an entirely wrong impression and there were inaccuracies in Jeffreys' figures. He felt that the article reflected (badly) on him. He questioned the wisdom of the article, stating that even if it was true that there had been a financial crisis, publication of the account could have shaken the faith of the people. He insists that there never was a financial crisis, nor even an approaching one. In his opinion, the only thing that could have caused such a crisis would have been a split between Jeffreys and the Executive. He also felt that the readers would judge the previous Executive of financial incompetence.[36] Twice in these notes he refers to the fact that the comments reflect on him and question his competency. He includes with his notes a table of figures showing the income to the movement from 1929 through to 1938. The only year in which there was a deficit was 1936, when there was a shortfall of £104. Every other year showed a surplus, which in 1938 was £2,808.[37] Jeffreys refers to EJ's discomfort over his article in a letter to Hathaway.[38] He feels that it is unnecessary for E J to see it as something that reflected on himself. Jeffreys acknowledges that it is a reflection on *the entire* old Executive, especially himself. Jeffreys genuinely felt that the movement at the time was in severe financial difficulties and had been miraculously delivered from it. E J was overly sensitive on this matter and the fact remains that the movement was greatly helped by the Jubilee Fund that was set up by Jeffreys.

Notes

[1] Liardon, R, *God's Generals: The Healing Evangelists* (Sarasota, FL: Robert Liardon Ministries), p82.

[2] Liardon, R, *The Healing Evangelists*, ibid, p82.

[3] Greenway, H W, *'Well done ... faithful servant'*, *Elim Evangel*, 23rd September 1973.

[4] Hudson, D N, ibid, 140.

[5] Hudson, D N, ibid.

[6] Carter, J, Obituary, E. J. Phillips, The Architect of Elim, *Redemption Tidings*, 11th October 1973.

[7] Carter, J, ibid.

[8] Hudson, D N, ibid, 140.

[9] Hudson, D N, ibid, 140.

[10] Hudson, D N, ibid.

[11] Greenway, 'Well done...faithful servant', ibid.

[12] Smith, He never shirked any duty, ibid.

[13] Hudson, D N, ibid.

[14] Edsor, Albert, *Set Your House in Order*, p18.

[15] This was the denomination that Jeffreys formed in 1940 and was a fellowship of locally governed churches built on 'the New Testament Pattern'.

[16] E J's illness lasted for about six years during which time he was often in hospital or else recovering at home.

[17] Hudson, D N, ibid.

[18] He was elected vice-president at the 1957 Elim Conference, the year he resigned as secretary-general. He became the President in 1958 and he only served for eight months owing to the change in the date of the 1959 Conference.

[19] Edsor, Albert, *Set Your House in Order*, pp198,199.

[20] Hathaway, W G Ministerial Circular 30 October 1937; Hudson, D N, ibid, p228.

[21] Letter Hathaway to Phillips, 12th November 1937.

[22] Handwritten letter from Phillips to Hathaway, 13th November 1937.

[23] Phillips to Hathaway, ibid.

[24] There were about four sections of churches within Elim. The largest was the EFGA; they were direct government churches. Phillips was convinced that Jeffreys wanted to put a limit on the number of Direct Government churches thus forcing all new churches into the self-governing section.

[25] Letter Phillips to Hathaway, 13th November 1937.

[26] 1935 Conference Resolution re the propagation of the British Israelism identity.

[27] Phillips to Hathaway, ibid.

[28] Phillips to Hathaway, ibid.

[29] Letter Hathaway to Phillips, 13th December 1937.

[30] Phillips to Hathaway, handwritten letter, 15th December 1937.

[31] Jeffreys, G, 'God Answers Prayer', *Elim Evangel*, 29th April 1938.

[32] Jeffreys, G, ibid.

[33] Jeffreys, G, ibid.

[34] Handwritten notes attached to *God Answers Prayer*, Phillips E J (Elim Archives).

[35] Information received from Cartwright D, Elim historian. Interview, 18th May 2011.

[36] Phillips, E J, ibid.

[37] Phillips, Table of Donations to Building Funds, Jubilee Funds and Surpluses 1929-1938 (Elim Archives).

[38] Letter, Jeffreys to Hathaway, 28th April 1938.

32

Two Other Reasons for the Split

British Israelism

E J was convinced that the main reason for the split in the movement was the pursuit of the doctrine of British Israelism by Jeffreys. He saw implications of this in almost every situation within the movement from 1934 onwards. It was first briefly discussed at the Northern Division Conference held in Glossop, October 24th-26th 1932, when Jeffreys made a proposal that Elim should admit the identity.[1] The subject was first discussed on a national scale within the movement at the 1933 Ministerial Conference. The minutes record: 'The subject of British Israelism was then discussed. On a show of hands about 16 signified they accepted the identity.'[2] The minutes then go on to record what was to become a consistent resolve of successive Conferences, namely, 'It was generally agreed that it should neither be preached nor attacked in our churches.' There was a further addition which appears not to have been acted upon: 'And that it should be referred to in the supplementary statement of belief.'

There was a major debate on the subject at the 1934 Conference. The speaker proposing an acceptance of the identity was John Leech, KC.[3] P N Corry, a member of the Executive Council, was designated to oppose Leech but indicated on the Tuesday of Conference that he would not be speaking. E J agreed to lead the opposition to Leech, and he stayed up most of the night preparing his speech.

The basic belief of British Israelism is that the British nation forms the lost ten tribes of Israel. According to Pollock, there is a modification to this theory.

> It is stated that Benjamin, just before the siege of Jerusalem, broke off from Judah and attached itself to the ten tribes; and that the tribe of Manasseh, identified by the advocates of this theory as the United States of America, broke off at the same time as the ten tribes, thus leaving the number of tribes at the figure of ten.[4]

Britain is identified as the tribe of Ephraim. The theory was adopted by some prominent evangelicals including Reader Harris, the founder of the Pentecostal League. Harris did not accept Pentecostal doctrine and renamed his movement 'The League of Prayer'. Boddy and Wigglesworth, well-known personalities in the early years of the Pentecostal movements in the UK, held meetings for Harris.[5]

According to Hudson, Jeffreys was unwilling to elaborate on his own beliefs concerning Britain's identification with Israel.[6] Jeffreys, however, was totally committed to the British Israelism identification. Hudson gives as the main reason for Jeffreys' commitment to British Israelism the influence of John Leech.[7] Leech (1857-1942) was highly influential in the development of the Elim Movement. He was appointed general-commissioner of the British-Israel Federation in July 1926.[8] Hudson quotes *The National Message & Banner's* list of Leech's achievements and these are fully listed here:

> Leech had been the First Honoursman of Trinity College, Dublin; the Plunket Gold Medallist for Oratory (Legal Debating); member of the Bar of Ireland, a King's Counsel, and a Bencher of the Inn of Court of Northern Ireland. He was also Senior Crown Prosecutor for County Longford and Chairman of the Incorporated

Council of Law reporting for Northern Ireland. He was an additional judge at Belfast Recorder's Court and the County Court of Antrim. He was Commissioner for the Reconstitution of Direct Electoral Divisions of Northern Ireland and the Chairman of Trade Boards. Until he left Dublin to live in Belfast, he was a member of the Dublin Diocesan Synod of the Church of Ireland and President of the Irish Church Union.[9]

It is clear that Jeffreys was closely connected with Leech and he invited the KC to form part of his Advisory Council for the Evangelistic Band, together with Thomas Hackett, a well-known Church of Ireland vicar. In a letter to Phillips in 1934, Jeffreys refers to his views on British Israelism as being the same as it had been for fifteen years.[10]

The 1934 Conference debate

E J took the place of P N Corry in the debate. Hudson gives an account of E J's speech gathered from his handwritten notes. He states that 'the pragmatic nature of Phillips's argument needs to be stressed. He presented no theological reaction at all'.[11] It is apparent that Hudson had not seen the transcript of the debate which the writer was privileged to see.[12] Unfortunately, Leech's speech is not covered in the notes, but E J's speech is given in full. It would appear that E J gave his pragmatic arguments as an introduction to his speech. He wanted to give his reasons as to why the British Israelism doctrine should not be allowed into Elim. In the debate itself, he went into a detailed theological examination of the doctrine and gave clear scriptural reasons as to why the identity of Britain being the remnants of the ten tribes should not be accepted. Mabel Dalton was E J's personal secretary and was the stenographer who was present at the conferences. Her notes cover the theological interaction in the debate with references to a number of ministers asking questions of clarification and stating their theological opinions.

The thrust of E J's theological approach was that the Israelites and Jews are one. In the discussion following Leech's speech, E J quoted 2 Chronicles 11:13: 'The priests and the Levites from all their districts throughout Israel sided with him.'[13] It was clear to E J that the priests and Levites are linked with Judah. He then quoted 2 Chronicles 15:9: 'Then he assembled all Judah and Benjamin and the people from Ephraim, Manasseh and Simeon, who had settled among them, for large numbers had come over to him from Israel when they saw that the LORD his God was with him.' This was as a result of King Asa's reform in Judah. Realising that these two references were prior to the Assyrian captivity, E J then quoted 2 Chronicles 34:9. By using this scripture, E J claimed that not all the ten tribes were taken into captivity: 'They gave Hilkiah the high priest the money that had been collected by the Levites who served as gatekeepers at the Temple of God. The gifts were brought by people from Manasseh, Ephraim, and from all the remnant of Israel, as well as from all Judah, Benjamin, and the people of Jerusalem.'[14] This reference is crucial because, according to Pollock, the tribe of Benjamin broke off and joined the ten tribes. He claimed that the tribe of Benjamin, originally belonging to Judah, just before the Babylonian siege of Jerusalem broke off from Judah, and attached itself to the ten northern tribes. E J then referred back to 1 Chronicles 9:1-3. He cryptically refers to verses 2 and 3 as follows: 'Now the first inhabitants that dwelt in their possessions in their cities were the Israelites' (who were supposed to be in captivity).[15] 'And in Jerusalem dwelt of the children of Benjamin, and of the children of Ephraim, and Manasseh' (who were supposed to be making their way across Europe to the British Isles).[16]

Following the discussion, E J then launched into his main speech. His argument was quite clearly summed up in his opening remarks:

> I believe that for the last 2000 years Israel and Judah are interchangeable terms, they are one people. I believe that

> the dictionary meaning of the word Jew is correct, that
> is that they are descendants of Jacob.

He admits that it did not always mean this as 'Jew' was first used in 2 Kings 25:25 after the rebellion. He then quoted Ezekiel 9:9 to prove that the prophet had in mind both Israel and Judah when he spoke of the sin of the nation. This was after the Assyrian captivity and just prior to the Babylonian captivity. He comments: 'The abominations committed in Jerusalem at that time previous to the Babylonian captivity were charged against Israel and Judah together.'[17] Referring to Ezra 1:1-4 he quite masterfully links the three kingdoms of Persia, Assyria and Babylon as all being under one government because one kingdom superseded the other. Persia conquered Babylon, which had conquered Assyria. Therefore, E J logically assessed that the ten tribes were as free as the two tribes to return to Jerusalem.[18] He then quotes Ezra 2:70: 'The priests, the Levites, the musicians, the gatekeepers and the temple servants settled in their own towns, along with some of the other people, and the rest of the Israelites settled in their towns.'[19] Reference is made to Nehemiah 11:1-3 that deals with the return of the people from captivity. One of every ten was to dwell at Jerusalem and the other 90 per cent were to dwell in other cities. Verses 3 and 4 state: 'These are the provincial leaders who settled in Jerusalem (now some Israelites, priests, Levites, temple servants and descendants of Solomon's servants lived in the towns of Judah, each on his own property in the various towns, while other people from both Judah and Benjamin lived in Jerusalem)'.[20] To E J it was clear that in Judah were the people of Judah, and in the towns outside the city were the Israelites.[21]

E J argues that in Ezra, Nehemiah and the New Testament the terms 'Israel' and 'Jews' are used interchangeably. The people are usually called Jews by the outside nations in their dealings with them, but in their dealings with God and in their dealings with one another they are called Israel. Jew is the common name; Israel is the sacred name for the same people.[22]

Turning to the New Testament, E J refers to Acts 2:5: 'There were dwelling in Jerusalem Jews, devout men' (KJV). He then turns to verse 22 where there is reference to the 'men of Israel'. Verse 36 is then quoted: 'Let all the house of Israel know assuredly, that God hath made the same Jesus, whom ye have crucified, both Lord and Christ' (KJV). Referring to the view of British Israelists, who maintain that Israel at this time was lost, he mischievously speculates on the foolishness of Peter in preaching over the heads of those to whom he was speaking and addressing his remarks to people wandering in Europe. Another reference is made to Israel in Acts 4:8 and again in verse 10. Referring to the birth of Christ he points out that in Matthew 2:2 Christ is referred to as 'King of the Jews' whereas in Matthew 2:6 reference is made to 'a Governor, that shall rule my people Israel' (KJV). E J convincingly claims that the terms 'King of the Jews' and 'the King of Israel' are used interchangeably.[23]

Among the other arguments he makes to prove that Britain cannot be descended from the ten-tribed nation of Israel, E J refers to the keeping of the Sabbath, which he insists is observed on the seventh day. According to Exodus 31:13,16, this commandment was given to the whole nation of Israel. The Jews, to this day, observe the Sabbath, our nation does not.[24]

Upon the conclusion of his speech, discussion was allowed from the floor of Conference.

The debate lasted for most of Wednesday, 19th September 1934. The Conference minutes record:

> Mr. John Leech gave reasons why he accepted British-Israelism and he was questioned, and his address was discussed. Pastor E.J. Phillips then gave the reasons why he considered it to be false teaching, and he was questioned and his address discussed. The question as to whether B.I. should be taught in our churches was then discussed, and it was decided, evidently unanimously, that it should neither be preached nor attacked in any Elim Church under Direct Government, nor should any

minister under Direct Government appear on any B.I. platform. As regards Elim Churches not under Direct Government, the majority were apparently of the opinion that it should be permissible to preach it within certain limits provided that it would not harm in any way the rest of the work.

The words 'evidently' and 'apparently' within the minutes give a certain ambiguity to the decisions of Conference, and this seems to have been exploited by Jeffreys and his followers in further debates on the subject. The voting which followed gives a clearer indication of the view of the ministers at the time. There were a total of 131 votes cast with only seventeen in favour of accepting the British Israel identity. Seventy-three rejected the identity while forty-one remained neutral. It is quite clear that E J defeated the highly gifted KC and did so, not on the basis of pragmatic argument, but by solid, thought-out, theological reasoning. Greenway and other leaders in Elim were of the opinion that Phillips saved the movement from being dragged into a situation where supplementary doctrinal issues would have caused it to lose sight of its main objective and seriously harmed its missional impact.[25]

Church government and the split

Having considered two of the main reasons for the split,[26] we now come to a consideration of what to Jeffreys and his supporters was the main reason for the schism within the movement – the issue of church government. Hudson states that publicly, 1936 was the year that Jeffreys was at the height of his power.[27] This was the year when Elim 'came of age': it celebrated its twenty-first anniversary. He was presented with two illuminated addresses, one on behalf of the ministers and the other on behalf of the laity. The writer would suggest that, in fact, by 1936 he had peaked as far as his power in Elim was concerned. From 1934 he virtually ceased his pioneering evangelistic crusades and concentrated on revisiting the larger churches that he had opened.

By the end of 1936, Jeffreys was considering his future as leader of the movement. Writing to E J he stated that for many years he had been feeling the weight of the responsibility of leading the work and the increased burden that it brought. He then stated that he felt that he should relinquish his position and withdraw his nominees from the Executive.[28] There was an obvious background to this letter, and some of this is revealed in notes written by E J about an interview he had with Jeffreys to discuss his letter. E J wrote that Jeffreys had three main concerns regarding his responsibility. These were i) the debts, ii) the Local Trustee scheme and iii) the ministers in case there was a split in the Conference.[29] That Jeffreys should have been talking about a split in the movement as far back as 1936 shows that he was, to a certain extent, bent on pursuing policies that would split the movement.

E J notes that he (Jeffreys) did not want their discussion to go outside the Executive, for he did not wish his letter to appear as an ultimatum. He was prepared to remain as leader under certain conditions but his preference was to resign, though he was prepared to remain as a 'spiritual father'. He gave E J his assurance that he was not of the opinion that things were getting out of his control. He also stated that he was not sorry that he had signed the Deed Poll and would not think of going back to the old position where he was solely in control of the movement. He certainly changed his position on this point and later attacked the Deed Poll. In a pamphlet on Elim Church Property[30] written after the split, he referred to the 1934 Deed Poll. He says that the nine members of the Executive, of which he and E J were two, signed the Deed Poll, which made them the governors of the Elim Alliance Church and house properties throughout the British Isles. He now realised that this secret method of acquiring control over church and house property was entirely wrong.

While it is clear that Jeffreys was greatly influenced by Dr Lewi Pethrus,[31] there is considerable doubt as to whether this was completely conviction-driven, or whether he saw his power slipping away and felt the need to turn the movement in another direction. In his letters around this time, it appears that Jeffreys is trying too hard to convince the Executive of his devotion to them and the movement. Time and again he writes that his suggestions must not be viewed in any way as an ultimatum. It is almost as if he protested too much! In a letter to E J he states:

> My release from the responsibility of leadership of the organisation is not going to interfere with our happy fellowship and co-operation in the spiritual side of the work which, thank God, we have experienced throughout the years. I shall be with you in any spiritual move you make for the extension of the Kingdom.[32]

Jeffreys drew up a scheme that he entitled 'Direct Government in Two Sections'. He proposed dividing the movement into two, the 'Jubilee Concentration' and the 'Forward Movement'.[33] The former was to consist of all self-supporting churches worshipping in buildings owned by the Alliance. The latter was to consist of all other churches at present under Direct Government, those who wished to come in from any other Section, and all churches in future. According to Jeffreys, his proposals would give security to the ministers in Section One, allow expansion of the work and help alleviate the debts. Each section would have its own ministerial conference and Executive Council but with a common Headquarters Council. All future ministers, students and probationers would be received into the second section. There would be a general conference for both sections.

E J's reply to Jeffreys' suggestions reveals his concerns over dividing the movement and the prospect of Jeffreys relinquishing his leadership.[34] E J stated that the scheme would entail extensive alterations to the Deed Poll.

The Deed Poll had become something of a 'sacred cow' to E J and he was defensive of it and sensitive to any efforts to get it changed. This reluctance to change the Deed Poll is reflected in the fact that there was only one Deed of Variation passed throughout the long years of his position as secretary-general. That was in 1942 when a Deed of Variation was necessitated as a result of the split and the changes made to the composition of the Annual Conference. Had he been less reluctant to change the Deed Poll, perhaps some of the later difficulties could have been avoided.

E J made a valid point about the concentration of the best and most experienced ministers being in the Jubilee Concentration. He felt that such a situation would result in inexperienced and unsuccessful men being in the Forward Movement and this would mean that inclusion of the Bible College, new probationers, all pioneering work and the future of the Elim work would be placed in their hands. It would appear that E J felt that Jeffreys' intention was to put a cap on the group consisting mainly of large churches and experienced ministers, while allowing the new section to grow unhindered. He may also have felt that he would have more control of the Forward Movement. Hudson suggests that Jeffreys was the one who was seeking a solution for the problem while Phillips' approach was a reactionary one.[35] The writer disagrees with this view. It is clear from his correspondence that E J did not want Jeffreys to leave the movement. He clearly felt that Jeffreys had stalled somewhat in his main gifting and was anxious that he concentrated once more on pioneering new churches.

> We hope very much that you will still have campaigns for Elim on a big scale in the homeland. With our difficulties all straightened out, the work could go forward again by leaps and bounds if we were to revert to the happy campaign days of a few years ago.[36]

By this time, Jeffreys had come to the opinion that he had heard from God and had divine instruction to 'set your house in order' (from Isaiah 38:1, NKJV). There is no doubt that this changed the whole atmosphere within the movement, and strongly influenced the close friends and supporters of Jeffreys. From this time onwards, the Executive Council were put in a very difficult position. If Jeffreys had received his instructions to reform the movement from God, then in opposing such reform, they were opposing God. It does not seem to have affected E J or the Executive Council too much because they did not mention his claim. However, the effect that such a revelation had upon his supporters was to aggravate the problem in the years that followed. His supporters took very entrenched positions, no doubt owing to the fact that their leader had said that he had received a specific revelation from God to reform the movement.

The basis of the revelation was to restore the Church to the 'New Testament Pattern'. This meant giving a large measure of local autonomy to each church, whereby they had full control of their buildings and finance. This became so ingrained in the minds of Jeffreys' supporters that they went so far as to suggest that that was how things were in the early days of the movement. Robert Tweed wrote an article in the mid-February 1943 edition of *The Pattern*[37] in which he spoke about the early days in Ireland. He stated that every church was a 'free church'. E J wrote to Tweed and expressed his amazement at such a statement.[38] E J reacted strongly to the article, even accusing Tweed of either losing his memory or propagating a lie. He firmly stated that central government was introduced into Elim by Mr Jeffreys himself. The letters between E J and Tweed reveal the sadness that resulted from the split. It is quite obvious that both men had a genuine appreciation and fondness for one another. This is borne out by the fact that Tweed and his wife were present at Phillips' funeral in Eastbourne in October 1973 and took part in the service.

Time and again Jeffreys referred to the 'New Testament Pattern' as regards the governance of the churches. In a circular to the ministers in July 1939, he gave an outline of his proposals.[39] It was a strange mixture of local and central government. He cites five reasons as to why he sent this circular independently of the Executive Council. Among these, he mentions his right as an apostle together with the fact that through him, doors had been opened to the ministry for a fairly large percentage of the ministers. It is fairly clear from Jeffreys' correspondence during this time that he was emphasising his leadership of the movement while at the same time trying to make out that he was on the same level as all the other ministers. In this letter, he writes:

> My desire to withdraw from the entrenchments of the Deed Poll has been born of a longing to be on the same level as the youngest minister in the Movement, to work with you as a brother, and not as one who has certain legal rights and dictatorial powers over you.[40]

E J certainly did not see Jeffreys' desire for local autonomy in this light. He was convinced that Jeffreys' desire for local church autonomy was to increase his power over the movement and to open the door to allow British Israelism teaching into Elim. E J clearly viewed Jeffreys as an autocrat. In a handwritten letter to Hathaway discussing a letter which he proposed to send to Jeffreys, he makes the point that if Jeffreys was to win by his current practice, things in the future would be more unbearable than in the past.[41] 'If the Conference lets him know plainly that they will tolerate no more of his nonsense and autocracy, there would be some hope for the work.'

The Conferences

The Conferences from 1934 through to 1940 were characterised by an increasing level of controversy with the lines of division within the movement being more clearly enhanced with each passing Conference. The Conference of 1934 saw the British Israelism identification being debated and an agreement passed that it should not be preached nor attacked in Direct Government churches. However, this did not prevent the subject from being raised at the 1935 Conference where the minutes record that a serious difference of opinion among members of the Executive Council was disclosed and the meeting broke up without any solution in sight.

E J expressed some concern over the suggestions that some members of the Executive and the Conference had been muzzled or coerced in the settlement which had been reached over British Israelism. He assured the meeting that this was not the case and that he was personally satisfied with the arrangements for the future of the work. Jeffreys also expressed satisfaction with the outcome because the work could proceed without further debts being incurred, and he was also satisfied because the subject of British Israelism was never to be brought up again.[42] However, the subject was discussed again at length at the 1937 Conference, when a proposal was passed confirming the decision of the 1935 Conference regarding British Israelism.[43]

The 1938 Conference was presented with Jeffreys' proposals to extend the scope of the Elim Foursquare Gospel Alliance, so that ministers not presently under Direct Government could come into the existing Ministerial Conference. A second proposal was put forward that would have had the effect of creating one inclusive movement under the constitution of the Foursquare Gospel Churches of the British Isles, with its name being changed to the Elim Church Incorporated.[44] In his handwritten notes, E J expressed a reluctance to vote against these proposals. Although he felt that these proposals would bring disaster to the work, he felt that he could not vote against because of Jeffreys' threat to resign and thought that this would split the work from top to bottom.[45]

The Conference minutes record that E J spoke on the proposals and argued that there were a number of matters that could not be left for a decision of the Conference. He maintained that such changes would require major alterations to the Deed Poll at considerable expense to the movement. The following proposal was put to the meeting:

> That instead of making the Ministerial Conference the governing body of the Alliance, the Executive Council delegates to the Ministerial Conference such powers as may be mutually decided upon.[46]

Jeffreys objected to the proposal and placed before the Conference an ultimatum that the Conference must introduce a new legislative body, or else he would have no alternative but to resign within six months. The minutes record that he also threatened to go to the churches with an explanation of why he resigned.

It is obvious that Jeffreys' ultimatum to the Conference on the Tuesday morning caused great tension. E J commented on the situation in his handwritten notes.[47] He was of the opinion that the ultimatum was a ploy to get more concessions from the Executive Council. He observes that no concessions were made. The Executive had met on the Monday night and had expressed a willingness to give certain powers to ministers. E J felt that Jeffreys wanted more concessions from the Executive but was reluctant to give ground himself. 'I repeat that the Executive has been as willing – and I say more willing than the Principal to give more power to the ministers.'[48]

By the time the 1939 Conference was due, it was obvious that schism in the movement was imminent. Owing to the onset of the war, the Conference was put back until late November. Correspondence between Jeffreys and E J clearly shows that there was deep suspicion of motives underlying action between them. In reply to a letter from Jeffreys, in which E J refers to Jeffreys' summing up of his (E J's) attitude towards him, he concurs with Jeffreys' understanding that E J had nothing against him.[49] This letter clearly shows E J's view of the way things had deteriorated within the movement and he clearly feels that Jeffreys must shoulder the bulk of the responsibility for the present state of affairs. The following points are made in the letter:

1. E J was of the opinion that Jeffreys had magnified the difficulties and dangers and overlooked the safety factors.

2. His main concern was that Jeffreys had flaunted the advice of trusted and proven men whom he had nominated as the first Executive Council, and disregarded their opinions and advice which had been influenced by the ministers of the movement with whom they had been in constant touch. There is an implication here that Jeffreys was out of touch with the ministers.

3. The continued policy of change had robbed the movement of any stability it may have possessed in the past and this had unsettled the ministers and people.

4. Referring to the various schemes that Jeffreys put forward, E J appealed to him not to do so in such a way that would drive his own loyal men into an opposite camp.

5. He finally appealed to Jeffreys to use the present Constitution to bring about any necessary changes without forcing a crisis over matters that had not become a major issue.[50]

In this same letter, E J sardonically refers to Jeffreys' belief in the British Israel identification by referring to Rehoboam who rejected the advice of trusted men, but instead, took the advice of those whose policy led him to a divided house and kingdom (see 1 Kings 12).

> That such should be the fate of our beloved Elim, God forbid. Think of the tragedy of it! Congregations divided, many returning to the denominational churches, and, sad

to say, returning to the world again, sick of the nauseating example of Christian brotherliness. What a tragedy![51]

While he clearly faced Jeffreys with the consequences of his actions, E J assured Jeffreys of his support in matters that would unify the movement.

The Conference was held from 20th November to 1st December 1939. Jeffreys refused to attend the Conference apart from occasional appearances and statements. E J apprised the ministers of the gravity of the situation facing the movement. He outlined the many changes that Jeffreys had made and proposed.[52] Some historians are of the opinion that E J set out to discredit Jeffreys in the eyes of the ministers in order to get them to reject any further changes. Such a view does not take into account E J's strong view that Jeffreys' evangelistic work should continue within Elim. While, by this time, he may have felt that a schism was unavoidable, it is the writer's opinion that E J battled to the last to avoid it.

He started his speech by referring to the many constitutional changes that had been made, claiming that on average, there had been a new constitution every three years.[53] He then outlined a whole raft of schemes and changes that the Executive Council and officers of the movement had had to contend with, schemes that had proved costly for the Alliance. In the course of this profound speech, E J went to the heart of the problem as he saw it, namely that Jeffreys was determined to get what he wanted. He was not fighting for a principle, but fighting for his own way. He (E J) made an interesting observation that seemed to have eluded Jeffreys, namely, that church members, especially evangelicals, are usually conservative, and will not tolerate frequent changes. 'All right in politics, but not here.'[54] E J refers to Jeffreys' inconsistency more than once in his speech. Referring to the Irish situation and the pressure by Jeffreys for Irish lay representation, E J refers to Jeffreys pressing for Irish property to be held by an Irish Executive whereas he opposed property on the mainland being held by the Executive Council. According to E J it was 'enough to make angels weep'.[55]

He also referred to the alleged financial crisis of 1937. As far as E J was concerned, the whole matter was vastly exaggerated. The accounts showed a loss of £104 in the year that the Jubilee Fund had raised nearly £7,000.[56] E J claimed that some ministers had been practically starving as a result of decisions made to pay off mortgages that had been arranged to clear over a period of fifteen years and could easily have been paid out of church surpluses. Such a statement would have influenced many ministers to sympathise with E J because he was addressing their personal financial difficulties. Some would believe that this was a cynical attempt by E J to carry the ministers with him. However, such a view is contrary to the integrity of the man that was clearly endorsed by many who knew him well.

E J finished the speech by concluding that Jeffreys was totally unfitted for the business side of the work of God. He claimed that Jeffreys was absolutely out of his depth in matters of organisation and business. E J's recommendation was that Jeffreys should give up the business side of the work completely and devote himself to evangelical ministry for which he was so gifted. The end of his speech was so significant that it is quoted at length:

> If the Principal would only take his hands off the government of the work, we would forget the past and I believe there would be a new lease of life for Elim. Left to ourselves, without interference, even now by the grace of God we can solve Elim's problems. I believe we could evolve a scheme for bringing the whole work together. But if he would give up his power to appoint nominees and promise not to interfere with the government of the work in any way, the work could be saved. If he would remain head of this work but with no more to say as to its government than King George VI has to the government of this land, then we would gladly work with him, and I believe once more the blessing of God would

> rest on the Elim work which we love and for which we
> have almost given our life's blood.[57]

It is quite evident from this speech that E J realised that Jeffreys' role as autocratic head of the movement would have to end. It was a devastating speech that revealed E J's deep frustrations, but also showed his firm conviction that Jeffreys had allowed his main gifting of an evangelist to be subverted by his desire to reform the movement. His plea was that Jeffreys might return to his evangelistic activity, remain the spiritual head of the movement, but leave the business and administrative side of the work to those who were better suited for the task.

Jeffreys had refused to attend the Conference, deciding instead to act through intermediaries. He appointed a committee of ten men who negotiated between himself and the Conference. They brought before the Conference eight points which Jeffreys wanted the movement to accept. Many of these were accepted and acted upon, but the main stumbling block was that of the Model Trust Deed.

It is evident from the minutes that E J had considerable influence upon the Conference. They record that he made a statement in reply to Jeffreys' circular of 11th July 1939, answering point by point and showing where many of them were incorrect.[58] E J then went on to speak about the adverse effects that the principal's various changes had had on the movement. He expressed his concerns at the cessation of definite pioneer evangelism. This was a crucial point as far as E J was concerned. He was strongly of the opinion that Elim was a missional movement and should continue to be so. The constant appeal for reform of the governmental structure of the movement was, in his opinion, digressing from what was the movement's *raison d'être*.

The outcome of the 1939 Conference was that George Jeffreys resigned from the Alliance and the Elim Church Incorporated. This was despite the fact that the Conference had embraced almost all his recommendations. On the vexed issue of lay representation, the Conference agreed in principle to the Conference being comprised of ministers and lay representatives on a 50/50 basis provided that there was a two-thirds approval of the ministers.[59] However, this was left in abeyance following the principal's resignation. The Conference placed on record its deep appreciation of George Jeffreys' untiring and loyal service to the cause of Christ as founder and leader of the Alliance. A proposal was passed calling on Jeffreys to accept the office of moderator or spiritual leader of the Alliance, and remain principal of the Elim Bible College.[60] The Conference then reconsidered the previous adjustment to Jeffreys' eight points. They maintained lay representation on the Elim Trust Corporation, they agreed on the establishment of presbyteries, the election of diaconates in local churches.[61] It was further decided that a Deed Poll of Trust be executed and that matters of doctrine be decided by the ministerial conference.[62] The Conference closed with the passing of a vote of confidence in the Executive Council.[63]

The minutes of the 1939 Conference have four references to E J and show him to have been very active in the conflict with George Jeffreys and the Executive Council. It is clear that the ministers, in the main, sided with E J and the Executive. The division within the movement had taken place and although Jeffreys agreed later to come back as the spiritual head of the movement, he finally resigned from all roles in November 1940 when he wrote a letter of resignation from the Elim Church Incorporated on the grounds that nothing had changed in the twelve months since his first resignation.[64]

The double blow of the schism between George Jeffreys and Elim and the devastation of the Second World War had disastrous effects upon the movement. Many prophesied that this would be the end of Elim. But, like a phoenix rising from its ashes, Elim would survive and grow. This story will be told in the second volume.

Notes

[1] Minutes of Northern Division Conference 1932.

[2] Minutes of the Ministerial Conference: 18th-22nd September 2011.

[3] John Leech was Dublin barrister and a long-time supporter of George Jeffreys. See chapter 8 for more information.

[4] Pollock, A J, *The British Israel Theory Briefly Tested by Scripture* (London: Central Truth Depot, n.d.), p2.

[5] Information received from Cartwright, D, by telephone, 19th May 2011.

[6] Hudson, D N, ibid, p185.

[7] Hudson, D N, ibid, p197.

[8] Hudson, D N, ibid, 198.

[9] John Leech, *The National Message & Banner, 18th September 1926,* 580, quoted by Hudson, D N, ibid.

[10] Letter Jeffreys to Phillips, 1st December 1934.

[11] Hudson, D N, ibid, p206.

[12] Mabel Dalton took down verbatim notes of Conference speeches.

[13] I have used the NIV translation because some of the words in some texts were not fully picked up by Miss Dalton.

[14] NLT.

[15] Phillips' parenthesis.

[16] Stenographer's translation, Dalton, M, ibid, pp48,49

[17] Dalton, M, ibid, p52.

[18] Dalton, M, ibid, p53.

[19] NIV.

[20] NIV.

[21] Dalton, M, ibid, p57.

[22] Dalton, M, ibid, p59.

[23] Dalton, M, ibid, p61.

[24] Dalton, M, ibid, pp64,65.

[25] Greenway, M, ibid.

[26] Hudson gives five main reasons for the split. Two of them are not dealt with in this book: the Irish situation and the World Revival Crusade.

[27] Hudson, D N, ibid, 239.

[28] Letter Jeffreys to Phillips, 9th December 1936.

[29] Phillips, Notes, 10th December 1936.

[30] Jeffreys, G, *Elim Church Property,* June 1942.

[31] Pethrus was the pastor of the Filadelfia Pentecostal Church in Stockholm, Sweden, which in 1939 was the largest Pentecostal church in the world with more than 6,000 members. There were more than 500 Pentecostal

assemblies in Sweden with Petrhus at the head. All the churches were self-governing.

32 Letter Jeffreys to Phillips, 9th December 1936.

33 Proposals re Direct Government with Letter from Jeffreys to Phillips, 15th December 1936.

34 Letter Phillips to Jeffreys, 30th December 1936.

35 Hudson, D N, ibid, p248.

36 Letter Phillips to Jeffreys, 8th February 1936.

37 *The Pattern*, February 1942. *The Pattern* was the official magazine of the Bible Pattern Fellowship. It was first published in pamphlet form in 1940.

38 Letter Phillips to Tweed, 6th March 1943.

39 Ministerial Circular, Jeffreys, 11th July 1939.

40 Ministerial Circular, Jeffreys, ibid.

41 Letter Phillips to Hathaway, 21st July 1939.

42 Conference Minutes 1935, p10.

43 Conference Minutes 1937, p8.

44 Conference Minutes 1938, p1.

45 Phillips, handwritten notes on 1938 Conference: Elim Archives.

46 1938 Conference Minutes, p2.

47 Phillips, handwritten notes of the proceedings of the 1938 Conference (Elim Archives).

48 Phillips, ibid.

49 Letter Phillips to Jeffreys, 29th August 1939.

50 Letter Phillips to Jeffreys, ibid.

51 Letter Phillips to Jeffreys, ibid.

52 Notes of Phillips' speech to Conference on 21st November 1939.

53 As mentioned previously, this was actually an incorrect statement because the first constitution in 1922 was merely a 'book of rules' for ministers and churches. The 1925 and 1929 editions were merely that: revisions of the 1922 rules.

54 Phillips, speech to 1939 Conference.

55 Phillips, ibid.

56 Phillips, ibid.

57 Phillips, ibid.

58 Ministerial Conference Minutes 1939, p2.

59 Minutes, ibid, p6.

60 Minutes, ibid, p7.

61 Hudson, D, N, ibid.

62 Conference Minutes, ibid, p8.

63 Conference Minutes, ibid, p9.

64 Hudson, D, N, ibid.

Bibliography

Published books

Anderson, Allan Heaton, *An Introduction to Pentecostalism, Second edition* (New York: Cambridge University Press, 2014).

Bartleman, Frank, *Azusa Street, Mission & Revival: The Birth of the Global Pentecostal Movement* (South Plainfield NJ: Bridge Publishing Inc, 1980).

Boulton, E C W, *George Jeffreys: A Ministry of the Miraculous* (London: Elim Publishing Office, 1928).

Boulton, E C W, *The Focused Life* (London: Elim Publishing Company Limited, 1932).

Brooks, Noel, *Fight for the Faith and Freedom* (London: Pattern Bookroom, 1948).

Cartwright, Desmond, *The Great Evangelists: The Remarkable lives of George and Stephen Jeffreys* (Basingstoke: Marshall, Morgan and Scott, Marshall Pickering, 1986).

Cartwright, Chris with Holdaway, Jan and David, *Defining Moments: 100 Years of the Elim Pentecostal Church* (Malvern: Elim Pentecostal Church, 2014).

Cauchi, Tony, *Revival Library*, CD Rom (Bishop's Waltham 2004).

Dayton, Donald, *Theological Roots of Pentecostalism* (Grand Rapids: MI, Bahn Academic, 2011).

Edsor, Albert, *Set Your House in Order: God's Call to George Jeffreys as the Founder of the Elim Pentecostal Movement* (Chichester: New Wine Press, 1989).

Evans, Eifion, *The Welsh Revival of 1904* (Bryntirion, Bridgend: Evangelical Press of Wales, 1993).

Frestadius, Simo, *Pentecostal Rationality: Epistemology and Theological Hermeneutics in the Foursquare Tradition* (London: T & T Clark, Bloomsbury Publishing Plc, 2020).

Gee, Donald, *The Pentecostal Movement, enlarged edition* (London: Elim Publishing Company, 1949).

Gee, Donald, *These Men I Knew* (Nottingham: Assemblies of God Publishing House, 1980).

Grudem, Wayne, *Systematic Theology, An Introduction to Biblical Theology* (Nottingham, Inter-varsity Press, 2003).

Hathaway, W G, *Elim Choruses, Books 1-18* (Eastbourne: Victory Press, 1966).

Jeffreys, Edward, *Stephen Jeffreys: The Beloved Evangelist* (London: Elim Publishing Company, 1946).

Jeffreys, George, *Pentecostal Rays* (London: Elim Publishing Company, 1933).

Jones, Brynmor, *Voices from the Welsh Revival* (Bryntirion, Bridgend: Evangelical Press of Wales, 1995).

Kay, William K, *Inside Story: A History of the British Assemblies of God* (Mattersley: Mattersley Hall Publishing, 1990).

Kay, William, *George Jeffreys: Pentecostal Apostle and Revivalist* (Cleveland TN: CTP Press, 2017).

Landau, Rom, *God is My Adventurer: A Book on Modern Mystics, Masters and Teachers* (London: Faber and Faber, 1935), Kindle edition.

Malcolmson, Keith, *Pentecostal Pioneers Remembered: British & Irish Pioneers of Pentecost* (USA: Xulon Press, 2008).

Massey, Richard, *Another Springtime: Donald Gee, Pentecostal Pioneer, A Biography* (Guildford: Highland Books, 1992).

Palmer, Chris, *The Emergence of Pentecostalism in Wales* (London: Apostolos Publishing, 2016).

Penn-Lewis, Jesee, *The Awakening in Wales* (London, Marshall Brothers, 1905).

Pride, Emrys, *Rhondda, My Valley Brave* (Risca, S Wales: Starling Press, 1975).

Redemption Hymnal (London: Elim Publishing Company Limited).

Robinson, James, *Pentecostal Origins: Early Pentecostal Origins in the Context of the British Isles* (Milton Keynes: Paternoster, 2005).

Robeck, Cecil M, *The Azusa Street Mission & Revival: The Birth of the Global Pentecostal Movement* (Nashville, TN: Thomas Nelson Inc, 2006).

Sutton, Mathew Arnold, *Aimee Semple McPherson and the Resurrection of Christian America* (London: Harvard University Press, Cambridge, Mass. 2007), Kindle Edition.

Taylor, Cyril, *My Life as a Social Entrepreneur* (Stroud: Camberley Publishing, 2013).

Usher, John, *Cecil Polhill, Missionary, Gentleman and Revivalsit – Volume 1 (1860-1914)* (Leiden, Netherlands: Brill Publications, 2020).

Warrington, Keith, *Pentecostal Perspectives* (Carlisle: Paternoster Press, 1998).

Unpublished Works

Canty, George, *History of Elim 1915-1983* (Malvern: Elim Archives).

Canty, George, *E J Phillips* (Paper written at the request of T G Hills, former field superintendent of Elim Pentecostal Church, passed on to Maldwyn Jones, Official Elim Historian 2019).

Carter, Jamys, 'An Historical Overview of women in ministry within the Elim Pentecostal Church in the first half of the twentieth century' *Journal of the European Pentecostal Theological Association* (August 2018.)

Cartwright, Desmond, *Some Evangelists: The Life and Ministry of George Jeffreys and P S Brewster in the Formation of the Elim Pentecostal Church*

(MA Dissertation in Pentecostal Charismatic History: Sheffield University (Date unknown)).

Elim Evangelistic Band Minute Book (Malvern: Kept in the office of the General Superintendent, Elim International Offices).

Elim Evangelistic Band, The Elim Pentecostal Alliance Churches, *Statement of Fundamental Truths and Arrangements for Incoming Members* (Malvern, Elim Archives).

Greenway, H W, *Meeting the Pentecostals: Personal Account* (Malvern: Elim Archives).

Hudson, Neil, *A Schism and its Aftermath: An Historical Analysis of Denominational Discerption in the Elim Pentecostal Church 1939-1940* (PhD Dissertation, King's College, 1999).

Jeffreys, George, *What We Believe: Elim Christ Church, Belfast – 1915* (Malvern: Elim Archives).

Jeffreys, George, *Deed Poll 1934 containing the Constitution of the Elim Pentecostal Church* (Malvern: Elim Archives).

Jones, Maldwyn, *An Analysis of the Role of E J Phillips and an Assessment of His Leadership in the Establishment of the Elim Pentecostal Church as a Coherent Christian denomination* (MA dissertation, Regents Bible College/Bangor University, 2011).

Lewis, I Wynne, *History of Elim Pentecostal Church* (Malvern: Elim Archives).

Niblett, Philip, *Ernest Charles William Boulton (1884-1959)* (Personal copy in possession of the author).

1934 Conference Debate: *Transcript of questions asked of John Leech on the British Israel Debate, and E J Phillips' speech in full, in opposition to Leech* (Personal copy in possession of the author).